readings
on
modern
sociology

prentice-hall international, inc., London

prentice-hall of australia, pty., ltd., Sydney

prentice-hall of canada, ltd., Toronto

prentice-hall of india (private) ltd., New Delhi

prentice-hall of japan, inc., Tokyo

readings
on
modern
sociology

Alex Inkeles
Harvard University

prentice-hall, inc./englewood cliffs, new jersey

prentice-hall readings in modern sociology series
Alex Inkeles, Editor

preface

In selecting materials for this set of *Readings on Modern Sociology,* I have taken as a first principle that they should be highly readable. Some of our more severe critics would claim that this standard must automatically exclude most of modern sociological writing. Yet I think the unprejudiced will acknowledge that with the exception of an occasional, and generally more technical, passage almost all articles in this collection are quite accessible to any serious reader.

While the test of readability is commendable, indeed necessary, it is hardly sufficient as a basis for selecting materials to represent modern sociology. The indispensable condition is some guiding principle which reflects a conception of the field. Fortunately my task is made light by virtue of the fact that this book is conceived as a companion to my essay *What Is Sociology?* which appears in the Prentice-Hall Series on The Foundations of Modern Sociology. In broad outline, therefore, these readings have been grouped to correspond to the main headings of that book. Limits of space obliged me to confine to one section on "Sociological Perspectives" materials covered in three chapters in my introductory essay. Beyond that, each chapter of *What Is Sociology?* has a corresponding part in these readings, on the themes: sociological analysis; models of society; conceptions of man; basic elements in social life; fundamental social processes; and modes of inquiry in sociology.

Since my essay deals at some length with definitions and explications of basic sociological concepts, I have excluded such material from the present collection. Rather than present people *talking about* sociology I have endeavored to show people *doing it*—through research and analysis of concrete social phenomena. Since these readings purport to deal with *modern* sociology, I have almost completely excluded the work of the founding fathers. This is not meant, however, to pass judgment on all such work as automatically other than modern in spirit. It is, rather, that I have taken the "modern" to mean essentially the *contemporary* in sociology.

These readings are meant only as an introduction to sociology, and obviously cannot serve the same role as a more thorough or encyclopedic treatment. The severe limits of space which appropriately apply in such a book do, however, present the editor with some difficult problems. Clearly it is not possible to represent all the fields in which sociologists work, since there is no aspect of social life which they do not analyze. Yet it seemed to me that even remotely to do justice to the wide and interesting range of contemporary sociological work I should give particular emphasis to the study of the institutions as treated in the section on "Elements in Social Structure." It is also not possible, within the boundaries of this book, to represent all the different styles of sociological analysis, ranging from the narrative and discursive through the clinical and analytical to the most formal and mathematical. Nevertheless, I have tried to represent a very wide range of such styles of work by choosing the articles so that they also serve to illustrate different modes of inquiry. In some cases I have listed a single article under two headings in the Table of Contents to highlight its relevance to a section other than the one in which it serves its main purpose. To the same end I have made numerous cross-references in the brief introductions which precede each Part and article.

Myself an author, I appreciate the pain writers feel on seeing their productions appear in truncated and often distorted "adaptations." As a reader I have often been disturbed by the parade of fragments and snippets of articles and chapters which are pasted together to yield a book of readings. Now as editor I have resolved not to perpetrate such violence on anyone's work. Almost without exception the articles and chapters in this book represent the complete text of the original unit as first presented by the author. In one case, substantial revision of the original was made by the author himself for this printing. In a few other cases, small excisions have been made to provide a smoother flow of the argument here appearing out of its original context.

Patricia Pajonas helped me search for suitable entries, and Susan Stokinger gave patient and intelligent assistance in preparing this book for publication. I am indebted to them both.

table of contents

Part 3
conceptions
of man
in society

Part 4
elements
of social
structure

Part 5
processes
in social
systems

**readings
on
modern
sociology**

Part 1

sociological perspectives

There is no one conception of sociology to which all who regard themselves as sociologists will subscribe. Even what is called the "classical tradition" is interpreted quite differently by those who urge us to continue its line. Emile Durkheim, whom everyone acknowledges as one of sociology's founding fathers, may be cited by some, on the basis of his research on suicide, as supporting the empirical approach; others will use his name to support the case for theory, pointing to Durkheim's writing on the division of labor; and yet others will argue that Durkheim is important mainly as a model of the sociologist as moralist and man of public responsibility. Of course these roles are not mutually exclusive, as Durkheim and Max Weber showed early in the twentieth century, as Robert Lynd demonstrated in the 'thirties, and as Daniel Bell and others are demonstrating today.

Sociology is a mansion of many rooms, and not all who dwell therein are on the best of terms. The common ground on which they stand is the conviction that society and social organization are worthy of serious and systematic study in their own right and can be understood through the accumulation of facts to which we apply the discipline of reason. But the path to such understanding, the precise aspects of society to be studied, and the objectives that should motivate investigation are the subject of endless discussion and no little disagreement. This is a condition that marks sociology and sets it apart from most of the natural sciences.

I suspect that most practicing sociologists today hold the same synthetic ideal: they would like to deal with some subject of great contemporary significance that also has important historical roots; to attack it with the most exquisitely wrought, advanced methods of mathematics and computer analysis, while still basing their work on direct, first-hand observation and displaying a keen clinical and intuitive sense of analysis; to test old theory and to advance dazzling new conceptions, while completely mastering the basic facts of concrete reality in every detail; to influence public policy, while still preserving scientific detachment and objectivity; and to be, in all this, always the humane man of letters, urbane, sophisticated, informed, and graciously conversant with the latest trends in art, music, and architecture.

The ideal is probably unattainable. Since only a more limited goal can realistically be achieved, there is understandably a lively competition for the crown of legitimacy and the pledge of allegiance. In this section I have presented pleas for four different approaches to the sociological role, each argued by a leading exponent for the conception of the sociologist as social critic, as expounder of social theory, as empirical researcher, and as humanist.

the sociologist as social critic

one

In the period after World War II, no one so completely captured the sociological imagination as did C. Wright Mills. He conducted a relentless and lonely campaign to persuade sociologists to turn away from what he considered the twin evils of "abstracted empiricism" and "grand theory," and to shift instead to historical problems and contemporary public *issues*. Both in his ideology and in his research he presented a sharp challenge to his colleagues to abandon what he called the "bureaucratic ethos" and to make sociology a special form of politically engaged social criticism.

The Sociological Imagination

C. WRIGHT MILLS

Nowadays men often feel that their private lives are a series of traps. They sense that within their everyday worlds, they cannot overcome their troubles, and in this feeling, they are often quite correct: What ordinary men are directly aware of and what they try to do are bounded by the private orbits in which they live; their visions and their powers are limited to the close-up scenes of job, family, neighborhood; in other milieux, they move vicariously and remain spectators. And the more aware they become, however vaguely, of ambitions and of threats which transcend their immediate locales, the more trapped they seem to feel.

Underlying this sense of being

C. Wright Mills, *The Sociological Imagination* (New York: Oxford University Press, Inc., 1959), pp. 3-13, 18-24. Copyright © 1959 by Oxford University Press.

trapped are seemingly impersonal changes in the very structure of continentwide societies. The facts of contemporary history are also facts about the success and the failure of individual men and women. When a society is industrialized, a peasant becomes a worker; a feudal lord is liquidated or becomes a businessman. When classes rise or fall, a man is employed or unemployed; when the rate of investment goes up or down, a man takes new heart or goes broke. When wars happen, an insurance salesman becomes a rocket launcher; a store clerk, a radar man; a wife lives alone; a child grows up without a father. Neither the life of an individual nor the history of a society can be understood without understanding both.

Yet men do not usually define the troubles they endure in terms of historical change and institutional contradiction. The well-being they enjoy, they do not usually impute to the big ups and downs of the societies in which they live. Seldom aware of the intricate connection between the patterns of their own lives and the course of world history, ordinary men do not usually know what this connection means for the kinds of men they are becoming and for the kinds of history-making in which they might take part. They do not possess the quality of mind essential to grasp the interplay of man and society, of biography and history, of self and world. They cannot cope with their personal troubles in such ways as to control the structural transformations that usually lie behind them.

Surely it is no wonder. In what period have so many men been so totally exposed at so fast a pace to such earthquakes of change? That Americans have not known such catastrophic changes as have the men and women of other societies is due to historical facts that are now quickly becoming "merely history." The history that now affects every man is world history. Within this scene and this period, in the course of a single generation, one sixth of mankind is transformed from all that is feudal and backward into all that is modern, advanced, and fearful. Political colonies are freed; new and less visible forms of imperialism installed. Revolutions occur; men feel the intimate grip of new kinds of authority. Totalitarian societies rise, and are smashed to bits—or succeed fabulously. After two centuries of ascendancy, capitalism is shown up as only one way to make society into an industrial apparatus. After two centuries of hope, even formal democracy is restricted to a quite small portion of mankind. Everywhere in the underdeveloped world, ancient ways of life are broken up and vague expectations become urgent demands. Everywhere in the overdeveloped world, the means of authority and of violence become total in scope and bureaucratic in form. Humanity itself now lies before us, the supernation at either pole concentrating its most coordinated and massive efforts upon the preparation of World War III.

The very shaping of history now outpaces the ability of men to orient themselves in accordance with cherished values. And which values? Even when they do not panic, men often sense that older ways of feeling and thinking have collapsed and that newer beginnings are ambiguous to the point of moral stasis. Is it any wonder that ordinary men feel they cannot cope with the larger worlds with which they are so suddenly confronted? That they cannot understand the meaning of their epoch for their own lives? That—in defense of selfhood—they become morally insensible, trying to remain altogether private men? Is it any wonder that they come to be possessed by a sense of the trap?

It is not only information that they need—in this Age of Fact, information often dominates their attention and overwhelms their capacities to assimilate it. It is not only the skills of reason that they need—although their struggles to acquire these often exhaust their limited moral energy.

What they need, and what they feel they need, is a quality of mind that will help them to use information and to develop reason in order to achieve lucid summations of what is going on in the world and of what may be happening within themselves. It is this quality, I am going to contend, that journalists and scholars, artists and publics, scientists and editors are coming to expect of what may be called the sociological imagination.

I

The sociological imagination enables its possessor to understand the larger historical scene in terms of its meaning for the inner life and the external career of a variety of individuals. It enables him to take into account how individuals, in the welter of their daily experience, often become falsely conscious of their social positions. Within that welter, the framework of modern society is sought, and within that framework the psychologies of a variety of men and women are formulated. By such means the personal uneasiness of individuals is focused upon explicit troubles and the indifference of publics is transformed into involvement with public issues.

The first fruit of this imagination—and the first lesson of the social science that embodies it—is the idea that the individual can understand his own experience and gauge his own fate only by locating himself within his period, that he can know his own chances in life only by becoming aware of those of all individuals in his circumstances. In many ways it is a terrible lesson; in many ways a magnificent one. We do not know the limits of man's capacities for supreme effort or willing degradation, for agony or glee, for pleasurable brutality or the sweetness of reason. But in our time we have come to know that the limits of "human nature" are frighteningly broad. We have come to know that every individual lives, from one generation to the next, in some society; that he lives out a biography, and that he lives it out within some historical sequence. By the fact of his living he contributes, however minutely, to the shaping of this society and to the course of its history, even as he is made by society and by its historical push and shove.

The sociological imagination enables us to grasp history and biography and the relations between the two within society. That is its task and its promise. To recognize this task and this promise is the mark of the classic social analyst.

It is characteristic of Herbert Spencer—turgid, polysyllabic, comprehensive; of E. A. Ross—graceful, muckraking, upright; of Auguste Comte and Émile Durkheim; of the intricate and subtle Karl Mannheim. It is the quality of all that is intellectually excellent in Karl Marx; it is the clue to Thorstein Veblen's brilliant and ironic insight, to Joseph Schumpeter's many-sided constructions of reality; it is the basis of the psychological sweep of W. E. H. Lecky no less than of the profundity and clarity of Max Weber. And it is the signal of what is best in contemporary studies of man and society.

No social study that does not come back to the problems of biography, of history, and of their intersections within a society has completed its intellectual journey. Whatever the specific problems of the classic social analysts, however limited or however broad the features of social reality they have examined, those who have been imaginatively aware of the promise of their work have consistently asked three sorts of questions:

1. What is the structure of this particular society as a whole? What are its essential components, and how are they related to one another? How does it differ from other varieties of social order? Within it, what is the meaning of any particular feature for its continuance and for its change?

2. Where does this society stand in human history? What are the mechanics by which it is changing? What is its place within and its meaning for the development of humanity as a whole? How does any particular feature we are examining affect, and how is it affected by, the historical period in which it moves? And this period—what are its essential features? How does it differ from other periods? What are its characteristic ways of history-making?

3. What varieties of men and

women now prevail in this society and in this period? And what varieties are coming to prevail? In what ways are they selected and formed, liberated and repressed, made sensitive and blunted? What kinds of "human nature" are revealed in the conduct and character we observe in this society in this period? And what is the meaning for "human nature" of each and every feature of the society we are examining?

Whether the point of interest is a great power state or a minor literary mood, a family, a prison, a creed—these are the kinds of questions the best social analysts have asked. They are the intellectual pivots of classic studies of man in society—and they are the questions inevitably raised by any mind possessing the sociological imagination. For that imagination is the capacity to shift from one perspective to another—from the political to the psychological; from examination of a single family to comparative assessment of the national budgets of the world; from the theological school to the military establishment; from considerations of an oil industry to studies of contemporary poetry. It is the capacity to range from the most impersonal and remote transformations to the most intimate features of the human self—and to see the relations between the two. Back of its use there is always the urge to know the social and historical meaning of the individual in the society and in the period in which he has his quality and his being.

That, in brief, is why it is by means of the sociological imagination that men now hope to grasp what is going on in the world, and to understand what is happening in themselves as minute points of the intersections of biography and history within society. In large part, contemporary man's self-conscious view of himself as at least an outsider, if not a permanent stranger, rests upon an absorbed realization of social relativity and of the transformative power of history. The sociological imagination is the most fruitful form of this self-consciousness. By its use men whose mentalities have swept only a series of limited orbits often come to feel as if suddenly awakened in a house with which they had only supposed themselves to be familiar. Correctly or incorrectly, they often come to feel that they can now provide themselves with adequate summations, cohesive assessments, comprehensive orientations. Older decisions that once appeared sound now seem to them products of a mind unaccountably dense. Their capacity for astonishment is made lively again. They acquire a new way of thinking, they experience a transvaluation of values: in a word, by their reflection and by their sensibility, they realize the cultural meaning of the social sciences.

II

Perhaps the most fruitful distinction with which the sociological imagination works is between "the personal troubles of milieu" and "the public issues of social structure." This distinction is an essential tool of the sociological imagination and a feature of all classic work in social science.

Troubles occur within the character of the individual and within the range of his immediate relations with others; they have to do with his self and with those limited areas of social life of which he is directly and personally aware. Accordingly, the statement and the resolution of troubles properly lie within the individual as a biographical entity and within the scope of his immediate milieu—the social setting that is directly open to his personal experience and to some extent his willful activity. A trouble is a private matter; values cherished by an individual are felt by him to be threatened.

Issues have to do with matters that transcend these local environments of the individual and the range of his inner life. They have to do with the organization of many such milieux into the institutions of an historical society as a whole, with the ways in which various milieux overlap and interpenetrate to form the larger structure of social and historical life. An issue is a public matter: some value cherished by publics is felt to be threatened. Often there is a debate about what that value really is and about what it is that really threatens it. This debate is often without focus if only because it is the very nature of an issue, unlike even widespread trouble, that it cannot very well be defined in terms of the immediate and everyday environments of ordinary men. An issue, in fact, often involves a crisis in institutional arrangements, and often too it involves what Marxists call "contradictions" or "antagonisms."

In these terms, consider unemployment. When, in a city of 100,000, only one man is unemployed, that is his personal trouble, and for its relief we properly look to the character of the man, his skills, and his immediate opportunities. But when in a nation of 50,000,000 employees, 15,000,000 men are unemployed, that is an issue, and we may not hope to find its solution within the range of opportunities open to any one individual. The very structure of opportunities has collapsed. Both the correct statement of the problem and the range of possible solutions require us to consider the economic and political institutions of the society, and not merely the personal situation and character of a scatter of individuals.

Consider war. The personal problem of war, when it occurs, may be how to survive it or how to die in it with honor; how to make money out of it; how to climb into the higher safety of the military apparatus; or how to contribute to the war's termination. In short, according to one's values, to find a set of milieux and within it to survive the war or make one's death in it meaningful. But the structural issues of war have to do with its causes; with what types of men it throws up into command; with its effects upon economic and political, family and religious institutions, with the unorganized irresponsibility of a world of nation-states.

Consider marriage. Inside a marriage a man and a woman may experience personal troubles, but when the divorce rate during the first four years of marriage is 250 out of every 1000 attempts, this is an indication of a structural issue having to do with the institutions of marriage and the family and other institutions that bear upon them.

Or consider the metropolis—the horrible, beautiful, ugly, magnificent sprawl of the great city. For many upper-class people, the personal solution to "the problem of the city" is to have an apartment with private garage under it in the heart of the city, and forty miles out, a house by Henry Hill, garden by Garrett Eckbo, on a hundred acres of private land. In these two controlled environments—with a small staff at each end and a private helicopter connection—most people could solve many of the problems of personal milieux caused by the facts of the city. But all this, however splendid, does not solve the public issues that the structural fact of the city poses. What should be done with this wonderful monstrosity? Break it all up into scattered units, combining residence and work? Refurbish it as it stands? Or, after evacuation, dynamite it and build new cities according to new plans in new places? What should those plans be? And who is to decide and to accomplish whatever choice is made? These are structural issues; to confront them and to solve them requires us to consider political and economic issues that affect innumerable milieux.

Insofar as an economy is so arranged that slumps occur, the problem of unemployment becomes incapable of personal solution. Insofar as war is inherent in the nation-state system and in the uneven industrialization of the world, the ordinary individual in his restricted milieu will be powerless—with or without psychiatric aid—to solve the troubles this system or lack of system imposes upon him. Insofar as the family as an institution turns women into darling little slaves and men into their chief providers and unweaned dependents, the problem of a satisfactory marriage remains incapable of purely private solution. Insofar as the overdeveloped megalopolis and the overdeveloped automobile are built-in features of the overdeveloped society, the issues of urban living will not be solved by personal ingenuity and private wealth.

What we experience in various and specific milieux, I have noted, is often caused by structural changes. Accordingly, to understand the changes of many personal milieux we are required to look beyond them. And the number and variety of such structural changes increase as the institutions within which we live become more embracing and more intricately connected with one another. To be aware of the idea of social structure and to use it with sensibility is to be capable of tracing such linkages among a great variety of milieux. To be able to do that is to possess the sociological imagination.

III

What are the major issues for publics and the key troubles of private individuals in our time? To formulate issues and troubles, we must ask what values are cherished yet threatened, and what values are cherished and supported, by the characterizing trends of our period. In the case both of threat and of support we must ask what salient contradictions of structure may be involved.

When people cherish some set of values and do not feel any threat to them, they experience *well-being*. When they cherish values but *do* feel them to be threatened, they experience a crisis—either as a personal trouble or as a public issue. And if all their values seem involved, they feel the total threat of panic.

But suppose people are neither aware of any cherished values nor experience any threat. That is the experience of *indifference*, which, if it seems to involve all their values, becomes apathy. Suppose, finally, they are unaware of any cherished values, but still are very much aware of a threat. That is the experience of *uneasiness*, of anxiety, which, if it is total enough, becomes a deadly, unspecified malaise.

Ours is a time of uneasiness and indifference—not yet formulated in such ways as to permit the work of reason and the play of sensibility. Instead of troubles—defined in terms of values and threats—there is often the misery of vague uneasiness; instead of explicit issues there is often merely the beat feeling that all is somehow not right. Neither the values threatened nor whatever threatens them has been stated; in short, they have not been carried to the point of decision. Much less have they been formulated as problems of social science.

In the 'thirties there was little doubt —except among certain deluded business circles that there was an economic issue which was also a pack of personal troubles. In these arguments about "the crisis of capitalism," the formulations of Marx and the many unacknowledged reformulations of his work probably set the leading terms of the issue, and some men came to understand their personal troubles in these terms. The values threatened were plain to see and cherished by all; the structural contradictions that threatened them also seemed plain. Both were widely and deeply experienced. It was a political age.

But the values threatened in the era after World War II are often neither widely acknowledged as values nor widely felt to be threatened. Much private uneasiness goes unformulated; much public malaise and many decisions of enormous structural relevance never become public issues. For those who accept such inherited values as reason and freedom, it is the uneasiness itself that is the trouble; it is the indifference itself that is the issue. And it is this condition, of uneasiness and indifference, that is the signal feature of our period.

All this is so striking that it is often interpreted by observers as a shift in the very kinds of problems that need now to be formulated. We are frequently told that the problems of our decade, or even the crises of our period, have shifted from the external realm of economics and now have to do with the quality of individual life—in fact with the question of whether there is soon going to be anything that can properly be called individual life. Not child labor but comic books, not poverty but mass leisure, are at the center of concern. Many great public issues as well as many private troubles are described in terms of "the psychiatric"— often, it seems, in a pathetic attempt to avoid the large issues and problems of modern society. Often this statement seems to rest upon a provincial narrowing of interest to the western societies, or even to the United States —thus ignoring two-thirds of mankind; often, too, it arbitrarily divorces the individual life from the larger institutions within which that life is enacted, and which on occasion bear upon it more grievously than do the intimate environments of childhood.

Problems of leisure, for example, cannot even be stated without considering problems of work. Family troubles over comic books cannot be formulated as problems without considering the plight of the contemporary family in its new relations with the newer institutions of the social structure. Neither leisure nor its debilitating uses can be understood as problems without recognition of the extent to which malaise and indifference now form the social and personal climate of contemporary American society. In this climate, no problems of "the private life" can be stated and solved without recognition of the crisis of ambition that is part of the very career of men at work in the incorporated economy.

It is true, as psychoanalysts continually point out, that people do often have "the increasing sense of being moved by obscure forces within themselves which they are unable to define." But it is *not* true, as Ernest Jones asserted, that "man's chief enemy and danger is his own unruly nature and the dark forces pent up within him." On the contrary: "Man's chief danger" today lies in the unruly forces of contemporary society itself, with its alienating methods of production, its enveloping techniques of political domination, its international anarchy—in a word, its pervasive transformations of the very "nature" of man and the conditions and aims of his life.

It is now the social scientist's foremost political and intellectual task— for here the two coincide—to make clear the elements of contemporary uneasiness and indifference. It is the central demand made upon him by other cultural workmen—by physical scientists and artists, by the intellectual community in general. It is because of this task and these demands, I believe, that the social sciences are becoming the common denominator of our cultural period, and the sociological imagination our most needed quality of mind.

* * * * *

V

It is my aim . . . to define the meaning of the social sciences for the cultural tasks of our time. I want to specify the kinds of effort that lie behind the development of the sociological imagination; to indicate its implications for political as well as for cultural life; and perhaps to suggest something of what is required to possess it. In these ways, I want to make clear the nature and the uses of the social sciences today, and to give a limited account of their contemporary condition in the United States.[1]

---

[1] I feel the need to say that I much prefer the phrase, "the social studies" to "the social sciences"—not because I do not like physical scientists (on the contrary, I do, very much), but because the word "science" has acquired great prestige and rather imprecise meaning. I do not feel any need to kidnap the prestige or to make the meaning even less precise by using it as a philosophical metaphor. Yet I suspect that if I wrote about "the social studies," readers would think only of high school civics, which of all fields of human learning is the one with which I most wish to avoid association. "The Behavioral Sciences" is simply impossible; it was thought up, I suppose, as a propaganda device to get money for social research from Foundations and Congressmen who confuse "social science" with "socialism." The best term would include history (and psychology, so far as it is concerned with human beings), and should be as noncontroversial as possible, for we should argue *with* terms, not fight *over* them. Perhaps "the human disciplines" would do. But never mind. With the hope of not being too widely misunderstood, I bow to convention and use the more standard "social sciences."

One other point: I hope my colleagues will accept the term "sociological imagination." Political scientists who have read my manuscript suggest "the political imagination"; anthropologists, "the anthropological imagination"—and so on. The term matters less than the idea. . . . By use of it, I do not of course want to suggest merely the academic discipline of "sociology." Much of what the phrase means to me is not at all expressed by sociologists. In England, for example, sociology as an academic discipline is still somewhat marginal, yet in much English journalism, fiction, and above all history, the sociological imagination is very well developed indeed. The case is similar for France: both the confusion and the audacity of French reflection since World War II rest upon its feeling for the sociological features of man's fate in our time, yet these trends are carried by men of letters rather than by professional sociologists. Nevertheless, I use "sociological imagination" because: (1) every cobbler thinks leather is the only thing, and for better or worse, I am a sociologist; (2) I do believe that historically the quality of mind has been more frequently and more vividly displayed by classic sociologists than by other social scientists; (3) since I am going to examine critically a number of curious sociological schools, I need a counter term on which to stand.

At any given moment, of course, "social science" consists of what duly recognized social scientists are doing—but all of them are by no means doing the same thing, in fact not even the same sort of thing. Social science is also what social scientists of the past have done—but different students choose to construct and to recall different traditions in their discipline. When I speak of "the promise of social science," I hope it is clear that I mean the promise as I see it.

Just now, among social scientists, there is widespread uneasiness, both intellectual and moral, about the direction their chosen studies seem to be taking. This uneasiness, as well as the unfortunate tendencies that contribute to it, are, I suppose, part of a general malaise of contemporary intellectual life. Yet perhaps the uneasiness is more acute among social scientists, if only because of the larger promise that has guided much earlier work in their fields, the nature of the subjects with which they deal, and the urgent need for significant work today.

Not everyone shares this uneasiness, but the fact that many do not is itself a cause for further uneasiness among those who are alert to the promise and honest enough to admit the pretentious mediocrity of much current effort. It is, quite frankly, my hope to increase this uneasiness, to define some of its sources, to help transform it into a specific urge to realize the promise of social science, to clear the ground for new beginnings: in short, to indicate some of the tasks at hand and the means available for doing the work that must now be done.

Of late the conception of social science I hold has not been ascendant. My conception stands opposed to social science as a set of bureaucratic techniques which inhibit social inquiry by "methodological" pretensions, which congest such work by obscurantist conceptions, or which trivialize it by concern with minor problems unconnected with publicly relevant issues. These inhibitions, obscurities, and trivialities have created a crisis in the social studies today without suggesting, in the least, a way out of that crisis.

Some social scientists stress the need for "research teams of technicians," others for the primacy of the individual scholar. Some expend great energy upon refinements of methods and techniques of investigation; others think the scholarly ways of the intellectual craftsmen are being abandoned and ought now to be rehabilitated. Some go about their work in accordance with a rigid set of mechanical procedures; others seek to develop, to invite, and to use the sociological imagination. Some—being addicts of the high formalism of "theory"—associate and disassociate concepts in what seems to others a curious manner; these others urge the elaboration of terms only when it is

clear that it enlarges the scope of sensibility and furthers the reach of reasoning. Some narrowly study only small-scale milieux, in the hope of "building up" to conceptions of larger structures; others examine social structures in which they try "to locate" many smaller milieux. Some, neglecting comparative studies altogether, study only one small community in one society at a time; others in a fully comparative way work directly on the national social structures of the world. Some confine their exact research to very short-run sequences of human affairs; others are concerned with issues which are only apparent in long historical perspective. Some specialize their work according to academic departments; others, drawing upon all departments, specialize according to topic or problem, regardless of where these lie academically. Some confront the variety of history, biography, society; others do not.

Such contrasts, and many others of similar kind, are not necessarily true alternatives, although in the heat of statesman-like controversy or the lazy safety of specialization they are often taken to be. . . . I am hopeful of course that all my own biases will show, for I think judgments should be explicit. But I am also trying, regardless of my own judgments, to state the cultural and political meanings of social science. My biases are of course no more or no less biases than those I . . . examine. Let those who do not care for mine use their rejections of them to make their own . . . explicit and . . . acknowledged. . . . Then the moral problems of social study—the problem of social science as a public issue—will be recognized, and discussion will become possible. Then there will be greater self-awareness all around —which is of course a precondition for objectivity in the enterprise of social science as a whole.

In brief, I believe that what may be called classic social analysis is a definable and usable set of traditions; that its essential feature is the concern with historical social structures; and that its problems are of direct relevance to urgent public issues and insistent human troubles. I also believe that there are now great obstacles in the way of this tradition's continuing—both within the social sciences and in their academic and political settings—but that nevertheless the qualities of mind that constitute it are becoming a common denominator of our general cultural life and that, however vaguely and in however a confusing variety of disguises, they are coming to be felt as a need.

Many practitioners of social science, especially in America, seem to me curiously reluctant to take up the challenge that now confronts them. Many in fact abdicate the intellectual and the political tasks of social analysis; others no doubt are simply not up to the role for which they are nevertheless being cast. At times they seem almost deliberately to have brought forth old ruses and developed new timidities. Yet despite this reluctance, intellectual as well as public attention is now so obviously upon the social worlds which they presumably study that it must be agreed that they are uniquely confronted with an opportunity. In this opportunity there is revealed the intellectual promise of the social sciences, the cultural uses of the sociological imagination, and the political meaning of studies of man and society.

VI

. . . Whatever may be true in such disciplines as political science and economics, history and anthropology, it is evident that in the United States today what is known as sociology has become the center of reflection about social science. It has become the center for interest in methods; and in it one also finds the most extreme interest in "general theory." A truly remarkable variety of intellectual work has entered into the development of the sociological tradition. To interpret this variety as A Tradition is in itself audacious. Yet perhaps it will be generally agreed that what is now recognized as sociological work has tended to move in one or more of three general directions, each of which is subject to distortion, to being run into the ground.

Tendency I

Toward a theory of history. For example, in the hands of Comte, as in those of Marx, Spencer, and Weber, sociology is an encyclopedic endeavor, concerned with the whole of man's social life. It is at once historical and systematic—historical, because it deals with and uses the materials of the past; systematic, because it does so in order to discern "the stages" of the course of history and the regularities of social life.

The theory of man's history can all too readily become distorted into a trans-historical strait jacket into which the materials of human history are forced and out of which issue prophetic views (usually gloomy ones) of the future. The works of Arnold Toynbee and of Oswald Spengler are well-known examples.

Tendency II

Toward a systematic theory of "the nature of man and society." For example, in the works of the formalists, notably Simmel and von Wiese, sociology comes to deal in conceptions intended to be of use in classifying all social relations and providing insight into their supposedly invariant features. It is, in short, concerned with a rather static and abstract view of the components of social structure on a quite high level of generality.

Perhaps in reaction to the distortion of Tendency I, history can be altogether abandoned: the systematic theory of the nature of man and of society all too readily becomes an elaborate and arid formalism in which the splitting of Concepts and their endless rearrangement becomes the central endeavor. Among what I . . . call Grand Theorists, conceptions have indeed become Concepts. The work of Talcott Parsons is the leading contemporary example in American sociology.

Tendency III

Toward empirical studies of contemporary social facts and problems. Although Comte and Spencer were mainstays of American social science until 1914 or thereabout, and German theoretical influence was heavy, the empirical survey became central in the United States at an early time. In part this resulted from the prior academic establishment of economics and political science. Given this, insofar as sociology is defined as a study of some special area of society, it readily becomes a sort of odd job man among the social sciences, consisting of miscellaneous studies of academic leftovers. There are studies of cities and families, racial and ethnic relations, and of course "small groups." . . . The resulting miscellany was transformed into a style of thought, which I . . . term "liberal practicality."

Studies of contemporary fact can easily become a series of rather unrelated and often insignificant facts of milieu. Many course offerings in American sociology illustrate this; perhaps textbooks in the field of social disorganization reveal it best. On the other hand, sociologists have tended to become specialists in the technique of research into almost anything; among them methods have become Methodology. Much of the work—and more of the ethos—of George Lundberg, Samuel Stouffer, Stuart Dodd, Paul F. Lazarsfeld are present-day examples. These tendencies—to scatter one's attention and to cultivate method for its own sake—are fit companions, although they do not necessarily occur together.

The peculiarities of sociology may be understood as distortions of one or more of its traditional tendencies. But its promises may also be understood in terms of these tendencies. In the United States today there has come about a sort of Hellenistic amalgamation, embodying various elements and aims from the sociologies of the several western societies. The danger is that amidst such sociological abundance, other social scientists will become so impatient, and sociologists be in such a hurry for "research," that they will lose hold of a truly valuable legacy. But there is also an opportunity in our condition: the sociological tradition contains the best statements of the full promise of the social sciences as a whole, as well as some partial fulfillments of it. The nuance and suggestion that students of sociology can find in their traditions are not to be briefly summarized, but any social scientist who takes them in hand will be richly rewarded. His mastery of them may readily be turned into new orientations for his own work in social science.

the sociologist as theorist

two

Talcott Parsons is generally acknowledged to be the leading sociological theorist in America, and his work has won worldwide attention. In this paper he presents the main outline that has guided his effort to elaborate a general theory of social systems. Special note should be taken of his discussion of the "action frame of reference," which is the core of his theoretical interest. The concepts of "structure" and "function" also loom large in this scheme. Critics of this approach would also call attention to the absence of references to conflict (see Chaps. 22 and 26), and to the fact that the theory here presented is mainly categorical or descriptive. No hypotheses or predictions, except perhaps at the most general level, are explicitly derived from the theory. For this reason the structural-functional approach is often called "static" and is held to be more a *perspective* on society than a scientific *theory*.

The Position of Sociological Theory

TALCOTT PARSONS

Objective and Approach

For the present purpose it seems best not to attempt a critical survey of relatively recent contributions to sociological theory. This has been done sufficiently recently in several places; for instance, the Symposium *Twentieth Century Sociology*, edited by Gurvitch and [W. E.] Moore, [Robert K.] Merton's paper in the fiftieth anniversary issue of the *American Journal of Sociology*, the excellent paper by Edward Shils on American sociology in the

British publication "Pilot Papers,"[1] and more sketchily by [Bernard] Barber and myself in the January, 1948, issue of the *American Journal of Sociology*. This decision is further justified by the fact that there have been relatively few publications of first-rate theoretical significance in recent years. This is of course, largely a consequence of the war and of the fact that so many people in the field have been preoccupied with work outside their normal professional interests. Rather than attempting such a critical survey, it seems more fruitful to present the outline of a positive orientation to the problem of sociological theory and a broad pro-

Talcott Parsons, "The Position of Sociological Theory," *American Sociological Review*, 13, No. 2 (April, 1948), 156-164.

[1] September, 1947.

gram for its development over the next few years. This is a wholly tentative attempt but can, it is hoped, serve as a focus for discussion and clarification of the fundamental methodological and theoretical problems involved. It seems to me that the time is ripe for such an attempt to deal with theory as a common task of the theoretically interested members of the professional group rather than with "theories," the critical discussion of the work of the conceptual schemes of a variety of different people. The time when the most important fact about theory in our field was its division into warring schools or the personal systems of individuals is, if not already completely passed, in my opinion, passing. We are in a position to agree on certain broad fundamentals of such a character that the large number of people who accept them can be working on common premises and, though their individual interests and contributions will differ and will cover a wide range, there is every prospect that they should converge in the development of a single major conceptual structure. It is as an attempt to assist in the implementation of this prospect that I should like to see this paper considered.[2]

---

[2] At the outset it seems appropriate to take cognizance of two of the points raised by Professor Merton . . . since these were addressed to the opening section of this paper.

First, I should like to express the heartiest agreement with his remarks about the relation between theory in contemporary sociology and the history of sociological theories. The latter have been predominantly ambitious, highly generalized syntheses created by individuals. Generally speaking, as total systems they have not proved usable by the contemporary research social scientists, and those smaller elements of them which are useful have for the most part become incorporated into more recent work in more usable form than the original. Hence as part of generalized training for sociological research, too much time devoted to sociological theory in this sense cannot be very profitable. This point is a direct extension of my own state-

A Few Basic Postulates

It seems possible to lay down a few fundamental propositions which can serve as general guiding lines for the more technical task of building a systematic treatment of sociological theory. I shall try to state these in sufficiently general form to leave room for a variety of different approaches in working out their implications in considerable detail. The following five seem to me the most essential of these basic postulates:

A. *Systematic theory itself is of fundamental importance to any science.*

---

ments of the changed orientation of the study of theory.

The second point, that the emphasis of the near future should be on "theories" rather than on "theory" raises more complex issues. It is perhaps well here to anticipate one of the closing statements of the present paper; namely, that it is not meant to present a system of theory but rather a program for the development of such a system. As such, it should be considered precisely as a framework within which the particular theories to which Merton refers can be developed. It is my contention that the time has passed when individual theories must be so particularistic that they must lack the common foundations which are necessary to make them building blocks in the same general conceptual structure, so that *theoretically* the development of our science may, to a degree hitherto unknown, become cumulative. The working out of such a framework is itself an essential and fruitful task. But it is quite true that there is danger of repetition of the old fallacy of premature closure of a theoretical system. Comte or Spencer all over again.

A crucial implication of the relation of particular special theories to such a generalized framework lies in the importance for every special theory of placing it in the framework of its role in a functioning *system*. To derive the immense benefits of this, a concept of system and its continual use are essential. But for this to be available it is not essential that every theoretical problem should be solved. On the contrary, the concept of system functions as a heuristic device to guide the formulation and empirical solution of such problems. It is, that is, a necessary basis for the most fruitful program of work in special theories as advocated by Merton.

There is, of course, no intention to deny that work which can be quite legitimately called scientific can develop without systematic theory. Morphologies, classifications, and empirical generalizations of various sorts have played very important parts in the development of a variety of sciences. The highest levels of scientific development, however, are not reached without conceptualization on the level of what is ordinarily called that of the theoretical system. The closer social science approaches to realizing this possibility, the more mature will it be considered as a science and the greater the predictive power which it will command.[3]

B. *The theoretical system which is basic to sociology must be broader than that of the science of sociology itself.* It must be a theory of social systems. There has historically been an important so-called "encyclopedic" view which considered sociology the synthesis of all our knowledge of human social behavior. This has the consequence of making economics, political science, etc., branches of sociology, which is not in accord either with current academic reality or with good analytical procedure. We must somehow work out a theoretical scheme which articulates our own field with others which are equally part of the same broader fundamental system.

C. *The systematic theory which is most fruitful for our field must conform with the "structural-functional" type, which is current in biological theory, notably physiology.* Intrinsically the type of theoretical system best exemplified by analytical mechanics is more desirable, but is not now attainable in our field either as a theoretical system as such or as a useful tool of empirical analysis over a wide range. The most notable attempt to develop

such a system was that of Pareto, which with all its merits has not proved very fruitful as a tool in empirical research. The most essential point about a structural-functional theory is that by the use of structural categories it simplifies dynamic problems to the point where a significant proportion of them become empirically manageable with the observational and analytical resources we can hope to command in the near future.

D. *The theory must be formulated within what may be called the "action" frame of reference.* It cannot, that is, be completely behavioristic in the sense of excluding all reference to the point of view of the actor himself and to what is imputed as belonging to his internal or subjective mental processes. This postulate is essential in order to make it possible to achieve a high degree of articulation with the motivational categories of contemporary psychology which deal with such things as attitudes, sentiments, goals, complexes, and the like.

E. *The theoretical system must so far as possible be framed in terms of genuinely operational concepts.* The ideal is to have theoretical categories of such a character that the empirical values of the variables concerned are the immediate products of our observational procedures. In relatively few fields of social science is any close approach to this yet possible, but with further development both on the theoretical side and in the invention of new observational and experimental procedures great progress in this direction is to be expected.

Some Methodological Prerequisites of the Formulation of a System

A. *Analysis of the action frame of reference.* In order to be clear about the implications of postulate *D* above, it is essential to work out some of the

---

[3] See qualification of this statement in note 2 above.

major features and implication[s] of the action schema. There are a variety of ways of doing this, but it has seemed on the whole most fruitful in the first instance to distinguish the orientation of the actor on the one hand, and the structure of the situation on the other. Though the situation includes both the physical environment and other persons, the point of view from which it must be analyzed for this purpose is not that of the physical or biological sciences as such, but the various types of significance of situational facts *to the actor*. This means that the analysis of the situation must be fully integrated with the analysis of action itself. Action, in turn, it seems convenient to analyze in terms of three fundamental modes of orientation, which may be called cognitive, goal directed, and affective, respectively. We can, that is, have an adequate analysis of the action of the individual only so far as we understand his action and his situation in terms of his attempts to know it cognitively, in terms of the goals he is striving to achieve, and in terms of his affective attitudes toward these components and toward the situation. This is a very broad and noncommital schema which is, in fundamental respects, in general current use.

B. *The functional prerequisites of the social system.* Somewhat analogous to the spelling out of the action frame of reference is an analysis of the functional prerequisites of the social system; that is, of a system of social action involving a plurality of interacting individuals. If the social system is to be the major unit of reference of the total theoretical schema as a whole, it must be treated in functional terms. It is assumed as a matter of empirical fact that it has either certain given characteristics as a system which differentiate it from other systems and from the nonsocial situation, or there is a relatively definite empirically observed pattern of change in these characteristics analogous to the pattern of maturation of the young organism. Functional requirements of the maintenance of any such pattern system or pattern line of change can be generalized to a certain degree. In the first place, of course, a social system must somehow provide for the minimum biological and psychological needs of a sufficient proportion of its component members. On a more strictly social level, there seem to be two primary fundamental foci of its functional prerequisites. One lies in the problem of order, in the problem of the coordination of the activities of the various members in such a way that they are prevented from mutually blocking each other's action or destroying one another by actual physical destruction of the organisms, and, on the other hand, they are sufficiently geared in with each other so that they do mutually contribute to the functioning of the system as a whole. The second focus is on adequacy of motivation. The system can only function if a sufficient proportion of its members perform the essential social roles with an adequate degree of effectiveness. If they are not adequately motivated to this minimum level of contribution to the system, the system itself, of course, cannot operate. A variety of further elaborations of the problem of functional prerequisites can be worked out from these starting points.

C. *The bases of structure in social systems.* A third fundamental methodological focus is in the nature of the structuring of the social system and the points of reference which must be considered in order to analyze that structuring. A structural category in its significance for a structural-functional system must be treated as a relatively stable patterning of the relationships of the parts, which in this connection may be treated either as component actors or as the roles in terms of which they participate in social relationships. One aspect of the structuring of the system must be what is conveniently called "institutionalization";[4] that is, the organization of action around sufficiently stable patterns so that it may be treated as structured from the point of view of the system. This theoretical function is to enable their assumption as constants for the treatment of limited dynamic problems. There are varying degrees of institutionalization of action in different parts of the total social system.

The second major aspect of the structuring of social systems is differentiation and the patterns according to which differentiation must be studied. This is a very complicated problem, and in general, treatment of it must be conceded to be in a rather unsatisfactory state. It is above all essential, however, that modes of differentiation be treated in terms of a system of categories which make different social structures comparable with each other on the structural level. Without this, any high level of dynamic generalization will prove to be impossible. The most promising lead to solving this problem seems to lie in the demonstration of the existence of certain invariant points of reference about which differentiated structures focus.[5] Some of these may lie in the external nonsocial situation of action; for instance, it is possible to systematize the comparison of kinship structures by using the fundamental biological facts of relatedness through biological descent as a set of invariant points of reference.[6] Seen in this light, social systems of kinship become as it were variations on the biological theme. In a somewhat comparable way, it is possible to treat certain elements of the structure of action in terms of the pursuit of specific goals and the social relationship complexes which grow out of that pursuit, as another set of invariant points of reference which makes structures in such areas as technology, exchange, property, organization, and the like, fundamentally comparable with each other. This is one aspect of the field which is in need of the most intensive analytical development.

The Main Conceptual Components of the Social System

In the terms most immediately relevant to the sociological level of theoretical analysis, it seems convenient to classify the major conceptual components under the following four categories:

A. The structure of the situation.

B. The cultural tradition.

C. Institutional structure.

D. Motivational forces and mechanisms.

A. *The role of the structure of the situation* has already been commented on above. Here it is necessary only to say that it is essential to keep continu-

---

[4] To avoid misunderstanding it should be clearly stated what concept of institutions and correspondingly of institutionalization is being employed in this paper. A pattern governing action in a social system will be called "institutionalized" insofar as it defines the main modes of the *legitimately expected* behavior of the persons acting in the relevant social roles, and insofar as conformity with these expectations is of strategic structural significance to the social system. An institutional pattern is thus a culture pattern (see below) to which a certain structured complex of motivations and social sanctions have become attached. It is an *ideal* pattern, but since conformity is legitimately expected it is not a "utopian" pattern. An institution is a complex of such institutional patterns which it is convenient to treat as a structural unit in the social system.

[5] See the mimeographed document "Toward a Common Language for the Area of Social Science," by J. T. Dunlop, M. P. Gilmore, C. Kluckhohn, T. Parsons, and O. H. Taylor, for a fuller discussion of this concept.

[6] Cf. Kingsley Davis, and W. L. Warner, "Structural Analysis of Kinship," *American Anthropologist*, 39 (1937).

ally in mind a distinction of two major levels. The first is the structure of the situation from the point of view of any given individual actor; the second, from the point of view of the functioning of the social system under consideration as a whole. Failure to distinguish these two levels was, for instance, the primary source of the dilemma into which Durkheim fell which was responsible for most of the controversy over the group mind problem. For the most part, the categorization of this area is relatively familiar. It should only be stated that there will be refinements and shifts of emphasis as a result of further development of the more distinctively sociological elements of the total theoretical system.

B. *The cultural tradition.* In general the usual anthropological definition of culture is applicable in this context.[7]

---

[7] There is, of course, no single standardized definition of culture accepted by all anthropologists. The theme of "social heredity" may, however, be considered the dominant one. The following are relatively typical samples:

Franz Boas, Encyclopedia of Social Science. Culture embraces all the manifestations of SOCIAL HABITS of a community, the REACTIONS of the INDIVIDUAL as affected by the habits of the group in which he lives, and the PRODUCTS of human activity as determined by these habits.

Ruth Benedict, 1931. The complex whole which includes all the HABITS acquired by man as a MEMBER OF SOCIETY.

Ralph Linton, 1936, Study of Man, p. 288. The sum total of IDEAS, CONDITIONED EMOTIONAL RESPONSES, and PATTERNS of HABITUAL BEHAVIOR which the members of that society have acquired through instruction or imitation and which they share to a greater or less degree.

Ralph Linton, Study of Man, p. 78. The SOCIAL HEREDITY is called culture. As a general term, culture means the total social heredity of mankind, while as a specific term a culture means a particular strain of social heredity.

Margaret Mead, 1937. The complex whole of TRADITIONAL BEHAVIOR which has been developed by the human race and is successively learned by each generation.

Culture in this sense consists in those patterns relative to behavior and the products of human action which may be transmitted, that is, passed on from generation to generation independently of the biological genes. It is an exceedingly varied and complex entity, and one of the most imperative theoretical tasks is to work out careful and analytical distinctions of the different elements which make it up and of their different relations to the levels of social structure and action. The difference from the usual anthropological usage of the concept culture lies in our interest in the particularly strategic role which is played by those elements in the cultural tradition which define ideal patterns governing the action of individuals. Their strategic significance derives from the fact that these are the patterns of culture which are susceptible of institutionalization, thereby forming components of the main structure of the social system itself. It clarifies discussion of this field, it seems to me, to make clear that there is not a substantive distinction between cultural and institutional patterns, but rather it should be held that all institutional patterns are cultural. However, only some cultural patterns become institutionalized and therefore have the special significance for the social system which institutions have. The distinction is one of functional relationship to the social system.

C. *Institutional structure.* This is that aspect of the conceptual analysis of the social system which is of closest relevance to the sociologist. Its most generalized role in the social system has been adequately described under C in the preceding section, and will be further elaborated below.

D. *Motivational forces and mecha-*

Bronislaw Malinowski, Encyclopedia of Social Science, Art. culture, pp. 621, 623. [Culture is] SOCIAL HERITAGE. Culture is a REALITY SUI GENERIS.

nisms. It is here that the psychological theory which is essential to the theory of social systems finds its place. It should be made quite clear that many elements of psychological theory are of only secondary relevance to the theory of social systems. This is true of a great deal of physiological psychology and also of the more idiosyncratic elements of the theory of personality. Fundamentally the basic concern of the theory of social systems is with those elements of motivation which deal with the motivation of typical or expected behavior in social roles, and those tendencies which motivate socially significant deviance. It is important to make clear that the very common statement that psychology provides certain premises or underlying assumptions for the theory of social systems is not correct. This psychological component does not constitute a set of assumptions which lie outside the system, but an indispensable component *of the system itself*. It seems to me that the relation between the psychological theory of motivation of social action and the sociological aspect of the theory of social systems is closely analogous to that between biochemistry and physiology. They are both inextricably interlocked in the same body of analytical thinking in such a way that they are only analytically distinguishable.

Institutions as the Theoretical Focus of Sociological Science

It has been stated above that sociology should not claim to be the encyclopedic science of all human social behavior, but should find a place *among* the various social sciences. In terms of this point of view, institutions constitute the logical focus of sociology. When, for instance, some of the difficulties associated with group mind problems are stripped away, I think this is what is left of Durkheim's emphasis on the study of society as a phenomenon *sui generis*. This point of view should not, however, be interpreted to mean that sociology should be confined to the formal classificatory treatment of the structure of institutions. I should prefer the formula that institutions are the *focus* of its interest and that almost any component of the social system which bears on the functional and dynamic problems of institutions should be defined as sociological. From this point of view, sociological theory would, it seems to me, fall principally into the five following divisions.

A. *The systematization of the study of the structural differentiation and integration of institutional patterns on a comparative basis*. This includes not simply formal morphology but the theoretical analysis of the relations of structure and structural variation to the functional needs of social systems. However, relatively speaking, this could be called "pure" or "formal" sociology. Its difference from the program of Simmel or von Wiese lies in its relations to the other branches of sociological theory rather than in a difference in specific content.[8] As has been remarked above, it is a grossly undeveloped part of sociological theory, and is much in need of attention. Promising beginnings, however, are to be found.

B. *The theory of the dynamic interrelationships of institutions and culture*. This is the major point of articulation between sociology and those aspects of anthropology which may be regarded as theoretically distinctive. What may be called the sociology of nonliterate societies cannot be regarded as distinctive of anthropology as a *theoretical* science. It would deal with

---

[8] Cf. the author's introduction to *Max Weber: The Theory of Social and Economic Organization*, Talcott Parsons, ed. (New York: Oxford University Press, 1947).

the selected processes and patterns of the institutionalization of different elements of culture which are not functionally appropriate for institutionalization, such as traditions of science or speculative philosophy or magic. It is within this field that primarily the sociology of knowledge and, for example, the sociology of religion should be placed.

C. *The theory of the motivation of institutional behavior.* In my opinion, this theory should center about the concept of role, which is the primary name for the focus of the integration of motivation of the individual within the social system. It also would include the sociologically relevant theory of the process of socialization and of what is sometimes called basic personality or character structure. Another important aspect is the theoretical analysis of the structural generalization of goals in institutional behavior. This whole field is, of course, one of the major points of articulation between the theory of social systems and psychology. One may perhaps speak of this and the next category as in a very broad sense constituting either "psychological sociology" or an essential part of social psychology.

D. *The theory of the motivation of deviant behavior and the problem of social control.* This branch of sociological theory within the general framework of a theory of motivation and institutional behavior would be particularly concerned with the dynamics of the balance between conforming and deviant behavior. It would analyze the sources of the motivation to deviant behavior in terms of their relations to the social status and role of the individuals concerned, and the strains placed upon them in those situations. Conversely, it would analyze the mechanisms of social control by which deviance is kept at a relatively low level.

It assumes both knowledge of institutional structure and of the basic motivation of institutional behavior as a starting point.[9]

---

[9] Professor [Theodore M.] Newcomb . . . questions the distinction between the above psychologically oriented branches of sociological theory. Of course no such classification as the present one can claim finality, and as among the five branches outlined here I should consider this the least important. There is a certain merit of symmetry in the scheme he suggests: A. Theoretical analysis of Institutional Structure itself. B. Relations of Institutions and Culture. C. Relation of Institutions and Motivation.

I should like to suggest, however, that my distinction is useful precisely from the point of view of sociological as distinguished from psychological theory. Psychologically the same fundamental scheme of motivational forces and mechanisms is involved. But in relation to the functioning of the social system there is an important difference of level. One deals with the motivational foundations of behavior in a given social system, the broad structuring of the motivational forces and its psychological determinants. The other deals with the more dynamic and microscopic balance of continuing adjustment processes. They tend to focus on rather different ranges of empirical phenomena, the latter above all on those of "social pathology." A certain relative distinction must be taken account of on whatever classificatory basis.

Newcomb also raised the question of the exact place of social psychology in the present scheme. In particular he suggested a neglect of the biological conditions of social behavior. Whether C and D of this classification should be taken to define the scope of social psychology may be taken to be an open question. It is meant to define a part of *sociological* theory, and social psychology may well be held to extend further in the biological direction. I should feel quite definitely that explicit theoretical analysis of the biological determinants of behavior should not be considered part of sociological theory as such.

The greatest care should of course be exercised always to take adequate account of the implications of the facts known about these determinants in all *empirical* generalizations about social phenomena. But this is quite a different matter from treating a theory of biological determinants as an integral part of sociological theory itself. The issue is essen-

E. The final branch of sociological theory according to this conception is the dynamic theory of institutional change. It is most important to realize that this from a theoretical point of view would involve a synthesis of all the other branches of the total theoretical system. It is impossible to understand the dynamics of change without a knowledge of the structural base from which any given process of change starts. It is also impossible to understand it without some knowledge of the possibilities of new definitions of the situation which are available in the cultural tradition. Finally, the motivation of any such change requires explicit analysis of the relevant motivational problems. This is above all true of the starting points of the process of change in terms of what, from the point of view of the initial starting point of a process of change, must be defined as deviant behavior. It must include an analysis of the ways in which deviant behavior becomes socially structured and linked with legitimizing cultural patterns. It is unquestionably the culminating synthetic aspect of the theoretical structure of our science, and high levels of achievement in this aspect must depend on the development of the tools in the other branches with which the theorist of dynamic change must work.[10]

---

tially one of methodological convenience and elegance—not one of empirical attention or neglect.

[10] It is scarcely necessary to point out that attempting to attain such levels of synthetic analytical generalization without the necessary empirically validated subsidiary particular "theories" of more restricted scope has been the major source of the instability of so many grand theoretical syntheses of the past, such as the great evolutionary schemes. It will require the development of very many of the restricted theories to which Merton refers before more than very restricted accomplishments on this level which are not unduly "speculative" become possible.

Conclusion

The point of view developed in this paper does not give sociological theory the most ambitious place ever claimed for it. It does, however, give it a key place in the total theory of social systems. It may be argued that institutions constitute as it were the structural "backbone" of social systems. The science which above all focuses on the study of this skeletal backbone is a strategically important part of any large-scale study of social phenomena. It can quite definitely be claimed that no other major tradition of social science fulfills this vitally important function in the whole. The nearest competitor would be social anthropology, but the concentration on the cultural point of view in anthropological tradition precludes recognition of its claim in this specific respect. There is a fundamental theoretical difference between the analysis of culture in the anthropological sense and the analysis of institutional structure of the social system. It is, however, of the first importance that the two should be satisfactorily articulated with each other.

A few words should also be said about the relations of sociological theory to two other important bodies of theory in the social field, economic theory and political theory. Economic theory, in my opinion, is concerned with the analysis of the determinants and consequences of certain distinctive dynamic processes of action within the social system, those responsive in certain ways to the stimuli of "prices" or "market conditions." These processes always presuppose an institutional framework within which they take place, and their strategic significance to the social system is a function of the particular character of this framework as well as of other factors. But whatever the role of an "institutional" point of view in many of the empirical branches of economics, in no case does *economic theory* as a distinctive conceptual scheme include a theory of institutions in the sense of this paper.

The case of political theory is different. Certainly one of its main interests has been in a particularly strategic complex of institutions in the above sense, namely those of government. But these have been treated in connection with dominant normative systems of ideas about what the role of government *should* be and of the history of both these ideas and the institutions. As a *theoretically distinctive* conceptual scheme of purely *empirical* social science which is not sociological, economic, anthropological, or psychological, I cannot see that there is such a thing as political theory. Its claim to distinctiveness must be couched in terms of a different level of considerations.

This problem makes it imperative to be quite clear that this paper has been couched in terms of the role of sociological *theory* as a conceptual scheme, not in terms of sociology as a total social science in its relation to others. I do believe that the place of sociology among the social sciences must rest *primarily* on the distinctive role of its *theory*. But, on the one hand, the sociologist working in an empirical field inevitably will and should deal with many things which are not in this theoretical sense distinctively sociological. This is true for instance of the student of population, where institutions are only part of the problem, or of at-titudes and public opinion. Correspondingly, many economists, political scientists, or anthropologists will be dealing in part with what is essentially applied sociological theory, since institutions are always to some degree empirically relevant to their interests and sometimes of crucial strategic significance. Indeed *every* important empirical field of social science is a field of application for the conceptual schemes of *all* the relevant theoretical disciplines. No academic organization of the disciplines can overcome this inherent logical cross- and interpenetration. In which disciplinary category a given empirical field is predominantly placed is usually mainly a matter of historical accident and pragmatic convenience, not of scientific principle.

In conclusion I recognize fully that what I have presented is not a system of sociological theory. It is rather a program for the development of such a system. It would be possible in the present state of knowledge to spell this out considerably further in the direction of formulating parts of the system itself. This occasion does not provide time to do this. I hope, however, that many theoretical workers will find this in its broad outline an acceptable approach, and will be able to contribute at many different points of the gradual building up of a well-integrated and keenly thought out system of concepts and their logical interrelations which within a reasonable period will earn for sociology a place as one of the more highly developed of the theoretical sciences.

the sociologist as empiricist

three

Those who consider themselves pure theorists often make light of what they regard as the puny efforts of those who want to make sociology mainly an empirical discipline. For their part the empiricists often make sport at the theorists' expense by calling attention to how abstract sociological theory is and how unconnected with any concrete social reality. Robert Merton, himself an outstanding theorist, is uniquely qualified to state the case for the relevance of empirical research to theoretical sociological concerns.

The Bearing of Empirical Research

ROBERT K. MERTON

History has a certain gift for outmoding stereotypes. This can be seen, for example, in the historical development of sociology. The stereotype of the social theorist high in the empyrean of pure ideas uncontaminated by mundane facts is fast becoming no less outmoded than the stereotype of the social researcher equipped with questionnaire and pencil and hot on the chase of the isolated and meaningless statistic. For in building the mansion of sociology during the last decades, theorist and empiricist have learned to work together. What is more, they have learned to talk to one another in the process. At times, this means only that a sociol-

Robert K. Merton, *Social Theory and Social Structure*, rev. ed. (New York: Free Press of Glencoe, Inc., 1957), pp. 102-117. Copyright 1957 by The Free Press, a corporation; copyright 1949 by The Free Press.

ogist has learned to talk to himself since increasingly the same man has taken up both theory and research. Specialization and integration have developed hand in hand. All this has led not only to the realization that theory and empirical research *should* interact but to the result that they *do* interact.

As a consequence, there is decreasing need for accounts of the relations between theory and research to be wholly programmatic in character. A growing body of theoretically oriented research makes it progressively possible to discuss with profit the actual relations between the two. And, as we all know, there has been no scarcity of such discussions. Journals abound with them. They generally center on the role of theory in research, setting forth, often with admirable lucidity, the functions of theory in the initiation, design, and prosecution of empirical inquiry. But since this is not a one-way relationship, since the two *interact*, it may be useful to examine the other direction of the relationship: the role of empirical research in the development of social theory. . . .

The Theoretic Functions of Research

With a few conspicuous exceptions, recent sociological discussions have assigned but one major function to empirical research: the testing or verification of hypotheses. The model for the proper way of performing this function is as familiar as it is clear. The investigator begins with a hunch or hypothesis, from this he draws various inferences, and these, in turn, are subjected to empirical test, which confirms or refutes the hypothesis.[1] But this is a logical model, and so fails, of course, to describe much of what actually occurs in fruitful investigation. It presents a set of logical norms, not a description of the research experience. And, as logicians are well aware, in purifying the experience, the logical model may also distort it. Like other models, it abstracts from the temporal sequence of events. It exaggerates the creative role of explicit theory just as it minimizes the creative role of observation. For research is not merely logic tempered with observation. It has its psychological as well as its logical dimensions, although one would scarcely suspect this from the logically rigorous sequence in which research is usually reported.[2] It is both the psychological

and logical pressures of research upon social theory which we seek to trace.

It is my central thesis that empirical research goes far beyond the passive role of verifying and testing theory: it does more than confirm or refute hypotheses. Research plays an active role: it performs at least four major functions which help shape the development of theory. It *initiates*, it *reformulates*, it *deflects*, and it *clarifies theory*.[3]

The Serendipity Pattern (The Unanticipated, Anomalous, and Strategic Datum Exerts Pressure for Initiating Theory)

Under certain conditions, a research finding gives rise to social theory. In a previous paper, this was all too briefly expressed as follows: "Fruitful empirical research not only tests theoretically derived hypotheses; it also originates new hypotheses. This might be termed the 'serendipity' component of research, i.e., the discovery, by chance or sagacity, of valid results which were not sought for."[4]

The serendipity[5] pattern refers to the

Ltd., 1936), 153. "A piece of research does not progress in the way it is 'written up' for publication."

[3] The fourth function, clarification, has been elaborated in publications by Paul F. Lazarsfeld.

[4] R. K. Merton, "Sociological Theory," *American Journal of Sociology*, **50** (1945), 469n. Interestingly enough, the same outlandish term "serendipity" which has had little currency since it was coined by Horace Walpole in 1754 has also been used to refer to this component of research by the physiologist Walter B. Cannon. See his *The Way of an Investigator* (New York: W. W. Norton & Company, Inc., 1945), Chap. 6, in which he sets forth numerous instances of serendipity in several fields of science.

[5] Since the foregoing note was first written in 1946, the word *serendipity*, for all its etymological oddity, has diffused far beyond the limits of the academic community. The marked speed of its diffusion can be illustrated by its most recent movement among

[1] See, for example, the procedural review of Stouffer's "theory of intervening opportunities" by G. A. Lundberg, "What Are Sociological Problems?" *American Sociological Review*, **6** (1941), 357-369.

[2] See R. K. Merton, "Science, Population and Society," *The Scientific Monthly*, **44** (1937), 170-171; the apposite discussion by Jean Piaget, *Judgment and Reasoning in the Child* (London: Routledge & Kegan Paul, Ltd., 1929), Chaps. 5, 9, and the comment by William H. George, *The Scientist in Action* (London: Williams & Norgate,

the pages of *The New York Times*. On May 22, 1949, Waldemar Kaempffert, science editor of the *Times*, had occasion to refer to serendipity in summarizing an article by the research scientist, Ellice McDonald—this, in an innermost page devoted to recent developments in science. Some three weeks later, on June 14, Orville Prescott, book reviewer of the daily *Times*, has evidently become captivated by the word, for in a review of a book in which the hero has a love of outlandish words, Prescott wonders if the hero knew the word serendipity. On Independence Day of 1949, serendipity wins full social acceptance. Stripped of qualifying inverted commas and no longer needing an appositive defining phrase, serendipity appears, without apology or adornment, on the front page of the *Times*. It achieves this prominence in a news dispatch from Oklahoma City, reporting an address by Sir Alexander Fleming, the discoverer of penicillin, at the dedication of the Oklahoma Medical Research Foundation. ("Sir Alexander's experience, which led to the development of modern disease-killing drugs," says the dispatch under the by-line of Robert K. Plumb, "is frequently cited as an outstanding example of the importance of serendipity in science. He found penicillin by chance, but had been trained to look for significance in scientific accidents.") In these travels from the esoteric page devoted to science to the less restricted columns of the book review to the popular front page, serendipity had become naturalized. Perhaps it would soon find its way into American abridged dictionaries.

This, then, is yet another instance in which a term, long unmet in common usage, has been recovered and put to fairly frequent use. . . . And here again, one might ask: what accounts for the cultural resonance in recent years of this contrived, odd-sounding, and useful word?

Questions of this order are being explored in a monographic study, by Elinor G. Barber and myself, of the sociological semantics involved in the cultural diffusion of the word *serendipity*. The study examines the social and cultural contexts of the coinage of the word in the eighteenth century; the climate of relevant opinion in which it first saw print in the nineteenth century; the patterned responses to the neologism when it was first encountered; the diverse social circles of littérateurs, physical and social scientists, engineers, lexicographers, and historians in which it has diffused; the changes of meaning it has undergone in the course of diffusion and the ideological uses to which it has been variously put.

fairly common experience of observing an *unanticipated, anomalous, and strategic* datum which becomes the occasion for developing a new theory or for extending an existing theory. Each of these elements of the pattern can be readily described. The datum is, first of all, unanticipated. A research directed toward the test of one hypothesis yields a fortuitous byproduct, an unexpected observation which bears upon theories not in question when the research was begun.

Secondly, the observation is anomalous, surprising,[6] either because it seems inconsistent with prevailing theory or with other established facts. In either case, the seeming inconsistency provokes curiosity; it stimulates the investigator to "make sense of the datum," to fit it into a broader frame of knowledge. He explores further. He makes fresh observations. He draws inferences from the observations, inferences depending largely, of course, upon his general theoretic orientation. The more he is steeped in the data, the greater the likelihood that he will hit upon a fruitful direction of inquiry. In the fortunate circumstance that his new hunch proves justified, the anomalous datum leads ultimately to a new or extended theory. The curiosity stimulated by the anomalous datum is temporarily appeased.

And thirdly, in noting that the unexpected fact must be strategic, i.e., that it must permit of implications which bear upon generalized theory, we are, of course, referring rather to what the observer brings to the datum than to the datum itself. For it obviously requires a theoretically sensitized ob-

[6] Charles Sanders Peirce had long before noticed the strategic role of the "surprising fact" in his account of what he called "abduction," that is, the initiation and entertaining of a hypothesis as a step in inference. See his *Collected Papers*, Vol. VI, pp. 522-528.

server to detect the universal in the particular. After all, men had for centuries noticed such "trivial" occurrences as slips of the tongue, slips of the pen, typographical errors, and lapses of memory, but it required the theoretic sensitivity of a Freud to see these as strategic data through which he could extend his theory of repression and symptomatic acts.

The serendipity pattern, then, involves the unanticipated, anomalous, and strategic datum which exerts pressure upon the investigator for a new direction of inquiry which extends theory. Instances of serendipity have occurred in many disciplines, but I should like to draw upon a recent sociological research for illustration. In the course of our research into the social organization of Craftown,[7] a suburban housing community of some 700 families, largely of working class status, we observed that a large proportion of residents were affiliated with more civic, political, and other voluntary organizations than had been the case in their previous places of residence. Quite incidentally, we noted further that this increase in group participation had occurred also among the parents of infants and young children. This finding was rather inconsistent with common sense knowledge. For it is well known that, particularly on the lower economic levels, youngsters usually tie parents down and preclude their taking active part in organized group life outside the home. But Craftown parents themselves readily explained their behavior. "Oh, there's no real problem about getting out in the evenings," said one mother who belonged to several organizations. "It's easy to find teenagers around here to take care of the kids. There are so many more teenagers around here than where I used to live."

The explanation appears adequate enough and would have quieted the investigator's curiosity, had it not been for one disturbing datum: like most new housing communities, Craftown actually has a very small proportion of adolescents—only 3.7 per cent for example, in the 15-19 year age group. What is more, the majority of the adults, 63 per cent, are under thirty-four years of age, so that their children include an exceptionally large proportion of infants and youngsters. Thus, far from [there] being many adolescents to look after the younger children in Craftown, quite the contrary is true: the ratio of adolescents to children under ten years of age is 1:10, whereas in the communities of origin, the ratio hovers about 1:1.5.[8]

We were at once confronted, then, by an anomalous fact which was certainly no part of our original program of observation. We manifestly did not enter and indeed could not have entered the field of research in Craftown with a hypothesis bearing upon an illusory belief in the abundance of teenage supervisors of children. Here was an observation both unanticipated and anomalous. Was it also strategic? We did not prejudge its "intrinsic" importance. It seemed no more and no less trivial than Freud's observation during the last war (in which he had two sons at the front) that he had misread a newspaper headline, "Die *Feinde* vor Görz" (The *Enemy* before Görz), as "Der *Friede* von Görz" (The *Peace* of

[7] Drawn from continuing studies in the Sociology and Social Psychology of Housing, under a grant from the Lavanburg Foundation.

[8] Essentially the same discrepancies in age distribution between Craftown and communities of origin are found if we compare proportions of children under ten with those between ten and nineteen. If we make children under five the basis of comparison, the disproportions are even more marked.

Görz). Freud took a trivial incident and converted it into a strategic fact. Unless the observed discrepancy between the subjective impressions of Craftown residents and the objective facts could undergo a somewhat similar transformation it had best be ignored, for it plainly had little "social significance."

What first made this illusion a peculiarly intriguing instance of a general theoretic problem was the difficulty of explaining it as merely the calculated handiwork of vested interests engaged in spreading a contrary-to-fact belief. Generally, when the sociologist with a conceptual scheme stemming from utilitarian theory observes a patently untrue social belief, he will look for special groups in whose interest it is to invent and spread this belief. The cry of "propaganda!" is often mistaken for a theoretically sound analysis.[9] But this is clearly out of the question in the present instance: there are plainly no special interest groups seeking to misrepresent the age distribution of Craftown. What, then, was the source of this social illusion?

Various other theories suggested points of departure. There was Marx's postulate that it is men's "social existence which determines their consciousness." There was Durkheim's theorem that social images ("collective representations") in some fashion reflect a social reality, although "it does not follow that the reality which is its founda-

tion conforms objectively to the idea which believers have of it." There was [Muzafer] Sherif's thesis that "social factors" provide a framework for selective perceptions and judgments in relatively unstructured situations. There was the prevailing view in the sociology of knowledge that social location determines the perspectives entering into perception, beliefs, and ideas. But suggestive as these general orientations were, they did not directly suggest *which* features of social existence, *which* aspects of the social reality, *which* social factors, *which* social location may have determined this seemingly fallacious belief.

The clue was inadvertently provided by further interviews with residents. In the words of an active participant in Craftown affairs, herself the mother of two children under six years of age:

My husband and I get out together much more. You see, there are more people around to mind the children. *You feel more confident about having some thirteen- or fourteen-year-old in here when you know most of the people. If you're in a big city, you don't feel so easy about having someone who's almost a stranger come in.*

This clearly suggests that the sociological roots of the "illusion" are to be found in the structure of community relations in which Craftown residents are enmeshed. The belief is an unwitting reflection, not of the statistical reality, but of the community cohesion. It is not that there are objectively more adolescents in Craftown, but more who are *intimately known* and who, therefore, *exist socially* for parents seeking aid in child supervision. Most Craftown residents having lately come from an urban setting now find themselves in a community in which proximity has developed into reciprocal intimacies. The illusion expresses the perspective

---

[9] To be sure, vested interests often do spread untrue propaganda, and this may reinforce mass illusions. But the vested-interest or priestly-lie theories of fallacious folk beliefs do not always constitute the most productive point of departure nor do they go far toward explaining the bases of acceptance or rejection of the beliefs. The present case in point, trivial though it is in any practical sense, is theoretically significant in showing anew the limitations of a utilitarian scheme of analysis.

of people for whom adolescents as potential child-care aides "exist" only if they are well known and therefore merit confidence. In short, perception was a function of confidence, and confidence, in turn, was a function of social cohesion.[10]

From the sociological viewpoint, then, this unanticipated finding fits into and extends the theory that social perception is the product of a social framework. It develops further the "psychology of social norms,"[11] for it is not merely an instance of individuals assimilating particular norms, judgments, and standards from other members of the community. The social perception is, rather, a byproduct, a derivative, of the structure of human relations.

This is perhaps sufficient to illustrate the operation of the serendipity pattern: an unexpected and anomalous finding elicited the investigator's curiosity, and conducted him along an unpremeditated bypath which led to a fresh hypothesis.

---

[10] Schedule data from the study provide corroborative evidence. In view of the exceptionally high proportion of young children, it is striking that 54 per cent of their parents affirm that it is "easier in Craftown to get people to look after our children when we want to go out" than it was in other places where they have lived; only 21 per cent say it is harder and the remaining 25 per cent feel there is no difference. Those who come from the larger urban communities are more likely to report greater ease in obtaining assistance in Craftown. Moreover, as we would expect from the hypothesis, those residents who are more closely geared in with Craftown, who identify themselves most fully with it, are more likely to believe it easier to find such aid; 61 per cent of these do so as against 50 per cent of those who identify with other communities, whereas only 12 per cent find it more difficult in comparison with 26 per cent of the latter group.

[11] Muzafer Sherif's book by this title should be cited as basic in the field, although it tends to have a somewhat limited conception of "social factors," *The Psychology of Social Norms* (New York: Harper & Row, Publishers, Inc., 1936).

The Recasting of Theory (New Data Exert Pressure for the Elaboration of a Conceptual Scheme)

But it is not only through the anomalous fact that empirical research invites the extension of theory. It does so also through the repeated observation of hitherto neglected facts. When an existing conceptual scheme commonly applied to a subject matter does not adequately take these facts into account, research presses insistently for its reformulation. It leads to the introduction of variables which have not been systematically included in the scheme of analysis. Here, be it noted, it is not that the data are anomalous or unexpected or incompatible with existing theory; it is merely that they had not been considered pertinent. Whereas the serendipity pattern centers in an apparent inconsistency which presses for resolution, the reformulation pattern centers in the hitherto neglected but relevant fact which presses for an extension of the conceptual scheme.

Examples of this in the history of social science are far from limited. Thus it was a series of fresh empirical facts which led [B.] Malinowski to incorporate new elements into a theory of magic. It was his Trobrianders, of course, who gave him the clue to the distinctive feature of his theory. When these islanders fished in the inner lagoon by the reliable method of poisoning, an abundant catch was assured and danger was absent. Neither uncertainty nor uncontrollable hazards were involved. And here, Malinowski noted, magic was not practiced. But in the open sea fishing, with the uncertain yield and its often grave dangers, the rituals of magic flourished. Stemming from these pregnant observations was his theory that magical belief arises to bridge the uncertainties in man's practical pursuits, to fortify confidence, to reduce anxieties, to open up avenues of escape from the seeming impasse. Magic was construed as a supplementary technique for reaching practical objectives. It was these empirical facts which suggested the incorporation of new dimensions into earlier theories of magic—particularly the relations of magic to the fortuitous, the dangerous, and the uncontrollable. It was not that these facts were *inconsistent* with previous theories; it was simply that these conceptual schemes had not taken them adequately into account. Nor was Malinowski testing a preconceived hypothesis—he was developing an enlarged and improved theory on the basis of suggestive empirical data.

For another example of this pressure of empirical data for the recasting of a specific theory we turn closer to home. The investigation dealt with a single dramatic instance of mass persuasion: broadcasting at repeated intervals over a span of eighteen hours, Kate Smith, a radio star, sold large quantities of war bonds in the course of a day. It is not my intention to report fully on the dynamics of this case of mass persuasion;[12] for present purposes, we are concerned only with the implications of two facts which emerged from the study.

First of all, in the course of intensive interviews many of our informants— New Yorkers who had pledged a bond to Smith—expressed a thorough disenchantment with the world of advertising, commercials, and propaganda. They felt themselves the object of manipulation—and resented it. They objected to being the target for advertising which cajoles, insists, and terrorizes. They objected to being engulfed in waves of propaganda proposing opinions and actions not in their own best

12 Robert K. Merton, M. Fiske, and Alberta Curtis, *Mass Persuasion* (New York: Harper & Row, Publishers, Inc., 1946).

interests. They expressed dismay over what is in effect a pattern of *pseudo-Gemeinschaft*—subtle methods of salesmanship in which there is the feigning of personal concern with the client in order to manipulate him the better. As one small business man phrased it, "In my own business, I can see how a lot of people in their business deals will make some kind of gesture of friendliness, sincerity, and so forth, most of which is phony." Drawn from a highly competitive, segmented metropolitan society, our informants were describing a climate of reciprocal distrust, of anomie, in which common values have been submerged in the welter of private interests. Society was experienced as an arena for rival frauds. There was small belief in the disinterestedness of conduct.

In contrast to all this was the second fact: we found that the persuasiveness of the Smith bond drive among these same informants largely rested upon their firm belief in the integrity and sincerity of Smith. And much the same was found to be true in a polling interview with a larger cross section sample of almost a thousand New Yorkers. Fully 80 per cent asserted that in her all-day marathon drive, Smith was *exclusively* concerned with promoting the sale of war bonds, whereas only 17 per cent felt that she was *also* interested in publicity for herself, and a negligible 3 per cent believed she was *primarily* concerned with the resulting publicity.

This emphasis on her sincerity is all the more striking as a problem for research in the molding of reputations because she herself appeared on at least six commercially sponsored radio programs each week. But although she is engaged in apparently the same promotional activities as others, she was viewed by the majority of our informants as the direct antithesis of all that these other announcers and stars represent. In the words of one devotee,

"She's sincere and *she really means anything* she ever says. It isn't just sittin' up there and talkin' and gettin' paid for it. She's different from what other people are."

Why this overwhelming belief in Smith's sincerity? To be sure, the same society which produces a sense of alienation and estrangement generates in many a craving for reassurance, an acute will to believe, a flight into faith. But why does Smith become the object of this faith for so many otherwise distrustful people? Why is she seen as genuine by those who seek redemption from the spurious? Why are her motives believed to rise above avarice and ambition and pride of class? What are the social-psychological sources of this image of Smith as sincerity incarnate?

Among the several sources, we wish to examine here the one which bears most directly upon a theory of mass persuasion. The clue is provided by the fact that a larger proportion of those who heard the Smith marathon war bond drive are convinced of her disinterested patriotism than of those who did not. This appears to indicate that the marathon bond drive enhanced public belief in her sincerity. But we must recognize the possibility that her devoted fans, for whom her sincerity was unquestioned, would be more likely to have heard the marathon broadcasts. Therefore, to determine whether the marathon did in fact extend this belief, we must compare regular listeners to her programs with those who are not her fans. Within each group, a significantly larger proportion of people who heard the marathon are convinced of Smith's exclusive concern with patriotic purposes.[13] This is as true for her devoted fans as for those who did not listen to her regular

programs at all. In other words, we have caught for a moment, as with a candid camera, a snapshot of Smith's reputation of sincerity in the process of being even further enhanced. We have frozen in mid-course the process of building a reputation.

But if the marathon increased the belief in Smith's sincerity, how did this come about? It is at this point that our intensive interviews, with their often ingenuous and revealing details, permit us to interpret the statistical results of the poll. The marathon had all the atmosphere of determined, resolute endeavor under tremendous difficulties. Some could detect signs of strain—and courageous persistence. "Her voice was not quite so strong later, but she stuck it out like a good soldier," says a discerning housewife. Others projected themselves into the vividly imagined situation of fatigue and brave exertion. Solicitous reports by her coadjutor, Ted Collins, reinforced the emphatic concern for the strain to which Smith was subjecting herself. "I felt, I can't stand this any longer," recalls one informant. "Mr. Collins' statement about her being exhausted affected me so much that I just couldn't bear it." The marathon took on the attributes of a sacrificial ritual.

In short, it was not so much what Smith *said* as what she *did* which served to validate her sincerity. It was the presumed stress and strain of an eighteen-hour series of broadcasts, it was the deed not the word which furnished the indubitable proof. Listeners might question whether she [was] not unduly dramatizing herself, but they could not escape the incontrovertible evidence that she was devoting the entire day to the task. Appraising the direct testimony of Smith's behavior, another informant explains that "she was on all day and the others weren't. So it seemed that she was sacrificing

---

[13] The statistical data will be found in *ibid.*, pp. 87-88.

more and was more sincere." Viewed as a process of persuasion, the marathon converted initial feelings of skepticism and distrust among listeners into at first a reluctant, and later, a full-fledged acceptance of Smith's integrity. The successive broadcasts served as a fulfillment in action of a promise in words. The words were reinforced by things she had actually done. The currency of talk was accepted because it was backed by the gold of conduct. The gold reserve, moreover, need not even approximate the amount of currency it can support.

This empirical study suggests that propaganda-of-the-deed may be effective among the very people who are distrustful of propaganda-of-the-word. Where there is social disorganization, anomie, conflicting values, we find propaganditis reaching epidemic proportions. Any statement of values is likely to be discounted as "mere propaganda." Exhortations are suspect. But the propaganda of the deed elicits more confidence. Members of the audience are largely permitted to draw their conclusions from the action—they are less likely to feel manipulated. When the propagandist's deed and his words symbolically coincide, it stimulates belief in his sincerity. Further research must determine whether this propaganda pattern is significantly more effective in societies suffering from anomie than in those which are more fully integrated. But not unlike the Malinowski case-in-point, this may illustrate the role of research in suggesting new variables to be incorporated into a specific theory.

The Refocusing of Theoretic Interest (New Methods of Empirical Research Exert Pressure for New Foci of Theoretic Interest)

To this point we have considered the impact of research upon the develop-

ment of particular theories. But empirical research also affects more general trends in the development of theory. This occurs chiefly through the invention of research procedures which tend to shift the foci of theoretic interest to the growing points of research.

The reasons for this are on the whole evident. After all, sound theory thrives only on a rich diet of pertinent facts and newly invented procedures help provide the ingredients of this diet. The new, and often previously unavailable, data stimulate fresh hypotheses. Moreover, theorists find that their hypotheses can be put to immediate test in those spheres where appropriate research techniques have been designed. It is no longer necessary for them to wait upon data as they happen to turn up—researches directed to the verification of hypotheses can be instituted at once. The flow of relevant data thus increases the tempo of advance in certain spheres of theory, whereas in others, theory stagnates for want of adequate observations. Attention shifts accordingly.

In noting that new centers of theoretic interest have followed upon the invention of research procedures, we do not imply that these alone played a decisive role.[14] The growing interest in the theory of propaganda as an instrument of social control, for example, is in large part a response to the changing historical situation, with its conflict of major ideological systems, new technologies of mass communication which have opened up new avenues for propaganda, and the rich research treasuries provided by business and government interested in this new weapon of war, both declared and undeclared. But this

[14] It is perhaps needless to add that these procedures, instruments, and apparatus are in turn dependent upon prior theory. But this does not alter their stimulating effect upon the further development of theory.

shift is also a byproduct of accumulated facts made available through such newly developed, and confessedly crude, procedures as content analysis, the panel technique, and the focused interview.

Examples of this impact in the recent history of social theory are numerous but we have time to mention only a few. Thus, the increasing concern with the theory of character and personality formation in relation to social structure became marked after the introduction of new projective methods; the Rorschach test, the thematic apperception test, play techniques, and story completions being among the most familiar. So, too, the sociometric techniques of Moreno and others, and fresh advances in the technique of the "passive interview" have revived interest in the theory of interpersonal relations. Stemming from such techniques as well is the trend toward what might be called the "rediscovery of the primary group," particularly in the shape of theoretic concern with informal social structures as mediating between the individual and large formal organizations. This interest has found expression in an entire literature on the role and structure of the informal group, for example, in factory social systems, bureaucracy, and political organizations. Similarly, we may anticipate that the recent introduction of the panel technique—the repeated interviewing of the same group of informants—will in due course more sharply focus the attention of social psychologists upon the theory of attitude formation, decisions among alternative choices, factors in political participation, and determinants of behavior in cases of conflicting role demands, to mention a few types of problems to which this technique is especially adapted.

Perhaps the most direct impact of research procedures upon theory has resulted from the *creation* of sociological statistics organized in terms of theoretically pertinent categories. Talcott Parsons has observed that numerical data are scientifically important only when they can be fitted into analytical categories and that "a great deal of current research is producing facts in a form which cannot be utilized by any current generalized analytical scheme."[15] These well-deserved strictures of a short while ago are proving progressively less applicable. In the past, the sociologist has largely had to deal with *precollected series* of statistics usually assembled for nonsociological purposes and, therefore, not set forth in categories directly pertinent to any theoretical system. As a result, at least so far as quantitative facts are concerned, the theorist was compelled to work with makeshift data bearing only a tangential relevance to his problems. This not only left a wide margin for error—consider the crude indices of social cohesion upon which Durkheim had to rely—but it also meant that theory had to wait upon the incidental and, at times, almost accidental availability of relevant data. It could not march rapidly ahead. This picture has now begun to change.

No longer does the theorist depend almost exclusively upon the consensus of administrative boards or social welfare agencies for his quantitative data. Tarde's programmatic sketch[16] a half century ago of the need for statistics in social psychology, particularly those dealing with attitudes, opinions, and

15 Talcott Parsons, "The Role of Theory in Social Research," *American Sociological Review*, 3 (1938), 19; cf. his *The Structure of Social Action* (New York: McGraw-Hill Book Co., Inc., 1937), 328-329n: ". . . in the social field most available statistical information is on a level which cannot be made to fit directly into the categories of analytical theory."

16 Gabriel Tarde, *Essais et mélanges sociologiques* (Paris, 1895), pp. 230-270.

sentiments, has become a half-fulfilled promise. So, too, investigators of community organization are creating statistics on class structure, associational behavior, and clique formations, and this has left its mark on theoretic interests. Ethnic studies are beginning to provide quantitative data which are reorienting the theorist. It is safe to suppose that the enormous accumulation of sociological materials during the war —notably by the Research Branch of the Information and Education Division of the War Department—materials which are in part the result of new research techniques, will intensify interest in the theory of group morale, propaganda, and leadership.[17] But it is perhaps needless to multiply examples.

What we have said does not mean that the piling up of statistics in itself advances theory; it does mean that theoretic interest tends to shift to those areas in which there is an abundance of *pertinent* statistical data.[18] Moreover, we are merely calling attention to this shift of focus, not evaluating it. It may very well be that it sometimes deflects attention to problems which, in a theoretic or humanistic sense, are "unimportant"; it may divert attention from problems with larger implications onto those for which there is the promise of immediate solutions. Failing a detailed study, it is difficult to come to any over-all assessment of this point. But the pattern itself seems clear enough in sociology as in other disciplines; as new and previously unobtainable data become available through the use of new techniques, theorists turn their analytical eye upon the implications of these data and bring about new directions of inquiry.

---

[17] As appears to be the case now that it has been published: S. A. Stouffer, *et al.*, *The American Soldier.*
[18] The statistical data also facilitate sufficient *precision* in research to put theory to determinate tests. . . .

The Clarification of Concepts (Empirical Research Exerts Pressure for Clear Concepts)

A good part of the work called "theorizing" is taken up with the clarification of concepts—and rightly so. It is in this matter of clearly defined concepts that social science research is not infrequently defective. Research activated by a major interest in methodology may be centered on the *design* of establishing causal relations without due regard for analyzing the variables involved in the inquiry. This methodological empiricism, as the design of inquiry without correlative concern with the clarification of substantive variables may be called, characterizes a large part of current research. Thus, in a series of effectively designed experiments Chapin finds that "the rehousing of slum families in a public housing project results in improvement of the living conditions and the social life of these families."[19] Or through controlled experiments, psychologists search out the effects of foster home placement upon children's performances in intelligence tests.[20] Or, again through experimental inquiry, researchers seek to determine whether a propaganda film has achieved its purpose of improving attitudes toward the British. These several cases, and they are representative of a large amount of research which has advanced social science method, have in common the fact that the empirical variables are not analyzed in terms of their conceptual ele-

---

[19] F. S. Chapin, "The Effects of Slum Clearance and Rehousing on Family and Community Relationships in Minneapolis," *American Journal of Sociology*, **43** (1938), 744-763.
[20] R. R. Sears, "Child Psychology," in Wayne Dennis, ed., *Current Trends in Psychology* (Pittsburgh: University of Pittsburgh Press, 1947), pp. 55-56. Sears' comments on this type of research state the general problem admirably.

ments.[21] As Rebecca West, with her characteristic lucidity, put this general problem of methodological empiricism, one might "know that A and B and C were linked by certain causal connections, but he would never apprehend with any exactitude the nature of A or B or C." In consequence, these researches advance the procedures of inquiry, but their findings do not enter into the repository of cumulative social science theory.

But in general, the clarification of concepts, commonly considered a province peculiar to the theorist, is a frequent result of empirical research. Research sensitive to its own needs cannot easily escape this pressure for conceptual clarification. *For a basic requirement of research is that the concepts, the variables, be defined with sufficient clarity to enable the research to proceed*, a requirement easily and unwittingly not met in the kind of discursive exposition which is often miscalled sociological theory.

The clarification of concepts ordinarily enters into empirical research in the shape of establishing *indices* of the variables under consideration. In nonresearch speculations, it is possible to talk loosely about "morale" or "social cohesion" without any clear conceptions of what is entailed by these terms, but they *must* be clarified if the researcher is to go about his business of systematically observing instances of low and high morale, of social cohesion or social cleavage. If he is not to be blocked at the outset, he must devise indices which are observable, fairly precise, and meticulously clear. The entire

movement of thought which was christened "operationalism" is only one conspicuous case of the researcher demanding that concepts be defined clearly enough for him to go to work.

This has been typically recognized by those sociologists who combine a theoretic orientation with systematic empirical research. Durkheim, for example, despite the fact that his terminology and indices now appear crude and debatable, clearly perceived the need for devising indices of his concepts. Repeatedly, he asserted that "it is necessary . . . to substitute for the internal fact which escapes us an external fact that symbolizes it and to study the former through the latter."[22] The index, or sign of the conceptualized item, stands ideally in a one-to-one correlation with what it signifies (and the difficulty of establishing this relation is of course one of the critical problems of research). Since the index and its object are so related, one may ask for the grounds on which one is taken as the index and the other as the indexed variable. As Durkheim implied and as Suzanne Langer has indicated anew, the index is that one of the correlated pair which is perceptible and the other, harder or impossible to perceive, is theoretically relevant.[23] Thus, attitude scales make available indices of otherwise not discriminable atti-

---

[21] However crude they may be, procedures such as the focused interview are expressly designed as aids for detecting possibly relevant variables in an initially undifferentiated situation. See R. K. Merton, M. Fiske, and P. L. Kendall, *The Focused Interview* (New York: The Free Press of Glencoe, Inc., 1956).

[22] Emile Durkheim, *Division of Labor in Society* (New York: The Macmillan Company, 1933), p. 66; also his *Les règles de la méthode sociologique* (Paris, 1895), pp. 55-58; *Le Suicide* (Paris: F. Alcan, 1930), p. 356; *et passim*. Cf. R. K. Merton, "Durkheim's *Division of Labor in Society*," *American Journal of Sociology*, **40** (1934), esp. 326-327, which touches on the problem of indices; for a greatly developed analysis, see Lazarsfeld and Rosenberg, eds., *The Language of Social Research*, introduction to Sec. I.

[23] Suzanne K. Langer, *Philosophy in a New Key* (New York: Penguin Books, 1948), pp. 46-47.

tudes, just as ecological statistics represent indices of diverse social structures in different areas.

What often appears as a tendency in research for quantification (through the development of scales) can thus be seen as a special case of attempting to clarify concepts sufficiently to permit the conduct of empirical investigation. The development of valid and observable indices becomes central to the use of concepts in the prosecution of research. A final illustration will indicate how research presses for the clarification of ancient sociological concepts which, on the plane of discursive exposition, have remained ill-defined and unclarified.

A conception basic to sociology holds that individuals have multiple social roles and tend to organize their behavior in terms of the structurally defined expectations assigned to each role. Further, it is said, the less integrated the society, the more often will individuals be subject to the strain of incompatible social roles. Type cases are numerous and familiar: the Catholic Communist subjected to conflicting pressures from party and church, the marginal man suffering the pulls of conflicting societies, the professional woman torn between the demands of family and career. Every sociological textbook abounds with illustrations of incompatible demands made of the multiselved person.

Perhaps because it has been largely confined to discursive interpretations and has seldom been made the focus of systematic research, this central problem of conflicting roles has yet to be materially clarified and advanced beyond the point reached decades ago. Thomas and Znaniecki long since indicated that conflicts between social roles *can* be reduced by conventionalization and by role segmentation (by assigning each set of role demands to different

situations).[24] And others have noted that frequent conflict between roles is dysfunctional for the society as well as for the individual. But all this leaves many salient problems untouched: on which grounds does one predict the behavior of persons subject to conflicting roles? And when a decision must be made, which role (or which group solidarity) takes precedence? Under which conditions does one or another prove controlling? On the plane of discursive thought, it has been suggested that the role with which the individual identifies most fully will prove dominant, thus banishing the problem through a tautological pseudosolution. Or, the problem of seeking to predict behavior consequent to incompatibility of roles, a research problem requiring operational clarification of the concepts of solidarity, conflict, role demands, and situation, has been evaded by observing that conflicts of roles typically ensue in frustration.

More recently, empirical research has pressed for clarification of the key concepts involved in this problem. Indices of conflicting group pressures have been devised and the resultant behavior observed in specified situations. Thus, as a beginning in this direction, it has been shown that in a concrete decision situation, such as voting, individuals subject to these cross pressures respond by delaying their vote decision. And, under conditions yet to be determined, they seek to reduce the conflict by escaping from the field of conflict: they lose interest in the political campaign. Finally, there is the intimation in these data that in cases of cross pressures upon the voter, it is socioeconomic position which is typically controlling.[25]

---

[24] W. I. Thomas and F. Znaniecki, *The Polish Peasant* (New York: Alfred A. Knopf, Inc., 1927), pp. 1866-1870, 1888, 1899ff.

[25] P. F. Lazarsfeld, B. Berelson, and Gaudet, *The People's Choice* (New York: Co-

However this may be, the essential point is that, in this instance, as in others, the very requirements of empirical research have been instrumental in clarifying received concepts. The process of empirical inquiry raises conceptual issues which may long go undetected in theoretic inquiry.

There remain, then, a few concluding remarks. My discussion has been devoted exclusively to four impacts of research upon the development of social theory: the initiation, reformulation, refocusing, and clarification of theory. Doubtless there are others.

lumbia University Press, 1948), Chap. 6 and the subsequent study by B. Berelson, P. F. Lazarsfeld, and W. N. McPhee, *Voting* (Chicago: University of Chicago Press, 1954).

Doubtless, too, the emphasis [here] lends itself to misunderstanding. It may be inferred that some invidious distinction has been drawn at the expense of theory and the theorist. That has not been my intention. I have suggested only that an explicitly formulated theory does not invariably precede empirical inquiry, that as a matter of plain fact the theorist is not inevitably the lamp lighting the way to new observations. The sequence is often reversed. Nor is it enough to say that research and theory must be married if sociology is to bear legitimate fruit. They must not only exchange solemn vows—they must know how to carry on from there. Their reciprocal roles must be clearly defined. This . . . is a short essay toward that definition.

the sociologist as humanist

four

There has always been a small, but highly articulate minority of sociologists who will offer allegiance neither to the camp of theory nor the banner of empiricism. Their plea is rather for the recognition of sociology as a humanistic study, closely linked to philosophy and chiefly concerned with human nature and man's experience and expression of his life condition. No one is better equipped to express this idea than the distinguished anthropologist and humane scholar Robert Redfield, whose concept of the "folk society" has been one of the leading ideas in social science for decades. (See Chap. 6.)

Sociology Among the Humanities

ROBERT REDFIELD

The identification with the natural sciences alone shelters the contempo-

Robert Redfield, "Social Science Among the Humanities," *Measure: A Critical Journal*, 1 (Winter, 1950), 62-67, 71-72.

rary American social scientist from a stimulation from philosophy and the arts and literature which social science needs. Partly because of this the sense of problem in American social science has diminished. Because small matters can be precisely done, large matters are left unconsidered. American political science has departed so far from philosophy that now in many departments of the subject central problems as to justice, or as to the relations of the individual and the state, get little attention. Anthropology, a science currently enjoying success in many fields of inquiry, has almost nothing considered to say as to the nature of human nature. And psychology, as Sidney Olivier complained, having named itself the science of the soul, substituted the study of behavior—which is another thing.

The stimulation which the social sciences can gain from the humanities can come from the arts and literatures themselves, and through an understanding of some of the problems which interest philosophers and the more imaginative students of the creative productions of mankind. It is not argued here that the humanities have ways of studying mankind which social scientists should adopt. It is not denied that many academic students of Chaucer or of the French language emphasize the mastery of formal method to a degree that they too are shut away from the humanity of man and from consideration of the important questions about man. Pedantry and formalism are weaknesses of humanistic learning as of social science. What is here asserted is that the arts and literatures of the world are sources of understanding of man in society from which social scientists may enrich their insights and their sense of problem. It is also asserted that among the professional humanists are many whose work is so similar to that of many social scientists in spirit and purpose as to suggest that some deliberate cultivation of their common interests, now that the scientific character of the social sciences is well established, would enrich and improve the work of both. Let the social scientists turn and talk for a time to their neighbors on their left.

What shall they find to talk about? What have they in common?

The answer is simple. They have humanity in common. Humanity is the common subject matter of those who look at men as they are represented in books or in works of art, and of those who look at men as they appear in institutions and in directly visible action. It is the central and essential matter of interest to social scientist and humanist alike. As physics is concerned with energy and matter, and biology with organisms and life processes, so social science is concerned with the way men and women feel and act and think. Allowing for the fact that there is an aspect of humanity which may be understood when it is seen as a part of all animal life, it is the more important fact that the human qualities of our kind are so notably distinct as to provide a special terrain for systematic inquiry. In this field the humanist and the social scientist work together—in Montaigne's day there was no separation. If, in grouping the academic disciplines, emphasis were given today to subject matter rather than to method, the social sciences and the humanities would be one group, distinct from the other sciences. For the humanity of man is not the concern of physicists or biologists; it is the subject matter of these two other kinds of specialists, now too firmly kept apart.

Humanity is the central subject matter of social scientist and humanist as it is the central interest of mankind. As human beings, we care about the human nature of man; it is more valued than is our animal nature; here theological doctrine restates the view of common sense. What matters to us all, what we live for, is sympathy, understanding, imagination, reason, tradition, aspiration, and personal and human associations. Without these we cannot really undertake to continue to exist, and in our hierarchies of values they are placed above the satisfactions to our physical and biological nature. These last-mentioned come first, in our demands, only because they must come first that better wants be satisfied; but all of us, from the Andaman Islands to New York City, know that companionship, a sense of participation in an effort felt worthwhile, and the confidence of those dear to us are more precious than the absolutely necessary food and shelter. In China, certainly a land where men are hard-pressed to find a livelihood, Confucius is reported to have replied to one who asked him what was necessary in the governing of a people that although food, force, and faith (or the confidence of the people) were necessary, the first two, as responsibilities of the state, might, at the worst, be dispensed with. But faith in one another we must have to become or to remain a society of human beings.

* * * * *

It seems that in spite of the exactions of scientific method, to which they are properly committed, social scientists cannot escape the fact that they are fundamentally concerned with states of mind. Social scientists are closest to their subject matter when they are concerned with feelings, sentiments, opinions, standards, and ideals. They are in fact usually concerned with these, even when the language does not apparently have that meaning. An "economic policy" means only that somebody intends something, and a "political machine" is only figuratively a machine—it is people, with hopes, ambitions, intentions, understandings. Neither a family nor a religion can be learned about by counting people or by measuring a house or a temple; these two are states of mind, and the

influence and relations of the states of mind of some people with respect to those of other people. By talking about "the origin of magic," or "the diffusion of matrilineal clans," even anthropologists managed to get some distance from a recognition of states of mind as their subject matter, as Dr. [Ruth] Benedict remarks. Under the influence of the scientific method that was adopted by students of humanity in the nineteenth century, humanity was cut into pieces of nature as much like plants and animals as they could be made. But as each fresh effort is made to understand humanity, "as it really is," the thing turns out to be made of states of mind.

* * * * *

To study states of mind, we need expressive documents. Whether we undertake the study of humanity as a student of the arts and of literature, or as a social scientist, we find or we make expressive documents. The materials of social science and of the humanities are essentially the same. A tool is expressive in that it shows the purpose of the user and perhaps something of the skill of the maker. Insofar as it is a work of fine art it shows something still more significant: something of the standards of technical performance and perhaps of aesthetic satisfaction. A personal letter is in many cases more richly expressive than a tool; and a curse, a chance remark, a word said in passion, a folktale, and a novel— these are very expressive indeed. The answers written in a questionnaire do not express so much. In 1948 there was a revival of discussion as to just what is expressed by a man who replies to a poll asking him how he will vote at the presidential election. What the student of the lives of men, considered separately as individuals or collectively as social groups, must have, is expressive materials. If he seeks to describe these lives in systematic generalizations, it is his business, surely, to report formally and numerically whatever can be so reported. The anthropologist makes a census, or part of one, counts the houses and the people in them, and hopes to get enough cases of marriage so that he can give some figures as to the proportion of cases in which the couple settle with the wife's parents to those in which the home is made with the husband's parents or somewhere else. Yet if he does only these things he will miss most of what he came for. When he gets a member of the group he is studying to talk or to write freely and naturally about the things that matter to him most—his family, his ambitions, his faith, and his doubts—then the anthropologist knows he has at hand the materials that are most necessary to his work.

These materials for the study of man in society by the social scientist are similar to and overlap the materials that are used by the humanistic scholar. Art expresses the standards of form, of beauty, and, in cases, the interests, political or religious, of the makers. And the materials of literature and philosophy are in part the same as those of sociology and in part are different but related. The materials for the study of Stoic philosophy are the writings of the Stoics, and the materials for the study of Navaho religion and thought are the texts of rituals, of life histories, and of interviews, written down by investigators or by Navahos themselves. The fact that the humanistic scholar generally stays at some university and draws his materials out of the library while the social scientist interviews the Indian or the Chicago precinct committeeman is not an important difference in this connection. Both are reading the words in which other men have expressed their states of mind, their schemes of values.

*   *   *   *   *

The common interest of social scientist and of creative artist exists similarly in the study of personality, the organization of human nature, and of culture in any particular individual. Here also it is the man of literature and art who has the longest interest in the subject. A personality wholly invented, like Madame Bovary or Huckleberry Finn, provides a record of a human individual that tells us much about the nature of human personality, of its development in relation to other personalities, and to events. A biography may be so written, as that by Hervey Allen on Edgar Allen Poe or that by Marquis James on Andrew Jackson, as to show much of those relationships between original temperament, personal associations, the culture of the community, and the happenings of circumstance, as equally concern the students of personality who are social scientists.

Part 2

models
of society

In this section we present some of the models of society that guide sociological theory and research. Just as there are different conceptions of the sociologist's role, so we find contrasting images of the nature of the social order, which is his subject matter. Indeed, one group of contemporary sociologists holds that this very concept of social order is misleading. To them the salient fact of social life is not order, but rather disorder or conflict. They have, accordingly, been designated as the "conflict school" of sociology. The chief target of their criticism is the "structural-functional" view, whose most prominent exponent, Talcott Parsons, we met in Part One. Examples of the work of the conflict school are represented later in Coser's article on terminating conflict (Chap. 22) and Richardson's study of the statistics of war (Chap. 26). In this section we include discussion of four other models of society—the modern evolutionary view, the bucolic image of the folk society, the classic characterization of the bureaucracy, and the "mass society" concept.

Sociological models of society are useful, indeed indispensable, yet they have great power to generate misunderstanding and fruitless controversy. This stems from the tendency of those who produce the models, and those who criticize them, to treat them as the real world rather than as the image of it they purport to be. Additional difficulty stems from the common monistic tendency of the model builder to argue for his as the *only* true conception of society. We urge our readers to keep in mind that a model is only a heuristic device, a representation of reality against which reality is to be tested. Experience in such testing reveals that most models are not especially productive of interesting research, and no one model is *the* key to all aspects of the complex design of social life. Yet many models offer interesting perspectives that other views neglect, and taken together they increase our awareness of the multifaceted nature of social organization.

the evolutionary model

five

The classic sociological model of society is the evolutionary model, which Auguste Comte and Herbert Spencer bequeathed to sociology. Our faith in the unerring, straight-line unfolding of human progress is today rather weak. Leslie White keeps the evolutionary concept alive by showing that mankind as a whole has clearly moved ahead in at least one respect—the harnessing of energy. White presents this view without becoming entangled in arguments about whether this is really "progress." And he resolves the old difficulties over the presumed inevitable stages of evolution by showing how the success of some groups permits others to skip stages of development and thus to share in the general advance.

Energy and Evolution

LESLIE A. WHITE

We turn now to a consideration of social systems in the process of cultural development. A social system is, as we have seen it must be, closely related to its underlying technological system. If a people are nomadic hunters—i.e., use certain technological instruments in certain ways in order to obtain food, furs, hides, and other need-serving materials —they will have one type of social system. If they lead a sedentary life, feeding upon rich beds of shellfish, or if they are pastoralists or intensive agriculturalists, or maritime traders, or industrialists, etc., they will have other

types of social systems. The process of military offense and defense and the technological means with which it is exercised also acts as a determinant of social organization, sometimes a very powerful one. Thus we see that the social system of a people is at bottom determined by the use of the technological means of subsistence and of offense and defense. Those social institutions not directly related to the technology are related indirectly; they serve to coordinate the various sectors of society with one another and to integrate them into a coherent whole.

The social systems of primitive peoples vary tremendously in detail because the specific circumstances of natural habitat and technology vary. But all social systems resting upon a human energy (i.e., prepastoral, preagricultural) basis belong to a common type. They are all relatively small and manifest a minimum of structural differentiation and specialization of function. We find no highly developed societies upon the primitive foundation of a technology powered by human energy alone.

The societies of pastoralists and agriculturalists in the early stages of these technological developments are likewise relatively simple, undifferentiated systems. As a matter of fact we may characterize all human social systems up to a certain point in the development of the agricultural, or farming-and-animal-husbandry, technology as *primitive society*: tribes based upon kinship ties, free access to the resources of nature for all, relatively little social differentiation and specialization, and a high degree of social equality. When, however, a certain point in the development of agriculture was reached, a profound change in social systems took place. This was the *social* aspect of the agricultural revolution. Let us trace the course of this social revolution in its main outlines at least.

Agriculture and animal husbandry are means of producing more food and other useful materials per unit of human energy than can be obtained by hunting, fishing, or gathering. When agriculture is combined with stock raising the energy resources for culture building are of course greater than when the cultivation of plants alone is practiced. Not only do flocks and herds supply meat, milk, wool, or hides, but their muscle power may be used to carry burdens, draw plows and carts, etc. All of the great civilizations of the Old World grew up on the basis of agriculture and animal husbandry. Since, however, it is the cultivation of cereals that is the basic factor in the new agriculture-and-animal-husbandry technology, we may for the sake of brevity speak of "the social consequences of a developing agricultural technology."

As the agricultural arts developed and matured, as plants were improved through selective breeding, as new techniques of cultivation, irrigation, drainage, rotation of crops, fertilization, etc., were introduced and improved, the amount of food produced increased. As the food supply was enlarged the population increased. Small tribes grew into large tribes and these into nations and empires; villages grew into towns and towns into cities.

Not only was *more food* produced by agricultural techniques than by hunting, fishing, and gathering, but more food per capita, more per unit of human labor expended. And, as the agricultural arts developed, the productivity of human labor in this field increased. It gradually became possible for a portion of the population to produce food for all. This meant that a portion of the population could be diverted from agriculture and turned into other channels, such as the industrial and aesthetic arts. As the agricultural technology advanced, more and more of the population could thus be withdrawn from the fields and put to work at other tasks and occupations. Society thus became divided along occupational lines, differentiated structurally and specialized functionally. This led to further social developments, as we shall see in a moment.

The mere increase in population had important consequences in another direction also. Tribes and clans were organized upon a basis of kinship ties; social relations were largely exercised in this form. This mechanism worked very well as long as the social units were relatively small; a clan or tribe could be effective as a mechanism of social organization and intercourse as long as its members were not exceedingly numerous, as long as social relations could be *personal*. But when, under the impetus of a developing agricultural technology and an increasing food supply, clan and tribal units grew to huge size, they tended to fall apart of their own weight. Primitive society tended therefore to disintegrate as a consequence of sheer increase in numbers. A new type of social organization was therefore required if chaos was to be averted. This new organization was found in the state. This was another consequence of the agricultural revolution.

The developing agricultural technology brought about a profound change in economic organization, also. In tribal society production, exchange, and consumption of wealth took place upon a personal, kinship basis; the economic organization was virtually identified with the kinship system. This type of economic organization worked well in a small society with a minimum of division of labor and with little differentiation of social structure along occupational lines. But as society became extensively differentiated, as a consequence of the increase in productivity of human labor in agriculture, a new type of economic system was required; a way of relating *classes* economically to one another must be devised. This can be done either in a feudal or a monetary-market system. In either case, however, we have a system in which property relations form the basis of social relations rather than the reverse, as was the case in tribal, kinship society.

On preliterate cultural levels there was of course some fighting between tribal groups. Competition for favored hunting and fishing grounds or other natural resources, vengeance for real or fancied (e.g., magical) injuries, led to a certain amount of intertribal conflict. But the factors necessary for large-scale and systematic and sustained warfare were lacking. These were supplied, however, as a consequence of the agricultural revolution. A high degree of development of the agricultural, metallurgical, ceramic, and other arts resulted in the production and accumulation of vast amounts of wealth. A rich nation's possessions together with the natural and human resources that made the wealth possible would constitute a rich prize to any people who could conquer it. Warfare became a profitable occupation. Thus we find, especially in Mesopotamia, a condition of almost chronic warfare: nations contending with one another for rich, fertile river valleys, the treasures of palace and temple, one nation conquering and looting another, new empires rising upon the ruins of old.

The social consequences of systematic and chronic warfare are significant: the formation of a professional military class, which in collaboration with political rulers and sometimes even autonomously, may become a powerful political force; the reduction of peoples of conquered nations to the status of slavery or serfdom; and the subordination of the masses at home to the imperatives of prolonged military conflict. Thus warfare tended powerfully to divide society into two major social classes: a relatively small ruling group who organized and directed the campaigns and to whom the overwhelming proportion of the wealth taken as booty went, and a large class who provided the "sinews of war"—the peasants, serfs, the common soldiers, etc. There was often but little difference between the lot of the masses at home and that of the masses of the vanquished nation after conquest and subjugation had been accomplished.

Warfare was not, however, the only means, or social process, that operated to divide societies of the post-agricultural revolutionary era into a small, wealthy, powerful, ruling class on the one hand, and a large class of peasants, serfs, or slaves on the other. The peaceful process of commerce, and especially the use of money, operated also to bring about the same end. Trade and commerce are means of concentrating wealth. In this competitive process the big merchants grew at the expense of the small ones. Wealth tended to gravitate into a few hands. Money lending is a particularly rapid and effective means of making the poor poorer and the wealthy richer. When interest rates range from say 30 to 100 per cent or even more, as they did in ancient times, the small borrowers rapidly sink into economic bondage to the money lenders. It was not at all uncommon in Greece before the reforms of Solon or Kleisthenes for a small farmer to sell his children into slavery in order to pay merely the interest on his loan, let alone the principal. Taxes levied by the ruling class through the mechanism of the state and exorbitant rents levied upon small tenants by large landlords also tended to reduce the masses to a condition of economic bondage and impotence.

Thus we see that the social, political, and economic effects of the technological revolution in agriculture were: the dissolution of the old social system of primitive society, the obsolescence of tribe and clan; the division of society into various occupational groups—guilds of artisans and craftsmen; the division of society horizontally into two major classes: a small, powerful, wealthy, ruling class and a large class, governed and exploited by the ruling class and held in bondage in one form or another by them. Civil society based upon property relations took the place of primitive society based upon kinship; the state replaced tribe and clan. The technological revolution in agriculture precipitated and carried through a revolution in the social, political, and economic sectors of culture. As the amount of energy harnessed and put to work per capita per year was increased by the development of the agricultural technology, society became more and more differentiated structur-

ally and increasingly specialized functionally. Concomitant with this trend was the emergence of a special social mechanism of coordination of functions and correlation of structures, a mechanism of integration and regulation. This political mechanism had two aspects, secular and ecclesiastic, sometimes closely related, sometimes distinct, but always present. We call this special mechanism of coordination, integration, and regulation the state-church. The evolution of civil society from the early metallurgical era to the present day, passing through a variety of forms of the state and class relations, is a story that we shall turn to presently. At this point we wish to return to a matter touched upon earlier.

If culture evolves when and as the amount of energy harnessed per capita per year increases, why did not culture continue to advance indefinitely as a consequence of the technological revolution in agriculture? As we have already seen, it did not. On the contrary, after attaining certain levels it ceased to advance and thereafter continued on a plateau until a new and powerful impetus came from the fuel revolution. Yet, agriculture as a technological process, as a mechanism of harnessing solar energy, was not developed to its technological limits by any means; it has not even yet reached those limits or even approached them very closely according to agronomists. Why, then, did technological progress in agriculture eventually slow down and virtually stop after so rapid a rise?

The answer seems to lie in the relationship between socioeconomic system and technological system established by the agricultural revolution. As we have noted, every social system rests upon and is determined by a technological system. But every technological system functions *within* a social system and is therefore *conditioned* by it. The social system created by the agricultural revolution affected the technological process so as eventually to "contain it" and to bring further progress in culture as a whole virtually to a standstill. This is how it was done.

The social system of civil society was, as we have seen, divided into a ruling class and an exploited class. The latter produced the wealth; the former appropriated so large a portion of it as to leave the latter with but minimum means of subsistence. No advantage would accrue to the producing class if they enlarged their production through increased efficiency; the increment would only be appropriated by the ruling class. On the other hand, the ruling class was not likely to resort to a long-range plan to improve the techniques of agricultural production. If they needed more than they were obtaining at the moment the need was immediate and a long-range plan would have been of no use. They would therefore resort to greater exactions from the producing class. But in many, if not most, instances, it would seem, the ruling class had ample for their needs. As a matter of fact, a great deal of evidence indicates that one of the problems they had to contend with was that of over-production rather than of insufficiency. Thus we see, especially in Egypt but also in Mesopotamia and elsewhere, the ruling class engaging in "conspicuous waste and consumption" and that on a grand scale. Palaces and temples were loaded with wealth and vast treasures were deposited with the dead in tombs. In addition to this, great public works programs—pyramids, monuments, temples, tombs, and palaces—were continually being built. It would appear that the ruling class was frequently confronted with the problem of overproduction and the threat of technological unemployment or a surplus of population among the lower classes. Their great public works programs, the wholesale disposition of

wealth in mortuary customs, etc., enabled them to solve both these problems with one stroke. Thus the social system tended to act as a damper on further increase in technological progress once a certain stage of development had been reached. In addition to the factors mentioned above, [V. G.] Childe has pointed out that the social system operated not only to concentrate wealth in the hands of the ruling minority but effectively prevented the fruits of technological progress from being distributed among the masses of the population. There was, consequently, no chance for the technology of production to expand quantitatively or to improve qualitatively.

We see, then, that the new agricultural technology resulted in a tremendous growth of culture in its initial stages. But in effecting this advance a social system was created that eventually curbed and contained the technological system in such a way as to bring progress virtually to a stop, despite the fact that the *technological* limits of agricultural development had not been even closely approximated. We may reasonably conclude, therefore, that human culture would never have gone substantially beyond the peaks achieved prior to the beginning of the Christian era had not the amount of energy harnessed per capita per year been considerably enlarged by tapping the forces of nature in a new form.

The fuel revolution was the culmination and synthesis of a number of streams of cultural elements that had been in progress of development for some time just as the agricultural revolution was the organized florescence of trends of earlier ages. And, like its predecessor, the fuel revolution brought about great social, political, and economic changes as a consequence of greatly augmenting the energy resources for culture building by harnessing solar energy in a new form, this time in coal, oil, and natural gas.

As in the case of the agricultural revolution, the new fuel technology resulted in a great increase in population. The population of Europe prior to the Coal Age grew only from 100,000,000 in 1650 to 187,000,000 in 1800. From 1800 to 1900, however, it increased to over 400,000,000. The population of England, to cite the country in which the industrial revolution got underway and in which it developed to a very great extent, increased 50 per cent between 1700 and 1800. But during the nineteenth century, it increased 260 per cent. In the two centuries prior to 1850, the population of Japan increased but 41 per cent. In the fifty years following 1872 —about the time industrialization began—however, the population increased over 80 per cent. Urban development was powerfully stimulated and accelerated by the new technology as it had been by the developing agricultural technology in the Bronze Age. The European feudal system—a rural, aristocratic, agricultural production for use economy—was rendered obsolete and replaced by an urban, parliamentary, industrial, production-for-sale-at-a-profit economy. Social structure became ever more differentiated and functions more specialized. The productivity of human labor increased as technology advanced. Farm populations decreased relatively and in some instances absolutely.

Changes occurred in the class structure of society also. The basic dichotomy—a minority ruling class and the majority of the population in a position of subordination and exploitation —remained, but the composition of these classes underwent radical change. Industrial lords and financial barons replaced the landed aristocracy of feudalism as the dominant element in the ruling class, and an urban, industrial proletariat took the place of serfs, peasants, or slaves as the basic element in the subordinate class. Industrial strife took the place of peasant revolts and uprisings of slaves and serfs of earlier days. And, in a new form, the state-church functioned as a coordinative and regulative mechanism to maintain the integrity of society by containing these class antagonisms and by mobilizing the resources of society for offense and defense.

We may pause at this point to take note of an interesting feature of the process of cultural evolution: *as culture evolves the rate of growth is accelerated.* As we have already seen, the rate of growth in late Neolithic and early Bronze times was much greater than in the Paleolithic and Eolithic Ages. The agricultural revolution required but a few thousand years to run its course. But the fuel revolution is only a century and a half or two centuries old at most, and already greater changes have been effected by it perhaps than by all earlier ages put together. The change is so rapid and we are so much in the midst of it that it is difficult to grasp the situation and to realize the profound and radical nature of the revolution, social and political as well as technological, through which we are passing. Twenty-seven years ago in *New Viewpoints in American History,* Professor A. M. Schlesinger compared the culture of the United States of Lincoln's day with that of Benjamin Franklin's on the one hand, and with the culture of 1922 on the other. He remarked that the daily life with which Lincoln was familiar was in most respects like that known to George Washington and Franklin. But our culture in 1922 would have been strange and bewildering to Lincoln had he returned to the American scene:

Buildings more than three or four stories high would be new. The plate-glass show windows of the stores, the electric street lighting, the moving-picture theaters, the electric elevators in the buildings, and especially the big department stores would be things in his day unknown. The smooth-paved streets and cement sidewalks would be new to him. The fast-moving electric streetcars and motor vehicles would fill him with wonder. Even a boy on a bicycle would be a curiosity. Entering the White House, someone would have to explain to him such commonplaces of modern life as sanitary plumbing, steam heating, friction matches, telephones, electric lights, the Victrola, and even the fountain pen. In Lincoln's day, plumbing was in its beginnings, coal-oil lamps and gas jets were coming into use, and the steel pen had only recently superseded the quill pen. The steel rail, the steel bridge, high-powered locomotives, refrigerator cars, artificial ice, the cream separator, the twine binder, the caterpillar tractor, money orders, the parcel post, rural free delivery, the cable, the wireless, gasoline engines, repeating rifles, dynamite, submarines, airplanes—these and hundreds of other inventions now in common use were all alike unknown.[1]

But consider the changes that have taken place—in transportation, medicine, communication, and in technology in general—since Schlesinger wrote in 1922! In warfare perhaps better than in other areas of our culture, is the dizzying rate of technological progress made dramatically apparent. The technology of the First World War looks quaint today, and some of the weapons and techniques introduced for the first time in World War II are already obsolete. One hardly dares to picture the next great military conflict; novelties already unveiled and others only intimated suggest all too vividly the distance that technological progress has gone since the days of Pearl

Harbor. And behind the scenes in the theatre of Mars are the great research laboratories and proving grounds, working under forced draft to develop and perfect new tools and techniques in all phases of our technology. The rate of cultural advance is now greater than ever before. "Our life," wrote the distinguished physicist, Arthur Holly Compton in 1940, "differs from that of two generations ago more than American life of that day differed from the civilized life at the dawn of written history."[2] And since Compton wrote these words, a profound and awful revolution—perhaps the most significant in all human history—has taken place: the harnessing of atomic energy.

But, even as in the case of the agricultural revolution and its aftermath, so in the Power Age the social system created by the new fuel technology came eventually to act as a brake upon further cultural advance. The price and profit system stimulated production and technological progress as long as the output could find a market. But, like the socioeconomic system of the Bronze Age, the new commercialism of the fuel era had its inherent limitations. No industrial nation had or could have purchasing power sufficient to keep and absorb its own output; the very basis of the industrial profit system was an excess in value of product over the cost of production in terms of wages paid to the industrial workers. Export of surplus was therefore essential; "we must export or die" is a cry of desperation heard from more than one nation in recent years. For a time new markets could be found abroad. But as the output of industrial nations increased with advances in technology, and as non-European nations such as Japan became industrialized and hence

[1] Arthur M. Schlesinger, *New Viewpoints in American History* (New York: The Macmillan Company, 1922), pp. 247-248. Copyright 1922 by The Macmillan Company.

[2] A. H. Compton, "Science Shaping American Culture," *Proceedings, American Philosophical Society*, 83 (1940), 576.

competitors for foreign markets, the international profit system began to bog down. The world market diminished as the industrial output increased. When goods could no longer be sold profitably abroad, production was curtailed at home. Entrepreneurs are disinclined to produce goods that cannot be sold at a profit. Factories, mills, and mines were closed. Millions of workers were thrown out of employment. Surplus goods were destroyed, agricultural production reduced. The awful plague of overproduction and unemployment, "starvation in the midst of plenty," settled upon the land. The social system was strangling the great technological machine of industry and paralyzing the body politic as a whole. The alternatives were stagnation and death or war and revolution. If the social system were able to contain the fuel technology and the commercial rivalries and class conflicts engendered by it, society would become stabilized in a more or less stagnant form of industrial feudalism. Should, however, the forces inherent in the new technology be able to surmount and overcome the restrictions of the price and parliamentary system, then culture could advance toward higher levels.

There is evidence aplenty that culture, powered by the mighty forces of fuel technology, is embarking upon the latter course. The first phase of the second great cultural revolution—the industrial revolution—has run its course and we are now entered upon the second phase, that of social, political, and economic revolution. And, as in the past, war is proving to be an effective means of profound political change. The system of free and individual enterprise in business and commerce is now virtually extinct. The gold standard is merely a memory of an era that is closed. The parliamentary system of government, a device designed to permit the greatest free-

dom for the growth of industrial and financial enterprise, is practically obsolete also. Private right is no longer significant chiefly as a means of freedom for growth as it was in the early days of commercialism. It now leads toward competitive rivalry, internecine strife, chaos, and paralysis. Concentrations of power without public responsibility among those who own or control vast wealth, or in the ranks of organized labor, are no longer compatible with the degree of unity, integrity, and strength that a nation must have if it is to compete successfully with its rivals in the international arena. The exigencies of national survival require the subordination of private right to general welfare, of part to whole. In short, the state, as the integrative and regulative mechanism of civil society, is destined to acquire ever-greater power and to wield more and more control. Social evolution is moving inexorably toward higher levels of integration, toward greater concentrations of political power and control.

On the international level, too, an interesting trend of social evolution can be discerned: movement toward ever-larger and larger political units. The agricultural technology replaced villages with cities, tribes with nations and empires. The modern fuel technology also is working toward larger political groupings, fewer concentrations of political power. The relatively recent trend toward amalgamation can be seen in the unification of Germany and Italy in the nineteenth century. The Treaty of Versailles attempted, with the "Balkanization of Europe," to oppose the age-old trend of social evolution by breaking the continent up into little pieces. One of the conspicuous and significant aspects of the Second World War in its initial phase was a movement toward the unification of Europe. A half-dozen or so world powers engaged in the First World

War; only two great powers emerged from the second. The competition for power narrows as contestants are eliminated. The logical conclusion is, however, not simply the domination of the world by a single nation—this would be but a transitional stage—but a single political organization that will embrace the entire planet and the whole human race. Toward such a denouement is our mighty power technology rapidly moving us.

But a new and ominous element has recently entered the picture: nuclear atomic energy for military purposes. Here again the significance of this new factor derives from the fact that a new source of energy has been harnessed and in awful form. Once more we are upon the threshold of a technological revolution. But the consequences of this new technological advance may possibly differ radically from those of the agricultural and the fuel revolutions. New technologies in the past have rendered old social systems obsolete but they have replaced them with new systems. The new nuclear technology, however, threatens to destroy civilization itself, or at least to cripple it to such an extent that it might require a century, a thousand, or ten thousand years to regain its present status. At least this is what eminent scientists and military men tell us; as laymen we are in a child's world of ignorance, with almost all the significant facts kept beyond our reach. The destruction of a few score of centers of science and industry in Europe and the United States would just about do for western civilization, and authorities assure us that this is well within the realm of possibility, not to say probability. The hope of the future, therefore, and the salvation of mankind and civilization would seem to lie in the emergence from the next war of a *victor*—not merely a survivor—and one with sufficient power and resources to organize the whole planet and the entire human species within a single social system.

We have thus presented a sketch of the evolution of the culture of mankind from the horizon of our prehuman forebears to the present time. It is a fascinating story of adventure and progress; of a species lifting itself up by its cultural bootstraps from the status of a mere animal to a radically new way of life, a way destined to win mastery over most other species and to exert a powerful and extensive control over the natural habitat. The origin of culture elevated the evolutionary process to a new plane. No longer was it necessary for the human animal to acquire new powers and techniques through the slow process of biological change; he now had an extrasomatic mechanism of adjustment and control that could grow freely of itself. Moreover, advances in one stream of cultural development could diffuse readily to other traditions so that all might share in the progress of each. Thus the story of man becomes an account of his culture.

Technology is the hero of our piece. This is a world of rocks and rivers, sticks and steel, of sun, air, and starlight, of galaxies, atoms, and molecules. Man is but a particular kind of material body who must do certain things to maintain his status in a cosmic material system. The means of adjustment and control, of security and survival, are of course technological. Culture thus becomes primarily a mechanism for harnessing energy and of putting it to work in the service of man, and, secondarily, of channelling and regulating his behavior not directly concerned with subsistence and offense and defense. Social systems are therefore determined by technological systems, and philosophies and the arts express experience as it is defined by technology and refracted by social systems. Cultural systems like those of the biological level are capable of growth. That is, the power to capture any energy is also the ability to harness more and still more of it. Thus cultural systems, like biological organisms, develop, multiply, and extend themselves. The sun is the prime mover; culture, a thermodynamic system operated by it. At least, solar energy has activated all cultural systems of history up to now, and it will continue to do so after terrestrial supplies of fissionable fuels have been exhausted— if civilization should survive and reach this point. But technology is still the leading character in our play, even though it may turn out to be a villain instead of the hero. Technology builds but it may also destroy. The belief and faith that civilization, won at such great cost in pain and labor, simply cannot go down in destruction because such an end would be too monstrous and senseless, is but a naïve and anthropocentric whimper. The cosmos does little know nor will it long remember what man has done here on this tiny planet. The eventual extinction of the human race—for come it will sometime—will not be the first time that a species has died out. Nor will it be an event of very great terrestrial significance.

But *man* may survive the coming holocaust of radioactivity even though his culture is tumbled to the level of Neolithic times, only to begin the long climb over again, this time perhaps by a somewhat different route; culture too may be able to profit from experience. But culture may *not* destroy or even critically wound itself with its new powers. Destruction is no more inevitable than salvation. Great though the devastation may—and will—be in the next test of strength in the international arena, the creative powers of the new technology may be sufficiently great to rise up from the ruins and to enclose the whole world in a single political embrace. Then and only then will the curse of war be lifted and the way made free and open for a fuller and richer life.

Our sketch of the evolution of culture is, it will be noted, wholly culturological. It does not resort to race, physical type, intelligence, a moral sense, the dignity of man, the spirit of progress or democracy, the individual —genius or otherwise—the rejection of the father, consciousness of kind, a set of instincts or "drives," social interaction, a basic personality structure, toilet training in infancy, or breast *vs.* bottle feeding and weaning, to account for the behavior and growth of this great extrasomatic tradition. We explain it in terms of culture itself. A thundershower or a tornado is explained in terms of antecedent and concomitant meteorological events; a clan or a constitution is likewise accounted for by citing its cultural antecedents and concomitants.

Culture is, as we have pointed out repeatedly, a stream of interacting elements; one trait reacts upon others and is affected by them in return. Some elements become obsolete and are eliminated from the stream; new elements are incorporated into it. New permutations, combinations, and syntheses are continually being formed. Whether we deal with a restricted portion of the cultural continuum such as the evolution of mathematics or the genealogy of the steam engine, or whether we encompass culture in its entirety, the principle of interpretation is the same: culture grows out of culture. In our sketch of the evolution of culture as a whole we deal with large categories: technology, social systems, and philosophies. We break technology down into energy and tool factors. We observe the action of each class of elements, their impact upon others, the effect of technology upon social systems, and the influence of economic and political institutions upon agriculture and steam-driven factories. We note the role that war as a culture process has played in the course of political change. And, finally, we see the fate of civilization delicately balanced in a scales to be tipped this way or that, we know not how, by the modern miracles of nuclear technology.

Culturology is the newest venture of science. After centuries of cultivation in the fields of astronomy, physics, and chemistry, after scores of years of tillage in physiology and psychology, science has at last turned to the most immediate and powerful determinant of man's *human* behavior: his culture. After repeated trials and as many failures it was discovered that culture cannot be explained psychologically; such interpretations are merely anthropomorphisms in scientific clothing. The explanation of culture is and must be culturological. The science of culture is young but full of promise. It is destined to do great things—if only the subject of its study will continue its age-old course: onward and upward.

the idyll of folk society

six

An idealized image that persists rather more tenaciously than most describes the small-scale society, based primarily on kinship and village ties, as yielding values of serenity, grace, dignity, cooperation, friendliness, and piety long since denied to us who live in the cold, impersonal, urban conglomerations of modern society. This idyllic image may be more wish than reality, as Oscar Lewis shows us with hard facts and firm analysis of the very villages about which Robert Redfield first formed his famous concept of the "folk society." This entry also may serve us as an example of the techniques for field research used by anthropological and sociological students of the small community, thus enlarging our perspective on the "modes of inquiry" described in Part Six.

Tepoztlán Restudied

OSCAR LEWIS

The Need for Restudies

Anthropologists who like to think that there is an element of science in the social sciences, including anthropology, have often called primitive societies the "laboratory" of the social scientists, where hypotheses about the

Oscar Lewis, "Tepoztlán Restudied: A Critique of the Folk-Urban Conceptualization of Social Change," *Rural Sociology*, **18** (1953), 121-134.

nature of man and society can be tested. While the experiments and observations of the natural scientist are generally repeated and checked independently by different observers, the reports of the anthropologists have to be accepted on their face value, and their reliability has to be judged in terms of the respect for and confidence in the author's integrity, the inner consistency of his work, and the extent to which it agrees with one's own preconceptions. If the analogy with the natural sciences is to be taken seriously, we must develop methods for checking the reliability of our observations and the validity of interpretation. Restudy is one such method. This point has been recognized by a number of anthropologists, but to date there have been very few restudies. The reasons for this are many. Perhaps most important have been the limited funds for field research, the time pressure to study tribes that were rapidly becoming extinct, the shortage of field workers, the greater appeal in studying a community never before studied, and finally, the lack of emphasis upon methodology.

Of course, there is some difference of opinion in regard to the value of restudies. Those who would emphasize the subjective element, the element of art in field work, tend to be skeptical about the methodological value of restudies. On the other hand, those who have greater faith in objective methods, in operational procedures for observation, are inclined to be more favorable toward restudies. The former would argue that all human beings make errors, that this can be taken for granted, and that we can learn more by going ahead with new studies than by concerning ourselves with past mistakes. The latter would argue that it is important to learn what kinds of errors have been made, particularly if the scientific aspect of anthropology is to grow stronger. The former would argue that we do not need to have a restudy to know that there is something wrong with a report. This can be determined in terms of our wider comparative knowledge, in terms of internal consistency, or in terms of whether it agrees with a particular school of thought. The latter would perhaps agree but add that this is not enough, that we need empirical evidence as to just what the facts are. Finally, some would suggest that there may be a further dichotomy involved—namely, the difference between those who hold that truth is relative and subjective and that each field worker is probably correct within the limits of the problem set and the materials selected for study, and those who hold that truth is absolute and objective and can be approximated more nearly by some methods than by others.

It must be emphasized that the objective and value of restudies is not to prove one man right and another wrong. It is not a matter of listing another's errors, in itself a distasteful and painful task, but rather of finding out what kind of errors tend to be made by what kind of people under what kind of conditions. Given a sufficiently large number of restudies, it might be possible to develop a theory of error of observation which would help to evaluate the role of the personal equation, personality, and ideological or cultural variables. If we could eventually arrive at generalizations in which we could say, given an anthropologist from such and such a cultural background, we can expect that his account of tribe X will be slanted in such and such a way, then we would have made some progress.

It may be useful to distinguish four types of restudies: (1) those restudies in which a second or third investigator goes to a community with the express design of re-evaluating the work of his predecessor; (2) those in which the same or an independent investigator goes to a community studied earlier this time to study cultural change, and utilizing the first report as a baseline against which to measure and evaluate change: (3) those in which one returns to study some aspect of the culture not studied earlier; and (4) those in which one studies more intensively, and perhaps from a new point of view, some aspect of the culture studied earlier. There is, of course, some overlapping between these types. All restudies are additive in a sense. However, it is a matter of emphasis in research design.

From the point of view of testing reliability, the first type would seem to be the most suitable, though not without its methodological difficulties. Communities change, and it is sometimes difficult to know to what extent differences in findings reflect changes in the culture. Much depends upon the area and community being restudied. In cases where many years have elapsed between the first and second study and where change has been rapid and profound, it may well be impossible to reconstruct the earlier condition with sufficient accuracy to make it useful for reliability purposes. On the other hand, there are many areas where change is relatively slow and superficial. Moreover, when too many years have not elapsed, it may be possible to interview the same informants as in the earlier study. Also, the use of village records and archive records can act as a control. Finally, much depends upon the amount of quantitative data in the first report. Where the amount is large, restudies have a more solid base for comparisons. Indeed, this is perhaps the major positive function of quantification.

To the present writer's knowledge, there is not a single published case of a restudy of the first type—i.e., where the express purpose was the interest in methodology, the interest in testing an earlier report. The recent restudy of Tepoztlán perhaps comes closest to this type, and in the following pages some aspects of this restudy will be discussed.

Differences Between Redfield's Study and the Restudy

In 1926, Robert Redfield first studied the village of Tepoztlán and gave us his pioneer work, *Tepoztlán—A Mexican Village.*[1] This book has since become a standard reference and a classic in the field of community studies. It is of particular importance in the history of community studies in that it contains Redfield's first statement on the nature of the folk society, and, at least implicitly, the concept of the folk-urban continuum, an hypothesis of societal change later made explicit in *The Folk Culture of Yucatan.*[2] The folk-urban conceptualization of culture change now enjoys great prestige among sociologists and anthropologists and has served as the theoretical frame of reference for many of the community studies done by Redfield's students.

Seventeen years after Redfield's study, the writer went to Tepoztlán to take another look, with the specific objective of studying the social, economic, political, and religious life of the community, with special emphasis upon an analysis of the changes which had occurred in the village since 1926. This involved a restudy of the village and a comparison of findings. Special attention, however, was given to those aspects of village life that Redfield had merely touched upon, such as demog-

[1] Robert Redfield, *Tepoztlán—A Mexican Village* (Chicago: University of Chicago Press, 1930).
[2] Robert Redfield, *The Folk Culture of Yucatan* (Chicago: University of Chicago Press, 1941).

raphy, the land problem, systems of agriculture, the distribution of wealth, standards of living, politics and local government, the life cycle of the individual, and interpersonal relations.

Readers who are familiar with the earlier study of Tepoztlán by Redfield will want to know how the findings compare. Such a comparison is made here, not only for a better understanding of Tepoztlán, but also because of its broader implications for anthropological method and theory. The questions are: To what extent and in what ways do the results obtained from the independent study of the same society by two anthropologists differ? What are the implications of such differences concerning the reliability and validity of anthropological reporting?

The differences in findings range from discrepancies in factual details to differences in the over-all view of Tepoztecan society and its people. The impression given by Redfield's study of Tepoztlán is that of a relatively homogeneous, isolated, smoothly functioning, and well-integrated society made up of a contented and well-adjusted people. His picture of the village has a Rousseauian quality which glosses lightly over evidence of violence, disruption, cruelty, disease, suffering, and maladjustment. We are told little of poverty, economic problems, or political schisms. Throughout his study we find an emphasis upon the cooperative and unifying factors in Tepoztecan society. The writer's findings, on the other hand, would emphasize the underlying individualism of Tepoztecan institutions and character, the lack of cooperation, the tensions between villages within the *municipio*, the schisms within the village, the pervading quality of fear, envy, and distrust in interpersonal relations.

Now let us consider some of these differences in more detail. Redfield's account of Tepoztlán stresses the role

of communal lands as a unifying factor within the village and the *municipio*. While this is certainly true, it is only part of the story. With the single exception of church lands, communal lands were and are individually operated, and the ideal of every Tepoztecan is to own his private plot of land. Furthermore, the communal lands have been a source of intervillage quarrels, and during the year that Redfield was in Tepoztlán these quarrels resulted in violence. Similarly, Redfield gives the impression that the *cuatequitl* (a traditional form of collective labor) was part and parcel of village life. He described a *cuatequitl*, which occurred during his stay, as if it were a common and regular occurrence. As a matter of fact, it was the first village *cuatequitl* of importance since the revolution, and there have been very few subsequent ones. The particular *cuatequitl* which Redfield observed was due to the curious circumstance whereby a local, socialistically oriented political faction, directed from Mexico City by a group of Tepoztecans who were members of the Confederación Regional de Obreros Mexicanos, locally known as "the Bolsheviki," revived the traditional *cuatequitl*. Before the Revolution, the village *cuatequitl* was not viewed simply as a voluntary, cooperative endeavor but was also associated with forced labor and imposition by the local *cacique* groups which ruled the village during the Díaz regime. In the Colonial period, the Spaniards similarly utilized the traditional *cuatequitl* as a source of labor. In short, Redfield's account of the cooperative aspects of village life needs to be modified somewhat in the light of other data.

Redfield portrayed Tepoztlán as a community of landowners and did not mention a land problem. But in the restudy it was found that over half of the villagers did not own private land, and that there was an acute shortage of good land and considerable population pressure in the face of dwindling agricultural resources. Redfield gave a rather glowing picture of Tepoztlán during the Díaz regime as having reached a period of great cultural florescence, but he failed to point out that this was limited to only a few Tepoztecans, and that the vast majority of Tepoztecans were illiterate, desperately poor, landless, and living under an oppressive political regime which forbade them to utilize their own communal resources. In this connection it is interesting to note that Tepoztlán was one of the first villages in the state of Morelos to join the Zapatista revolt against the Díaz regime. Redfield apparently viewed the Mexican revolution as having had the effect of halting the tendency for the merging of social class differences; but the writer found that the Revolution had a marked leveling influence, economically, socially, and culturally.

Redfield presented only the positive and formal aspects of interpersonal relations, such as forms of greeting and the respect-relations of *compadres*; he failed to deal with some of the negative and disruptive aspects of village life, such as the fairly high incidence of stealing, quarrels, and physical violence. An examination of the local records revealed that, in the year that Redfield lived in the village, there were 175 reported cases of crimes and misdemeanors in the local court. Most of these cases were offenses against person and property. Since not all cases reach the local authorities, this number is indicative of considerable conflict.

Redfield described local politics as a game, but it appears that politics was a very serious affair which frequently led to violence. The year Redfield was there, the political schisms culminated in open violence bordering on civil war, and it was this situation which finally resulted in Redfield's leaving the village.

Another important difference between the findings concerns Redfield's delineation of the social structure of the village in terms of what he called the *tontos*, or representative of folk culture, and the *correctos*, or representative of city ways. It should be pointed out that Tepoztecans do not conceive of these terms as designations of social classes, in the sense used by Redfield, nor did they twenty years ago. Tepoztecans use the words as descriptive adjectives, with *tonto* meaning stupid, backward, foolish, or ignorant, and with *correcto* meaning well mannered, well bred, proper, or correct. The poorest, least educated, and most conservative man may be *correcto* to a Tepoztecan if he is polite and behaves in the accepted manner. Similarly a well-educated, acculturated man may be called *tonto* if he permits himself to be fooled by others or dominated by his wife. Within any one family, some of the members may be considered *tonto* and others *correcto*, depending almost entirely upon personality traits and manners.

But, granting that the degree of exposure to and influence of city ways is an important criterion in making for status differences in Tepoztlán, it is by no means the only one, and certainly not the most significant one in terms of the actual operation of the many status distinctions in the village. Among status distinctions which were then, and are today, more meaningful to Tepoztecans are those of rich and poor, landowners and landless, owners of private lands and holders of *ejidos*, *ejidatarios* and *comuneros*, farmers in hoe culture and farmers in plow culture, sons of *caciques* and sons of ex-Zapatistas, to mention but a few.

Furthermore, the concept of *tontos* and *correctos*, as social classes representing different cultural levels, led to

46662

misunderstanding of the local political situation. The opposing political factions in the village during Redfield's stay were not composed of *tontos* on the one side and *correctos* on the other. The leaders on both sides included highly acculturated and little acculturated individuals, as did the members at large. A study of the personnel of each of the local government administrations (*ayuntamientos*) from 1926 to 1947 gives no support to Redfield's statement that politics, like the religious fiestas, are in the hands of the *tontos*.

The use of the terms *tonto* and *correcto* to designate social groups, which did not and do not exist and operate as such, makes much of Redfield's analysis of Tepoztecan society oversimplified, schematic, and unreal. There is a much wider range of custom and belief among the so-called *tontos* than was reported by Redfield; and by the same token there was less of a gap between the *tontos* and *correctos*. While Redfield's concept would tend to make for two cultures, the writer sees Tepoztlán as a single culture, with more and less acculturated individuals in close and frequent contact, each influencing the other, as they have for the past four hundred years.

Reasons for Differences

More important than the differences in findings is the question of how to explain these differences. In a sense, it is inevitable that different students studying the same society will arrive at different conclusions. Certainly the personal factor, and what Redfield has recently referred to as the element of art in social science, cannot be overlooked. Nevertheless the differences in findings on Tepoztlán are of such magnitude as to demand some further and more detailed explanation.

Some of the differences in the two sets of data can be explained by changes which have occurred in the village in the interim of nearly twenty years between the studies. Other differences result from the difference in the general scope of the two studies. The present study had the advantage of having Redfield's pioneer work to start with, the assistance of Mexican personnel, more than twice the amount of time for field work, and the new approaches and methods, especially in the field of culture and personality, developed during the past twenty years. The much greater emphasis upon economic analysis in this study also reflects a fairly recent trend in anthropology. In addition, this study was based on the testimony of well over one hundred informants, as compared with about a half-dozen used by Redfield. This revealed a wide range of individual differences and enabled more thorough checking of data.

Still other differences, such as those summarized, must be attributed for the most part to differences in theoretical orientation and methodology, which in turn influenced the selection and coverage of facts and the way in which these facts were organized. A re-examination of Redfield's book, in the light of the more recent field observations in the village, suggests that the concept of the folk culture and folk-urban continuum was Redfield's organizing principle in the research. Perhaps this helps to explain his emphasis on the formal and ritualistic aspects of life rather than the everyday life of the people and their problems, on evidence of homogeneity rather than heterogeneity and the range of custom, on the weight of tradition rather than deviation and innovation, on unity and integration rather than tensions and conflict.

Redfield's interest was primarily in the study of a single cultural process: the evolution from folk to urban, rather than a well-rounded ethnographic account. He only incidentally considered Tepoztlán in its historical, geographical, and cultural context in Morelos and Mexico, and attempted rather to place Tepoztlán within the broader, more abstract context of the folk-urban continuum.

The questions he asked of his data were quite different from those asked in this study. For example, he was not concerned with determining just what Tepoztlán is typical of, in relation to rural Mexico; nor was he concerned with determining how a study of Tepoztlán might reveal some of the underlying characteristics and problems of Mexico as a whole. Thus, the revolution in Tepoztlán is not analyzed in terms of its social, economic, and political effects upon the village, nor in terms of what light it might throw upon the nature of the revolution as a whole, but rather in regard to the more limited question of the emergence of Zapata as a "folk hero."

Comparison with Redfield's Yucatan Findings: Disorganization

To what extent does the trend of change found in the present study of Tepoztlán fall within the categories suggested by Redfield in his study, *The Folk Culture of Yucatan?* He postulates that with increased urban influences there is greater disorganization, secularization, and individualization. Taking each separately, we shall consider the family first, as an example of disorganization. Redfield summarized the broad trends of change in family organization as follows:

As one goes from Tusik toward Merida there is to be noted a reduction in the stability of the elementary family; a decline in the manifestation of patriarchal or matriarchal authority; a disappearance of institutions expressing cohesion in the great family; a reduction in the strength and importance of respect relationships, especially for elder brothers and for elder people generally; an increasing vagueness of the conventional outlines of appropriate behavior toward relatives; and a shrinkage in the applicability of kinship terms primarily denoting members of the elementary family toward more distant relatives or toward persons not relatives.[3]

The first generalization that can be made in the case of Tepoztlán is that, despite the increased city influences in the last seventeen years, the stability of the nuclear family has not been seriously modified. The family remains strong and cohesive, separations have not noticeably increased, and divorce is all but nonexistent. The extended family is relatively weak but continues to serve in cases of emergency. This weakness, however, is not a recent phenomenon. Quarrels between husband and wife and wife-beating occur with some frequency; but this, too, seems to be an old pattern. The tensions and quarrels within families reflect a type of family organization, as well as Tepoztecan personality, but are not necessarily symptoms of disorganization.

Parental authority remains strong in Tepoztlán despite the elimination of arranged marriages and the increase in elopements. Parents continue to have control over their children, in many cases even after marriage. On about a sixth of the house sites there are joint families, and about half of these are extended families in which married sons are treated as children subject to the authority of the parents (*hijos de familia*).

Although about half of the marriages now begin as elopements, which flout the authority of the parents, the old form of asking for the girl's hand by the boy's parents continues. In any case, elopements do not lead to disor-

---

[3] *Ibid.*, p. 211.

ganization, for most elopements end in marriage, and the couple make peace with their parents. Assuming that elopements are an old trait, as seems to be indicated, here we have a case in which urban influence has intensified an old trait rather than caused its breakdown. Moreover, because Redfield found practically no elopements in Tusik and many elopements in Merida, he associated elopements with urbanism and disorganization. But this assumes what has still to be proved. In Tepoztlán, which is much less urban than Merida, by Redfield's own standards, we find a much higher proportion of elopements than in Merida. Furthermore, in Tzintzuntzan, an even more isolated village, Foster found that 90 per cent of the marriages began as elopements. And he cites documentary evidence for the antiquity of this pattern.[4] Beals, in another connection, has also called attention to a pattern of change different from that reported by Redfield. Beals writes:

Cherán, like many Indian communities of Mexico, is increasingly influenced by the town and the city. Nevertheless, the process again seems significantly different from those hitherto described by Redfield. In Cherán there is no distinction of *los tontos* and *los correctos*, *mestizo* and *indio*, or *ladino* and *indio*, although such may exist in some Tarascan towns with an appreciable *mestizo* population. Nor does the neat diminishing order of city, town and village hold in this area. Cherán is probably more influenced by Gary (Indiana), Mexico City, and Morelia (possibly in diminishing order) than it is by Uruapan and Patzcuaro. Indeed, it is quite probable that fundamentally Cherán is more progressive, more in touch with the modern world, than is *mestizo* Patzcuaro with its conscious idealization of a Colonial past.[5]

[4] George M. Foster, *Empire's Children: The People of Tzintzuntzan* (Mexico: Imprenta Nueva Mundo, 1948), p. 429.
[5] Ralph L. Beals, *Cherán: A Sierra Taras-*

The desire of young couples to become independent of their parents and to set up their own homes reflects a greater individualism but does not necessarily imply a breakdown in family life. On the contrary, the lesser role of the in-laws and the greater dependence of the husband and wife upon each other, plus the fact that they are each of their own choice, may make for better marriage relations and greater family stability.

Although it is true that some outer forms of respect have been discarded, the fundamental respect status of elders remains. Perhaps the single exception has been the decline in the respect accorded to elder brothers. But it is questionable whether the elder brother in Tepoztlán ever enjoyed the special position that he had in Maya society.

There seems to be no evidence of any marked change in the reciprocal behavior of relatives, perhaps because such changes have occurred so far back in history that informants have no memory of them today. As stated previously, the extended family is weak, and seems to have been so for many generations. The same may be said for the use of kinship terms, which have not changed in recent history. In surrounding villages, which generally conserve older culture elements, kinship terms are used in substantially the same way as in Tepoztlán.

In the examples cited, it is clear that changes have occurred in the village, but these changes do not necessarily imply disorganization. Rather, they involve a new kind of organization or reorganization.

Secularization

The second conclusion of the study in Yucatan showed a clear trend toward secularization:

can Village, Institute of Social Anthropology, Publication No. 2 (Washington, D.C.: Smithsonian Institution, 1946), pp. 211f.

The conclusion has been reached that the city and town exhibit greater secularization than do the villages. The principal facts offered in support of this conclusion are . . . the separation of maize from the context of religion and its treatment simply as a means of getting food or money; the increase in the number of specialists who carry on their activities for a practical livelihood relative to those that carry on traditional activities which are regarded as prerogatives and even moral duties to the community; the change in the character of the institution of *guardia* whereby from being an obligation, religiously supported, to protect a shrine and a god it becomes a mere job in the town hall; the (almost complete) disappearance of family worship; the decline in the sacramental character of baptism and marriage; the conversion of the pagan cult from what is truly religious worship to mere magic or even superstition; the decline in the veneration accorded the *santos*; the change in the *novena* in which from being a traditional form expressive of appeal to deity, it becomes a party for the fun of the participants; the alteration in the festival of the patron saint in which it loses its predominant character as worship and becomes play and an opportunity for profit; the separation of ideas as to the cause and cure of sickness from conceptions as to moral or religious obligation.[6]

The data from Tepoztlán do not enable a careful comparison on each of the cited points. However, many of the data are comparable and show the trend toward secularization noted. The attitude toward corn in Tepoztlán combines both the secular and religious. Certainly corn is viewed as the basic crop, both for subsistence and for trade. But the religious aspects have not been entirely lopped off. The corn is still blessed in the church on San Isidro's Day, and some families still burn incense in the home and address

a prayer to the corn before planting. Some also make the sign of the cross when planting the first seed. Moreover, on the Day of San Miguel, crosses are still placed at the four corners of the *milpa* to ward off the winds. From informants' accounts, it appears that these customs were more widespread before the revolution. It is difficult to say how much change has occurred since 1926, for Redfield did not report on this subject.

The study of occupational changes and division of labor in Tepoztlán showed that most of the old "folk specialists" have continued and even increased in number, side by side with the increase in the new specialists. There were more *curaderos*, *chirimiteros*, fireworks-makers, and mask-makers in 1944 than in 1926, and there seemed to be every indication that these occupations would continue. The only exceptions are the *huehuechiques*, who must be able to speak Nahuatl, and those *chirimiteros*, who are being displaced by the more modern variety. However, the rate of increase in what Redfield would call the secular specialists has been much greater than that of the "folk specialists." To this extent, the independent findings for Yucatan and Tepoztlán agree. But it should be noted that before the revolution there were more shoemakers, carpenters, saddle-makers, and other artisans than in 1926 or 1944. Were it not for the specific historical information to explain this phenomenon, one might conclude that with increasing urban contacts there is a decrease in the number of specialists. The reason for this decrease has been, rather, the destruction of many neighboring *haciendas* which were formerly supplied by labor from Tepoztlán, and the abolition of the *cacique* class which had offered a market for the products of the artisans.

In Tepoztlán there does not appear to have been any appreciable decline

<hr/>

[6] *The Folk Culture of Yucatan, op. cit.*, p. 352.

in the sacramental character of baptism and marriage. At any rate, both are considered important and are standard practices. Despite the legalization of secular marriage, church marriage is still considered the best marriage by most Tepoztecans.

Similarly, there is no evidence of any decline in the veneration of the *santos;* the *novena* continues to be an appeal to the deity rather than a party for fun; the patron saints of the *barrios* are still regarded as protectors and are worshiped as such. Nor have *barrio* fiestas become primarily an occasion for profit. In fact, Tepoztecans do not show the marked commercial spirit reported in Mitla by [Mrs. Elsie] Parsons, and in communities of the Guatemalan highlands by Sol Tax. Unlike Parsons' experiences in Mitla, the researchers were never besieged by questions about the cost of things, nor did they ever witness Tepoztecans haggling among themselves or with strangers.

Individualization

The third conclusion of the Yucatan study pertains to the trend toward individualization, or individualism, as one goes from folk to urban. The specific facts found in the study of the four communities are given as follows:

. . . The relative decrease in importance of specialized functions which are performed on behalf of the community and the relative increase of specialties discharged for the individual's own benefit; the development of individual rights in land and in family estates; the diminution or disappearance of collective labor and of the exchange of services in connection with civic enterprises and religious worship; the decreasing concern of the family or of the local community in the making and the maintaining of marriages; the becoming less common of the extended domestic family; the lessening of emphasis and of conventional definition of the respect relationships

among kin; the decline in family worship and the disappearance of religious symbols expressive of the great family; the decrease in the tendency to extend kinship terms with primary significance for members of the elementary family to more remote relatives or to persons unrelated genealogically; the increasing vagueness of the conventional outlines of appropriate behavior toward relatives; the change in the nature of marriage and baptism rites so as less to express the linkage of the families and more to concern the immediately involved individuals only; the decline in relative importance of the *santo* patron of the local community; the suggested relation of the increase in sorcery to the separation of individuals, especially of women, from the security of familial groups.[7]

Some of the items listed above were also listed under the categories of disorganization and secularization and have been treated earlier. The development of individual rights in land may date back to the Spanish Conquest. Cortés and his heirs owned land in Tepoztlán and rented it out to Tepoztecans as early as 1580. In the past twenty or thirty years there have been no changes in the direction of the private ownership of the communal resources. The persistence of the communal land, which still accounts for over four-fifths of all the area of the *municipio,* is impressive.

The trend toward the breakdown of collective labor is seen clearly in Tepoztlán, particularly in connection with the difficulty in getting *barrio* members to turn out for the plowing and planting of the *barrio* fields. In 1947, three of the *barrios* had rented out the land and used the rental for the *barrio.* On the whole, many of our findings for Tepoztlán might be interpreted as confirming Redfield's more general finding for Yucatan, particularly with regard to the trend toward secularization and individualization,

---

[7] *Ibid.,* p. 355.

perhaps less so with regard to disorganization.

Limitations of the Folk-Urban Concept

Since the concept of the folk society as an ideal type is, after all, a matter of definition, there can be no quarrel with it as such, provided that it can be shown to have heuristic value. On the basis of the restudy of Tepoztlán, however, it seems necessary to point out a number of limitations found in the conceptual framework of the folk-urban continuum, both as a scheme for the study of culture change, and for cultural analysis. These criticisms can be discussed under seven related points.

1. The folk-urban conceptualization of social change focuses attention primarily on the city as the source of change, to the exclusion or neglect of other factors of an internal or external nature. So-called folk societies have been influencing each other for hundreds of years and out of such interaction has come cultural change. The archaeological record in Tepoztlán, as well as in other parts of Mexico, indicates quite clearly a great mingling of people and cultures, which dates back at least a thousand years before the Spanish Conquest. Tepoztlán itself was first conquered by the Toltecs and later by the Aztecs, and with each conquest came new influences, new religious ideas, and new customs.

Another example of nonurban factors in culture change can be seen in the case of Tepoztlán and other parts of Latin America, where the introduction of rural culture elements was at least as far-reaching in effect as any changes brought about by later urban influences. Similarly, we find that the Mexican agrarian revolution (particularly in its Zapatista phase) was a profound influence for change, but can hardly be classified as an urban influence. It is evident that the folk-urban continuum concept covers only one of a wide variety of situations which may lead to culture change. In the case of Tepoztlán, to study the urban factors alone would give us only a partial picture of culture change.

2. It follows that in many instances culture change may not be a matter of folk-urban progression, but rather an increasing or decreasing heterogeneity of culture elements. For example, we have seen that the incorporation of Spanish rural elements—such as the plow, oxen, plants, and many folk beliefs—did not make Tepoztlán more urban but instead gave it a more varied rural culture. The introduction of plow culture in Tepoztlán did not eliminate the older system of hoe culture but gave the Tepoztecans an alternative and, in some ways, a more efficient method of farming, making for greater heterogeneity in the economic life and in the forms of social relationships.

3. Some of the criteria used in the definition of the folk society are treated by Redfield as linked or interdependent variables, but might better be treated as independent variables. Sol Tax, in his study of Guatemalan societies, has shown that societies can be both culturally well organized and homogeneous and, at the same time, highly secular, individualistic, and commercialistic. He has also shown that interpersonal relations in a small and homogeneous society can be characterized by formalism and impersonality. His findings are supported by the present study. Moreover, this study shows other possible combinations of variables. Thus, whereas Tax found family disorganization as a concomitant of commercialism, in Tepoztlán the family remains strong, and there is little evidence of family disorganization. Moreover, collective forms of land tenure exist side by side with private land ownership and individual working of the land.

4. The typology involved in the folk-urban classification of societies tends to obscure one of the most significant findings of modern cultural anthropology, namely, the wide range in the ways of life and in the value systems among so-called primitive peoples. The "folk society," as used by Redfield, would group together food-gathering, hunting, pastoral, and agricultural peoples, without distinction. To apply the term "folk society" to high cultures like that of the Aztecs (Tepoztlán was part of this high-culture area) and at the same time to apply it to simple food-gathering peoples like the Shoshone robs the term of its discriminatory value. Also, to write of a "folk element" in Tepoztlán in 1926 (the so-called *tontos*) as if it were identical with the folk element of the pre-Hispanic days neglects all the cultural influences to which this element has been subjected in the intervening 400 years and blurs many distinctions which have to be made. Similarly, it would put into one category societies which are as different culturally and psychologically as the Arunta and the Eskimo, the Dobu and the Ba Thonga, the Zuni and the Alorese, the Dahomey and the Navaho. Indeed, one might argue that the folk-urban classification is not a cultural classification at all, since it rides roughshod over fundamental cultural differences—i.e., differences in the ethos of a people. The point is that in attitudes and value systems, folk societies may resemble some urban societies much more than they resemble other folk societies. For example, the individualism and competitiveness of the Blackfoot Indians remind one much more of American urban value systems than of Zuni values. This suggests that the criteria used in the folk-urban classification are concerned with the purely formal aspects of society and are not necessarily the most crucial for cultural analysis.

What has been said of the folk end of the folk-urban formula applies also to the urban end. Focusing only on the formal aspects of urban society reduces all urban societies to a common denominator and treats them as if they all had the same culture. Thus, Greek, Egyptian, Roman, Medieval, and twentieth-century American and Russian cities would all be put into the same class. To take but one example, there are obvious and significant differences between American and Russian urban culture, and in all probability these two "urban influences" would have a very different effect upon a preliterate society exposed to them.

It should be clear that the concept "urban" is too much of a catch-all to be useful for cultural analysis. Moreover, it is suggested here that the question posed by Redfield—What happens to an isolated homogeneous society when it comes into contact with an urbanized society?—cannot possibly be answered in a scientific way because the question is too general and the terms used do not give us the necessary data. What we need to know is what kind of an urban society, under what conditions of contact, and a host of other specific historical data.

5. The folk-urban classification has serious limitations in guiding field research because of the highly selective implications of the categories themselves and the rather narrow focus of problem. The emphasis upon essentially formed aspects of culture leads to neglect of psychological data and, as a rule, does not give insight into the character of the people. We have already seen how this approach has influenced the selection, interpretation, and organization of the data in Redfield's study of Tepoztlán.

6. The folk-urban conceptualization

of social change as developed by Redfield assumes a uniform, simultaneous, and unilateral change in all institutions, which is reminiscent of early evolutionary theory. Moreover, it tells us nothing about the rate of change.

7. Finally, underlying the folk-urban dichotomy as used by Redfield is a system of value judgments which contains the old Rousseauian notion of primitive peoples as noble savages, and the corollary that with civilization has come the fall of man. This type of value system is particularly prone to influence the interpretation of a given cultural change as to whether it shall be called disorganization or simply reorganization. Since the concept of disorganization is one of the three key concepts in Redfield's folk-urban hypothesis, it can be seen how directly this value system may affect the interpretation. This is not, of course, an objection to the fact of values *per se*, but rather to the failure to make them explicit, as well as to this particular value system. Redfield's values suggest what Lovejoy and Boas have called "cultural primitivism," which they define as "the discontent of the civilized with civilization, or with some conspicuous and characteristic feature of it."[8]

These authors show that primitivism has existed in various forms throughout the recorded history of mankind.

Of direct, or even indirect, influence of the classical primitivistic tradition there is probably little. But since the beginning of the present century, western man has become increasingly skeptical concerning the nineteenth-century "myth of progress," increasingly troubled with the misgivings about the value of the outcome of civilization thus far, about the future to which it tends, and about

himself as the author of it all; and similar doubts and apprehensions found expression two millennia or more ago. In spite of the more complex and sophisticated general ideology of the contemporary exponents of these moods, there are striking parallels to be observed between certain of the texts that follow (i.e., Greek, Roman, and Indian) and some passages in such writings as Freud's *Civilization and Its Discontents* and Spengler's *Man and Technics*.[9]

Again and again in Redfield's writings there emerges the value judgment that folk societies are good and urban societies bad. It is assumed that all folk societies are integrated while urban societies are the great disorganizing force. In his introduction to [Horace] Miner's *St. Denis* study, Redfield suggests that the usual view of peasant life "as something to be escaped, an ignominy to be shunned" may be wrong. He finds that the habitant of St. Denis has order, security, faith, and confidence, "because he has culture." In another essay, "The Folk Society and Culture" in *Eleven Twenty-Six*, he contrasts the "organization and consistency which gives a group moral solidarity" with "the impaired moral organization of the urban society." Even in his most recent study, which to this writer represents a great departure from his earlier thinking, in that he is less concerned with formalism and categories and more concerned with people, we find the old values reappearing. "Progress" and urbanization now are seen as inevitable, but they are still evil.[10]

Conclusions

The limitations in the folk-urban conceptualization of social change

---

[8] Arthur A. Lovejoy and George Boas, *Primitivism and Related Ideas in Antiquity* (Baltimore: Johns Hopkins University Press, 1935), p. 7.

[9] *Ibid.*, p. 10.
[10] Robert Redfield, *A Village that Chose Progress, Chan Kom Revisited* (Chicago: University of Chicago Press, 1950), p. 178.

stand out even more clearly when we compare the results of this type of analysis with the results obtained by another method—namely, a combined historical-functional approach, in which the categories for analysis of change grow out of the historical data from a given situation. From this point of view, the history of culture change in Tepoztlán may be divided into three major periods: (1) from the Spanish Conquest to about 1910; (2) from 1910 to about 1930; (3) from 1930 to the present. No single formula will explain the whole range of phenomena embraced by these periods. Indeed, it appears that each period is characterized by a different rate of change and by varying degrees of change within different institutions. In some periods we find both destructive and constructive aspects, disorganization and reorganization. In one period, the technological changes affect primarily the lives of women; in another, primarily the lives of men.

During the first period, change was on the whole gradual but far-reaching, touching all aspects of life from material culture and technology to social organization, economics, and religion. The changes during this period were the result of outside influence and consisted of the transformation of the culture by the superimposition of Spanish culture—consisting of both urban and rural elements—on the native culture, with a resultant fusion of the two. During the second period, the changes were caused by a combination of external and internal factors, and changes were more rapid and violent, affecting primarily the social and political organization. The third period was in a sense a continuation of the second, with the changes primarily in the fields of communication, literacy, education, consumption patterns, and values, and with economics, social organization, and religion remaining quite stable. In all periods, particularly in the field of material culture, the new culture elements tended not to supplant the old but to be added to them, thus making for a richer and more heterogeneous culture.

This discussion can be summarized in three general conclusions: (1) There is a need for more independent restudies in anthropology and, if possible, simultaneous studies of the same community or region by different investigators. (The writer would welcome an independent restudy of Tepoztlán twenty years hence.) (2) The approach to community and regional studies must be of the broadest possible type in which the community is seen in its geographical and historical contacts rather than as an independent isolate. (3) The checking of a specific hypothesis in the course of a community study is certainly worthwhile, but one must be aware of the highly selective role of the hypothesis itself in directing the gathering of data. It may be that what is left out, because of the limiting needs of the hypothesis, is all-important for an understanding of the total cultural situation.

bureaucracy

seven

The most seminal of all the models of modern society has been Max Weber's paradigm for describing bureaucracy, and it is therefore included as the only work of the classic writers of sociology found in this volume. Like most classic models, it too has been extended, challenged, and in part replaced. Much of the research on modern, large-scale organizations calls into question the extent to which these social units in fact follow the Weberian model. While this may seem to invalidate the model as a description of empirical reality, the research nevertheless serves to emphasize how useful it has been to have Weber's clear model of bureaucracy as a standard against which to judge contemporary organizations.

The Characteristics of Bureaucracy

MAX WEBER

Characteristics of Bureaucracy

Modern officialdom functions in the following specific manner:

I. There is the principle of fixed and official jurisdictional areas, which are generally ordered by rules, that is, by laws or administrative regulations.

1. The regular activities required for the purposes of the bureaucratically governed structure are distributed in a fixed way as official duties.

2. The authority to give the commands required for the discharge of these duties is distributed in a stable way and is strictly delimited by rules concerning the coercive means, physical, sacerdotal, or otherwise, which may be placed at the disposal of officials.

3. Methodical provision is made for the regular and continuous fulfillment of these duties and for the execution of the corresponding rights; only persons who have the generally regulated qualifications to serve are employed.

In public and lawful government these three elements constitute "bureaucratic authority." In private economic domination, they constitute bureaucratic "management." Bureaucracy, thus understood, is fully developed in political and ecclesiastical communities only in the modern state, and, in the private economy, only in the most advanced institutions of cap-

H. H. Gerth and C. Wright Mills, eds., *From Max Weber: Essays in Sociology* (New York: Oxford University Press, Inc., 1946), pp. 196-204. Copyright 1946 by Oxford University Press.

italism. Permanent and public office authority, with fixed jurisdiction, is not the historical rule but rather the exception. This is so even in large political structures such as those of the ancient Orient, the Germanic and Monogolian empires of conquest, or of many feudal structures of state. In all these cases, the ruler executes the most important measures through personal trustees, table companions, or Court servants. Their commissions and authority are not precisely delimited and are temporarily called into being for each case.

II. The principles of office hierarchy and of levels of graded authority mean a firmly ordered system of super- and subordination in which there is a supervision of the lower offices by the higher ones. Such a system offers the governed the possibility of appealing the decision of a lower office to its higher authority, in a definitely regulated manner. With the full development of the bureaucratic type, the office hierarchy is monocratically organized. The principle of hierarchical office authority is found in all bureaucratic structures: in state and ecclesiastical structures as well as in large party organizations and private enterprises. It does not matter for the character of bureaucracy whether its authority is called "private" or "public."

When the principle of jurisdictional "competency" is fully carried through, hierarchical subordination—at least in public office—does not mean that the "higher" authority is simply authorized to take over the business of the "lower." Indeed, the opposite is the rule. Once established and having fulfilled its task, an office tends to continue in existence and be held by another incumbent.

III. The management of the modern office is based upon written documents ("the files"), which are preserved in their original or draft form.

There is, therefore, a staff of subaltern officials and scribes of all sorts. The body of officials actively engaged in a "public" office, along with the respective apparatus of material implements and the files, make up a "bureau." In private enterprise, "the bureau" is often called "the office."

In principle, the modern organization of the civil service separates the bureau from the private domicile of the official, and, in general, bureaucracy segregates official activity as something distinct from the sphere of private life. Public monies and equipment are divorced from the private property of the official. This condition is everywhere the product of a long development. Nowadays, it is found in public as well as in private enterprises; in the latter, the principle extends even to the leading entrepreneur. In principle, the executive office is separated from the household, business from private correspondence, and business assets from private fortunes. The more consistently the modern type of business management has been carried through the more are these separations the case. The beginnings of this process are to be found as early as the Middle Ages.

It is the peculiarity of the modern entrepreneur that he conducts himself as the "first official" of his enterprise, in the very same way in which the ruler of a specifically modern bureaucratic state spoke of himself as "the first servant" of the state.[1] The idea that the bureau activities of the state are intrinsically different in character from the management of private economic offices is a continental European notion and, by way of contrast, is totally foreign to the American way.

IV. Office management, at least all specialized office management—and such management is distinctly modern

---

[1] Frederick II of Prussia.

—usually presupposes thorough and expert training. This increasingly holds for the modern executive and employee of private enterprises, in the same manner as it holds for the state official.

V. When the office is fully developed, official activity demands the full working capacity of the official, irrespective of the fact that his obligatory time in the bureau may be firmly delimited. In the normal case, this is only the product of a long development, in the public as well as in the private office. Formerly, in all cases, the normal state of affairs was reversed: official business was discharged as a secondary activity.

VI. The management of the office follows general rules, which are more or less stable, more or less exhaustive, and which can be learned. Knowledge of these rules represents a special technical learning which the officials possess. It involves jurisprudence, or administrative or business management.

The reduction of modern office management to rules is deeply embedded in its very nature. The theory of modern public administration, for instance, assumes that the authority to order certain matters by decree—which has been legally granted to public authorities—does not entitle the bureau to regulate the matter by commands given for each case, but only to regulate the matter abstractly. This stands in extreme contrast to the regulation of all relationships through individual privileges and bestowals of favor, which is absolutely dominant in patrimonialism, at least insofar as such relationships are not fixed by sacred tradition.

The Position of the Official

All this results in the following for the internal and external position of the official:

I. Officeholding is a "vocation." This is shown, first, in the requirement of a firmly prescribed course of training, which demands the entire capacity for work for a long period of time, and in the generally prescribed and special examinations which are prerequisites of employment. Furthermore, the position of the official is in the nature of a duty. This determines the internal structure of his relations, in the following manner: Legally and actually, officeholding is not considered a source to be exploited for rents or emoluments, as was normally the case during the Middle Ages and frequently up to the threshold of recent times. Nor is officeholding considered a usual exchange of services for equivalents, as is the case with free labor contracts. Entrance into an office, including one in the private economy, is considered an acceptance of a specific obligation of faithful management in return for a secure existence. It is decisive for the specific nature of modern loyalty to an office that, in the pure type, it does not establish a relationship to a *person*, like the vassal's or disciple's faith in feudal or in patrimonial relations of authority. Modern loyalty is devoted to impersonal and functional purposes. Behind the functional purposes, of course, "ideas of culture values" usually stand. These are *ersatz* for the earthly or supramundane personal master: ideas such as "state," "church," "community," "party," or "enterprise" are thought of as being realized in a community; they provide an ideological halo for the master.

The political official—at least in the fully developed modern state—is not considered the personal servant of a ruler. Today, the bishop, the priest, and the preacher are in fact no longer, as in early Christian times, holders of purely personal charisma. The supramundane and sacred values which they offer are given to everybody who seems to be worthy of them and who asks for them. In former times, such leaders acted upon the personal command of their master; in principle, they were responsible only to him. Nowadays, in spite of the partial survival of the old theory, such religious leaders are officials in the service of a functional purpose, which in the present-day "church" has become routinized and, in turn, ideologically hallowed.

II. The personal position of the official is patterned in the following way:

1. Whether he is in a private office or a public bureau, the modern official always strives and usually enjoys a distinct *social esteem* as compared with the governed. His social position is guaranteed by the prescriptive rules of rank order and, for the political official, by special definitions of the criminal code against "insults of officials" and "contempt" of state and church authorities.

The actual social position of the official is normally highest where, as in old civilized countries, the following conditions prevail: a strong demand for administration by trained experts; a strong and stable social differentiation, where the official predominantly derives from socially and economically privileged strata because of the social distribution of power; or where the costliness of the required training and status conventions are binding upon him. The possession of educational certificates . . . are usually linked with qualification for office. Naturally, such certificates or patents enhance the "status element" in the social position of the official. For the rest this status factor in individual cases is explicitly and impassively acknowledged; for example, in the prescription that the acceptance or rejection of an aspirant to an official career depends upon the consent ("election") of the members of the official body. This is the case in the German army with the officer corps. Similar phenomena, which promote this guild-like closure of officialdom, are typically found in patrimonial and, particularly, in prebendal officialdoms of the past. The desire to resurrect such phenomena in changed forms is by no means infrequent among modern bureaucrats. For instance, they have played a role among the demands of the quite proletarian and expert officials (the *tretyj* element) during the Russian revolution.

Usually the social esteem of the officials as such is especially low where the demand for expert administration and the dominance of status conventions are weak. This is especially the case in the United States; it is often the case in new settlements by virtue of their wide fields for profit making and the great instability of their social stratification.

2. The pure type of bureaucratic official is *appointed* by a superior authority. An official elected by the governed is not a purely bureaucratic figure. Of course, the formal existence of an election does not by itself mean that no appointment hides behind the election—in the state, especially, appointment by party chiefs. Whether or not this is the case does not depend upon legal statutes but upon the way in which the party mechanism functions. Once firmly organized, the parties can turn a formally free election into the mere acclamation of a candidate designated by the party chief. As a rule, however, a formally free election is turned into a fight, conducted according to definite rules, for votes in favor of one of two designated candidates.

In all circumstances, the designation of officials by means of an election among the governed modifies the strictness of hierarchical subordination. In principle, an official who is so elected has an autonomous position opposite the superordinate official. The elected official does not derive his position "from above" but "from below," or at least not from a superior authority of the official hierarchy but from powerful party men ("bosses"), who also determine his further career. The career of the elected official is not, or at least not primarily, dependent upon his chief in the administration. The official who is not elected but appointed by a chief normally functions more exactly, from a technical point of view, because, all other circumstances being equal, it is more likely that purely functional points of consideration and qualities will determine his selection and career. As laymen, the governed can become acquainted with the extent to which a candidate is expertly qualified for office only in terms of experience, and hence only after his service. Moreover, in every sort of selection of officials by election, parties quite naturally give decisive weight not to expert considerations but to the services a follower renders to the party boss. This holds for all kinds of procurement of officials by elections, for the designation of formally free, elected officials by party bosses when they determine the slate of candidates, or the free appointment by a chief who has himself been elected. The contrast, however, is relative: substantially similar conditions hold where legitimate monarchs and their subordinates appoint officials, except that the influence of the followings are then less controllable.

Where the demand for administration by trained experts is considerable, and the party followings have to recognize an intellectually developed, educated, and freely moving "public opinion," the use of unqualified officials falls back upon the party in power at the next election. Naturally, this is more likely to happen when the officials are appointed by the chief. The demand for a trained administration now exists in the United States, but in the large cities, where immigrant votes are "corraled," there is, of course, no educated public opinion. Therefore, popular elections of the administrative chief and also of his subordinate officials usually endanger the expert qualification of the official as well as the precise functioning of the bureaucratic mechanism. It also weakens the dependence of the officials upon the hierarchy. This holds at least for the large administrative bodies that are difficult to supervise. The superior qualification and integrity of federal judges, appointed by the President, as over against elected judges in the United States is well known, although both types of officials have been selected primarily in terms of party considerations. The great changes in American metropolitan administrations demanded by reformers have proceeded essentially from elected mayors working with an apparatus of officials who were appointed by them. These reforms have thus come about in a "Caesarist" fashion. Viewed technically, as an organized form of authority, the efficiency of "Caesarism," which often grows out of democracy, rests in general upon the position of the "Caesar" as a free trustee of the masses (of the army or of the citizenry), who is unfettered by tradition. The "Caesar" is thus the unrestrained master of a body of highly qualified military officers and officials whom he selects freely and personally without regard to tradition or to any other considerations. This "rule of the personal genius," however, stands in contradiction to the formally "democratic" principle of a universally elected officialdom.

3. Normally, the position of the official is held for life, at least in pub-

lic bureaucracies; and this is increasingly the case for all similar structures. As a factual rule, *tenure for life* is presupposed, even where the giving of notice or periodic reappointment occurs. In contrast to the worker in a private enterprise, the official normally holds tenure. Legal or actual life tenure, however, is not recognized as the official's right to the possession of office, as was the case with many structures of authority in the past. Where legal guarantees against arbitrary dismissal or transfer are developed, they merely serve to guarantee a strictly objective discharge of specific office duties free from all personal considerations. In Germany, this is the case for all juridical and, increasingly, for all administrative officials.

Within the bureaucracy, therefore, the measure of "independence," legally guaranteed by tenure, is not always a source of increased status for the official whose position is thus secured. Indeed, often the reverse holds, especially in old cultures and communities that are highly differentiated. In such communities, the stricter the subordination under the arbitrary rule of the master, the more it guarantees the maintenance of the conventional seigneurial style of living for the official. Because of the very absence of these legal guarantees of tenure, the conventional esteem for the official may rise in the same way as, during the Middle Ages, the esteem of the nobility of office[2] rose at the expense of esteem for the freemen, and as the king's judge surpassed that of the people's judge. In Germany, the military officer or the administrative official can be removed from office at any time, or at least far more readily than the "independent judge," who never pays with loss of his office for even the grossest offense against the "code

of honor" or against social conventions of the salon. For this very reason, if other things are equal, in the eyes of the master stratum the judge is considered less qualified for social intercourse than are officers and administrative officials, whose greater dependence on the master is a greater guarantee of their conformity with status conventions. Of course, the average official strives for a civil service law, which would materially secure his old age and provide increased guarantees against his arbitrary removal from office. This striving, however, has its limits. A very strong development of the "right to the office" naturally makes it more difficult to staff them with regard to technical efficiency, for such a development decreases the career opportunities of ambitious candidates for office. This makes for the fact that officials, on the whole, do not feel their dependency upon those at the top. This lack of a feeling of dependency, however, rests primarily upon the inclination to depend upon one's equals rather than upon the socially inferior and governed strata. The present conservative movement among the Badenia clergy, occasioned by the anxiety of a presumably threatening separation of church and state, has been expressly determined by the desire not to be turned "from a master into a servant of the parish."[3]

4. The official receives the regular *pecuniary* compensation of a normally fixed *salary* and the old age security provided by a pension. The salary is not measured like a wage in terms of work done, but according to "status," that is, according to the kind of function (the "rank") and, in addition, possibly, according to the length of service. The relatively great security

---

[2] "Ministerialen."

[3] Written before 1914. (German editor's note.)

of the official's income, as well as the rewards of social esteem, make the office a sought-after position, especially in countries which no longer provide opportunities for colonial profits. In such countries, this situation permits relatively low salaries for officials.

5. The official is set for a *career* within the hierarchical order of the public service. He moves from the lower, less important, and lower paid to the higher positions. The average official naturally desires a mechanical fixing of the conditions of promotion: if not of the offices, at least of the salary levels. He wants these conditions fixed in terms of "seniority," or possibly according to grades achieved in a developed system of expert examinations. Here and there, such examinations actually form a character *indelebilis* of the official and have lifelong effects on his career. To this is joined the desire to qualify the right to office and the increasing tendency toward status group closure and economic security. All of this makes for a tendency to consider the offices as "prebends" of those who are qualified by educational certificates. The necessity of taking general personal and intellectual qualifications into consideration, irrespective of the often subaltern character of the educational certificate, has led to a condition in which the highest political offices, especially the positions of "ministers," are principally filled without reference to such certificates.

mass society

eight

The rational and orderly image of modern social life suggested in Weber's model of bureaucracy has been challenged by the depravity of totalitarian societies. And in the democracies that have escaped this more severe fate many analysts see a world of alienation, of cheapened standards, of stifling uniformity, which they sum up in the model of "mass society"—a concept whose applicability to the United States Daniel Bell judiciously assesses for us. Through his analysis we learn how to test the adequacy of a model both logically and empirically.

The U.S. as a Mass Society

DANIEL BELL

. . . A sombre melancholy weighed on people's souls. . . . It would sometimes

Daniel Bell, *The End of Ideology* (New York: Free Press of Glencoe, Inc., 1960), pp. 21-36. Copyright © 1960 by The Free Press, a corporation.

seem as if this period had been particularly unhappy, as if it had left behind only the memory of violence, of covetousness and moral hatred. . . . The feeling of general insecurity [was heightened] by the chronic form wars were apt to take, by the constant menace of the dangerous classes, by the mistrust of justice. . . . It was, so to say, bad form to praise the world and life openly. It was fashionable to see only its suffering and misery, to discover everywhere the signs of decadence and the near end —in short to condemn the times or to despise them.

—J. H. Huizinga, *The Waning of the Middle Ages*

The sense of a radical dehumanization of life which has accompanied events of the past few decades has given rise to the theory of "mass society." One can say that, Marxism apart, it is probably the most influential social theory in the western world today. While no single individual has stamped his name on it—to the extent that Marx is associated with the transformation of personal relations under capitalism into commodity values, or Freud with the role of the irrational and unconscious in behavior—the theory is central to the thinking of the principal aristocratic, Catholic, or Existentialist critics of modern society. These critics—Ortega y Gasset, Paul Tillich, Karl Jaspers, Gabriel Marcel, Emil Lederer, Hannah Arendt, and others—have been concerned less with the general conditions of freedom in society than with the freedom of the *person* and with the possibility, for some few persons, of achieving a sense of individual self in our mechanized society. And this is the source of their appeal.

The conception of the "mass society" can be summarized as follows: The revolutions in transport and communications have brought men into closer contact with each other and bound them in new ways; the division of labor has made them more interdependent; tremors in one part of society affect all others. Despite this greater interdependence, however, individuals have grown more estranged from one another. The old primary group ties of family and local community have been shattered; ancient parochial faiths are questioned; few unifying values have taken their place. Most important, the critical standards of an educated élite no longer shape opinion or taste. As a result, mores and morals are in constant flux, relations between individuals are tangential or compartmentalized, rather than organic. At the same time, greater mobility, spatial and social, intensifies concern over status. Instead of a fixed or known status, symbolized by dress or title, each person assumes a multiplicity of roles and constantly has to prove himself in a succession of new situations. Because of all this, the individual loses a coherent sense of self. His anxieties increase. There ensues a search for new faiths. The stage is thus set for the charismatic leader, the secular messiah, who, by bestowing upon each person the semblance of necessary grace and of fullness of personality, supplies a substitute for the older unifying belief that the mass society has destroyed.

In a world of lonely crowds seeking individual distinction, where values are constantly translated into economic calculabilities, where in extreme situations shame and conscience can no longer restrain the most dreadful excesses of terror, the theory of the mass society seems a forceful, realistic description of contemporary society, an accurate reflection of the *quality* and *feeling* of modern life. But when one seeks to apply the theory of mass society, analytically, it becomes very slippery. Ideal types, like the shadows in Plato's cave, generally never give us more than a silhouette. So, too, with the theory of "mass society." Each of the statements making up the theory, as set forth in the second paragraph above, might be true, but they do not follow necessarily from one another. Nor can we say that all the conditions described are present at any one time or place. More than that, there is no organizing principle—other than the general concept of a "breakdown of values"—that puts the individual elements of theory together in a logical, meaningful—let alone historical—manner. And when we examine the way the "theory" is used by those who employ it, we find ourselves even more at a loss.

In trying to sort out the ambiguities in the use of the phrase, we can distinguish perhaps five different, and sometimes contradictory, usages:

1. *Mass as undifferentiated number.* As commonly used in the term "mass media," "mass" implies that standardized material is transmitted to "all groups of the population uniformly."[1] As understood generally by sociologists, a *mass* is a heterogeneous and undifferentiated audience, as opposed to a *class*, or any parochial and relatively homogeneous segment. Some sociologists have been tempted to go further and make "mass" a rather pejorative term. Because the mass media subject a diverse audience to a common set of cultural materials, it is argued that these experiences must necessarily lie outside the personal—and therefore meaningful—experiences to which the individual responds directly. A movie audience, for example, is a "mass" because the individuals looking at the screen are, in the words of the American sociologist Herbert Blumer, "separate, detached, and anonymous." The mass "has no social organization, no body of custom and tradition, no established set of rules or rituals, no organized group of senti-

ments, no structure of status roles and no established leadership."[2]

To become part of the mass is to be divorced—or "alienated"—from oneself. And the instruments which project the dominant social values that men (and women and children) choose as their *imago*, or ideal image and desire—television, radio, and the movies—impose a mass response on their audience.

2. *Mass as the judgment by the incompetent.* As first introduced by the late Ortega y Gasset in 1931, in his famous *Revolt of the Masses*, the terms "masses" and "mass" had a far different meaning than the usage implied by the term "mass media" and its invidious connotations. For Ortega, the word "mass" did not designate a group of persons—the masses were not the workers, even though the revolutionary movements of the time had equated the two—but the low *quality* of modern civilization, resulting from the loss of a commanding position by the "gentlemen" who once made up the educated élite. Modern taste, for Ortega, represents the judgment of the unqualified. Modern life "makes a *tabula rasa* of all classicism." Nothing that is in the past can be "any possible model or standard." Even "the famous Renaissance reveals itself as a period of narrow provincialism—why not use the word?—ordinary." Modern culture, since it disowns the past, seeks a "free expression of its vital desires"; it becomes, therefore, an unrestrained "spoiled child" with no controlling standards, "no limit to its caprice."[3] In Ortega, one finds the most sweep-

---

[1] For a neutral discussion of the idea of "mass" in "mass media," see, e.g., Paul F. Lazarsfeld and Patricia Kendall, "The Communication Behavior of the Average American," in *Mass Communication*, Wilbur Schramm, ed. (Urbana: University of Illinois Press, 1949).

[2] Herbert Blumer, "Collective Behavior," in *New Outlines of the Principles of Sociology*, A. M. Lee, ed. (New York, 1936). For a further discussion, see Eliot Friedsen, "Research and the Concept of the Mass," *American Sociological Review* (June, 1953).

[3] José Ortega y Gasset, *The Revolt of the Masses* (New York: W. W. Norton & Company, Inc., 1932), pp. 18-19, 39.

ing attack against all "modernity." His is the disdain of the humanist for the vulgar.

3. *Mass as the mechanized society.* In German romanticism, in its idealization of nature and the pastoral, one finds the source of much of the protest against modern life. For these writers —and the poets and critics Ernst and Friedrich George Juenger can be taken as typical—the dehumanizing element is technology.[4] The mass society is a mechanical society. Society has become an "apparatus." The machine impresses its style on man, makes life mathematical and precise; existence takes on a masklike character: the steel helmet and the welder's face guard symbolize the individual's disappearance into his technical function. The regulated, functional man emerges as a new type, hard and ruthless, a cog in the technological press.

4. *The mass as the bureaucratized society.* Less romantic, but equally critical, are those theorists who see extreme rationalization and extreme bureaucratization—the *overorganization* of life—as the salient features of the mass society. The idea of "rationalization" goes back to Hegel and Marx, and along with it the notions of "estrangement" or "alienation," "reification," and the "fetishism of commodities"—all of which express the thought that in modern society man has become a "thing," an object manipulated by society, rather than a subject who can remake life in accordance with his own desires. In our time, Georg Simmel, Max Weber, and Karl Mannheim have developed and elaborated these concepts. In Mannheim's work—notably in his *Man and Society in an Age of Reconstruction*— the diverse strands are all brought together.

Mannheim's argument, put schematically, runs as follows: modern, large-scale organization, oriented exclusively to efficiency, creates hierarchies that concentrate all decisions at the top. Even technical decisions are removed from the shop floor and centered in specialized bodies that have no direct contact with work. Since the concern is solely with efficiency, rather than human satisfactions, all solutions to problems are defined in relation to this single value. Mannheim calls this "functional rationality," or direct means-ends relationships, in contrast to "substantial rationality," which is the application of reason to human affairs.[5]

This concentration of decision making not only creates conformity but stunts the initiative of subordinates and leaves them unsatisfied in their personal needs for gratification and esteem. (In effect, the demand for submission to extreme rationality deprives the individual of the power to act rationally; i.e., in accordance with reason. This frustration seeks release in irrational ways.) Normally, the routinization of one's job dulls the edge of frustration and provides some security. But when unemployment looms, the helplessness becomes sharpened, and self-esteem is threatened. Since individuals cannot rationally locate the source of their frustration (i.e., the impersonal bureaucratic system itself), they will, under these circumstances, seek scapegoats and turn to fascism.

---

[4] Friedrich George Juenger, *The Failure of Technology* (Chicago: Henry Regnery Co., 1948).

[5] Karl Mannheim, *Man and Society in an Age of Reconstruction* (London: Routledge & Kegan Paul, Ltd., 1940), pp. 53-67. Mannheim uses several other terms to round out his analysis. Modern society, he says, is based on "fundamental democratization," a term that is fuzzy, but close to Ortega's idea of "massification." Because of "fundamental democratization," i.e., the idea that culture should belong to all and that each man's opinion is as good as the next man's, the "creative élites," through whom culture is sustained, have no means of functioning.

5. *The mass as mob.* While for Mannheim, and the neo-Marxists, mass society is equated with monolithic bureaucratization, for Emil Lederer and Hannah Arendt it is defined by the elimination of difference, by uniformity, aimlessness, alienation, and the failure of integration.

In Lederer's view, society is made up of many social groups united by function or self-interest, some rational in purpose, some irrational. So long as society is stratified, these groups can impose only partial control, and irrational emotions are restricted. But when the lines dividing social groups break down, the people become volatile and febrile "masses," ready to be manipulated by a leader.[6]

Hannah Arendt, perhaps because she writes a decade later, sees the masses as already overspilling the bounds. The masses are those who, because of indifference or simply sheer number, do not belong to "political parties or municipal governments or professional organizations or trade unions"—in short, organizations that exist to satisfy a common interest—and they "form the majority of those large numbers of neutral, politically indifferent people who never join a party or hardly ever go to the polls."

Such people already stand "outside" of society. The revolt of the masses is a revolt against the "loss of social status along with which [is] lost the whole sector of communal relationships in whose framework common sense makes sense. . . . The masses [become] obsessed by a desire to escape from reality because in their essential homelessness they can no longer bear its accidental incomprehensible aspects."[7]

And so, because modern life sunders all social bonds, and because the techniques of modern communication have perfected the means whereby propaganda can manipulate the masses, the "age of the masses" is now upon us.

What strikes one first about these varied uses of the concept of mass society is how little they reflect or relate to the complex, richly striated social relations of the real world. Take Blumer's example of the movie audience as "separate, detached, and anonymous." Presumably, a large number of individuals, because they have been subjected to similar experiences, now share some common psychological reality in which the differences between individual and individual become blurred; accordingly we get the sociological assumption that each person is now of "equal weight," and therefore a sampling of what such disparate individuals say they think constitutes "*mass opinion.*" But is this so? Individuals are not *tabulae rasae.* They bring varying social conceptions to the same experience and go away with dissimilar responses. They may be silent, separate, detached, and anonymous while watching the movie, but afterward they talk about it with friends and exchange opinions and judgments. They are once again members of particular social groups. Would one say that several hundred or a thousand individuals home alone at night, but all reading the same book, constitute a "mass"?

Because romantic feeling colors critical judgment, the attacks on modern life often have an unduly strong emotional charge. The image of "facelessness," for example, is given a metaphysical twist by Gabriel Marcel:

The individual, in order to belong to the mass . . . has had to . . . divest

[6] Emil Lederer, *The State of the Masses* (New York: W. W. Norton & Company, Inc., 1940), pp. 23-40.

[7] Hannah Arendt, *The Origins of Totali-* *tarianism* (New York: Harcourt, Brace & World, Inc., 1951), pp. 305, 341-342.

himself of that substantial reality which was linked to his initial individuality. . . . The incredibly sinister role of the press, the cinema, the radio has consisted in passing that original reality through a pair of flattening rollers to substitute for it a superimposed pattern of ideas, an image with no real roots in the deep being of the subject of this experiment.[8]

Perhaps terms like "original reality" and "real roots in the deep being" have a meaning that escapes an empiricist temper, but without the press, the radio, etc., etc.—and they are not monolithic—in what way, short of being everywhere at once, can one learn of events that take place elsewhere? Or should one go back to the happy ignorance of earlier days?

Some of the images of life in the mass society, as presented by its critics, border on caricature. According to Ernst Juenger, traffic demands traffic regulations, and so the public becomes conditioned to automatism. Karl Jaspers has written that in the "technical mass order" the home is transformed "into a lair or sleeping place." Even more puzzling is the complaint against modern medicine. "In medical practice . . . patients are now dealt with in the mass according to the principle of rationalization, being sent to institutes for technical treatment, the sick being classified in groups and referred to this or that specialized department. . . . The supposition is that, like everything else, medical treatment has become a sort of manufactured article."[9]

The attack on the mass society sometimes widens into an attack on science itself. For Ortega, "the scientific man is the prototype of the mass man," because science, by encouraging specialization, has made the scientist "hermetic and self-satisfied within his limitations." Ortega draws from this the sweeping conclusion that "the most immediate result of this unbalanced specialization has been that today, when there are more 'scientists' than ever, there are much less 'cultured' men than, for example, about 1750."[10] But how is one to verify such a comparison between 1750 and the present? Even if we could establish comparable categories, surely Ortega would have been the first to shy away from statistical comparisons. Moreover, can we assume that because a man specializes in his work, he is unable, in his leisure and in reflection, to appreciate culture? And what is "culture"? Would not Ortega admit that we have more knowledge of the world than in 1750—knowledge not only of nature but of the inner life of man? Is knowledge to be divorced from culture, or is "true culture" a narrow area of classical learning in which eternal truths reside?

One could argue, of course, that reading a book, to cite my previous example, is a qualitatively different experience from going to a movie. But this leads precisely to the first damaging ambiguity in the theory of the mass society. Two things are mixed up in that theory: a judgment regarding the *quality* of modern experience—with much of which any sensitive individual might agree—and a presumed scientific statement concerning the disorganization of society created by industrialization and by the demand of the masses for equality. It is the second of these statements with which this essay quarrels.

Behind the theory of social disorganization lies a romantic—and somewhat false—notion of the past, which

[8] Gabriel Marcel, *Man Against Mass Society* (Chicago: Henry Regnery Co., 1952), pp. 101-103.

[9] Karl Jaspers, *Man in the Modern Age* (London: Routledge & Kegan Paul, Ltd., 1951), p. 65.

[10] Ortega, *op. cit.*, p. 124.

sees society as having once been made up of small, "organic," close-knit communities (called *Gemeinschaften* in the terminology of the sociologists) that were shattered by industrialism and modern life, and replaced by a large, impersonal, "atomistic" society (called *Gesellschaft*) that is unable to provide the basic gratifications, and call forth the loyalties, that the older communities knew.[11] These distinctions are, however, completely riddled by value judgments. Everyone is against atomism and for "organic living." But if we substitute, with good logic, the term "total" for "organic," and "individualistic" for "atomistic," the whole argument looks quite different. In any case, a great weakness in the theory is its lack of history-mindedness. The transition to a mass society, if it be such, was not effected suddenly, explosively, within a single lifetime, but took generations to mature. In its sociological determinism, the hypothesis overlooks the human capacity for adaptiveness and creativeness, for ingenuity in shaping new social forms. Such new forms may be trade unions whose leaders rise from the ranks—there are 50,000 trade union locals in this country that form little worlds of their own—or the persistence under new conditions of ethnic groups and solidarities.

But more than mere contradictions in usage, ambiguities in terminology, and a lack of historical sense are involved in the theory of the mass so-

11 This antithesis, associated with the German sociologist Tonnies, is central to almost every major modern social theory: Weber's traditional-rational behavior, Durkheim's mechanical-organic solidarity, Redfield's folk-urban society, and so on. Sometimes this distinction is presumed to be an historical one, describing societies in some undefined past as against the present; sometimes it is used as an ahistorical, analytic distinction, setting up two ideal types in contrast with each other. The result, however, is confusion.

ciety. It is at heart a defense of an aristocratic cultural tradition—a tradition that does carry with it an important but neglected conception of liberty—and a doubt that the large mass of mankind can ever become truly educated or acquire an appreciation of culture. Thus, the theory often becomes a conservative defense of privilege. This defense is at times so extreme as to pose a conflict between "culture" and "social justice." The argument (reminiscent of the title of Matthew Arnold's book *Culture and Anarchy*) is made that any attempts at social betterment must harm culture. And, while mainly directed against "bourgeois" society, the theory also strikes at radicalism and its egalitarian notions.

The fear of the "mass" has its roots in the dominant conservative tradition of western political thought, which in large measure still shapes many of the political and sociological categories of social theory—i.e., in authoritarian definitions of leadership and in the image of the "mindless masses." The picture of the "mass" as capable only of violence and excess originates with Aristotle's *Politics*. In his threefold typology, democracy is equated with the rule of *hoi polloi*—who are easily swayed by demagogues—and which must degenerate into tyranny. This notion of the masses, developed in Hellenistic times, was deepened by the struggles between plebes and aristocracy in the Roman republic, and by the efforts of the Caesars to exploit mob support; and the image of the insensate mob fed by "bread and circuses" became deeply imprinted on history. (From Plutarch, for example, came the description of the fickle masses and the wily tribunes that was drawn upon so directly by Shakespeare in his tragedy *Coriolanus*.) Early Christian theory justified its fear of the masses with a theory about human nature. In the religious terms of Augustine—as, later, in the secularized version of Hobbes— the Earthly City bore an ineradicable stain of blood; in Paradise there was neither private property nor government; property and police were the consequence of the Fall of Man; property and police were signs, therefore, not of man's civilization but of his corruption; they were necessary means of keeping man in check.

But it was the French revolution that transplanted the image of the "mindless masses" into modern consciousness. The destruction of the *ancien régime* and the rallying cry of "equality" sharpened the fear of conservative, and especially Catholic, critics that traditional values (meaning political, social, and religious dogma) would be destroyed.[12] For a Tocqueville and an Acton, there was an irreducible conflict between liberty and equality; liberty guaranteed each man the right to be different, whereas equality meant a "leveling" of tastes to the lowest common denominator. For a Max Scheler, as well as an Ortega, the mass society meant a "democracy of the emotions," which could unleash only irrational forces. For the Catholic de Maistre, as for the Anglican T. S. Eliot, the equality of men meant the destruction of the harmony and authority so necessary to a healthy, integrated society.[13] From this tradition-

alist point of view, Nazism has been characterized not as a reaction against, but the inevitable end product of, democracy. Hitler is seen as a replica of the classical demagogue swaying the mindless masses and leading them in nihilistic revolt against the traditional culture of Europe.

Important as these conceptions are, as reminders of the meaning of liberty, and of excellence, they reflect a narrow conception of human potentialities. The question of social change has to be seen against the large political canvas. The starting point of modern politics, as Karl Mannheim has pointed out, came after the Reformation, when chiliasm, or religiously inspired millennial striving to bring about heaven on earth, became an expression of the demands for social and economic betterment of the lower strata of society.[14] Blind resentment of things as they were was thereby given principle, reason, and eschatological force, and directed to definite political goals. The equality of all souls became the equality of all individuals and the right of everyone, as enlightened by progressive revelation, to make a judgment on society.

Comte, the father of modern sociology, expressed great horror at the idea of this universal right to one's own opinion. No community could exist, he wrote, unless its members had a certain degree of confidence in one another, and this, he said, was incom-

[12] For a discussion of the roots of the idea of the "mindless masses" in western social theory, see my essay, "Notes on Authoritarian and Democratic Leaders," in *Studies in Leadership*, Alvin Gouldner, ed. (New York: Harper & Row, Publishers, Inc., 1950).

[13] In a brilliant essay, "Daydreams and Nightmares: Reflections on the Criticism of Mass Culture," *Sewanee Review*, 65 (1957), Edward Shils points to the curious convergence of both conservative and neo-Marxist critics in their attacks on mass culture. In this respect, the radical has taken over uncritically the aristocratic view that the past was dominated by a high culture that is now being debauched. In fact, as Shils points out,

the lives of most people were brutalized by long hours of work at arduous labor, while the entry of the "mass" into society has resulted in the extension of culture—of art, music, and literature—to a degree hitherto undreamed of. This argument is elaborated by Professor Shils in a paper prepared for the Tamiment Conference on Mass Culture (June, 1959), which appears in *Daedalus* (Spring, 1960).

[14] Karl Mannheim, *Ideology and Utopia* (New York: Harcourt, Brace & World, Inc., 1936), pp. 190-197.

patible with the right of everyone to submit the very foundations of society to discussion whenever he felt like it. In calling attention to the dangers of free criticism, Comte pointed to the decline in public morals as evidenced by the increase of divorces, the effacement of traditional class distinctions, and the ensuing impudence of individual ambitions. It was part of the function of government, he thought, to prevent the diffusion of ideas and the anarchic spread of intellectual freedom.[15]

Modern society, apparently, does not bear Comte out: though the foundations of privilege go on being challenged in the name of justice, society does not collapse. Few moralists would now uphold the bleak view once expressed by Malthus, that "from the inevitable laws of human nature some human beings will be exposed to want. These are the unhappy persons who in the great lottery of life have drawn a blank."[16] The most salient fact about modern life—capitalist and communist —is the ideological commitment to social change. And by change is meant the striving for material, economic betterment, greater opportunity for individuals to exercise their talents, and an appreciation of culture by wider masses of people. Can any society deny these aspirations?

It is curious that in these "aristocratic" critiques of modern society, refracted as they are through the glass of an idealized feudal past, democracy is identified with equality alone. The role of constitutionalism and of the rule of law, which, with universal suffrage, are constituent elements of the western democratic structure, are overlooked. The picture of modern culture as debauched by concessions to popular taste—a picture that leaves out the great rise in the general appreciation of culture—is equally overdrawn. If it is granted that mass society is compartmentalized, superficial in personal relations, anonymous, transitory, specialized, utilitarian, competitive, acquisitive, mobile, and status-hungry, the obverse side of the coin must be shown, too—the right to privacy, to free choice of friends and occupation, status on the basis of achievement rather than of ascription, a plurality of norms and standards, rather than the exclusive and monopolistic social controls of a single dominant group. For if, as Sir Henry Maine once put it, the movement of modern society has been from status to contract, then it has been, in that light, a movement from a fixed place in the world to possible freedom.

The early theorists of the mass society (Ortega, Marcel) focused attention on the "deterioration of excellence," while the later theorists (Mannheim, Lederer, Arendt) called attention to the way in which the overorganization and, at the same time, the disruption of the social fabric facilitated the rise of fascism. Recently, in the light of Communist successes, the argument has been advanced that the mass society, because it cannot provide for the individual's real participation in effective social groups, is particularly vulnerable to Communist penetration, and that the mass organization, because it is so unwieldy, is peculiarly susceptible to Communist penetration and manipulation.[17] Certainly, the Communists have scored enormous successes in infiltration, and their "front organization" may be counted as one of the great political inventions

---

[15] Auguste Comte, *Cours de philosophie positive*, 2d ed. (Paris, 1864), Books IV-V.

[16] T. R. Malthus, *An Essay on Population* (in the University of Chicago readings) Book III, Chapter II.

[17] Philip Selznick, *The Organizational Weapon* (New York: McGraw-Hill Book Co., Inc., 1952), pp. 275-308.

of our century. But without discounting Communist techniques, the real problem here lies less with the "mass society" as such (aside from the excuse it affords disaffected intellectuals for attacks on modern culture) than with the capacity or incapacity of the given social order to satisfy the demands for social mobility and higher standards of living that arise once social change is under way. This is the key to any radical appeal.

It is not poverty *per se* that leads people to revolt; poverty most often induces fatalism and despair, and a reliance, embodied in ritual and superstitious practices, on supernatural help. *Social tensions are an expression of unfulfilled expectations*. It is only when expectations are aroused that radicalism can take hold. Radical strength is greatest (and here the appeal of Communism must be seen as a variant of the general appeal of radicalism) in societies where awareness of class differences runs deep, expectations of social advancement outstrip possibilities, and the establishments of culture fail to make room for aspiring intellectuals.

It is among industrial workers rather than apathetic peasants (in Milan rather than Calabria), among frustrated intellectuals rather than workers long unionized (e.g., India), that radicalism spreads. Resentment, as Max Scheler once noted, is among the most potent of human motives; it is certainly that in politics. It is in the advanced industrial countries, principally the United States, Britain, and northwestern Europe, where national income *has* been rising, where mass expectations of an equitable share in that increase are relatively fulfilled, and where social mobility affects ever-greater numbers, that extremist politics have the least hold. It may be, as the late Joseph Schumpeter pessi-

mistically believed,[18] that in newly awakened societies, like Asia's, the impatient expectations of key social strata, particularly the intellectuals, may so exceed the actual possibilities of economic expansion that Communism will come to look like the only plausible solution to the majority.[19] Whether this will happen in India and Indonesia is one of the crucial political questions of the next decade. But at any rate it is not the mass society, but the inability, pure and simple, of any society to meet impatient popular expectations that makes for a strong response to radical appeals.

From the viewpoint of the mass-society hypothesis, the United States ought to be exceptionally vulnerable to the politics of disaffection. In our country, urbanization, industrialization, and democratization have eroded older primary and community ties on a scale unprecedented in social history. Yet, though large-scale unemployment during the depression was more prolonged and more severe here than in any country in western Europe, the Communist movement never gained a real foothold in the United States,

18 Joseph Schumpeter, *Capitalism, Socialism and Democracy* (New York: Harper & Row, Publishers, Inc., 1942), pp. 145-156.
19 As Morris Watnick has pointed out in a pioneering study (in the University of Chicago symposium *The Progress of Underdeveloped Areas*), the Communist parties of Asia are completely the handiwork of native intellectuals. The history of the Chinese Communist party from Li Ta-Chao and Ch'en Tu-hsu, its founders, to Mao Tse-tung and Liu Shao-Chi, its present leaders, "is virtually an unbroken record of a party controlled by intellectuals." This is equally true of India, "where in 1943, eighty-six of 139 [Communist] delegates were members of professional and intellectual groups." The same pattern also holds true "for the Communist parties of Indochina, Thailand, Burma, Malaya, and Indonesia, all of which show a heavy preponderance of journalists, lawyers, and teachers among the top leadership."

nor has any fascist movement on a European model arisen. How does one explain this?

It is asserted that the United States is an "atomized" society composed of lonely, isolated individuals. One forgets the truism, expressed sometimes as a jeer, that Americans are a nation of joiners. There are in the United States today at least 200,000 voluntary organizations, associations, clubs, societies, lodges, and fraternities, with an aggregate (but obviously overlapping) membership of close to 80,000,000 men and women. In no other country in the world, probably, is there such a high degree of voluntary communal activity, expressed sometimes in absurd rituals, yet often providing real satisfactions for real needs.[20]

"It is natural for the ordinary American," wrote Gunnar Myrdal, "when he sees something that is wrong to feel not only that there should be a law against it, but also that an organization should be formed to combat it."[21] Some of these voluntary organizations are pressure groups—business, farm, labor, veterans, trade associations, the aged, etc.—but thousands more are like the National Association for the Advancement of Colored People, the American Civil Liberties Union, the League of Women Voters, the American Jewish Committee, the Parent-Teachers Associations, local community-improvement groups, and so on, each of which affords hundreds of individuals concrete, emotionally shared activities.

Equally astonishing are the number of ethnic group organizations in this country carrying on varied cultural, social, and political activities. The number of Irish, Italian, Jewish, Polish, Czech, Finnish, Bulgarian, Bessarabian, and other national groups, their hundreds of fraternal, communal, and political groups, each playing a role in the life of America, is staggering.[22]

Even in urban neighborhoods, where anonymity is presumed to flourish,

---

[20] Between 30 and 40,000,000 of the 80,-000,000 United States joiners work at their voluntary jobs. In 1950, 2,000,000 volunteer workers pounded sidewalks for the Community Chests (the fund-raising and disbursing bodies in each community for local hospitals and social service agencies) and raised $200 million. Other thousands raised over $100 million for the United Jewish Appeal, $67 million for the Red Cross, $30 million for the National Foundation for Infantile Paralysis, $20 million for the National Tuberculosis Association, $13,600,000 for the American Cancer Society—in all about a billion dollars a year for philanthropy. In 1950 there were 17,000 conventions—national, regional, or state, but not counting district or local—held in the United States, attended by 10,000,000 persons. In Atlantic City, famed seaside resort, 244,000 individuals went to 272 conventions ranging from the American Academy of Periodontology to the Telephone Pioneers of America. (Figures compiled by Fortune magazine research staff.)

[21] Gunnar Myrdal, An American Dilemma (New York: Harper & Row, Publishers, Inc., 1944).

[22] In December, 1954, for example, when the issue of Cyprus was first placed before the United Nations, the Justice for Cyprus Committee, "an organization of American citizens," according to its statement, took a full-page advertisement in The New York Times (December 15) to plead the right of that small island to self-determination. Among the groups listed in the Justice for Cyprus Committee were: The Order of Ahepa, the Daughters of Penelope, the Pan-Laconian Federation, the Cretan Federation, the Pan-Messian Federation, the Pan-Icarian Federation, the Pan-Epirotic Federation of America, the Pan-Elian Federation of America, the Dodecanesian League of America, the Pan-Macedonian Association of America, the Pan-Samian Association, the Federation of Sterea Ellas, the Cyprus Federation of America, the Pan-Arcadian Federation, the GAPA, and the Federation of Hellenic Organizations. We can be sure that if, in a free world, the question of the territorial affiliation of Ruthenia were to come up before the United Nations, dozens of Hungarian, Rumanian, Ukrainian, Slovakian, and Czech "organizations of American citizens" would rush eagerly into print to plead the justice of the claims of their respective homelands to Ruthenia.

the extent of local ties is astounding. Within the city limits of Chicago, for example, there are eighty-two community newspapers with a total weekly circulation of almost 1,000,000; within Chicago's larger metropolitan area, there are 181. According to standard sociological theory, these local papers providing news and gossip about neighbors should slowly decline under the pressure of the national media. Yet the reverse is true. In Chicago, the number of such newspapers has increased 165 per cent since 1910; in those forty years, circulation has jumped 770 per cent. As sociologist Morris Janowitz, who studied these community newspapers, observed: "If society were as impersonal, as self-centered and barren as described by some who are preoccupied with the one-way trend from *Gemeinschaft* to *Gesellschaft* seem to believe, the levels of criminality, social disorganization and psychopathology which social science seeks to account for would have to be viewed as very low rather than (as viewed now) alarmingly high."[23]

It may be argued that the existence of such a large network of voluntary associations says little about the cultural level of the country concerned. It may well be, as Ortega maintains, that cultural standards throughout the world have declined (in everything?—in architecture, dress, design?), but nonetheless a greater proportion of the population today participates in worthwhile cultural activities. This has been almost an inevitable concomitant of the doubling—*literally*—of the American standard of living over the last fifty years.[24]

The rising levels of education have meant a rising appreciation of culture. In the United States, more dollars are spent on concerts of classical music than on baseball. Sales of books have doubled in a decade.[25] There are over

[23] Morris Janowitz, *The Community Press in an Urban Setting* (New York: The Free Press of Glencoe, Inc., 1952), pp. 17-18. More recent research, particularly by British sociologists, has questioned the idea that the modern society inevitably tears down primary ties. As Peter Willmott put it succinctly: "Stereotypes die hard, even among sociologists. Ever since Tonnies and Durkheim proclaimed the decline of the family, the notion has persisted that in urban industrial societies it is rootless and atomized, confined to parents and dependent children, isolated from relatives. Only in recent years has this impression been challenged—by field inquiries in London and other English cities, even in such unlikely places (one would have thought) as Detroit and San Francisco. These have suggested that the kindred may be an important source of companionship and support in the heart of the modern city" ("Kinship and Social Legislation," *British Journal of Sociology*, [June, 1958], 126). The chief British studies are those by Michael Young and Willmott, in Bethnal Green, entitled *Family and Kinship in East London* (Lon-

don: Routledge & Kegan Paul, Ltd., 1957), and the researches of the Institute of Community Studies, headed by Michael Young, particularly Peter Townsend, *The Family Life of Old People* (London: Routledge & Kegan Paul, Ltd., 1957). Among the American studies cited by Willmott are: *A Social Profile of Detroit: 1955* (Ann Arbor: University of Michigan Press, 1956); Morris Axelrod, "Urban Structure and Social Participation," *American Journal of Sociology* (February, 1956); Wendell Bell and M. D. Boar, "Urban Neighborhoods and Informal Social Relations," *American Journal of Sociology* (January, 1957).

[24] For a scholarly summary on American living standards, see William Fielding Ogburn, "Technology and the Standard of Living in the United States," *American Journal of Sociology* (January, 1955), 380-386. Data on cultural participation can be found in F. B. Turek, "The American Explosion," *Scientific Monthly* (September, 1952).

[25] Malcolm Cowley, in his essay on "Cheap Books for the Millions," points out that there were few book clubs in 1931, when a broad survey of the book publishing industry was made, while in 1953 there were seventy-four clubs that recommended books for adults. "The fear had been," he writes, "that the clubs would encourage a general uniformity of taste in the American public, and instead they were, to some extent, encouraging a diversity" (*The Literary Situation*

1,000 symphony orchestras, and several hundred museums, institutes, and colleges are purchasing art in the United States today. Various other indices can be cited to show the growth of a vast middlebrow society. And in coming years, with steadily increasing productivity and leisure, the United States will become an even more active "consumer" of culture.[26]

[New York: The Viking Press, Inc., 1955], p. 101).

[26] Some further ambiguity in the use of the mass-society concept derives from the confusions in the use of the anthropological and the humanist meanings of the word "culture." Thus some critics point to the "breakdown" of local folk or regional practices—speech differences, cooking, songs, dances, humor—and their replacement by uniform national patterns as an indication of the leveling of the mass society and of the decline of culture. These changes, which are real, are meaningful, however, only in anthropological usage, as a change from parochial to more universal cultural forms. But such changes are not *necessarily* a judgment about the humanist quality of the culture. (It is curious that in the past the breakdown of rustic forms was seen as a necessary prelude to the growth of a "high culture." Today the breakdown of the rustic forms is seen as part of the destruction of humanist culture.) The distinctions should be made clear. The anthropological concept of culture is relativistic. It implies no judgment of any one culture and cannot be used as a stick to criticize "high culture." The fact that the nature of satisfactions has changed from country dances and folksy humor to Brazilian sambas and Broadway flippancy is analytically a different question than that of the character of the culture. As these criticisms are made, one deals with the presumed disorganization of society, the other with the quality of the culture. Again, it is the purpose of this essay to point out that the invocation of the notion of tradition (*Gemeinschaft*, etc.) to make a judgment about the disorganization of the society is scientifically spurious and conceals a value. The other criticism, which is serious, lies outside the scope of this essay. [For a discussion of the issues of "high" vs. "middlebrow" culture, see Clement Greenberg, "The Plight of Our Culture," *Commentary* (June-July, 1953). See also Mary McCarthy, "America the Beautiful," *Commentary* (September, 1947).]

It has been argued that the American mass society imposes an excessive conformity upon its members. But it is hard to discern who is conforming to what. The *New Republic* cries that "hucksters are sugar-coating the culture." The *National Review*, organ of the "radical right," raises the banner of iconoclasm against the domination of opinion making in our society by "the liberals." *Fortune* decries the growth of "organization man." Each of these tendencies exists, yet in historical perspective there is probably less conformity to an over-all mode of conduct today than at any time within the last half-century in America. True, there is less bohemianism than in the 'twenties (though increased sexual tolerance) and less political radicalism than in the 'thirties (though the New Deal enacted sweeping reforms). But does the arrival at a political dead center mean the establishment, too, of a dead norm? I do not think so. One would be hard put to find today the "conformity" *Main Street* exacted of Carol Kennicott thirty years ago. With rising educational levels, more individuals are able to indulge a wider variety of interests. ("Twenty years ago you couldn't sell Beethoven out of New York," reports a record salesman. "Today we sell Palestrina, Monteverdi, Gabrielli, and Renaissance and Baroque music in large quantities.")

The curious fact, perhaps, is that no one in the United States defends conformity. Everyone is against it, and probably everyone always was. Thirty-five years ago, you could easily rattle any middle-class American by charging him with being a "Babbitt." Today you can do so by accusing him of conformity. The problem is to know who is accusing whom. In December, 1958, the *Reader's Digest* (circulation 12,000,000) reprinted an article from *Woman's Day* (circulation 5,000,000) with the title, "The Danger of Being

Too Well-Adjusted." The point of the article is that great men were not adjusted, and the article quotes a psychiatrist who says that "we've made conformity into a religion"; we ought to remember, however, that each child is different "and ought to be."

Such citation is no proof that there is not "conformity" in the middle class; but if there is, there is also a great deal of anxiety and finger-pointing about it. Certainly those who live on the margin of society—the Upper Bohemians, whose manners soon become the style for the culture—seek frantically to find different ways of emphasizing their nonconformity. In Hollywood, where Pickfair society in the 'twenties counterfeited a European monarchy (and whose homes crossed Louis XIV with Barnum & Bailey), "nonconformity," according to *Life* magazine (in its jumbo Entertainment issue of December 22, 1958—readership 25,000,000), "is now the key to social importance and that Angry Middle-Aged man, Frank Sinatra, is its prophet and reigning social monarch." The Sinatra set, *Life* points out, deliberately mocks the old Hollywood taboos and is imitated by a host of other sets that eagerly want to be nonconformist as well. Significantly—a fact *Life* failed to mention—the reigning social set and its leaders, Sinatra, Dean Martin, Sammy Davis, Jr., are all from minority groups and from the wrong side of the tracks. Sinatra and Martin are Italian, Davis a Negro. In earlier times in American life, a minority group, having bulled its way to the top, would usually ape the style and manners of the established status community. In Hollywood, the old status hierarchies have been fragmented, the new sets celebrate their triumph by jeering at the pompous ways of the old.

At the margins of the literary life, and a different social phenomenon, are the Beatniks, a hopped-up, jazzed-up, souped-up, self-proclaimed group of outcasts who are rebelling against the "highly organized academic and literary movement employment agency of the Neoanti-reconstructionist [who form] a dense crust of custom over American cultural life." But the singular fact is, as Delmore Schwartz recently argued, that these Beatniks are imaginary rebels, "since the substance of their work is a violent advocacy of a nonconformism which they already possess . . . since nonconformism of almost every variety had become acceptable and respectable and available to everyone. Unlike the Bohemianism of the past, which had to attack the dominant Puritanism and Victorianism of respectable society in a variety of forms, including the censorship of books, Prohibition, and a prudery enforced by the police, the new nonconformism has no genuine enemy . . . hence the new rebel bears a great deal of resemblance to a prize fighter trying to knock out an antagonist who is not in the ring with him."[27] The additional sardonic fact is that the man in the gray flannel suit, the presumed target of the Beatniks, is, as Russell Lynes pointed out, especially if he is in advertising, or the entertainment media, an Upper Bohemian himself. The job is accepted as a means of obtaining an income in order to sport and flaunt his presumed, idiosyncratic tastes in dress, food, travel, and the like.[28] The prob-

[27] Delmore Schwartz, "The Present State of Poetry," in *American Poetry at Mid-Century* (The Whittall Lectures, Library of Congress, 1958), p. 26.
[28] "In the richly appointed Lake Shore Drive apartment of Chicago Financier Albert Newman, the guests chatted animatedly, gazed at the original Picasso on the wall, and the Monet, the Jackson Pollock. On tables and shelves stood Peruvian fertility symbols, jade bracelets, sculptures that looked like the superstructure of a Japanese battleship. . . . [The guests] had come to meet thirty-two-

lem for all these multiple sets is not conformity but added novelty.

To add one more paradox, the early theorists of mass society [e.g., (Georg) Simmel] condemned it because in the vast metropolitan honeycombs people were isolated, transient, anonymous to each other. Americans, sensitive as they are to the criticism of others, took the charge to heart and, in building the postwar suburbs, sought to create fraternity, communality, togetherness, only to find themselves accused of conformity. In the new, recent trend of people returning to the city, it is clear that, in recoil, people will once again establish barriers and will thus bring on the charge, in the next inspection by European sociology, of anonymity, isolation and soullessness, and anomie.

One hears the complaint that divorce, crime, and violence demonstrate a widespread social disorganization in the country. But the rising number of divorces may indicate not the disruption of the family but a freer, more individualistic basis of choice and the emergence of the "companionship" marriage. And as regards crime, . . . there is actually much *less* crime and violence (though more vicarious violence through movies and TV, and more "windows" onto crime, through the press) than was the case twenty-

five and fifty years ago. Certainly Chicago, San Francisco, and New York were much rougher and tougher cities in those years. But violent crime, which is usually a lower-class phenomenon, was then contained within the ecological boundaries of the slum; hence one can recall quiet, tree-lined, crime-free areas and feel that the tenor of life was more even in the past. But a cursory look at the accounts of those days—the descriptions of the gang wars, bordellos, and street-fighting in San Francisco's Barbary Coast, New York's Five Points, or Chicago's First Ward—would show how much more violent the actual life of those cities was in the past.

At this point, it becomes quite apparent that such large-scale abstractions as "the mass society," with the implicit diagnosis of social disorganization and decay that derive from them, are rather meaningless without standards of comparison. Social and cultural change is probably greater and more rapid today in the United States than in any other country, but the assumption that social disorder and anomie inevitably attend such change is not borne out in this case.

This may be due to the singular fact that the United States is probably the first large society in history to have change and innovation "built into" its culture. Almost all human societies, traditionalist and habit-ridden as they have been and still are, tend to resist change. The great efforts to industrialize underdeveloped countries, increase worker mobility in Europe, and broaden markets—so necessary to the raising of productivity and standards of living—are again and again frustrated by ingrained resistance to change. Thus, in the Soviet Union, change has been introduced only by dint of wholesale coercion. In the United States—a culture with no feudal tradition, with a pragmatic ethos, as expressed by Jef-

---

year-old Allen Ginsberg of Paterson, N.J., author of a celebrated, chock-full catalogue called *Howl* ("I saw the best minds of my generation destroyed by madness, starving hysterical naked."). . . . At length Poet Ginsberg arrived wearing blue jeans and a checked black-and-red lumberjacking shirt with black patches. . . . With the crashing madness of a Marx Brothers scene run in reverse, the Beatniks [Ginsberg and two friends] read their poetry, made their pitch for money for a new Beatnik magazine, *The Big Table*, and then stalked out. . . . The trio was an instant hit with the literary upper crust. . . . [The next evening] at the Sherman Hotel, the Beatniks read more poetry for a curious crowd of 700 (who paid $1 and up) . . ." (*Time*, February 9, 1959).

ferson, that regards God as a "workman"; with a boundless optimism and a restless eagerness for the new that have been bred out of the original conditions of a huge, richly endowed land —change, and the readiness to change, have become the norm. This indeed may be why those consequences of change predicted by theorists basing themselves on European precedent find small confirmation.

The mass society is the product of change—and is itself change. It is the bringing of the "masses" into a society, from which they were once excluded. But the *theory* of the mass society affords us no view of the relations of the parts of the society to each other that would enable us to locate the sources of change. We may not have enough data on which to sketch an alternative theory, but I would argue that certain key factors, in this country at least, deserve to be much more closely examined than they have been: the change from a society once geared to frugal saving and now impelled to spend dizzily; the breakup of family capitalism, with the consequent impact on corporate structure and political power; the centralization of decision making, politically, in the state, and, economically, in a group of large corporate bodies; the rise of status and symbol groups replacing specific interest groups—these indicate that new social forms are in the making and, with them, still greater changes in the complexion of life under mass society. With these may well come new status anxieties—aggravated by the threats of war—changed character structures, and new moral tempers.

The moralist may have his reservations or give approval—as some see in the breakup of the family the loss of a source of essential values, while others see in the new, freer marriages a healthier form of companionship—but the singular fact is that these changes emerge in a society that is now providing one answer to the great challenge posed to western—and now world— society over the last 200 years: how, within the framework of freedom, to increase the living standards of the majority of people and at the same time maintain or raise cultural levels. For these reasons, the theory of the mass society no longer serves as a description of western society but as an ideology of romantic protest against contemporary life.

Part 3

conceptions
of man
in society

Although the sociologist takes society as his main object of study, he finds he cannot long operate unless his work is also guided by some systematic conception of the nature of man, of his psychic development and functioning. The image of man most common in sociology pictures him as reflecting in his psyche the social forms and values typical for his culture and his position in society. The Freudian conception has won few adherents. Other theories of man, however, have found a more friendly reception in sociology, especially those that stress themes such as the man's need for social relatedness, his modes of moral functioning, and his social adaptation. Sociologists have also shown great interest in the "authoritarian personality" syndrome, which Daniel Levinson discusses.

It would be a mistake, furthermore, to assume that the interaction between psychology and sociology has been limited to sociological borrowing of personality theory. Sociology has much to offer psychology in understanding how social forces affect the development of the person and his later functioning. The process of child rearing and child development, as Aberle and Naegele show, is much influenced by the social status of the father. And, as David Riesman argues, the types of men emerging in any population may reflect in their personalities many of the salient characteristics of the social order in which they live. These perspectives are more systematically brought together in studies in social psychology, which some feel will in the future emerge as the key discipline of the behavioral sciences.

freud and sociology

nine

Freud stressed man's "destructive, anti-social, anti-cultural tendencies" rooted in instinctual drives. Despite the almost universal acceptance of Freud's image, sociologists continue to see man mainly as the sum total of the *social* roles in which society has cast him. It is this image that Dennis Wrong has dubbed the "oversocialized conception of man." He offers us both a concise summary of the Freudian view and an incisive critique of the common sociological perspective on man.

The Over-Socialized Conception of Man

DENNIS H. WRONG

What is the answer of contemporary sociological theory to the Hobbesian question? There are two main answers, each of which has come to be understood in a way that denies the reality and meaningfulness of the question. Together they constitute a model of human nature, sometimes clearly stated, more often implicit in accepted concepts, that pervades modern sociology. The first answer is summed up in the notion of the "internalization of social norms." The second, more commonly employed or assumed in empirical research, is the view that man is essentially motivated by the desire to achieve a positive image of self by winning acceptance or status in the eyes of others.

The following statement represents,

Dennis H. Wrong, "The Oversocialized Conception of Man," *American Sociological Review*, **26** (April, 1961), 185-193.

briefly and broadly, what is probably the most influential contemporary sociological conception—and dismissal —of the Hobbesian problem: "To a modern sociologist imbued with the conception that action follows institutionalized patterns, opposition of individual and common interests has only a very limited relevance or is thoroughly unsound."[1] From this

[1] Francis X. Sutton, *et al.*, *The American Business Creed* (Cambridge: Harvard University Press, 1956), p. 304. I have cited this study and, on several occasions, textbooks and fugitive articles rather than better-known and directly theoretical writings because I am just as concerned with what sociological concepts and theories are taken to mean when they are actually used in research, teaching, and introductory exposition as with their elaboration in more self-conscious and explicitly theoretical discourse. Since the model of human nature I am criticizing is partially implicit and "buried" in our concepts, cruder and less qualified illustrations are as relevant as the formulations of leading theorists. I am also aware that some older theorists, notably [Charles H.] Cooley and [Robert M.] MacIver, were shrewd and worldly-wise enough to

writer's perspective, the problem is an unreal one: human conduct is totally shaped by common norms or "institutionalized patterns." Sheer ignorance must have led people who were unfortunate enough not to be modern sociologists to ask, "How is order possible?" A thoughtful bee or ant would never inquire, "How is the social order of the hive or ant-hill possible?" for the opposite of that order is unimaginable when the instinctive endowment of the insects insures its stability and built-in harmony between "individual and common interests." Human society, we are assured, is not essentially different, although conformity and stability are there maintained by noninstinctive processes. Modern sociologists believe that they have understood these processes and that they have not merely answered but disposed of the Hobbesian question, showing that, far from expressing a valid intimation of the tensions and possibilities of social life, it can only be asked out of ignorance.

*   *   *   *   *

What has happened is that internalization has imperceptibly been equated with "learning," or even with "habit formation" in the simplest sense. Thus when a norm is said to have been "internalized" by an individual, what is frequently meant is that he habitually both affirms it and conforms to it in his conduct. The whole stress on inner conflict, on the tension between powerful impulses and superego controls the behavioral outcome of which cannot be prejudged, drops out of the picture. And it is this that is central to Freud's view, for in psychoanalytic terms to say that a

reject the implication that man is ever fully socialized. Yet they failed to develop competing images of man which were concise and systematic enough to counter the appeal of the oversocialized models.

norm has been internalized, or introjected to become part of the superego, is to say no more than that a person will suffer guilt feelings if he fails to live up to it, not that he will in fact live up to it in his behavior.

The relation between internalization and conformity assumed by most sociologists is suggested by the following passage from a recent, highly-praised advanced textbook: "Conformity to institutionalized norms is, of course, 'normal.' the actor, having internalized the norms, feels something like a need to conform. His conscience would bother him if he did not."[2] What is overlooked here is that the person who conforms may be even more "bothered," that is, subject to guilt and neurosis, than the person who violates what are not only society's norms but his own as well. To Freud, it is precisely the man with the strictest superego, he who has most thoroughly internalized and conformed to the norms of his society, who is most wracked with guilt and anxiety.[3]

*   *   *   *   *

Recent discussions of "deviant behavior" have been compelled to recognize these distinctions between social demands, personal attitudes toward them, and actual conduct, although they have done so in a laboriously taxonomic fashion.[4] They represent, however, largely the rediscovery of

---

[2] Harry M. Johnson, Sociology: A Systematic Introduction (New York: Harcourt, Brace & World, Inc., 1960), p. 22.

[3] Sigmund Freud, Civilization and Its Discontents (New York: Doubleday & Co., 1958), pp. 80-81.

[4] Robert Dubin, "Deviant Behavior and Social Structure: Continuities in Social Theory," American Sociological Review, 24 (April, 1959), 147-164; Robert K. Merton, "Social Conformity, Deviation, and Opportunity Structures: A Comment on the Contributions of Dubin and Cloward," ibid., 178-189.

what was always central to the Freudian concept of the superego. The main explanatory function of the concept is to show how people repress themselves, imposing checks on their own desires and thus turning the inner life into a battlefield of conflicting motives, no matter which side "wins," by successfully dictating overt action. So far as behavior is concerned, the psychoanalytic view of man is less deterministic than the sociological. For psychoanalysis is primarily concerned with the inner life, not with overt behavior, and its most fundamental insight is that the wish, the emotion, and the fantasy are as important as the act in man's experience.

Sociologists have appropriated the superego concept, but have separated it from any equivalent of the Freudian id. So long as most individuals are "socialized," that is, internalize the norms and conform to them in conduct, the Hobbesian problem is not even perceived as a latent reality. Deviant behavior is accounted for by special circumstances: ambiguous norms, anomie, role conflict, or greater cultural stress on valued goals than on the approved means for attaining them. Tendencies to deviant behavior are not seen as dialectically related to conformity. The presence in man of motivational forces bucking against the hold social discipline has over him is denied.

Nor does the assumption that internalization of norms and roles is the essence of socialization allow for a sufficient range of motives underlying conformity. It fails to allow for variable "tonicity of the superego," in Kardiner's phrase.[5] The degree to which conformity is frequently the result of coercion rather than conviction is minimized.[6] Either someone has internalized the norms, or he is "unsocialized," a feral or socially isolated child, or a psychopath. Yet Freud recognized that many people, conceivably a majority, fail to acquire superegos. "Such people," he wrote, "habitually permit themselves to do any bad deed that procures them something they want, if only they are sure that no authority will discover it or make them suffer for it; their anxiety relates only to the possibility of detection. Present-day society has to take into account the prevalence of this state of mind."[7] The last sentence suggests that Freud was aware of the decline of "inner-direction," of the Protestant conscience, about which we have heard so much lately. So let us turn to the other elements of human nature that sociologists appeal to in order to explain, or rather explain away, the Hobbesian problem.

Man the Acceptance-Seeker[8]

The superego concept is too inflexible, too bound to the past and to in-

[5] Abram Kardiner, *The Individual and His Society* (New York: Columbia University Press, 1939), pp. 65, 72-75.

[6] C. Wright Mills, *The Sociological Imagination* (New York: Oxford University Press, 1959), pp. 39-41; Ralf Dahrendorf, *Class and Class Conflict in Industrial Society*, pp. 157-165.

[7] Freud, *op. cit.*, pp. 78-79.

[8] In many ways I should prefer to use the neater, more alliterative phrase "status-seeker." However, it has acquired a narrower meaning than I intend, particularly since Vance Packard appropriated it, suggesting primarily efforts, which are often consciously deceptive, to give the appearance of personal achievements or qualities worthy of deference. "Status-seeking" in this sense is, as Veblen perceived, necessarily confined to relatively impersonal and segmental social relationships. "Acceptance" or "approval" convey more adequately what all men are held to seek in both intimate and impersonal relations according to the conception of the self and of motivation dominating contemporary sociology and social psychology. I have, nevertheless, been unable to resist the occasional temptation to use the term "status" in this broader sense.

dividual biography, to be of service in relating conduct to the pressures of the immediate situation in which it takes place. Sociologists rely more heavily therefore on an alternative notion, here stated—or, to be fair, overstated—in its baldest form: "People are so profoundly sensitive to the expectations of others that all action is inevitably guided by these expectations."[9]

Parsons' model of the "complementarity of expectations," the view that in social interaction men mutually seek approval from one another by conforming to shared norms, is a formalized version of what has tended to become a distinctive sociological perspective on human motivation. Ralph Linton states it in explicit psychological terms: "The need for eliciting favorable responses from others is an almost constant component of [personality]. Indeed, it is not too much to say that there is very little organized human behavior which is not directed toward its satisfaction in at least some degree."[10]

The insistence of sociologists on the importance of "social factors" easily

leads them to stress the priority of such socialized or socializing motives in human behavior.[11] It is frequently the

---

[11] When values are "inferred" from this emphasis and then popularized, it becomes the basis of the ideology of "groupism" extolling the virtues of "togetherness" and "belongingness" that have been attacked and satirized so savagely in recent social criticism. David Riesman and W. H. Whyte, the pioneers of this current of criticism in its contemporary guise, are both aware, as their imitators and epigoni usually are not, of the extent to which the social phenomenon they have described is the result of the diffusion and popularization of sociology itself. See on this point Robert Gutman and Dennis H. Wrong, "Riesman's Typology of Character," in Seymour M. Lipset and Leo Lowenthal, eds., *Culture and Social Character* (New York: Free Press of Glencoe, Inc., 1961); and William H. Whyte, *The Organization Man* (New York: Simon & Schuster, Inc., 1956), Chaps. 3-5. As a matter of fact, Riesman's "inner-direction" and "other-direction" correspond rather closely to the notions of "internalization" and "acceptance-seeking" in contemporary sociology as I have described them. Riesman even refers to his concepts initially as characterizations of "modes of conformity," although he then makes the mistake, as Robert Gutman and I have argued, of calling them character types. But his view that all men are to some degree both inner-directed and other-directed, a qualification that has been somewhat neglected by critics who have understandably concentrated on his empirical and historical use of his typology, suggests the more generalized conception of forces making for conformity found in current theory. See David Riesman, Nathan Glazer, and Reuel Denny, *The Lonely Crowd* (New York: Doubleday & Co., 1953), pp. 17ff. However, as Gutman and I have observed: "In some respects Riesman's conception of character is Freudian rather than neo-Freudian: character is defined by superego mechanisms and, like Freud in *Civilization and Its Discontents*, the socialized individual is defined by what is forbidden him rather than by what society stimulates him to do. Thus in spite of Riesman's generally sanguine attitude toward modern America, implicit in his typology is a view of society as the enemy both of individuality and of basic drive gratification, a view that contrasts with the at least potentially benign role assigned it by neo-Freudian thinkers like Fromm and Horney." Gutman and Wrong,

---

[9] Sutton *et al., op. cit.,* p. 264. Robert Cooley Angell, in *Free Society and Moral Crisis* (Ann Arbor: University of Michigan Press, 1958), p. 34, points out the ambiguity of the term "expectations." It is used, he notes, to mean both a factual prediction and a moral imperative, e.g., "England expects every man to do his duty." But this very ambiguity is instructive, for it suggests the process by which behavior that is nonnormative and perhaps even "deviant" but nevertheless "expected" in the sense of being predictable, acquires over time a normative aura and becomes "expected" in the second sense of being socially approved or demanded. Thus [Talcott] Parsons' "interaction paradigm" provides leads to the understanding of social change and need not be confined, as in his use of it, to the explanation of conformity and stability. . . .

[10] Ralph Linton, *The Cultural Background of Personality* (New York: Appleton-Century-Crofts, 1945), p. 91.

task of the sociologist to call attention to the intensity with which men desire and strive for the good opinion of their immediate associates in a variety of situations, particularly those where received theories or ideologies have unduly emphasized other motives such as financial gain, commitment to ideals, or the effects on energies and aspirations of arduous physical conditions. Thus sociologists have shown that factory workers are more sensitive to the attitudes of their fellow workers than to purely economic incentives; that voters are more influenced by the preferences of their relatives and friends than by campaign debates on the "issues"; that soldiers, whatever their ideological commitment to their nation's cause, fight more bravely when their platoons are intact and they stand side by side with their "buddies."

It is certainly not my intention to criticize the findings of such studies. My objection is that their particular selective emphasis is generalized—explicitly or, more often, implicitly—to provide apparent empirical support for an extremely one-sided view of human nature. Although sociologists have criticized past efforts to single out one fundamental motive in human conduct, the desire to achieve a favorable self-image by winning approval from others frequently occupies such a position in their own thinking. The following "theorem" has been, in fact, openly put forward by Hans Zetterberg as "a strong contender for the position as the major Motivational Theorem in sociology":[12]

An actor's actions have a tendency to become dispositions that are related to the occurence [sic] of favored uniform evaluations of the actor and/or his actions in his action system.[13]

Now Zetterberg is not necessarily maintaining that this theorem is an accurate factual statement of the basic psychological roots of social behavior. He is, characteristically, far too self-conscious about the logic of theorizing and "concept formation" for that. He goes on to remark that "the maximization of favorable attitudes from others would thus be the counterpart in sociological theory to the maximization of profit in economic theory."[14] If by this it is meant that the theorem is to be understood as a heuristic rather than an empirical assumption, that sociology has a selective point of view which is just as abstract and partial as that of economics and the other social sciences, and if his view of theory as a set of logically connected formal propositions is granted provisional acceptance, I am in agreement. (Actually, the view of theory suggested at the beginning of this paper is a quite different one.)

But there is a further point to be made. Ralf Dahrendorf has observed that structural-functional theorists do not "claim that order *is based on* a general consensus of values, but that it *can be conceived of in terms of* such consensus and that, if it is conceived of in these terms, certain propositions follow which are subject to the test of specific observations."[15] The same may be said of the assumption that people seek to maximize favorable evaluations by others; indeed this assumption has already fathered such additional concepts as "reference group" and "circle of significant others." Yet the question must be raised as to whether we really wish to, in effect, define sociology by

---

"Riesman's Typology of Character," p. 4 (typescript).

[12] Hans L. Zetterberg, "Compliant Actions," *Acta Sociologica*, **2** (1957), 189.

[13] *Ibid.*, 188.

[14] *Ibid.*, 189.

[15] Dahrendorf, *Class and Class Conflict, op. cit.*, p. 158.

such partial perspectives. The assumption of the maximization of approval from others is the psychological complement to the sociological assumption of a general value consensus. And the former is as selective and one-sided a way of looking at motivation as Dahrendorf and others have argued the latter to be when it determines our way of looking at social structure. The oversocialized view of man of the one is a counterpart to the overintegrated view of society of the other.

Modern sociology, after all, originated as a protest against the partial views of man contained in such doctrines as utilitarianism, classical economics, social Darwinism, and vulgar Marxism. All of the great nineteenth- and early twentieth-century sociologists[16] saw it as one of their major tasks to expose the unreality of such abstractions as economic man, the gain-seeker of the classical economists; political man, the power-seeker of the Machiavellian tradition in political science; self-preserving man, the security-seeker of Hobbes and Darwin; sexual or libidinal man, the pleasure-seeker of doctrinaire Freudianism; and

even religious man, the God-seeker of the theologians. It would be ironical if it should turn out that they have merely contributed to the creation of yet another reified abstraction in socialized man, the status-seeker of our contemporary sociologists.

Of course, such an image of man is, like all the others mentioned, valuable for limited purposes so long as it is not taken for the whole truth. What are some of its deficiencies? To begin with, it neglects the other half of the model of human nature presupposed by current theory: moral man, guided by his built-in superego and beckoning ego-ideal.[17] In recent years sociologists have been less interested than they once were in culture and national character as backgrounds to conduct, partly because stress on the concept of "role" as the crucial link between the individual and the social structure has directed their attention to the immediate situation in which social interaction takes place. Man is increasingly seen as a "role-playing" creature, responding eagerly or anxiously to the expectations of other role-players in the multiple group settings in which he finds himself. Such an approach, while valuable in helping us grasp the complexity of a highly differentiated social structure such as our own, is far too often generalized to serve as a kind of ad hoc social psychology, easily adaptable to particular sociological purposes.

---

[16] Much of the work of Thorstein Veblen, now generally regarded as a sociologist (perhaps the greatest America has yet produced), was, of course, a polemic against the rational, calculating homo economicus of classical economics and a documentation of the importance in economic life of the quest for status measured by conformity to arbitrary and shifting conventional standards. Early in his first and most famous book Veblen made an observation on human nature resembling that which looms so large in contemporary sociological thinking: "The usual basis of self-respect," he wrote, "is the respect accorded by one's neighbors. Only individuals with an aberrant temperament can in the long run retain their self-esteem in the face of the disesteem of their fellows." The Theory of the Leisure Class (New York: Mentor Books, 1953), p. 38. Whatever the inadequacies of his psychological assumptions, Veblen did not, however, overlook other motivations to which he frequently gave equal or greater weight.

[17] Robin M. Williams, Jr., writes: "At the present time, the literature of sociology and social psychology contains many references to 'Conformity'—conforming to norms, 'yielding to social pressure,' or 'adjusting to the requirements of the reference group' . . . ; the implication is easily drawn that the actors in question are motivated solely in terms of conformity or nonconformity, rather than in terms of 'expressing' or 'affirming' internalized values . . ." (his italics). "Continuity and Change in Sociological Study," American Sociological Review, 23 (December, 1958), 630.

But it is not enough to concede that men often pursue "internalized values" remaining indifferent to what others think of them, particularly when, as I have previously argued, the idea of internalization has been "hollowed out" to make it more useful as an explanation of conformity. What of desire for material and sensual satisfactions? Can we really dispense with the venerable notion of material "interests" and invariably replace it with the blander, more integrative "social values"? And what of striving for power, not necessarily for its own sake —that may be rare and pathological— but as a means by which men are able to *impose* a normative definition of reality on others? That material interests, sexual drives, and the quest for power have often been overestimated as human motives is no reason to deny their reality. To do so is to suppress one term of the dialectic between conformity and rebellion, social norms and their violation, man and social order, as completely as the other term is suppressed by those who deny the reality of man's "normative orientation" or reduce it to the effect of coercion, rational calculation, or mechanical conditioning.

The view that man is invariably pushed by internalized norms or pulled by the lure of self-validation by others ignores—to speak archaically for a moment—both the highest and the lowest, both beast and angel, in his nature. Durkheim, from whom so much of the modern sociological point of view derives, recognized that the very existence of a social norm implies and even creates the possibility of its violation. This is the meaning of his famous dictum that crime is a "normal phenomenon." He maintained that "for the originality of the idealist whose dreams transcend his century to find expression, it is necessary that the originality of the criminal, who is below the level

of his time, shall also be possible. One does not occur without the other."[18] Yet Durkheim lacked an adequate psychology and formulated his insight in terms of the actor's cognitive awareness rather than in motivational terms. We do not have Durkheim's excuse for falling back on what Homans has called a "social mold theory" of human nature.[19]

Social but Not Entirely Socialized

I have referred to forces in man that are resistant to socialization. It is not my purpose to explore the nature of these forces or to suggest how we ought best conceive of them as sociologists— that would be a most ambitious undertaking. A few remarks will have to suffice. I think we must start with the recognition that *in the beginning there is the body*. As soon as the body is mentioned the specter of "biological determinism" raises its head and sociologists draw back in fright. And certainly their view of man is sufficiently disembodied and nonmaterialistic to satisfy Bishop Berkeley, as well as being desexualized enough to please Mrs. Grundy.

Am I, then, urging us to return to the older view of a human nature divided between a "social man" and a "natural man" who is either benevolent, Rousseau's noble savage, or sinister and destructive, as Hobbes regarded him? Freud is usually represented, or misrepresented, as the chief modern proponent of this dualistic conception which assigns to the social order the purely negative role of blocking and redirecting man's "imperious

[18] Emile Durkheim, *The Rules of Sociological Method* (Chicago: University of Chicago Press, 1938), p. 71.
[19] George C. Homans, *The Human Group* (New York: Harcourt, Brace & World, Inc., 1950), pp. 317-319.

biological drives."[20] I say "misrepresented" because, although Freud often said things supporting such an interpretation, other and more fundamental strains in his thinking suggest a different conclusion. John Dollard, certainly not a writer who is oblivious to social and cultural "factors," saw this twenty-five years ago: "It is quite clear," he wrote, ". . . that he (Freud) does not regard the instincts as having a fixed social goal; rather, indeed, in the case of the sexual instinct he has stressed the vague but powerful and impulsive nature of the drive and has emphasized that its proper social object is not picked out in advance. His seems to be a drive concept which is not at variance with our knowledge from comparative cultural studies, since his theory does not demand that the 'instinct' work itself out with mechanical certainty alike in every varying culture."[21]

So much for Freud's "imperious biological drives!" When Freud defined psychoanalysis as the study of the "vicissitudes of the instincts," he was confirming, not denying, the "plasticity" of human nature insisted on by social

scientists. The drives or "instincts" of psychoanalysis, far from being fixed dispositions to behave in a particular way, are utterly subject to social channelling and transformation and could not even reveal themselves in behavior without social molding any more than our vocal cords can produce articulate speech if we have not learned a language. To psychoanalysis man is indeed a social animal; his social nature is profoundly reflected in his bodily structure.[22]

But there is a difference between the Freudian view on the one hand and both sociological and neo-Freudian conceptions of man on the other. To Freud man is a *social* animal without being entirely a *socialized* animal. His very social nature is the source of conflicts and antagonisms that create resistance to socialization by the norms of any of the societies which have existed in the course of human history. "Socialization" may mean two quite distinct things; when they are confused an oversocialized view of man is the result. On the one hand socialization means the "transmission of the culture," the particular culture of the society an individual enters at birth; on the other hand the term is used to mean the "process of becoming human," of acquiring uniquely human attributes from interaction with others.[23] All men are socialized in the

---

[20] Robert K. Merton, *Social Theory and Social Structure*, rev. ed. (New York: The Free Press of Glencoe, Inc., 1957), p. 131. Merton's view is representative of that of most contemporary sociologists. See also Hans Gerth and C. Wright Mills, *Character and Social Structure* (New York: Harcourt, Brace & World, Inc., 1953), pp. 112-113. For a similar view by a "neo-Freudian," see Erich Fromm, *The Sane Society* (New York: Holt, Rinehart & Winston, Inc., 1955), pp. 74-77.

[21] John Dollard, *Criteria for the Life History* (New Haven: Yale University Press, 1935), p. 120. This valuable book has been neglected, presumably because it appears to be a purely methodological effort to set up standards for judging the adequacy of biographical and autobiographical data. Actually, the standards serve as well to evaluate the adequacy of general theories of personality or human nature and even to prescribe in part what a sound theory ought to include.

---

[22] One of the few attempts by a social scientist to relate systematically man's anatomical structure and biological history to his social nature and his unique cultural creativity is Weston La Barre's *The Human Animal* (Chicago: University of Chicago Press, 1954). See especially Chaps. 4-6, but the entire book is relevant. It is one of the few exceptions to Paul Goodman's observation that anthropologists nowadays "commence with a chapter on physical anthropology and then forget the whole topic and go on to culture." See his "Growing up Absurd," *Dissent*, **7** (Spring, 1960), 121.

[23] Paul Goodman has developed a similar distinction. *Ibid.*, 123-125.

the over-socialized conception of man   95

latter sense, but this does not mean that they have been completely molded by the particular norms and values of their culture. All cultures, as Freud contended, do violence to man's socialized bodily drives, but this in no sense means that men could possibly exist without culture or independently of society.[24] From such a standpoint, man may properly be called, as Norman Brown has called him, the "neurotic" or the "discontented" animal and repression may be seen as the main characteristic of human nature as we have known it in history.[25]

But isn't this psychology and haven't sociologists been taught to forswear psychology, to look with suspicion on what are called "psychological variables" in contradistinction to the institutional and historical forces with which they are properly concerned? There is, indeed, as recent critics have complained, too much "psychologism" in contemporary sociology, largely, I think, because of the bias inherent in our favored research techniques. But I do not see how, at the level of theory, sociologists can fail to make assumptions about human nature.[26] If our assumptions are left implicit, we will inevitably presuppose of a view of man that is tailor-made to our special needs; when our sociological theory overstresses the stability and integration of society we will end up imagining that man is the disembodied, conscience-driven, status-seeking phantom of current theory. We must do better if we really wish to win credit outside of our ranks for special understanding of man, that plausible creature[27] whose wagging tongue so often hides the despair and darkness in his heart.

---

[24] Whether it might be possible to create a society that does not repress the bodily drives is a separate question. See Herbert Marcuse, *Eros and Civilization* (Boston: The Beacon Press, 1955); and Norman O. Brown, *Life Against Death* (New York: Random House, Inc., 1960). Neither Marcuse nor Brown [is] guilty in their brilliant, provocative, and visionary books of assuming a "natural man" who awaits liberation from social bonds. They differ from such sociological Utopians as Fromm, *op. cit.*, in their lack of sympathy for the desexualized man of the neo-Freudians. For the more traditional Freudian view, see Walter A. Weisskopf, "The 'Socialization' of Psychoanalysis in Contemporary America," in Benjamin Nelson, ed., *Psychoanalysis and the Future* (New York: National Psychological Association for Psychoanalysis, 1957), pp. 51-56; Hans Meyerhoff, "Freud and the Ambiguity of Culture," *Partisan Review*, **24** (Winter, 1957), 117-130.

[25] Brown, *op. cit.*, pp. 3-19.

[26] "I would assert that very little sociological analysis is ever done without using at least an implicit psychological theory." Alex Inkeles, "Personality and Social Structure," in Robert K. Merton, *et al.*, eds., *Sociology Today* (New York: Basic Books, Inc., 1959), p. 250.

[27] Harry Stack Sullivan once remarked that the most outstanding characteristic of human beings was their "plausibility."

socialization

ten

Since the sociologist sees the *social* formation of man as critical, it follows that he should emphasize in man's early training those features of that experience which prepare him for the social roles he will later assume as an adult. To illustrate the process of *socialization*, therefore, I have chosen a paper by David Aberle and Kaspar Naegele in which they highlight for us the ways in which middle-class fathers shape the training of their sons in accord with their image of the qualities that will later make for success in a middle-class occupational world. We should note the difference between this environment and the stark socialization experience of lower-class Negroes described by Allison Davis and John Dollard in Chap. 13.

Raising Middle-Class Sons

DAVID F. ABERLE   KASPAR D. NAEGELE

This paper will consider the relationship between the occupational role of the middle-class male and his aims and concerns in the socialization of his children. The approach is deliberately one-sided. We will deal almost entirely with fathers, and scarcely at all with mothers, and we will highlight other aspects of the socialization process at the expense of such matters as feeding practices, toilet training, and sexual training.[1] There is no intention of denying the worth of approaches other than that exemplified here. We wish only to stress what seem to be neglected, though obvious and common sense aspects of the question of socialization.

David F. Aberle and Kaspar D. Naegele, "Middle-Class Fathers' Occupational Role and Attitudes Toward Children," *American Journal of Orthopsychiatry*, 22 (April, 1952), 366-378. Slightly revised. Copyright, the American Orthopsychiatric Association, Inc.

[1] In one sense these matters are universal. In all societies the child is eventually weaned and toilet trained, and some regulation is imposed on sexual expression. Means and goals of training, of course, vary widely. But regardless of the degree to which these particular disciplines are regarded as crucial, it is probable that the techniques used and the goals pursued with respect to any *specific* socialization problem are in part reflections of general parental value attitudes. Techniques and goals in socialization reflect a commitment to a style of life. This is a convenient assumption, however, and not a proven fact, and should not prevent researchers from being alert to apparent or real contradictions and inconsistencies in parents' socialization practices.

Approaches to the Question
of Socialization

We will define socialization for the purpose at hand as the process of inculcating in individuals the skills, traits, and value attitudes associated with the performance of present or anticipated roles.[2] There are a number of ways of stating problems concerning socialization. One approach is to ask what are the *effects* of certain types of socialization experience. Considerable strides have been made along these lines, in analyzing, for example, the effects of "basic disciplines" such as weaning, toilet training, and sexual training. The effects of aggression and dependency training are also receiving attention. Some work has been undertaken regarding the effects of particular kinds of parent-child relationships on the socialization process. When attention is turned to the *causes* of certain types of treatment of the child, there is a tendency in psychiatric and mental health work to investigate the causes of *pathological* parental behavior, and to find its sources in the childhood experiences of the parents: to see that in various complex and unconscious ways parents are repeating, or undoing, or working out problems derived from their own childhood. There is no desire to eliminate either of these approaches. But the focus here will be on an aspect of socialization so obvious that it is sometimes forgotten: the relationship between the adult role of the individual and his orientation to his children.

In every society parents aim to raise their children to become adults capable of assuming the typical adult roles and of being integrated into the social system. Consequently we can expect that within any given social group there will be similarities in the goals and practices of socialization. Similarity of goals depends partly upon the relative uniformity of the parents' long-range expectations as to what sorts of positions the children will ultimately occupy and what consequent skills, attitudes, and qualities they must ultimately possess, and partly on the relative uniformity of the definition of the succession of roles intermediate between infancy and adulthood.[3] Similarities in means depend partly on the fact that they "make sense" to the parents in terms of the goals hoped for, and partly on the effects of having one's efforts inspected by one's neighbors. (In addition to these conscious and semiconscious expectations, parents are influenced by a variety of unconscious factors, derived from both idiosyncratic and general experience. Furthermore, any particular socialization regime has consequences for personality unanticipated by the socializing agents. These unanticipated consequences sometimes take the form of particular types of deviations common in the society, sometimes of "quirks" commonly found in "normal" members of the group.) All in all, child rearing is future-oriented to an important extent. The picture of the desired end product is importantly influenced by the parents' experiences in the adult world, as well as by their

---

[2] This is not presented as a universally useful definition. One may equally well analyze socialization from the point of view of the person socialized, rather than from that of the socializer, or as a reciprocal process, involving mutual learning. In terms of our definition, socialization efforts are directed at individuals throughout life, whenever new roles are taken on or anticipated. It is assumed that the impact of early experiences with socializing agents and practices is of very great importance.

[3] There may be major inconsistencies between the expectations for, say, a twelve-year-old boy in a particular society, and expectations for that same boy's behavior as an adult. This involves complexities beyond the scope of this paper.

childhood experiences. When adult experience changes under the impact of major social change, there is reason to believe that there will ultimately, though not necessarily immediately, be shifts in the socialization pattern as well. The adult's experiences tell him what attitudes, skills, and qualities his child must have to fit into the adult role system. And the parent is likely to consider his child's *present* behavior as a prognostication of his probable adult behavior. The parent's evaluation of the child's behavior, however, proceeds not only by direct extrapolation, but also by vaguer, and less conscious processes, in which the connection between present and future behavior is more indirectly and symbolically reckoned.

These rather obvious matters are sometimes forgotten by the psychiatrically oriented—or rather, fall far into the background—in the interests of analyzing more complex and interesting problems of psychopathological behavior. But it is with these things in mind that we shall approach the question of the middle-class father. And perhaps it should be said that one reason we are stressing the father is that he, too, is forgotten or recedes into the background in the face of the overwhelming focus on the mother in recent work.

The Research Project

This presentation is based on data collected in the course of research carried out for the Human Relations Service, a group interested in preventive psychiatry, located in a suburb of Boston, with both clinical and research functions. The Service is headed by Dr. Erich Lindemann and financed by the W. T. Grant Foundation. The authors of this paper, respectively a social anthropologist and a sociologist, have recently completed interviews with both parents in a series of more than twenty families. Each family had at least one child in a particular nursery school in the community. The parents were selected for our research because after meetings of their group where members of the Human Relations Service spoke, they expressed willingness to serve as subjects. The group is middle class by our subjective impressions, and by rating according to Warner's Index of Status Characteristics. The members range from upper middle class to lower middle class. Incomes run from about $20,000 per annum to about $3700. One family lives in a two-family house, and the remainder in single-family dwellings, all in "good" neighborhoods. For the most part the fathers are professional men, major and minor executives of medium to large business concerns, owners of businesses, and salesmen (not including house-to-house sales). Only one man is on an hourly wage rate, and the group includes no skilled, semiskilled, or unskilled laborers. Most of the men are college educated, and the remainder have technical training beyond the high school level. Most of the wives are college educated. The school itself is "progressive." All of the men have risen in status in the course of their careers, and almost all feel that they have not yet reached their ceilings.

Since the families are middle class, what is said here is restricted in its implications to the middle class, with no necessary assumption that the remarks that follow have wider application, and some reason to believe that they do not. Most of the families are "normal," in the sense that few parents have sought or appear to need psychiatric advice, few children have appeared in psychiatric facilities, and there are no startling deviations from the norm in the patterning of adult roles.

* * * * *

One of us (D.F.A.) interviewed the fathers in these families, seeing them ordinarily for two evening-long interviews in their homes. The other (K.D.N.) interviewed the mothers. Information regarding the mothers . . . is used only for background data here.

The Separation of Occupation and Parental Role

That part of the project which was concerned with the fathers had as its aim the investigation of the relationship between the father's occupational role and his behavior in the home. More specifically, it was hoped that a connection could be established between the particular satisfactions and strains of each father's occupational setting and his behavior toward his wife and children. While minor relationships of this kind seem to exist, the data appear to illuminate somewhat more general questions. Before discussing them, we must stress the tentative character of subsequent remarks. The investigation was exploratory in nature, and the number of cases small. Matters which turned out to be quite important later on were not included in the initial interview schedule. And that schedule was long enough so that some questions were overlooked in interviewing some fathers.

It became clear in the course of research that the relationship which some fathers could see between their job situation and their behavior in the home was trivial, that some fathers could find no connection, and that still others flatly rejected the idea that there could be any connection. There is good reason for this. In the first place, many features of our social system stress the *separation* of the occupational and the domestic role. In urban, middle-class America, there is a deliberate boundary between home and job. This only seems obvious because we all participate in this sort of setup. In the majority of the world's societies, production and consumption units overlap greatly, and the extended or nuclear family is likely to be a basic organized unit of production and consumption. In our middle-class society, universalistic standards ideally govern the selection of individuals for occupational positions: competence—what you can do—rather than who you are, is, or ideally should be crucial for occupational recruitment, advancement, or firing. Family connections are theoretically irrelevant to the allocation of occupational role in the majority of middle-class occupations. There are institutional barriers against nepotism in many organizations, personal fortune and company funds are kept distinct, and of course place of employment and home are ordinarily separate. One's home life may actually affect job performance, positively or negatively. But the effects of home life are treated as irrelevant in many organizations, or as intrusive: something to be recognized only in order to dispel it—such is the role of the psychological consultant in many firms. For many reasons, modern complex industrial bureaucratic society requires this separation, institutionalizes it, makes of it a virtue—and the fathers in our group respond in terms of this norm.

Second, a man is bewildered when he is asked to consider the relationship of his behavior and attitudes on the job to those in the home. For him the two worlds are incommensurable. The occupational world is one of clearly delimited responsibility and authority, of judgment of individuals on the basis of what they can do, rather than who they are, of initiative and persistence, usually of competition, and a world where aggressiveness—in the layman's sense—pays off. In the domestic world, however, there are no such clear-cut limits on authority and responsibility; children are to be loved and cared for because they are one's children, and not because of their accomplishments or deserts; competition and aggressiveness are considered inappropriate techniques for gaining one's ends; and ideally emotional warmth, relaxation, and the like are to be maximized. Thus the techniques required for dealing with other individuals and making a success in the occupational world differ point by point from the techniques for dealing with wife and children and making a success of family life and the raising of sons and daughters. It is true that the standards of the occupational world "infect" behavior in the family in many ways, not all of which can be mentioned here. But in terms of ideal patterns, the two spheres are far apart. Hence the unwillingness or inability of fathers to see a relationship need not surprise us. But neither need it deter us from seeking a connection. When we consider the investment of time and affect in the occupational sphere, we are entitled to assume that the eight or more hours a day spent on the job may affect behavior during the other hours of the day. We shall see that while the father attempts to leave the office behind him at home, he *represents* the occupational world to his family (this is particularly clear in the interviews with mothers) and evaluates his children in terms of his occupational role.

Expectations for Children

We would assume that fathers in this group would be oriented toward their sons in terms of an expectation that they will ultimately occupy positions in the middle-class occupational structure, and toward their daughters with the expectation that they will not. The data confirm this assumption. Without exception fathers desire college training for their boys. One father says that one of his sons may not be college material, and that in this case he should not take up space in college —but he considers this a shocking statement. For girls, the majority of fathers plan a college education, but there is considerably more willingness to admit that the child may not go, either because she does not want to, or because she may get married first.

As for the sons' future occupation, fathers always say initially that they have "no plans" for their children. Further questioning always shows that "no plans" means that any occupation is all right, *if* it is a middle-class occupation. It means that either a professional or a business career is all right. (In the same way, "no plans" with regard to college means any *good* college, usually with certain limitations as to what constitutes a good college.) Skilled wage work is never mentioned. This drastic limitation is completely unconscious for the fathers. From their point of view this restriction is identical with "no plans." It might be mentioned that if fathers were asked whether academic work represented a possible career for the boy, they tended to reject it. One accepted it as a possibility; one said that it would be fine for his oldest son, since he was shy, irresponsible, bookish, and needed a woman to look after him. Three rejected it contemptuously. It is evident from the rejections, as well as from one of the acceptances, that it is not just a matter of meager financial reward: many a middle-class father does not consider the academic role to exemplify appropriate masculine behavior.[4]

[4] For present purposes the middle class is treated as if it were homogeneous. In fact, as

As for the daughters, over half of the fathers who discussed the point would accept the possibility of a career for their daughters, but only as a possibility. Most of these men would prefer that their daughters marry, or expect them to, and the remainder of the group reject a career out of hand. Only two fathers wanted their daughters to know how to earn a livelihood, and both of them [had] wives who [were] working or [had worked] during married life.

These findings are "normal" and "obvious" only because we are so deeply imbedded in the life which these fathers represent. Note that no father envisages downward mobility for his son. Also, though many of our fathers come from social and occupational backgrounds quite different from those they now occupy, it is their own present status, derived from adult experience, which they project into the future for their children. So far, then, our assumptions are supported by the data.[5]

One complication is introduced. Fathers do expect their sons to move in the same general occupational world that they do. But in our society occupational choice is theoretically free, and particular occupational positions are achieved, not inherited. Fathers *should* not, and in most cases *cannot* if they would, plan their children's precise future—since almost no one can guarantee a particular niche to his son. That means that fathers cannot foresee *exactly* what skills, values, and personality traits are going to be useful for their sons—something that is possible in many other societies. Nor can they plan precisely what steps their sons should take to reach this unknown future. Consequently, in evaluating their sons' present behavior they can only focus on general character traits conducive to success, on symbolic manifestations of those traits, and on a modicum of success in school as an almost essential step toward middle-class occupational status. A different future, marriage, is envisaged for girls, and we can expect a different evaluation of present behavior.

Evaluation of Behavior: Concerns

In the light of fathers' expectations for the future, let us examine some typical concerns that fathers express about the present behavior of their children. It must be stated at once that when we say that a child's behavior is a matter of concern to the father, this does not mean that the child is, or will become a problem by psychiatric standards. It means only that the child's behavior is disvalued, is a matter of worry and mild anxiety, is something that the parent would like to change, for the sake of the child (though his own convenience may also be involved). It should also be mentioned that it is possible for a father to become seriously concerned over behavior which a clinician might consider normal, to overlook behavior

[I.] Rosow has pointed out, there are undoubtedly subdivisions within any class as regards style of life and life goals, some of which may cut across class lines. Nevertheless, our particular group is fairly homogeneous with respect to the matters discussed here. Additional complexities are therefore overlooked, but their possible importance deserves mention.

[5] That is not to say that all lower-class fathers will project lower-class futures for their sons. The orientation of an individual to the total social system in which he participates is more complex than that. Fathers of whatever class may hold upward social mobility as a value. If a lower-class father does so, he will project middle-class status for his son. When he does so, however, his picture of middle-class status and its demands, and his consequent evaluation of his child's conduct should be affected by his lower-class status and experience. It should not be identical with that of the middle-class father. This is an empirical question well worth analysis, but one on which we have no information.

which might be considered portentous by a clinician, and to pass off some troubling behavior on the assumption that it is "just a stage."

Fifty-six children are involved: twenty-nine boys and twenty-seven girls. The age range is from thirteen years to a few months for boys, and from ten years to a few months for girls. Fathers may not subject very young infants to evaluative comment of the sort we are about to discuss, but this begins early in the child's life. There are many more statements of concern involving boys, and the emotional strength of these concerns is considerably greater with respect to boys than with respect to girls.

The question of securing obedience, and of annoyance at disobedience runs through virtually all the interviews and will not be discussed. The recurrent concerns expressed involve lack of responsibility and initiative, inadequate performance in school, insufficiently aggressive or excessively passive behavior, athletic inadequacies, overconformity, excitability, excessive tearfulness, and the like, . . . and "childish" behavior.[6] In all of these categories more boys were objects of concern than girls; in some, many more boys, and in some no girls were mentioned. Of course no parent expressed concern about all these things in any one child, or even in any one family. But the total tendency clearly indicates that such behaviors as have been mentioned are negatively evaluated when they appear in male children. Simi-

larly, satisfactory performance in these areas of behavior was more often mentioned for boys than for girls. Fathers are pleased if their boys display responsibility and initiative, perform well in school, stand up for themselves, show athletic ability, emotional stability, and so on. Only one father does not want his boys to be particularly athletic. Far less concerns, we have said, are expressed regarding girls. Satisfactions with girls, though they do include school performance, moral sexual behavior, and the like, seem to focus strongly on the girls' being "nice," "sweet," pretty, affectionate, and well liked. For both boys and girls, of course, fathers hope for normal personalities, good adjustment, likeability, and popularity.

But all of the traits we have mentioned as matters of concern are—from the father's point of view—prognosticators, direct or indirect, of adult traits which will interfere with success in middle-class occupational life. The ideal-typical successful adult male in the middle-class occupational role should be responsible, show initiative, be competent, be aggressive, be capable of meeting competition. He should be emotionally stable and capable of self-restraint. These qualities are part of the value structure of the occupational world, they are involved in the role definitions of that world, and fathers' discussions of their own jobs show that these qualities have great significance for them. This does a great deal to explain the difference between the father's concern with his son's behavior and with his daughter's. He worries about failures in these areas and is happy over successes, because of his future expectations for his sons. He does not worry so much about his daughters because they will occupy different roles, toward which he has a somewhat vaguer orientation. Occupational career is not taken seriously,

---

[6] Sexual disciplines were discussed rarely with mothers, almost never with fathers. This limitation came about partly because of the newness of the Human Relations Service and its insecure position in the community. People had expressed fears that the Service aimed either at another Kinsey report or another Middletown, and at the time it seemed important to minimize such fears. In addition, however, the problem under analysis required other emphases.

marriage is the primary hope and expectation, the same sorts of demands are not made, and the father does not seem to fuss too much as to whether his young daughter will ultimately be a good mate. If she is a sweet little girl, this is enough. We do find that there is some concern with these matters in girls, and that one father is disturbed by his daughter's lack of aggressiveness. But by and large, though the girls are undoubtedly *less* athletic, *less* aggressive, and *more* tearful and emotional than the boys, this does not bother the father. These qualities do not predict failure in the adult feminine role—quite the reverse. In fact some fathers are troubled if their daughters are bossy—a term not used for any of the boys. Though we know that some of the boys are holy terrors in their play groups, no father shows any concern lest his son be a bully, and some proudly mention that they guess the boy is a bit of a devil. (It might be noted that though the "bad boy" is a stereotype of American life, ambivalently but never wholly negatively regarded, there is no corresponding stereotype for a girl, the phrase "bad girl" having quite different connotations.) We will not deal here with mothers' concerns, but it can be said that mothers do react to what they consider excessive aggression in boys, and that mothers show more concern with girls than do fathers.

Fathers' concern with athletic ability and the rare expressions of concern require a little further discussion. This is a case of indirect and symbolic meaning of present behavior. Fathers are not concerned with athletics because they want their boys to grow up to be professional athletes, but because failure along these lines seems to symbolize for the father inability to be properly aggressive and competitive, now and in the future.

Projection into the future is not in-tended as a total explanation of the father's concerns. A son's present failures reflect on the father as a father, and this is important. In addition, we see conscious and half-conscious identification with sons in several fathers, and it is undoubtedly present in many more. Some of our most critical or most concerned fathers remark that the boy is "like me," or "reminds me of myself when I was his age." In a sense, we might say that whereas the father's present situation represents to him his son's probable future situation (broadly speaking), the son's present behavior may represent to the father his own past. This identification may produce nurturant behavior. But the identification may result in a highly ambivalent reaction: perhaps difficulties now observed in the son were once successfully overcome by the father, sometimes after a struggle, and these may now be unconsciously reactivated. The identification may thus intensify the degree to which the father attempts to counteract the disturbing behaviors in his son, attempting at the same time to stifle the same tendencies in himself.

It might be mentioned that our sample indicates that fathers become more concerned with male first-born children than with female first-born children, and that subsequent male children, whether they follow boys or girls, are less likely to be foci of concern for fathers. This might be partly connected with the identification phenomenon noted above, since conscious identification is mentioned more often in connection with male first-born children than with other sons. But there are many—too many—other ways to interpret this particular finding, and on the basis of our small sample we are reluctant to choose among them.[7]

[7] Thus [R. R.] Sears indicates that first-born children are more dependent. If this were so, then we would expect fathers to

We see a good deal of evidence, then, for the belief that fathers' attitudes toward their sons' behavior are different from those toward their daughters'. It is relatively easy to account for a good deal of this difference on the basis of the fact that the father is oriented toward his son as the future occupant of a middle-class occupational role, for which certain behaviors are of great importance—something about which he has direct experience —and toward his daughter as the future occupant of a different middle-class role, that of mother and wife, for which his own standards are less exacting and less well formed in terms of the girl's present behavior.

This does not mean that because the father uses present behavior as a prognosticator for the future it is a good prognosticator. It has been pointed out that he may well stress the unimportant, disregard fairly severe symptoms, and at times simply reckon present behavior as a "stage." Nor do our findings mean that boys are subject to more strains than girls, or are more likely to be problems in adult life, or the reverse. They only point to a particular relationship: that between father's occupational role, his future expectations for his children, and his evaluation of their conduct. The nature of that relationship has been discussed. What are its broader implications?

Theoretical Implications

On the theoretical level, it is hoped that this paper points to the desirability of much more minute inquiries

react more negatively to the dependency feelings of male first-born children than to those of female first-borns. Also, [E. M.] Duvall asserts that parents are more self-conscious about the raising of their first children. But the literature on birth order and personality is so loaded with contradictions as to make these speculations hazardous. . . .

aimed at relating socialization practices (about which we have said little), aims of socialization, parents' evaluation of children's behavior at various age levels, and parents' long-range expectations, to parents' adult roles, occupational and other, and to the values connected with those roles. Let us turn our attention not only to the *effects* of socialization practices in a group, but to the *causes* of those patterns. For, far from being fortuitous with respect to the remainder of the social system, many or most of those patterns are somehow integrated with it. The broad outlines of some of these relationships are recognized and have been explored empirically, as in the work of [A.] Davis and [R. J.] Havighurst, who have compared certain socialization practices as between class and caste groups and related those practices to the social position of the parents. The present paper works within a class, rather than by comparing two classes, and gives explicit attention to differences of expectations as between boys and girls. A tremendous amount of work, however, remains to be done on these and on more subtle and intricate issues.

Many questions in this general area pressed for our attention in the course of research. Some have been omitted here for lack of space, and some because the data were insufficient for extended discussion. But a few might be mentioned as suggestive of the sorts of problems remaining for analysis. Parents often express a certain ambivalence regarding the use of physical techniques in discipline—an ambivalence probably related to middle-class rejection of force as a means of settling interpersonal tensions or organizational difficulties. This rejection, in turn, has ramifications in the characteristics of role systems in the middle class. The question of means of socialization, largely neglected here, brings to mind the disagreements we sometimes saw between husband and wife as to what means shall be used, and the problem of analyzing to what extent these differences reflect a real difference of opinion regarding goals, and to what extent only a disagreement as to the path to be followed to reach a jointly agreed-upon goal. If the latter is the case, what are the factors which make one technique more congenial to the father, and a different one to the mother? We find a close relationship between these disagreements and another striking phenomenon: faddism in child-rearing techniques. Much of the faddism seems to center about two apparently opposed techniques of child rearing. One (the older) stresses scheduled feeding, early sphincter training, and in general responsibility and self-control. The other (and more recent) emphasizes demand feeding, late sphincter training, and concern for spontaneity and lack of severe inhibitions. Do these two approaches in fact reflect utterly diverse values, or are they simply two aspects of the same general value: individualism, with its responsibility aspect and its freedom aspect, here, as in other areas of life, in tension with each other?

Regardless of the issues about which faddism centers, we must ask how it is possible to have fads in child-training procedures. One factor seems to be the high valuation in our society placed on antitraditionalism, which is associated with the stress on science, rationalism, and progress. This antitraditionalistic attitude opens up the possibility of experimentation, change, and faddism in child training, as in other aspects of social life—though there are other social reasons for the existence of faddism as a general phenomenon. A thorough analysis of faddism in child rearing would also involve analysis of the adult feminine role in our society. These examples and partial interpretations only suggest the wealth of problems lying ready [at] hand. So, finally, this paper represents a very small contribution to a very large potential field: the relating of socialization practices to general American values, to class values, to role orientations, and the like, with due regard for the effects of adult, as well as childhood experiences, in determining parents' attitudes and behavior toward children, and with due attention to unconscious and symbolic connections as well as conscious ones.

Practical Implications

The approach used in this paper has implications for preventive psychiatric work, as well as for research. We see that fathers consider their sons' present behavior directly or symbolically indicative of probable future behavior, but we know that they may overstress minor defections and overlook serious symptoms. This stresses the need for pushing forward current work in educating the public. To insure rapid referral of disturbed children, and perhaps even more important, to allay parental anxieties, guidance must be provided not only to mothers, but also to fathers, which will give them a more precise understanding of the prognostic significance of present behavior for the future.

The matter of faddism, briefly touched on here, highlights another practical issue. In a sense the specialist views child training as a technological problem and believes that, like other technological problems, it can at least be improved by scientific analysis, which, he expects, can provide more effective techniques than those of common sense. Many middle-class parents have absorbed this attitude. Technological change always creates some discomfort in those who have to learn new ways, and parents are no exception. Lacking the security derived from the belief that customary behavior is adequate, they seek security by following to the hilt—or attempting to follow—the current recommendations of specialists, who now assume for the parents the authority once vested in tradition. These recommendations change, and parents attempt to change with them. In this way faddism grows out of insecurity and the use of the specialist's recommendations in the effort to attain fixity. But along with the effort to follow the specialist goes an ambivalence toward him—for, it seems, each psychiatrist is held responsible for the shifts of opinion of the last twenty years. Thus faddism poses three problems for preventive psychiatry: the careful evaluation of their recommendations, to test their validity; the assuaging of the anxiety created in parents by "styles" in child rearing; and fence-mending with respect to public relations.

One last point stands out with great clarity. In the course of research we found what many other workers must have observed: fathers with an ultimate faith in psychiatry and preventive psychiatry, but with marked resistance to some of the advice they had received in public meetings conducted by psychiatrically oriented—and well-qualified—individuals. Their complaints, in addition to faddism, seemed to center about excessive self-consciousness induced in parents, and too much emphasis on spontaneity and deinhibition, rather than discipline and responsibility. In the light of what has been said about the occupational sphere and about fathers' concerns, these complaints become intelligible. It would be too limited a view to consider such complaints only as manifestations of hostility toward the children. Rather, the "spontaneity" regime threatens the fathers because to them it means the possibility of raising children who cannot adapt to the world as the fathers know it. From a practical point of view, then, efforts to educate parents regarding socialization practices must be accompanied by at least equally intensive efforts to understand the meaning to the parents of the socialization practices they now use, to understand the threats which a change would mean to them, and to show them (when such is the case) that their goals are not subverted, but supported by suggested changes. Otherwise, we can anticipate reactions to attempted change in the form of ambivalence, overcomplicated performance, resistance, or rejection of the changes proposed.

types of men

eleven

The middle-class man to whom Aberle and Naegele introduced us is of course a type, and only one among many. The sociologists' interest in personality has manifested itself most distinctively in the parade of various "types of men" they have conceived and described. Today's sociologists have not forsaken this interesting game, and to represent it I have chosen perhaps the most famous of all the contemporary types—the "tradition-," "inner-," and "other-directed" men of David Riesman's *The Lonely Crowd*.

Inner, Other, and Tradition Directed

DAVID RIESMAN   NATHAN GLAZER

REUEL DENNEY

Character and Society

What is the relation between social character and society? How is it that every society seems to get, more or less, the social character it "needs"? Erik H. Erikson writes, in a study of the social character of the Yurok Indians, that ". . . systems of child training . . . represent unconscious attempts at creating out of human raw material that configuration of attitudes which is (or once was) the optimum under the tribe's particular natural conditions and economic-historic necessities."[1]

From "economic-historic necessities"

David Riesman, Nathan Glazer, and Reuel Denney, *The Lonely Crowd*, abridged ed. (New York: Doubleday & Co., 1953), pp. 19-42. Reprinted by permission of Yale University Press.

[1] "Observations on the Yurok: Childhood and World Image," *University of California Publications in American Archaeology and Ethnology*, **35** (1943), iv.

to "systems of child training" is a long jump. Much of the work of students of social character has been devoted to closing the gap and showing how the satisfaction of the largest "needs" of society is prepared, in some half-mysterious way, by its most intimate practices. Erich Fromm succinctly suggests the line along which this connection between society and character training may be sought: "In order that any society may function well, its members must acquire the kind of character which makes them *want* to act in the way they *have* to act as members of the society or of a special class within it. They have to *desire* what objectively is *necessary* for them to do. *Outer force* is replaced by *inner compulsion*, and by the particular kind of human energy which is channeled into character traits."[2]

[2] "Individual and Social Origins of Neurosis," *American Sociological Review*, **9** (1944), 380; reprinted in *Personality in Na-*

Thus, the link between character and society—certainly not the only one, but one of the most significant, and the one I choose to emphasize in this discussion—is to be found in the way in which society insures some degree of conformity from the individuals who make it up. In each society, such a mode of insuring conformity is built into the child, and then either encouraged or frustrated in later adult experience. (No society, it would appear, is quite prescient enough to insure that the mode of conformity it has inculcated will satisfy those subject to it in every stage of life.) I shall use the term "mode of conformity" interchangeably with the term "social character"—though certainly conformity is not all of social character: "mode of creativity" is as much a part of it. However, while societies and individuals may live well enough—if rather boringly—without creativity, it is not likely that they can live without some mode of conformity—even be it one of rebellion.

My concern in this book is with two revolutions and their relation to the "mode of conformity" or "social character" of western man since the Middle Ages. The first of these revolutions has in the last 400 years cut us off pretty decisively from the family- and clan-oriented traditional ways of life in which mankind has existed throughout most of history; this revolution includes the Renaissance, the Reformation, the Counter-Reformation, the industrial revolution, and the political revolutions of the seventeenth, eighteenth, and nineteenth centuries. This revolution is, of course, still in process, but in the most advanced countries of the world, and particularly in America, it is giving way to another sort of

revolution—a whole range of social developments associated with a shift from an age of production to an age of consumption. The first revolution we understand moderately well; it is, under various labels, in our texts and our terminology; this book has nothing new to contribute to its description, but perhaps does contribute something to its evaluation. The second revolution, which is just beginning, has interested many contemporary observers, including social scientists, philosophers, and journalists. Both description and evaluation are still highly controversial; indeed, many are still preoccupied with the first set of revolutions and have not invented the categories for discussing the second set. . . . I [shall] try to sharpen the contrast between, on the one hand, conditions and character in those social strata that are today most seriously affected by the second revolution, and, on the other hand, conditions and character in analogous strata during the earlier revolution; in this perspective, what is briefly said about the traditional and feudal societies which were overturned by the first revolution is in the nature of backdrop for these later shifts.

One of the categories I make use of is taken from demography, the science that deals with birth rates and death rates, with the absolute and relative numbers of people in a society, and their distribution by age, sex, and other variables, for I tentatively seek to link certain social and characterological developments, as cause and effect, with certain population shifts in western society since the Middle Ages.

It seems reasonably well established, despite the absence of reliable figures for earlier centuries, that during this period the curve of population growth in the western countries has shown an S-shape of a particular type (as other countries are drawn more closely into

ture, *Society and Culture*, Clyde Kluckhohn and Henry Murray, eds. (New York: Alfred A. Knopf, Inc., 1948).

the net of western civilization, their populations also show a tendency to develop along the lines of this S-shaped curve). The bottom horizontal line of the S represents a situation where the total population does not increase or does so very slowly, for the number of births equals roughly the number of deaths, and both are very high. In societies of this type, a high proportion of the population is young, life expectancy is low, and the turnover of generations is extremely rapid. Such societies are said to be in the phase of "high growth potential"; for should something happen to decrease the very high death rate (greater production of food, new sanitary measures, new knowledge of the causes of disease, and so on), a "population explosion" would result, and the population would increase very rapidly. This in effect is what happened in the West, starting with the seventeenth century. This spurt in population was most marked in Europe, and the countries settled by Europeans, in the nineteenth century. It is represented by the vertical bar of the S. Demographers call this the stage of "transitional growth," because the birth rate soon begins to follow the death rate in its decline. The rate of growth then slows down, and demographers begin to detect in the growing proportion of middle-aged and aged in the population the signs of a third stage, "incipient population decline." Societies in this stage are represented by the top horizontal bar of the S, again indicating, as in the first stage, that total population growth is small—but this time because births and deaths are low.

The S-curve is not a theory of population growth so much as an empirical description of what has happened in the West and in those parts of the world influenced by the West. After the S runs its course, what then? The developments of recent years in the United States and other western countries do not seem to be susceptible to so simple and elegant a summing up. "Incipient population decline" has not become "population decline" itself, and the birth rate has shown an uncertain tendency to rise again, which most demographers think is temporary.[3]

It would be very surprising if variations in the basic conditions of reproduction, livelihood, and survival chances, that is, in the supply of and demand for human beings, with all it implies in change of the spacing of people, the size of markets, the role of children, the society's feeling of vitality or senescence, and many other intangibles, failed to influence character. My thesis is, in fact, that each of these three different phases on the population curve appears to be occupied by a society that enforces conformity and molds social character in a definably different way.

The society of high growth potential develops in its typical members a social character whose conformity is insured by their tendency to follow tradition: these I shall term *tradition-directed* people and the society in which they live *a society dependent on tradition-direction*.

The society of transitional population growth develops in its typical members a social character whose conformity is insured by their tendency to acquire early in life an internalized set of goals. These I shall term *inner-directed* people and the society in which they live *a society dependent on inner-direction*.

Finally, the society of incipient population decline develops in its typical members a social character whose

---

[3] The terminology used here is that of Frank W. Notestein. See his "Population— The Long View," in *Food for the World*, Theodore W. Schultz, ed. (Chicago: University of Chicago Press, 1945).

conformity is insured by their tendency to be sensitized to the expectations and preferences of others. These I shall term *other-directed* people and the society in which they live one *dependent on other-direction*.

Let me point out, however, before embarking on a description of these three "ideal types" of character and society, that I am not concerned here with making the detailed analysis that would be necessary before one could prove that a link exists between population phase and character type. Rather, the theory of the curve of population provides me with a kind of shorthand for referring to the myriad institutional elements that are also—though usually more heatedly—symbolized by such words as "industrialism," "folk society," "monopoly capitalism," "urbanization," "rationalization," and so on. Hence when I speak here of transitional growth or incipient decline of population in conjunction with shifts in character and conformity, these phrases should not be taken as magical and comprehensive explanations.

My reference is as much to the complex of technological and institutional factors related—as cause or effect—to the development of population as to the demographic facts themselves. It would be almost as satisfactory, for my purposes, to divide societies according to the stage of economic development they have reached. Thus, Colin Clark's distinction between the "primary," "secondary," and "tertiary" spheres of the economy (the first refers to agriculture, hunting and fishing, and mining; the second to manufacturing; the third to trade, communications, and services) corresponds very closely to the division of societies on the basis of demographic characteristics. In those societies which are in the phase of "high growth potential," the "primary" sphere is dominant (for example,

India); in those that are in the phase of "transitional" growth, the "secondary" sphere is dominant (for example, Russia); in those that are in the phase of "incipient decline," the "tertiary" sphere is dominant (for example, the United States). And, of course, no nation is all of a piece, either in its population characteristics or its economy—different groups and different regions reflect different stages of development, and social character reflects these differences.

High Growth Potential: Tradition-Directed Types

The phase of high growth potential characterizes more than half the world's population: India, Egypt, and China (which have already grown immensely in recent generations), most preliterate peoples in Central Africa, parts of Central and South America, in fact most areas of the world relatively untouched by industrialization. Here death rates are so high that if birth rates were not also high the populations would die out.

Regions where the population is in this stage may be either sparsely populated, as are the areas occupied by many primitive tribes and parts of Central and South America; or they may be densely populated, as are India, China, and Egypt. In either case, the society achieves a Malthusian bargain with the limited food supply by killing off, in one way or another, some of the potential surplus of births over deaths —the enormous trap which, in Malthus' view, nature sets for man and which can be peaceably escaped only by prudent cultivation of the soil and prudent uncultivation of the species through the delay of marriage. Without the prevention of childbirth by means of marriage postponement or other contraceptive measures, the population must be limited by taking the life of living beings. And so societies have "invented" cannibalism, induced abortion, organized wars, made human sacrifice, and practiced infanticide (especially female) as means of avoiding periodic famine and epidemics.

Though this settling of accounts with the contradictory impulses of hunger and sex is accompanied often enough by upheaval and distress, these societies in the stage of high growth potential tend to be stable at least in the sense that their social practices, including the "crimes" that keep population down, are institutionalized and patterned. Generation after generation, people are born, are weeded out, and die to make room for others. The net rate of natural increase fluctuates within a broad range, though without showing any long-range tendency, as is true also of societies in the stage of incipient decline. But unlike the latter, the average life expectancy in the former is characteristically low: the population is heavily weighted on the side of the young, and generation replaces generation far more rapidly and less "efficiently" than in the societies of incipient population decline.

In viewing such a society we inevitably associate the relative stability of the man-land ratio, whether high or low, with the tenacity of custom and social structure. However, we must not equate stability of social structure over historical time with psychic stability in the life span of an individual: the latter may subjectively experience much violence and disorganization. In the last analysis, however, he learns to deal with life by adaptation, not by innovation. With certain exceptions conformity is largely given in the "self-evident" social situation. Of course nothing in human life is ever really self-evident; where it so appears it is because perceptions have been narrowed by cultural conditioning. As the

precarious relation to the food supply is built into the going culture, it helps create a pattern of conventional conformity which is reflected in many, if not in all, societies in the stage of high growth potential. This is what I call tradition-direction.

A Definition of Tradition-Direction

Since the type of social order we have been discussing is relatively unchanging, the conformity of the individual tends to be dictated to a very large degree by power relations among the various age and sex groups, the clans, castes, professions, and so forth —relations which have endured for centuries and are modified but slightly, if at all, by successive generations. The culture controls behavior minutely, and, while the rules are not so complicated that the young cannot learn them during the period of intensive socialization, careful and rigid etiquette governs the fundamentally influential sphere of kin relationships. Moreover, the culture, in addition to its economic tasks, or as part of them, provides ritual, routine, and religion to occupy and to orient everyone. Little energy is directed toward finding new solutions of the age-old problems, let us say, of agricultural technique or "medicine," the problems to which people are acculturated.

It is not to be thought, however, that in these societies, where the activity of the individual member is determined by characterologically grounded obedience to traditions, the individual may not be highly prized and, in many instances, encouraged to develop his capabilities, his initiative, and even, within very narrow time limits, his aspirations. Indeed, the individual in some primitive societies is far more appreciated and respected than in some sectors of modern society. For the individual in a society dependent on tradition-direction has a well-defined functional relationship to other members of the group. If he is not killed off, he "belongs"—he is not "surplus," as the modern unemployed are surplus, nor is he expendable as the unskilled are expendable in modern society. But by very virtue of his "belonging," life goals that are *his* in terms of conscious choice appear to shape his destiny only to a very limited extent, just as only to a limited extent is there any concept of progress for the group.

In societies in which tradition-direction is the dominant mode of insuring conformity, relative stability is preserved in part by the infrequent but highly important process of fitting into institutionalized roles such deviants as there are. In such societies a person who might have become at a later historical stage an innovator or rebel, whose belonging, as such, is marginal and problematic, is drawn instead into roles like those of the shaman or sorcerer. That is, he is drawn into roles that make a socially acceptable contribution, while at the same time they provide the individual with a more or less approved niche. The medieval monastic orders may have served in a similar way to absorb many characterological mutations.

In some of these societies certain individuals are encouraged toward a degree of individuality from childhood, especially if they belong to families of high status. But, since the range of choice, even for high-status people, is minimal, the apparent social need for an individuated type of character is also minimal. It is probably accurate to say that character structure in these societies is very largely "adjusted," in the sense that for most people it appears to be in tune with social institutions. Even the few misfits "fit" to a degree; and only very rarely is one driven out of his social world.

This does not mean, of course, that the people are happy; the society to whose traditions they are adjusted may be a miserable one, ridden with anxiety, sadism, and disease. The point is rather that change, while never completely absent in human affairs, is slowed down as the movement of molecules is slowed down at low temperature; and the social character comes as close as it ever does to looking like the matrix of the social forms themselves.

In western history the Middle Ages can be considered a period in which the majority were tradition-directed. But the term tradition-directed refers to a common element, not only among the people of precapitalist Europe, but also among such enormously different types of people as Hindus and Hopi Indians, Zulus and Chinese, North African Arabs and Balinese. There is comfort in relying on the many writers who have found a similar unity amid diversity, a unity they express in such terms as "folk society" (as against "civilization"), "status society" (as against "contract society"), "*Gemeinschaft*" (as against "*Gesellschaft*"), and so on. Different as the societies envisaged by these terms are, the folk, status, and *Gemeinschaft* societies resemble each other in their relative slowness of change, their dependence on family and kin organization, and—in comparison with later epochs—their tight web of values. And, as is now well recognized by students, the high birth rate of these societies in the stage of high growth potential is not merely the result of a lack of contraceptive knowledge or techniques. A whole way of life—an outlook on chance, on children, on the place of women, on sexuality, on the very meaning of existence—lies between the societies in which human fertility is allowed to take its course and toll and those which prefer to pay other kinds of toll to cut down on fertility by calculation, and, conceivably, as Freud and other observers have suggested, by a decline in sexual energy itself.

Transitional Growth:
Inner-Directed Types

Except for the West, we know very little about the cumulation of small changes that can eventuate in a breakup of the tradition-directed type of society, leading it to realize its potential for high population growth. As for the West, however, much has been learned about the slow decay of feudalism and the subsequent rise of a type of society in which inner-direction is the dominant mode of insuring conformity.

Critical historians, pushing the Renaissance ever back into the Middle Ages, seem sometimes to deny that any decisive change occurred at all. On the whole, however, it seems that the greatest social and characterological shift of recent centuries did indeed come when men were driven out of the primary ties that bound them to the western medieval version of tradition-directed society. All later shifts, including the shift from inner-direction to other-direction, seem unimportant by comparison, although, of course, this latter shift is still underway and we cannot tell what it will look like when—if ever—it is complete.

A change in the relatively stable ratio of births to deaths, which characterizes the period of high growth potential, is both the cause and consequence of other profound social changes. In most of the cases known to us a decline takes place in mortality prior to a decline in fertility; hence there is some period in which the population expands rapidly. The drop in death rate occurs as the result of many interacting factors, among them sanitation, improved communications (which permit government to operate over a wider area and also permit easier transport of food to areas of shortage from areas of surplus), the decline, forced or otherwise, of infanticide, cannibalism, and other inbred kinds of violence. Because of improved methods of agriculture the land is able to support more people, and these in turn produce still more people.

Notestein's phrase, "transitional growth," is a mild way of putting it. The "transition" is likely to be violent, disrupting the stabilized paths of existence in societies in which tradition-direction has been the principal mode of insuring conformity. The imbalance of births and deaths puts pressure on the society's customary ways. A new slate of character structures is called for or finds its opportunity in coping with the rapid changes—and the need for still more changes—in the social organization.

A Definition of Inner-Direction

In western history the society that emerged with the Renaissance and Reformation and that is only now vanishing serves to illustrate the type of society in which inner-direction is the principal mode of securing conformity. Such a society is characterized by increased personal mobility, by a rapid accumulation of capital (teamed with devastating technological shifts), and by an almost constant *expansion*: intensive expansion in the production of goods and people, and extensive expansion in exploration, colonization, and imperialism. The greater choices this society gives—and the greater initiatives it demands in order to cope with its novel problems—are handled by character types who can manage to live socially without strict and self-evident tradition-direction. These are the inner-directed types.

The concept of inner-direction is intended to cover a very wide range of types. Thus, while it is essential for the study of certain problems to differentiate between Protestant and Catholic countries and their character types, between the effects of the Reformation and the effects of the Renaissance, between the puritan ethic of the European north and west and the somewhat more hedonistic ethic of the European east and south, while all these are valid and, for certain purposes, important distinctions, the concentration of this study on the development of modes of conformity permits their neglect. It allows the grouping together of these otherwise distinct developments because they have one thing in common: *the source of direction for the individual is "inner" in the sense that it is implanted early in life by the elders and directed toward generalized but nonetheless inescapably destined goals.*

We can see what this means when we realize that, in societies in which tradition-direction is the dominant mode of insuring conformity, attention is focused on securing external *behavioral* conformity. While behavior is minutely prescribed, individuality of character need not be highly developed to meet prescriptions that are objectified in ritual and etiquette—though to be sure, a social character *capable* of such behavioral attention and obedience is requisite. By contrast, societies in which inner-direction becomes important, though they also are concerned with behavioral conformity, cannot be satisfied with behavioral conformity alone. Too many novel situations are presented, situations which a code cannot encompass in advance. Consequently the problem of personal choice, solved in the earlier period of high growth potential by channeling choice through rigid social organization, in the period of transi-

tional growth is solved by channeling choice through a rigid though highly individualized character.

This rigidity is a complex matter. While any society dependent on inner-direction seems to present people with a wide choice of aims—such as money, possessions, power, knowledge, fame, goodness—these aims are ideologically interrelated, and the selection made by any one individual remains relatively unalterable throughout his life. Moreover, the means to those ends, though not fitted into as tight a social frame of reference as in the society dependent on tradition-direction, are nevertheless limited by the new voluntary associations—for instance, the Quakers, the Masons, the Mechanics' Associations—to which people tie themselves. Indeed, the term "tradition-direction" could be misleading if the reader were to conclude that the force of tradition has no weight for the inner-directed character. On the contrary, he is very considerably bound by traditions: they limit his ends and inhibit his choice of means. The point is rather that a splintering of tradition takes place, connected in part with the increasing division of labor and stratification of society. Even if the individual's choice of tradition is largely determined for him by his family, as it is in most cases, he cannot help becoming aware of the existence of competing traditions—hence of tradition as such. As a result he possesses a somewhat greater degree of flexibility in adapting himself to ever-changing requirements and in return requires more from his environment.

As the control of the primary group is loosened—the group that both socializes the young and controls the adult in the earlier era—a new psychological mechanism appropriate to the more open society is "invented": it is what I like to describe as a psychological gyroscope.[4] This instrument, once it is set by the parents and other authorities, keeps the inner-directed person, as we shall see, "on course" even when tradition, as responded to by his character, no longer dictates his moves. The inner-directed person becomes capable of maintaining a delicate balance between the demands upon him of his life goal and the buffetings of his external environment.

This metaphor of the gyroscope, like any other, must not be taken literally. It would be a mistake to see the inner-directed man as incapable of learning from experience or as insensitive to public opinion in matters of external conformity. He can receive and utilize certain signals from outside, provided that they can be reconciled with the limited maneuverability that his gyroscope permits him. His pilot is not quite automatic.

[Johan] Huizinga's *The Waning of the Middle Ages* gives a picture of the anguish and turmoil, the conflict of values, out of which the new forms slowly emerged. Already by the late Middle Ages people were forced to live under new conditions of awareness. As their self-consciousness and their individuality developed, they had to make themselves at home in the world in novel ways. They still have to.

Incipient Decline of Population: Other-Directed Types

The problem facing the societies in the stage of transitional growth is that of reaching a point at which resources become plentiful enough or are utilized effectively enough to permit a rapid accumulation of capital. This rapid accumulation has to be achieved even

_____
[4] Since writing the above I have discovered Gardner Murphy's use of the same metaphor in his volume *Personality* (New York: Harper & Row, Publishers, Inc., 1947).

while the social product is being drawn on at an accelerated rate to maintain the rising population and satisfy the consumer demands that go with the way of life that has already been adopted. For most countries, unless capital and techniques can be imported from other countries in still later phases of the population curve, every effort to increase national resources at a rapid rate must actually be at the expense of current standards of living. We have seen this occur in the U.S. S.R., now in the stage of transitional growth. For western Europe this transition was long-drawn-out and painful. For America, Canada, and Australia—at once beneficiaries of European techniques and native resources —the transition was rapid and relatively easy.

The tradition-directed person, as has been said, hardly thinks of himself as an individual. Still less does it occur to him that he might shape his own destiny in terms of personal, lifelong goals or that the destiny of his children might be separate from that of the family group. He is not sufficiently separated psychologically from himself (or, therefore, sufficiently close to himself), his family, or group to think in these terms. In the phase of transitional growth, however, people of inner-directed character do gain a feeling of control over their own lives and see their children also as individuals with careers to make. At the same time, with the shift out of agriculture and, later, with the end of child labor, children no longer become an unequivocal economic asset. And with the growth of habits of scientific thought, religious and magical views of human fertility—views that in an earlier phase of the population curve made sense for the culture if it was to reproduce itself —give way to "rational," individualistic attitudes. Indeed, just as the rapid accumulation of productive capital requires that people be imbued with the "Protestant ethic" (as Max Weber characterized one manifestation of what is here termed inner-direction), so also the decreased number of progeny requires a profound change in values—a change so deep that, in all probability, it has to be rooted in character structure.

As the birth rate begins to follow the death rate downward, societies move toward the epoch of incipient decline of population. Fewer and fewer people work on the land or in the extractive industries or even in manufacturing. Hours are short. People may have material abundance and leisure besides. They pay for these changes, however—here, as always, the solution of old problems gives rise to new ones —by finding themselves in a centralized and bureaucratized society and a world shrunken and agitated by the contact—accelerated by industrialization—of races, nations, and cultures.

The hard enduringness and enterprise of the inner-directed types are somewhat less necessary under these new conditions. Increasingly, *other people* are the problem, not the material environment. And as people mix more widely and become more sensitive to each other, the surviving traditions from the stage of high growth potential—much disrupted, in any case, during the violent spurt of industrialization—become still further attenuated. Gyroscopic control is no longer sufficiently flexible, and a new psychological mechanism is called for.

Furthermore, the "scarcity psychology" of many inner-directed people, which was socially adaptive during the period of heavy capital accumulation that accompanied transitional growth of population, needs to give way to an "abundance psychology" capable of "wasteful" luxury consumption of leisure and of the surplus product. Unless people want to destroy the sur-

plus product in war, which still does require heavy capital equipment, they must learn to enjoy and engage in those services that are expensive in terms of manpower but not of capital —poetry and philosophy, for instance.[5] Indeed, in the period of incipient decline, nonproductive consumers, both the increasing number of old people and the diminishing number of as yet untrained young, form a high proportion of the population, and these need both the economic opportunity to be prodigal and the character structure to allow it.

Has this need for still another slate of character types actually been acknowledged to any degree? My observations lead me to believe that in America it has.

A Definition of Other-Direction

The type of character I shall describe as other-directed seems to be emerging in very recent years in the upper middle class of our larger cities: more prominently in New York than in Boston, in Los Angeles than in Spokane, in Cincinnati than in Chillicothe. Yet in some respects this type is strikingly similar to *the* American, whom Tocqueville and other curious and astonished visitors from Europe, even before the Revolution, thought to be a new kind of man. Indeed, travelers' reports on America impress us with their unanimity. The American is said to be shallower, freer with his money, friendlier, more uncertain of himself and his values, more demanding of approval than the European. It all adds up to a pattern which, without stretching matters too far, resembles the kind of character that a number of social scientists have seen as developing a contemporary, highly industrialized, and bureaucratic America:

[5] These examples are given by Allan G. B. Fisher, *The Clash of Progress and Security* (London: Macmillan & Co., Ltd., 1935).

Fromm's "marketer," Mills's "fixer," Arnold Green's "middle-class male child."[6]

It is my impression that the middle-class American of today is decisively different from those Americans of Tocqueville's writings who nevertheless strike us as so contemporary, and much of this book will be devoted to discussing these differences. It is also my impression that the conditions I believe to be responsible for other-direction are affecting increasing numbers of people in the metropolitan centers of the advanced industrial countries. My analysis of the other-directed character is thus at once an analysis of the American and of contemporary man. Much of the time I find it hard or impossible to say where one ends and the other begins. Tentatively, I am inclined to think that the other-directed type does find itself most at home in America, due to certain unique elements in American society, such as its recruitment from Europe and its lack of any feudal past. As against this, I am also inclined to put more weight on capitalism, industrialism, and urbanization—these being international tendencies—than on any character-forming peculiarities of the American scene.

Bearing these qualifications in mind, it seems appropriate to treat contemporary metropolitan America as our illustration of a society—so far, perhaps, the only illustration—in which other-direction is the dominant mode of insuring conformity. It would be premature, however, to say that it is already the dominant mode in Amer-

ica as a whole. But since the other-directed types are to be found among the young, in the larger cities, and among the upper income groups, we may assume that, unless present trends are reversed, the hegemony of other-direction lies not far off.

If we wanted to cast our social character types into social class molds, we could say that inner-direction is the typical character of the "old" middle class—the banker, the tradesman, the small entrepreneur, the technically oriented engineer, etc.—while other-direction is becoming the typical character of the "new" middle class—the bureaucrat, the salaried employee in business, etc. Many of the economic factors associated with the recent growth of the "new" middle class are well known. They have been discussed by James Burnham, Colin Clark, Peter Drucker, and others. There is a decline in the numbers and in the proportion of the working population engaged in production and extraction—agriculture, heavy industry, heavy transport—and an increase in the numbers and the proportion engaged in white collar work and the service trades. People who are literate, educated, and provided with the necessities of life by an ever-more efficient machine industry and agriculture, turn increasingly to the "tertiary" economic realm. The service industries prosper among the people as a whole and no longer only in court circles.

Education, leisure, services, these go together with an increased consumption of words and images from the new mass media of communications. While societies in the phase of transitional growth begin the process of distributing words from urban centers, the flow becomes a torrent in the societies of incipient population decline. This process, while modulated by profound national and class differences, connected with differences in literacy

---

[6] See Erich Fromm, *Man for Himself* (New York: Holt, Rinehart & Winston, Inc., 1947); C. Wright Mills, "The Competitive Personality," *Partisan Review*, 13 (1946), 433; Arnold Green, "The Middle-Class Male Child and Neurosis," *American Sociological Review*, 11 (1946), 31. See also the work of Jurgen Ruesch, Martin B. Loeb, and coworkers on the "infantile personality."

and loquacity, takes place everywhere in the industrialized lands. Increasingly, relations with the outer world and with oneself are mediated by the flow of mass communication. For the other-directed types political events are likewise experienced through a screen of words by which the events are habitually atomized and personalized—or pseudopersonalized. For the inner-directed person who remains still extant in this period the tendency is rather to systematize and moralize this flow of words.

These developments lead, for large numbers of people, to changes in paths to success and to the requirement of more "socialized" behavior both for success and for marital and personal adaptation. Connected with such changes are changes in the family and in child-rearing practices. In the smaller families of urban life, and with the spread of "permissive" child care to ever-wider strata of the population, there is a relaxation of older patterns of discipline. Under these newer patterns the peer group (the group of one's associates of the same age and class) becomes much more important to the child, while the parents make him feel guilty not so much about violation of inner standards as about failure to be popular or otherwise to manage his relations with these other children. Moreover, the pressures of the school and the peer group are reinforced and continued—in a manner whose inner paradoxes I shall discuss later—by the mass media: movies, radio, comics, and popular culture media generally. Under these conditions types of character emerge that we shall here term other-directed. . . . *What is common to all the other-directed people is that their contemporaries are the source of direction for the individual— either those known to him or those with whom he is indirectly acquainted, through friends and through the mass*

media. This source is, of course, "internalized" in the sense that dependence on it for guidance in life is implanted early. The goals toward which the other-directed person strives shift with that guidance: it is only the process of striving itself and the process of paying close attention to the signals from others that remain unaltered throughout life. This mode of keeping in touch with others permits a close behavioral conformity, not through drill in behavior itself, as in the tradition-directed character, but rather through an exceptional sensitivity to the actions and wishes of others.

Of course, it matters very much who these "others" are: whether they are the individual's immediate circle or a "higher" circle or the anonymous voices of the mass media; whether the individual fears the hostility of chance acquaintances or only of those who "count." But his need for approval and direction from others—and contemporary others rather than ancestors— goes beyond the reasons that lead most people in any era to care very much what others think of them. While all people want and need to be liked by some of the people some of the time, it is only the modern, other-directed types who make this their chief source of direction and chief area of sensitivity.[7]

It is perhaps the insatiable force of this psychological need for approval that differentiates people of the metropolitan, American upper middle class, whom we regard as other-directed, from very similar types that have appeared in capital cities and among other classes in previous historical

[7] This picture of the other-directed person has been stimulated by, and developed from, Erich Fromm's discussion of the "marketing orientation" in *Man for Himself, op. cit.*, pp. 67-82. I have also drawn on my portrait of "The Cash Customer," *Common Sense,* **11** (1942), 183.

periods, whether in Imperial Canton, in eighteenth- and nineteenth-century Europe, or in ancient Athens, Alexandria, or Rome. In all these groups fashion not only ruled as a substitute for morals and customs, but it was a rapidly changing fashion that held sway. It could do so because, although the mass media were in their infancy, the group corresponding to the American upper middle class was comparably small and the élite structure was extremely reverberant. It can be argued, for example, that a copy of *The Spectator* covered its potential readership more thoroughly in the late eighteenth century than *The New Yorker* covers its readership today. In eighteenth- and nineteenth-century English, French, and Russian novels, we find portraits of the sort of people who operated in the upper reaches of bureaucracy and had to be prepared for rapid changes of signals. Stepan Arkadyevitch Oblonsky in *Anna Karenina* is one of the more likeable and less opportunistic examples, especially striking because of the way Tolstoy contrasts him with Levin, a moralizing, inner-directed person. At any dinner party Stepan manifests exceptional social skills; his political skills as described in the following quotation are also highly social:

Stepan Arkadyevitch took in and read a liberal newspaper, not an extreme one, but one advocating the views held by the majority. And in spite of the fact that science, art, and politics had no special interest for him, he firmly held those views on all subjects which were held by the majority and by his paper, and he only changed them when the majority changed them—or, more strictly speaking, he did not change them, but they imperceptively changed of themselves within him.

Stepan Arkadyevitch had not chosen his political opinions or his views; these political opinions and views had come to him of themselves, just as he did not choose the shapes of his hats or coats, but simply took those that were being worn. And for him, living in a certain society—owing to the need, ordinarily developed at years of discretion, for some degree of mental activity—to have views was just as indispensable as to have a hat. If there was a reason for his preferring liberal to conservative views, which were held also by many of his circle, it arose not from his considering liberalism more rational, but from its being in closer accord with his manner of life. . . . And so liberalism had become a habit of Stepan Arkadyevitch's, and he liked his newspaper, as he did his cigar after dinner, for the slight fog it diffused in his brain.

Stepan, while his good-natured gregariousness makes him seem like a modern middle-class American, is not fully other-directed. This gregariousness alone, without a certain sensitivity to others as individuals and as a source of direction, is not the identifying trait. Just so, we must differentiate the nineteenth-century American, gregarious and subservient to public opinion though he was found to be by Tocqueville, Bryce, and others, from the other-directed American as he emerges today, an American who in his character is more capable of and more interested in maintaining responsive contact with others both at work and at play. This point needs to be emphasized, since the distinction is easily misunderstood. The inner-directed person, though he often sought and sometimes achieved a relative independence of public opinion and of what the neighbors thought of him, was in most cases very much concerned with his good repute and, at least in America, with "keeping up with the Joneses." These conformities, however, were primarily external, typified in such details as clothes, curtains, and bank credit. For, indeed, the conformities were to a standard, evidence of which was provided by the "best people" in one's milieu. In contrast with this pattern, the other-directed person, though he has his eye very much on the Joneses, aims to keep up with them not so much in external details as in the quality of his inner experience. That is, his great sensitivity keeps him in touch with others on many more levels than the externals of appearance and propriety. Nor does any ideal of independence or of reliance on God alone modify his desire to look to the others—and the "good guys" as well as the best people—for guidance in what experiences to seek and in how to interpret them.

The Three Types Compared

One way to see the structural differences between the three types is to see the differences in the emotional sanction or control in each type.

The tradition-directed person feels the impact of his culture as a unit, but it is nevertheless mediated through the specific, small number of individuals with whom he is in daily contact. These expect of him not so much that he be a certain type of person but that he behave in the approved way. Consequently the sanction for behavior tends to be the fear of being *shamed*.

The inner-directed person has early incorporated a psychic gyroscope which is set going by his parents and can receive signals later on from other authorities who resemble his parents. He goes through life less independent than he seems, obeying this internal piloting. Getting off course, whether in response to inner impulses or to the fluctuating voices of contemporaries, may lead to the feeling of *guilt*.

Since the direction to be taken in life has been learned in the privacy of the home from a small number of guides and since principles, rather than details of behavior, are internalized, the inner-directed person is capable of great stability. Especially so when it turns out that his fellows have gyro-

scopes too, spinning at the same speed and set in the same direction. But many inner-directed individuals can remain stable even when the reinforcement of social approval is not available—as in the upright life of the stock Englishman isolated in the tropics.

Contrasted with such a type as this, the other-directed person learns to respond to signals from a far wider circle than is constituted by his parents. The family is no longer a closely knit unit to which he belongs but merely part of a wider social environment to which he early becomes attentive. In these respects the other directed person resembles the tradition-directed person: both live in a group milieu and lack the inner-directed person's capacity to go it alone. The nature of this group milieu, however, differs radically in the two cases. The other-directed person is cosmopolitan. For him the border between the familiar and the strange— a border clearly marked in the societies depending on tradition-direction—has broken down. As the family continuously absorbs the strange and so reshapes itself, so the strange becomes familiar. While the inner-directed person could be "at home abroad" by virtue of his relative insensitivity to others, the other-directed person is, in a sense, at home everywhere and nowhere, capable of a rapid if sometimes superficial intimacy with and response to everyone.

The tradition-directed person takes his signals from others, but they come in a cultural monotone; he needs no complex receiving equipment to pick them up. The other-directed person must be able to receive signals from far and near; the sources are many, the changes rapid. What can be internalized, then, is not a code of behavior but the elaborate equipment needed to attend to such messages and occasionally to participate in their circulation. As against guilt-and-shame controls, though of course these survive, one prime psychological lever of the other-directed person is a diffuse *anxiety*. This control equipment, instead of being like a gyroscope, is like a radar.[8]

[8] The "radar" metaphor was suggested by Karl Wittfogel.

personality and social action

twelve

The personality game, if such it is, becomes really serious for the sociologist only when he can show convincingly how personality makes a difference in social action. Such demonstrations are, unfortunately, few in number. Social psychologists are, however, learning to measure personality in ways maximally relevant to social analysis and with an economy and precision that permit collecting large numbers of cases by the survey method. D. J. Levinson illustrates the approach by showing how the authoritarian personality syndrome influences the individual's orientations toward foreign policy.

Authoritarianism and Foreign Policy

DANIEL J. LEVINSON

Attempts to understand the foreign policy of particular nations or the course of international relations generally have traditionally been guided almost entirely by historical-sociological points of view. The chief foci of analysis have been in the realms of power politics, geopolitics, national economic interests, and the like. Recently, we have seen a growing interest in the role of psychological factors in international relations.[1] This interest stems in part from the recognition of "irrationality" in foreign policy viewpoints. However, it would seem overly narrow to limit our psychological concern to the problem of irrationality. The thesis of this paper is that every foreign policy orientation, whatever its degree of rationality and constructiveness, has, to an appreciable extent, a psychological foundation in the personalities of its adherents. This is not to say that foreign policy is purely an individual matter or merely a reflection of intrapersonal dynamics. I would argue,

Daniel J. Levinson, "Authoritarian Personality and Foreign Policy," *Journal of Conflict Resolution*, 1 (March, 1957), 37-47.

[1] G. Almond, *The American People and Foreign Policy* (New York: Harcourt, Brace & World, Inc., 1950); G. F. Kennan, "The Illusion of Security," *Atlantic Monthly* (August, 1954), 31-34; O. Klineberg, *Tensions Affecting International Understanding*, Social Science Research Council Bulletin 62 (New York: Social Science Research Council, 1950).

rather, for the development of a socio-psychological approach, one that gives due recognition to individual (and modal) personality while yet taking account of broader social forces.

My aim here is to consider certain psychological factors in various foreign policy orientations within the United States. Specifically, I wish to consider some of the ways in which psychological processes, operating in large numbers of individuals, influence the degree of support given to various foreign policy orientations. Although the present analysis is limited to the United States, its guiding principles can be applied to other nations as well.

In the analysis of the total process of formation, implementation, and change of foreign policy, there are several focal points which can be studied independently, though each must ultimately be understood in relation to the others. First, we may focus on the processes by which *basic policy decisions* are made and the determinants of various high-level policy orientations. Subjects of study would include "top" State Department meetings, foreign ministers' conferences, meetings of United Nations bodies, and the like. A second focus might be on the *production and distribution of foreign policy ideology*, in forms intended for mass consumption and having the purpose of justifying or opposing specific policy stands. The most obvious subject of study here is the mass media of communication, which provide the most potent means for the widespread distribution of ideology. Third, we may study the *consumption of foreign policy ideology*, that is, the various ways in which individuals selectively assimilate the diverse viewpoints with which they are constantly bombarded. This part of the total process—what might be considered the "public opinion" aspect—is the chief concern of this paper.

"Nationalism" and "Internationalism" as Ideological Orientations

The study of American foreign policy orientations is complicated from the start by the fact that the American people tend, for the most part, to be relatively unsophisticated about and only partially involved in foreign policy issues. There is, of course, a keen interest in the more dramatic events, such as the Korean War, the conscription bills, and the periodic American-Russian flareups. Nevertheless, we are relatively unconcerned and uninformed about the less dramatic but equally significant issues such as U.N. policy, the Point Four program, and the like. Historical and current sociological reasons for this are not hard to find: America has only recently come of age internationally; the understanding of international relations requires an ability and a readiness to think in terms of institutional abstractions to which Americans are only just getting accustomed; our newspapers and other communications media tend to perpetuate the existing confusion and ideological immaturity.

However, despite the relative lack of crystallized viewpoints, there does seem to exist a variety of general policy orientations or approaches. For certain purposes the existing foreign policy orientations can be grouped along a continuum between two opposing extremes—nationalism and internationalism: in the center are the "middle-of-the-road" viewpoints, which represent constructive synthesis, compromise, or ambivalent shifting between the nationalist and internationalist extremes; in one direction we have increasing degrees of internationalism, and in the other direction increasing degrees of nationalism.

To say that nationalism-internationalism is one *dimension* of foreign policy ideology is not, of course, to say that this is the only dimension or in all contexts the most significant one. There are, clearly, numerous forms of nationalism and internationalism; and there may well be important similarities among those who hold extreme views at opposite ends of the continuum. Moreover, in certain newly industrializing countries, such as India, Israel, and Burma, we may find conjointly in many individuals a fierce emphasis on national sovereignty and a broadly internationalistic (collaborative, multilateral, pro-U.N.) ideology. Certain modifications of the present analysis would no doubt be required for its extension to these and other social contexts. This analysis applies most directly to the United States at mid-century as a period in which "extremists" are few and moderation prevails in virtually all ideological domains. The prototypic forms of nationalism and internationalism, as they are conceived to exist within this social context, may be briefly delineated; a fuller exposition is given elsewhere.[2]

Nationalism may be seen as a facet of a broader ethnocentric orientation. It is, so to speak, ethnocentric thinking in the sphere of international relations. Like other forms of ethnocentrism, it is based on a rigid and pervasive distinction between in-groups and out-groups. The primary in-group in this case is the American nation; all other nations are potential out-groups, the focal out-groups at any given time being those nations whose aims are seen, rightly or wrongly, as different from ours. The American nation as a symbol is glorified and idealized; it is regarded as superior to other nations in all important aspects. Great emphasis is placed on such concepts as national honor and national sovereignty.

Other nations are seen as inferior, envious, and threatening. At the worst, they are likely to attack us; at best, they seek alliances only to pursue their own selfish aims and to "play us for a sucker." Ethnocentric ideas about human nature rationalize a belief in the inevitability of war. "Human nature being what it is and other 'races' being what they are," so the reasoning goes, "some nation is bound to attack us sooner or later." Given this "jungle" conception of international relations, our best policy is to be militarily the strongest of all nations, so that none will dare attack us.

Perhaps the two main forms that American nationalism has taken are *isolationism* and *imperialism*, though the two often go together. The guiding image of isolationism has been that of "Fortress America": its aim is a nation which is militarily impregnable and culturally isolated. Imperialism, on the other hand, is prepared to make foreign alliances and commitments, and it frequently uses internationalist terminology. Its aim, however, is the kind of "American Century" in which the development and reconstruction of other nations can proceed only on terms set by us, for our supposed economic and strategic advantage. Isolationism and imperialism sometimes merge into a single approach as the lines of American military defense are conceived to move outward into Europe and Asia and as we extend support to all governments, whatever their character, in exchange for military support.

An especially dramatic image exemplifying a nationalistic conception of the world situation has been provided by Robert Oppenheimer and discussed by Walter Lippmann.[3] The image is that of the United States and the So-

[2] Almond, *op. cit.*; D. J. Levinson, "An Approach to the Theory and Measurement of Ethnocentricism," *Journal of Psychology,* **28** (1949), 19-39.

[3] W. Lippmann, column appearing in the *Boston Globe* (October 7, 1953).

viet Union as "two scorpions in a bottle—each capable of killing the other but only at the risk of his own life." Lippmann suggests that this image gives "a radically false picture of the atomic situation and it is an unmistakable symptom of a dangerous American neurosis." Its falseness lies, as Lippmann points out, in its neglect of the other nations that are so directly involved in the course of world events. In conceiving of American-Soviet relations primarily in military terms and in focusing chiefly on questions of self-defense and enemy annihilation, those who adopt this image fail to utilize existing possibilities of diplomacy, alliance, and negotiation toward constructive cooperation. To say, as Lippmann does, that this orientation is a "neurotic" one is to imply more than that it is false or harmful. A neurotic outlook reflects the activation, perhaps by a highly stressful social environment, of character traits, unconscious anxieties, and reality-distorting modes of ego defense that are of long standing in the individual personality. Without becoming preoccupied with the issue of neurosis as such, I shall turn shortly to a consideration of the inner psychological bases of this conception of world affairs.

It is difficult to formulate a generic conception of *internationalism* that will hold for the great variety of ideologies falling under this rubric. One common characteristic is the wish to minimize the barriers now existing between nations and to promote full exchange—of ideas, commodities, cultural ways—among all nations. Either military activity is rejected entirely (pacifism), or, more commonly, it is accepted as a last resort after all other means of settling disputes have been used. Great emphasis is placed on the reduction of national sovereignty and on the establishment of an international organization like the U.N. More-over, the U.N. is conceived of not merely as a means of settling disputes but, more important, as a mechanism for the economic and cultural development of all nations. This approach does not necessarily assume that there will be no conflict between nations, in either the near or the distant future; but it does assume that conflict, when it does occur, can be dealt with in a nondestructive, nonautocratic manner.

From the point of view of modern social science, the basic tenets of internationalism are presumably more "rational"—more soundly based on our knowledge of history, social organization, and human nature—than are those of nationalism. It would be unwise, however—and it is certainly not my intent—to regard internationalism as having a monopoly on truth and goodness. Its hopefulness regarding the long-range possibilities of world peace often leads to a naïve optimism concerning what can be achieved in the short run. The dislike of force may lead to unrealistic military policies. And, more generally, the social effectiveness of internationalism or any other ideology is influenced (and often impaired) to a high degree by the individual personalities and organizational policies of its adherents. My concern here is with the nature and the sociopsychological determinants of these viewpoints rather than with their rationality or effectiveness.

Given these admittedly sketchy and incomplete formulations of nationalism and internationalism, let me turn to my central problems: How can we assess nationalism and internationalism as generalized orientations in the individual? What sociopsychological differences are there, if any, between those who stand at opposite ends of this foreign policy continuum? In what sense can we speak of psychological determinants of foreign policy ideology?

The Measurement of Nationalism and Internationalism

I shall attempt a partial answer to these questions on the basis of work reported in *The Authoritarian Personality*,[4] as well as a more recent study of my own. Two opinion-attitude scales were developed, at different times, to provide a measure of nationalism that might then be correlated with measures of other psychological and sociological variables. The construction of both scales was guided by the conceptions of nationalism and internationalism just presented. The first scale, developed during the war years, expressed nationalistic ideas concerning the inevitability of war, the importance of militarization, the restriction of immigration, the punishment of conscientious objectors, and so on.

In 1951 I developed a second "Internationalism-Nationalism Scale" dealing with then current controversial issues.[5] This scale is presented in Table 1. Its twelve items cover a variety of problems relating to our role in the U.N., emphasis on military *vs.* economic aid to other countries, our choice of allies in the cold war, and so on. For example: "We need more leaders who, like MacArthur, have the morals and the strength to put our national honor above appeasement" (item 1). Item 9 was included because it seemed that the current attack on freedom of thought was an aspect of the nationalistic orientation: "In these troubled times, if we are to be strong and united against our common enemy, we must have more laws and safeguards against

the spreading of dangerous ideas." Item 10 represents a presumably internationalist viewpoint: "One main trouble with American foreign policy today is that there is too much concern with military force and too little concern with political negotiation and economic reconstruction."

The scale was administered and scored in the same manner as those presented in *The Authoritarian Personality* research. Subjects were allowed three degrees of agreement ($+1$, $+2$, $+3$) and three degrees of disagreement with each item. The items were scored on a 1-7 scale, the higher scores being given for agreement with "nationalistic" items and for disagreement with "internationalistic" items. The subject's total scale score is his mean item score multiplied by 10. The possible range of scores is thus 10-70 points, with a hypothetical mid-point at 40.

This Internationalism-Nationalism (IN) Scale was administered in 1951 to two classes in education and one in social relations at the Harvard University summer session. The eighty-four subjects included some college undergraduates, a few graduate students in education, and a considerable number of persons in teaching and related community work. This sample is thus somewhat more diversified than the usual college sample, but it shows some homogeneity in the direction of high educational level and moderate income. On the IN Scale it earned a mean of 31.8 (slightly on the "internationalist" side of the mid-point), an S.D. of 12.5, and a range of 10-64. There were, in other words, wide individual differences in scale scores.

The reliability and internal consistency of the IN Scale were relatively high. The split-half reliability for the total sample was .86; the test-retest correlation for one of the education classes retested after six weeks was .90.

---

[4] T. W. Adorno, Else Frenkel-Brunswik, D. J. Levinson, and R. N. Sanford, *The Authoritarian Personality* (New York: Harper & Row, Publishers, Inc., 1950).

[5] I wish to thank Miss Lora W. Heims and Mr. Paul E. Sapir for their assistance in various phases of this study.

TABLE 1   The Internationalism-Nationalism (IN) Scale

Item*		Mean†	D.P.‡
1	We need more leaders like MacArthur, who have the morals and the strength to put our national honor above appeasement	3.1	4.2
2	If it weren't for Russia and her satellites, the world would be headed toward peace and prosperity by now	3.4	3.5
3*	In the long run, it would be to our best interest as a nation to spend less money for military purposes and more money for education, housing, and other social improvements	2.6	2.2
4	The immigration of foreigners to this country should be kept down so that we can provide for Americans first	3.4	3.8
5	The only way peace can be maintained is to keep America so powerful and well armed that no other nation will dare to attack us	3.2	4.1
6*	Our best policy in China would be to forget about Chiang Kai-shek and to work for a coalition between the Communists and the "center" parties	4.8	3.1
7	If the United Nations doesn't show more signs of getting tough with Russia soon, America must be prepared to carry on the fight by itself	3.4	3.3
8	While we should give military aid to countries which are prepared to fight our enemies, we ought to cut down on foreign economic help, or else the other countries will just play us for a sucker	3.3	3.2
9	In these troubled times, if we are to be strong and united against our common enemy, we must have more laws and safeguards against the spreading of dangerous ideas	3.0	3.8
10*	One main trouble with American foreign policy today is that there is too much concern with military force and too little concern with political negotiation and economic reconstruction	3.0	2.4
11	In view of America's moral and material superiority, it is only right that we should have the biggest say in deciding United Nations policy	2.4	2.8
12	The first principle of our foreign policy should be to join forces with any country, even if it is not very democratic, just as long as it is strongly anti-Communist	2.8	2.4

° Items marked with an asterisk take an "internationalist" position as here defined; the others represent a "nationalist" position.

† Responses are scored on a 1-7 scale; 7 points are given for strong agreement on the nationalistic items and for strong disagreement on the internationalistic items [see (1)].

‡ The "D.P." is the "Discriminatory Power" of an item, i.e., its ability to discriminate between high and low scorers on the total scale. It is obtained by subtracting the item mean earned by the low group (bottom quarter of the total scale distribution) from the mean of the high group (top quarter). All D.P.'s are significantly greater than zero (at beyond the 1 per cent level of confidence).

Internal consistency was assessed by the Discriminatory Power (D.P.) technique.[6] Item means and D.P.'s are presented in Table 1. An item's D.P. indicates its ability to discriminate between high and low scores (top and bottom quarters) on the total scale. All twelve of the items discriminate adequately (beyond the 1 per cent level); no items had to be rejected on this ground. Thus each item may be said to represent an aspect of a broader ideological pattern, though some items are more central than others in the sense of reflecting more of the unifying core. A reading of the most discriminating items—Nos. 1, 4, 5, and 9—gives perhaps the clearest indication of the diversity in literal content, as well as the unity in underlying theme, within this ideological domain. The scale properties indicate that most persons are relatively (though by no means entirely) consistent in taking either a nationalist or an internationalist position in the sense noted above, and individuals can be ranked with fair accuracy along a nationalist-internationalist continuum.

[6] R. Likert, "A Technique for the Measurement of Attitudes," *Archives of Psychology*, **160** (1932), 1-55.

Sociopsychological Correlates of Nationalism and Internationalism

There is a gradually accumulating body of evidence concerning the kinds of personal characteristics that tend to be associated with preference for a strongly nationalistic viewpoint. In briefly defining nationalism, I suggested that it is a facet of a broader ethnocentric approach in which the distinction between "in-groups" and "out-groups" plays a central part. A derivative hypothesis is that those who tend most strongly to fear and derogate other nations will exhibit similar beliefs and feelings about various *intranational* groups, such as Negroes, Jews, foreigners, lower socioeconomic groupings, and the like. This hypothesis was supported in our original research by correlations averaging about .7 between nationalism and other sections of the Ethnocentrism (E) Scale, as well as by interview material. In my 1951 study, the IN Scale correlated .77 with a sixteen-item E Scale derived from the earlier form. Findings such as these support the view that extreme nationalism is a form of "pseudopatriotism." Although nationalists glorify America as a symbol, they are inclined to regard most of the American population as an alien out-group. They are activated, it would seem, less by love of Americans and their heritage than by a sense of hostility and anxiety regarding other nations and "outsiders" generally. Internationalists, being under less compulsion either to glorify their own nation or to condemn others, show a more genuine attachment to their cultural traditions.

Nationalists and internationalists show characteristic differences in ideology spheres apparently far removed from foreign policy and intergroup relations. Nationalism is associated, for example, with an autocratic orientation toward child rearing, husband-wife relations, and other aspects of family life. Nationalists are inclined to conceive of the family in hierarchical terms. They regard the husband as properly dominant over the wife, the parents as strong authorities requiring obedience and respect above all from their children. They tend to be moralistic and disciplinarian in their child-rearing methods and to be guided by rigidly conventionalized definitions of masculinity and femininity. Evidence in this direction was obtained in the analysis of clinical interviews of high- versus low-scoring subjects on the Ethnocentrism Scale.[7] The Traditional Family Ideology (TFI) Scale was developed specifically to measure this pattern of thought. Correlations of .6-.7 between this scale and the E Scale were obtained in several samples.[8] In the 1951 study described above, I obtained a correlation of .65 between the IN and the TFI scales. These findings are consistent with the earlier formulations of Reich, Fromm, Erikson, and Dicks[9] and others writing on nationalism in various European countries.

Again, nationalism is associated with certain patterns of religious ideology, notably those that may be characterized as fundamentalistic or conventionalistic. In these religious orientations God is regarded as a kind of power figure who rewards the virtuous and

---

[7] *The Authoritarian Personality, op. cit.,* especially the chapters by Adorno and Frenkel-Brunswik.

[8] D. J. Levinson and Phyllis E. Huffman, "Traditional Family Ideology and Its Relation to Personality," *Journal of Personality,* **23** (1955), 251-273.

[9] W. Reich, *The Mass Psychology of Fascism* (New York: Orgone Institute Press, 1946); Erich Fromm, *Escape from Freedom* (New York: Holt, Rinehart & Winston, Inc., 1941); E. H. Erikson, "Hitler's Imagery and German Youth," *Psychiatry* (1942), 475-493; H. V. Dicks, "Personality Traits and National Socialist Ideology," *Human Relations,* 3 (1950), 111-154.

punishes the sinful and who can be directly appealed to or ingratiated. Great emphasis is placed on the efficacy of ritual, and the precepts of the in-group religious authority are taken literally and unquestioningly. The Religious Conventionalism Scale, developed by Lichtenberg and the author to measure this outlook, correlated .52 with the IN Scale. Slightly lower correlations, of the order of .3-.4, have been obtained between various measures of nationalism and of politicoeconomic conservatism; for example, in the sample described above, the IN Scale correlated .34 with a variant of the Politico-Economic Conservatism Scale reported by Adorno, *et al.*

These and related findings provide substantial evidence that foreign policy orientation is part of a broader ideological context. Nationalism appears most commonly within an autocratic approach to the social world. This approach embraces not only the domain of international relations but the individual's views concerning religion, family, politics, and other aspects of social life as well.

What are the sources of this complex ideological patterning? The sources are to be found, no doubt, both within the individual and in his social environment. With regard to *intraindividual* sources, I would speak for the following postulate: The individual's approach to the external, social world will in significant degree reflect his approach to himself—his self-conceptions, character traits, modes of dealing with inner conflict, and the like.[10] A corollary hypothesis in the present case is that *an autocratic approach to problems of social organization will most often be found within an authoritarian personality structure.*

This hypothesis can be derived from an analysis of the psychological qualities that are directly represented in nationalism and related viewpoints. Such characteristics as punitiveness, stereotypy, fear of moral contamination, submission to powerful authority, and exaggerated fear of weakness—in their extreme form, features of authoritarian personality—make recurrent appearances in nationalistic thought. However, adequate testing of this hypothesis requires the independent assessment of personality variables in persons supporting various ideological positions. Various types of empirical work have been carried out along these lines, no one of them fully conclusive but each contributing to the general picture. Among the more directly relevant studies are Erikson's analysis of *Mein Kampf*[11] and Dicks's work on German prisoners of war[12] and Russian *émigrés.*[13]

In *The Authoritarian Personality*, personality variables were assessed by means of clinical interviews, projective techniques, and more structured devices. The so-called F Scale, developed in this research, gives a quantitative, though crude, measure of authoritarianism that can be applied in survey-type studies. Correlations of the order of .5-.7 were obtained between the F Scale and the Ethnocentrism Scale in a variety of samples. In the study of the IN Scale, described earlier, a 12-item F Scale (Form FERPT) correlated .60 with IN. Similar findings have been obtained with a smaller number of F- and IN-type items in a series of nationwide samples surveyed during the period 1948-52 by the Survey Research Center, University of Michigan (cf. Janowitz and Marvick

---

[10] D. J. Levinson, "Idea Systems in the Individual and Society," in K. Benne, ed., *Frontiers in the Study of Human Relations* (in press).

[11] Erikson, "Hitler's Imagery," *op. cit.*
[12] Dicks, "Personality Traits," *op. cit.*
[13] H. V. Dicks, "Observations on Contemporary Russian Behavior," *Human Relations,* **5** (1952), 111-175.

and Lane).[14] Lane found, for example, that in 1952 a significantly larger proportion of authoritarians than of equalitarians (by the criterion of the F score) preferred to deal with the Korean crisis either by pulling out of Korea altogether or by bombing Manchuria and China; the equalitarians more often preferred a policy of working toward a peaceful settlement. The general conclusion that seems warranted by the various clinical, survey, and other studies is that personal authoritarianism constitutes an important inner source (though by no means the only source) of the disposition toward nationalism and related ideologies.

In addition to their anchorage in the personality, ideologies are developed, utilized, and to various degrees altered in response to diverse social influences. What a man believes depends in large part on the ideological opportunities and demands presented by a variety of membership groups and reference groups. Thus in the 1951 study of the IN Scale, as in many similar studies, various political and religious groupings were found to differ in their average degree of nationalism. The Republicans had a significantly higher (more nationalistic) mean IN score than the Democrats or the independents, the group means being 39.3, 30.6, and 28.6, respectively. With regard to religious grouping, the Catholics had an IN mean of 38.7, the

Protestants a mean of 32.8, the Jews 30.1, and those with no affiliation 21.2. In the case of religious attendance (regardless of affiliation), those who attend services weekly had an IN mean of 36.2, those who attend occasionally, 30.9, and the nonattenders, 25.3. Findings of this sort have been obtained in a large number of surveys which used various types of items and scales. It should be noted, however, that, while these and other groupings show significant differences in *average* score, the degree of individual variation within every major grouping is large indeed. An individual's membership in a particular social group does not, in itself, provide a very adequate basis for prediction of his outlook.

In attempting to generalize from the foregoing research, it should be kept in mind that the samples used have for the most part represented limited sections of the national population, namely, the more highly educated, the urban, the "middle class." Relationships among ideology, personality, and social context have been less intensively studied in the case of the less educated, the very poor and the wealthy, and those in rural and other regions farther removed from university centers. Lubell,[15] for example, has pointed out that the strongest isolationist vote over the years has been registered in counties that are predominantly German-American and/or Catholic and/or rural in composition. It remains for further research to determine whether the widespread isolationist sentiment in these areas is a direct function of tradition and social pressure or whether personal authoritarianism is an equally important factor in facilitating the acceptance of isolationist doctrine. Evidence of gross differences in authoritarianism (F score) in vari-

14 M. Janowitz and D. Marvick, "Authoritarianism and Political Behavior," *Public Opinion Quarterly*, **17** (1953), 185-201; R. E. Lane "Political Personality and Electoral Choice," *American Political Science Review*, **49** (1955), 173-190. Significant relationships between brief measures of authoritarianism and nationalism have been found as well in a study of seven western European nations. The study was carried out by the Organization for Comparative Social Research; this particular analysis was made by Stein Rokkan, Arthur Couch, and the author. . . .

15 S. Lubell, "The Politics of Revenge," *Harper's Magazine* (April, 1956).

ous social strata (distinguished by class, education, and age) has been given by Janowitz and Marvick.

It would appear that the "functionality" of ideology for the person—the degree to which his social views are imbedded in and serve to maintain other aspects of his personality—will vary with the person and with the social setting. One individual holds a nationalistic outlook in part because the images and relationships it portrays reflect so well his unconscious fantasies; the ideology is deeply gratifying and anxiety binding. Another individual holds a roughly similar outlook on the basis of a more superficial acceptance of what is "given" in his social environment; in this case, personality factors may play a relatively incidental role in the formation and maintenance of ideology.

One of the major systematic questions in the study of ideology is this: What are the conditions that maximize the role of personality as a determinant of ideology formation? I shall mention two such conditions: first, that his society presents the individual with a reasonable degree of *choice*, that is, with a range of legitimized ideological alternatives from which to select, and, second, that the individual be *personally involved* in ideological issues. In other words, the greater the degree of choice and the greater the involvement in choosing, the more heavily will the person's ideology be influenced by deep-lying personality characteristics.

Given a reasonable degree of choice and involvement, the following types of influence of personality on ideology are found. (*a*) *Receptivity*. Each individual is receptive to only a limited number of the total range of available ideologies. (*b*) *Immanence*. A person's freely verbalized ideology, with regard to foreign policy, religion, or whatever, can be viewed as a personal document.

Like other personal documents, it will be found to express in its thematic and formal qualities many of the person's central personality characteristics. Personality is to varying degrees immanent in ideology. (*c*) *Relative consistency*. A person's ideology regarding various social issues (foreign policy, the family, and so on) will show consistency not necessarily in a logical sense but in the sense that similar values, conflicts, and the like will be reflected throughout.

Nationalism, Internationalism, and Modal Personality Patterns

I should like to conclude by mentioning briefly a few implications of the foregoing theory and data for the analysis of "American national character" and American foreign policy[16] The classic descriptions of "American character" by De Tocqueville, Bryce, and others have brought out two sharply contrasting sides. On the one hand, they find such traits as anxious conformism, emphasis on socially defined success, a tendency to "escape into the crowd" rather than to look within, an emphasis on work over leisure, on quantity over quality, on varied activity rather than deep experience. On the other hand, however, they find genuine humanitarianism, capacity for self-awareness, aesthetic sensitivity, readiness to identify with the underdog, and the like. The former traits have been shown in various studies to characterize authoritarian personalities, while the latter traits characterize equalitarian personalities. There are, of course, many Americans who possess both types of characteris-

16 For a more general discussion see Almond, *op. cit.*, and A. Inkeles and D. J. Levinson, "National Character: The Study of Modal Personality and Sociocultural Systems," in G. Lindzey, ed., *Handbook of Social Psychology* (Cambridge, Mass.: Addison-Wesley Press, 1954).

tics and who maintain various forms of compromise or conflictful balance between them. However, if the accumulated research has any validity, there are also many individuals who have predominantly one or the other character structure and its associated ideological orientations.

According to this conception, "American character" can be schematically represented as falling along a trimodal distribution, the modes representing authoritarian, equalitarian, and "in-between" patterns. The last mode is conceived as a composite of the first two, and each mode contains numerous subvariants. Like all typologies, this one needs to be applied with discrimination; for certain purposes, other bases of analysis will be more useful.

There is one analysis of American history and mentality which exemplifies this approach without benefit—or hindrance—of current technical jargon. It is V. L. Parrington's monumental work, *Main Currents in American Thought*.[17] In Parrington's view—and he documents it well—a major dynamic in America's intellectual and institutional history has been the conflict, partially synthesized but never fully resolved, between authoritarian and equalitarian conceptions of man and society. He finds evidence for this dialectic in the European intellectual traditions transplanted in America by the colonists; in the development of our political, economic, and religious systems; in our artistic and scientific endeavors.

The recurrent conflict so well described by Parrington has never been more dramatically evident than in our present ideas and policies concerning international relations. Both domestic and international conditions have conspired to intensify our anxieties and with them our authoritarian trends. The decline of capitalism in other nations, the rapid rise of Soviet Russia as a world power, the growth of revolutionary anticapitalist movements in the industrially undeveloped nations, the threat of total destruction by atomic warfare, the fear of depression and mass unemployment if war production is curtailed—these and other factors have operated to intensify our nationalistic-chauvinistic potentialities, which are further reinforced and given ideological form by nationalistic leaders in politics, in the mass media, and in other strategic positions.

Similar conclusions, stemming from a somewhat different theoretical and observational base, have been expressed by G. F. Kennan. In 1954, speaking of the widespread tendency to regard "total military security" as the foundation of American foreign policy, he pointed out:

. . . It is precisely these subjective factors—factors relating to the state of mind of many of our own people—rather than the external circumstances, that seem to constitute the most alarming component of our situation. It is such things as the lack of flexibility in outlook, the stubborn complacency about ourselves and our society, the frequent compulsion to extremism, the persistent demand for absolute solutions, the unwillingness to accept the normal long-term hazards and inconveniences of power—it is these things in the American character that give added gravity to a situation which would in any case be grave enough.[18]

One symptom of the trend toward authoritarianism is the rapid decrease in ideological choice now available to the general population. The relative standardization of ideology in the press, as well as the intimidation of

---

[17] V. L. Parrington, *Main Currents in American Thought*, 3 vols. (New York: Harcourt, Brace & World, Inc., 1943).

[18] Kennan, *op. cit.*, 32.

teachers, government employees, writers, and others, have led toward an artificial homogenizing of public opinion. This process is dangerous not merely because of the threat to civil liberties and intellectual freedom, but also because it goes hand-in-hand with pressures toward nationalism in our foreign policy. For these and other reasons, our inner predispositions toward internationalism are hindered from achieving full ideological expression.

I have perhaps seemed to underestimate the strength of equalitarian forces in the present social scene. However, in this period, when almost any form of ideological deviance may be called "subversive," it is to be kept in mind that American character has its authoritarian as well as its democratic side. It is unrealistic and, ultimately, dangerous to make the casual assumption that America will *necessarily* constitute a democratic force in world affairs and that our foreign policy will automatically be such as to reduce international tensions. The kind of world role that America plays will depend in no small part on our ability to create the conditions under which our underlying equalitarian potentials can become ideologically and institutionally kinetic.

Part 4

elements
of
social
structure

As most commonly used, the term "social structure" refers to the organization of society, in particular to the way in which its major institutions, or substructures, are related to each other. The institutions are membership units that relate individuals and sets of individuals to each other. Each of these institutional substructures is generally assumed to be organized around some central problem or purpose of social life. Each is conceived of as a structure or system in its own right, but also as a substructure of that larger and complete system, the self-sufficient society, which is the ultimate object of sociological analysis.

Despite the lack of a standard and uniformly accepted list of institutions on which all sociologists agree, most sociological analysis returns again and again to the same basic set. Of these I have in this section included articles on the family, organized religion, the community, the economy, and the polity. I have also included readings on the individual and the small group—although neither is an institution—in recognition of the widely held view that these two are fundamental building blocks in any social structure. Lack of space rather than any judgment as to their importance forced me to exclude other institutions, among them educational organizations, such as the school and college, and those concerned with welfare, such as the hospital.

I should call attention to the fact that the largest units of social structure considered in this part are the polity and the economy, both of which are substructures of society. But the society itself may be taken as the unit of structural analysis, as in my paper on Soviet Russia in Chap. 23 and Daniel Bell's analysis of the United States in Chap. 8. Indeed, we may say that the societies of the world are themselves but substructures in a global social structure whose patterns of conflict are examined by L. F. Richardson in Chap. 26.

the individual

thirteen

The sociologist's prime concern with institutions as the basic elements of social structure leads to neglect of the individual. When sociologists do discuss the individual, he usually bears a distinctive stamp. The typical sociological approach to the individual is to depict him as mirroring in his *personal* experience the concrete forms of the *general* condition of men of his particular place and time. Allison Davis and John Dollard give us a characteristic, but powerful, example of such analysis by making clear what it means to be a Negro, and poor, in the American South. Their account also serves to illustrate the process of *socialization,* in this case a process markedly different from that experienced in the middle-class white families discussed by Aberle and Naegele in Chap. 10.

How It Feels to Be Lower Caste

ALLISON DAVIS   **JOHN DOLLARD**

It is difficult for a white person to understand the feelings of Negroes in their lower-caste positions. In the first place, as soon as he begins to live in the South, a white person is taught the social dogma of *his* caste with regard to Negroes. On every hand, he hears that Negroes are inherently childish and primitive. He is taught that they lie and steal impulsively, "like children," that they are unable to control their sexual urges, and that they share none of the complex social and economic ambitions of white people.

Allison Davis and John Dollard, *Children of Bondage* (Washington, D.C.: American Council on Education, 1940), pp. 237-255.

Since Negroes are primitive and child-like, the story runs, they accept their restricted opportunities as matters of course (although children themselves do not do so), and consequently they feel no pain or deprivation in performing the heaviest, dirtiest work, or in undergoing the severest discriminations. In many essential points, the southern dogma concerning Negroes is the same as that held by the slave-owning classes almost a century ago.

The second difficulty which white people meet in understanding the experience of Negroes as lower-caste people is the *rigidity* which the caste system has attained in the South. Negroes and whites, for example, seldom have face-to-face relationships, except in necessary economic transactions. In those immediate relations which they do have with whites, Negroes must always act deferentially. In life, this means that the colored individual seldom expresses to white people, by word or by action, the frustration or resentment which he may feel toward them. On the contrary, he must dramatize his subservience by using deferential forms of address, and by accepting without open aggression those punishments with which the whites subordinate him. To a white person who observes Negro behavior from his own caste position, therefore, Negroes may appear perfectly accommodated and "happy." Even in Old City, Mississippi, the caste system appears to work very smoothly, except when it has to be oiled at times by a whipping or a lynching.

Yet we know that Negroes in the Deep South are continually expressing to each other the sharpest antagonisms against whites and the deepest sense of frustration over their position in society. They verbalize these tabooed feelings only to their colored friends or to colored interviewers, and to northern white men, that is, to members of those groups which will not *punish* them for such expressions. In order to penetrate the rigid surface of the caste system in our own South, and to get at the human experiences and motivation which are imbedded in the tough, protective layers of custom, we must talk with people on their own terms, therefore, and live in their part of the society. As realists, we wish to pierce the dogma of the "childish Negro" (who at the same time is completely tough-skinned), and to obtain a face-to-face experience with children who have been living as lower-caste persons in America. In order to do so, one must break his own caste bonds—long

enough at any rate to enable him to participate in these experiences of Negro children with white people.

In both New Orleans and Natchez, a general form of subordination which Negroes meet from whites is that of being addressed by their first names. In November, 1938, a colored school teacher in New Orleans entered one of the leading stores on Canal Street to buy a suit. She is a brown-skinned woman, nineteen years old, of the upper-middle class. A white female clerk showed her one suit and left her. No other clerk returned to wait upon her. The colored woman then left the store and went to a small shop which catered to middle-class whites. There she was waited upon and purchased a rather expensive suit. Finally she gave her name and address so that the suit might be delivered to her.

After writing down the information, the white saleswoman said, "Margaret, what time do you want this purchase delivered?" Neither woman had ever seen the other before that time.

The Negro woman later stated to the interviewer, who was her close friend, "I saw red. I was so mad. But I couldn't say a thing before all those white people. I made up my mind right then, though, that I'd never go there again to be insulted."

An even more frequent use of the caste punishments is in work situations, since most Negroes work directly under whites. The caste system enables the white employer or supervisor to maintain a stricter discipline over Negroes than over white workers because it allows him (1) to use physical violence or the threat of violence against Negroes, and (2) to pay them less. In June, 1938, Riley Martin, a dark-skinned boy, sixteen years old, of the upper-lower class in New Orleans, delivered a package for the white drugstore which employed him. He rang the bell of a small, yellow frame house. A white woman, apparently of lower-middle class, opened the door.

"What's this?" she asked. "From Jones' Drug Store?"

"Yes, ma'am. Perfume."

"How much is it?"

"It's seventy-five cents."

"Well, wait till I open it." She untied the package, and drew out a dark green bottle. The stopper was chipped just at the mouth of the bottle. The woman turned red and glared at the boy. "You dropped it and cracked it and tried to slip it over on me. Nigger, I'll fix you! I'll telephone your store, and tell the manager!"

When the boy returned to the store, Mr. Heiner, the manager, yelled at him from the prescription counter, "Come here, nigger!"

He went back to the counter. Mr. Heiner jerked the bottle from him and examined it.

"You broke this. Well, I'm taking this out of your pay, and you'll be a good, long time paying for it. You might *think* you're getting by with this, but you're not. You black bastard!" Then he slapped the boy.

The boy told the colored female interviewer that he "got mad" at this point, but admitted that he took no aggressive action. "I didn't do nothin'. He was a man." When she pointed out that he had been openly aggressive recently toward a colored male teacher, the boy answered, "Yes, ma'am, but Mr. Heiner was a white man. I was scared he might send me to jail."

In the same way, the great majority of our upper-class and middle-class adolescents reported that they "did nothing" when they were called "nigger" or threatened by white people, but insisted at the same time that they "felt mad" or "saw red." A usual response for children of these classes was that of Milton DePuy, a colored Creole boy of thirteen, light-brown in color and of the upper-middle class.

Milton said that he hated white people because they thought they were "cute" and because they did not "want you to go places where they go." He then cited an experience he had had with white people on a bus in New Orleans. On buses and streetcars in this city, white and colored people are separated into two groups by a movable sign ("screen"). White people must sit in front of this sign, colored people behind it. One day Milton was sitting on the second seat behind the sign; there was one vacant seat between him and the section for whites, and one vacant seat behind him.

"A lot of white people got on and wanted me to move back, so they could take my seat. I didn' say a word. I kep' my mouth closed. They said I must've been deaf. I just sat there with my mouth closed."

Lower-class Negro children, however, are usually more aggressive in similar caste situations. Lower-class colored boys and girls are trained to fight by their own families, as well as by their neighborhood cliques; they are habituated early to the use of their fists and are consequently much more likely to resist physical aggression by whites than are upper-class and middle-class Negro adolescents. Lower-class children, moreover, have generally had rock and fist fights with white children and they will usually strike out if pushed beyond the normal demands of the local caste system. It is the *lower-class whites*, furthermore, with whom they fight; the parents of these white children do not object to fighting and consider it a test of manhood for white and colored children to fight each other at this age. Such fights were allowed by lower-class white parents in both Natchez and New Orleans. A lower-class white father in the latter city said to a colored mother who complained to him that his young son had beaten her son in a fight, "Well, I tell yuh. I don' have time to be both'ring with children's mess. Both boys are the same size, an' about the same age. When Waldo (colored) beat hell outtuh A. J. (white), I didn't say nothin' tuh you, an' now that A. J. has beat hell outtuh Waldo, I ain' gonnuh do nothin' about that."

These habit structures learned as a child are sometimes carried over into late adolescence, as in the case of John Simmons, a lower-class Negro male, nineteen years old and reddish-yellow in color, who worked on a bridge construction job. He held the position of foreman of a colored gang.

One day a white man, working with a white gang on the same job, yelled at Simmons, "Hey! You red albinah son of a bitch!"

Simmons cursed back at the white man. The white man picked up a crowbar, and walked toward Simmons, Simmons grabbed a two-by-four piece of wood and yelled, "You tek anuthuh step toward me, an' I'll bus' yo' haid with this boa'd!"

The white man stopped and turned back. Simmons, in reciting the incident to the interviewer, said, "There wuz some othuh white men on the bridge, but they wuz down at the othuh end, an' I knowed they couldn' ketch me. Man, I wuz goin' tuh kill him with that boa'd, an' go on 'bout my business."

On a second occasion, Simmons was struck by a white employer. He knocked the white man down and ran. Other white men threw bottles at him and chased him, but he escaped. That night he was arrested by the sheriff.

Simmons' father told the white sheriff, "Some white man hit my boy."

The sheriff answered, "You mean, yore boy hit a *white* man." Simmons was fined by the court.

As a rule, upper-class and middle-class Negroes who do not work for whites experience little of this kind of direct subordination from white people, except in stores or in public carriers. At times, however, even children of these classes have terrifying experiences with white people.

One of our students, a light-brown, upper-class girl of thirteen, who was exceptionally small for her age, went bicycling with a group of upper-class girls in the spring of 1938. On their way to the home of a friend who lived in a predominantly white middle-class neighborhood, they rode their bicycles on the sidewalk. This practice is common in the city.

The girls had been at their friend's home only a short time when a police patrol wagon drove up to the house, and three white policemen came to the door. Their friend's mother went to the door, and was told that a complaint had made to the police against some "nigger" girls who had been riding their bicycles on the sidewalk.

The colored mother asked, "Why do you bring a patrol wagon and come with three policemen? They are just little girls."

"Well, we had a complaint. A white lady called up and said a gang of niggers was riding their bicycles all over the sidewalk."

"A gang of niggers? This is a group of nice little girls and they are all from nice families."

The white policemen appeared to be a little ashamed and agreed to drop the matter if the girls would not ride on the sidewalk again. The mother, who had become increasingly angry, closed the dialogue by remarking, "Well, the next time the white girls around here ride on the sidewalk, I'm going to call you up. I'm going to ask for the patrol wagon to come for a bunch of white girls. I hope you'll be sure to come."

More terrifying was the experience

of another upper-class girl, Phyllis Logan, with the white police. One night in May, 1939, she was riding home from the movies in the family automobile with her father, mother, and sister. Her father is medium-brown in color, her mother white-skinned with light eyes. A car behind them tried to pass but the street was too narrow. The car followed, passed them at an intersection, and then pulled over sharply, forcing Mr. Logan to stop his car.

Two white men in civilian clothes got out of the other car. One of them stuck a pistol into the side of the girls' father. Their mother screamed. One of the white men said, "Why'n hell didn' you get over and let us pass? You're under arrest." Then they made Phyllis' father get into their car.

Since the white men had shown no police badges, and wore no uniforms, Phyllis and her sister and their parents believed the men were thugs. Mrs. Logan began to weep but the girls were too frightened to make any sound. A crowd of white people had gathered but no one interfered when Mr. Logan was taken away by the two white men.

Then, as the women sat helpless, firmly convinced that Mr. Logan was dead, an upper-class white man and his wife got out of their car and came over to the Logans. They expressed their sympathy and offered to drive the women to various police stations to discover whether the two white men had actually been policemen. The Logans went with them.

After a two-hour search, they found Mr. Logan. During this whole time, the mother wept, and Phyllis and her sister sat stunned. They finally discovered him locked up in a distant police station. He was released upon the demand of the white protector. No action was taken against the policemen, however, because no white peo-ple would testify against them—not even the upper-class white man and his wife.

In relating the incident to the interviewer, Phyllis concluded, "That was the worst experience of my life. It is like a horrible nightmare. Mother is still a wreck. Nice world, huh?"

In order to understand the caste sanctions as training, we must see them at the moment of their impact upon the individual. In the personal experience of a white person or of a Negro in the South, the caste controls appear as sanctions defining the conditions under which he may reach the basic biological and social goals. They are experienced as privileges and punishments which facilitate or block the road to certain basic goals. These elementary goals may be defined simply. They are:

1. freedom of movement;
2. the acquiring and spending of money, which are necessary instrumental acts to obtaining food, shelter, and clothing;
3. the securing of sexual responses;
4. avoidance of being struck, and of other forms of physical punishment;
5. avoidance of threats which arouse anticipation of punishment (that is, fear);
6. access to instrumental techniques which secure money—namely, education, apprenticeship, and political participation.

If we are to attempt to see the caste system as it appears to the individual living under its controls, we must hereafter think in terms of these fundamental motives which are common to all human beings in our society.

As a result of the physical caste marks with which he is born, the white individual is freed to a large degree from interference in seeking these goals. Indeed, his efforts to make the goal responses are facilitated by the society; his path is eased by powerful legal, economic, educational, and political privileges, as compared with that of the Negro individual.[1]

This finding runs counter to the widespread social dogma which states that the southern Negro does not experience his caste restrictions as punishments. The dogma, popular as it may be, is not borne out by the thousands of pages of interviews which have been recorded for Negroes of all social classes in Old City and its rural background, in Natchez, and in New Orleans. Within their conversation groups these Negroes in the Deep South were often found detailing the instances in which they had been threatened or humiliated by white people and expressing great hostility and resentment toward the local white group. In fact, the antagonism voiced by the local white people toward Negroes, although it was certainly violent and fully supported by group approval, was scarcely more violent than that which Negroes, including the youngest adolescents, expressed to the white group as a whole.

When one gathers detailed accounts of these emotional reactions of Negroes to the impact of caste controls, it is not difficult to understand the basis of their frustrations and their consequent verbal aggression. Indeed, it becomes clear that only a vested societal interest in caste can account for the established dogma that most Negroes are completely "accommodated" to their caste status and that they are simple-natured, childlike beings with childish needs. It is necessary for the society to

inculcate strong defensive teachings of this kind to prevent general human recognition of the basic deprivations and frustrations which life in a lower caste involves. But it is certain that the sting of caste is deep and sharp for most Negroes.

For example, when a skilled Negro worker seeks a job in the planing mill which employs most of the working population of Old City, he finds that all of the well-paid positions are closed to him. If he is hired, he soon learns that he is being paid at a much lower hourly rate than are white men doing the same kind of work.[2] The Negro worker, however, must pay the same price as the white worker for the pound of pork or the bag of cowpeas which he buys, the same price for his shoes or pair of overalls (if he is to get the same quality), and the same price for his children's schoolbooks (which the city does not supply). Therefore, the imposition of a lower wage scale is experienced as a basic punishment—as a deprival of food or clothing, or of access to social techniques for acquiring money. The Negro experiences this punishment as a *caste* deprivation, moreover, because he discovers that it is not administered to white men.

His path to the sexual goal responses is likewise restricted. The Negro male learns by punishment, or by identifying with the punishment of other Negroes, that while he is not allowed to seek sexual relationships with white women, the society does permit white men to seek such relationships with Negro women. In actual situations observed in Southerntown and Old City, this taboo meant that a Negro man could not attack a white man who

---

[1] In this caste context, a privilege is the presentation to the individual by society of a more direct and less punished route to certain goals. Furthermore, it is the offering to the white individual of certain goal responses which are completely blocked for Negroes, such as higher technical training or political office.

[2] If the sociologist analyzes the payroll of this mill, he finds that the few colored men who are employed as skilled workers receive an hourly wage which is only one-fourth as large as that paid to white men who perform similar work.

sought out his wife or daughter. He must submit and let the woman go if she wishes. The authors observed several such incidents at firsthand; one interviewer lived in the home of a colored family whose daughter was constantly sought by an important white municipal official. The girl fought her own battle for status successfully (she would have lost rank in the colored group if she had accepted the white man as a lover), but her father and brother could not defend her without risking their lives. The great value which the white man attaches to his cross-caste sexual privileges is indicated by the persistence with which he defends them. In Old City, a Negro minister who protested in his church against the numerous liaisons between white men and colored women was visited the next day by a group of white businessmen who warned him not to mention this subject again, under threat of being made to leave the city. On the other hand, it is certainly a basic deprivation to the Negro man to be unable to protect his daughter, wife, or sweetheart from the white man's sexual advances.

The caste controls likewise withhold from Negroes legal protection against physical attack and the threats of such attack by white persons. By punishment, the Negro individual is trained not to demand certain occupational, sexual, political, and social privileges. This training usually takes place through identification with other Negroes who have received such punishment. The example of a Negro who has been beaten, whipped, or shot by a white planter or by a white mob operates to make all other Negroes in the community *anticipate* that such punishment would come to them if they should violate the caste sanctions. On the other hand, the patronage and the protection which the "good Negro" receives also act to maintain the

caste system. By imitating these well-accommodated Negroes, the colored man or woman learns to avoid punishment and to seek only those rewards (substitute goals) which *are* possible within his caste position if he follows the prescribed route.

Both the numerical indices from the census and the observed behavior of Negroes and whites toward each other make it clear that the Negro child in New Orleans or Natchez lives in a caste system which from his birth severely limits his opportunities for economic advancement and for social training. The rewards which the society offers him in the fields of occupational and political status are very few. His opportunities for education, moreover, are greatly inferior to those of the white child, and his incentive to grasp the available opportunities is weak because the society systematically withholds from him the rewards which it offers to the white child.

At an early age, he learns that the economic and social restrictions upon him as a lower-caste person are maintained by powerful threats of the white society, and that any efforts to rise out of his caste position will be severely punished. Both in the city and in the country, the disabilities which his caste suffers are maintained primarily by a system of force. This superior physical and legal power of the white caste is not left to his imagination but is dramatized periodically for the whole society in the form of beatings and lynchings.

The whipping and killing of Negroes by whites as a punishment for resisting caste demands occur in both Natchez and New Orleans. It is not necessary to have a large number of such demonstrations in order to intimidate the Negro population. To be able to understand this fact, we must remember that human beings learn to accept restrictions by means of identifying with other persons within the family or group who *have been punished* for not learning the required behavior.

The study of Old City and its plantation background revealed that the caste taboos were more numerous and the punishments for infractions more severe in the rural areas than in the city itself. The severity of the controls upon Negroes increased in direct proportion to the distance of the rural area from a large town or city. For example, in Rural County, which had no village of more than 1000 inhabitants, white planters frequently whipped their colored tenants and they considered the Negroes in Old City, just forty miles away, "spoiled" and "sassy." One prominent white planter complained that these urban Negroes did not even know how to act toward a white man; as proof, he cited the attempt of a colored businessman in Old City to shake hands with him.

In Old City itself, however, a colored boy five years old was severely beaten by a white man who accused the child of "making advances" to the white man's equally young daughter. In New Orleans, the largest city in the South, the local white newspapers reported five colored men killed by white policemen between 1936 and 1938. Three of these men were killed in city jails while awaiting trial. The other two were shot while in custody. All were accused of having attacked white men or women. By means of detailed accounts in the newspapers, these symbolic "legal lynchings" were made known to the colored population and served as a means of further intimidation.

As has been stated, mob whippings and lynchings occur in the rural environs of Natchez and New Orleans. It is difficult to write about these matters with scientific objectivity, but the authors will limit themselves to the facts, as given by the New Orleans white radio stations and newspapers, concerning a lynching in Ruston, Louisiana, which occurred while this research study was in progress.

On October 12, 1938, two radio stations in New Orleans began to announce several times daily that an unidentified Negro man who had been accused of murdering a white man was being hunted by a mob of whites at Ruston. Both the radio stations and the white newspapers also announced that a lynching was "feared." On the second day, the radio stations reported that a mob composed of "1500 armed white men" was searching for the accused, but unidentified, colored man.[3]

On the afternoon of the second day, a Negro man was lynched after reputedly confessing the crime to 1500 armed white men. Five days later, the parish grand jury, composed of white residents, brought in a verdict that the "evidence is conclusive that W. C. Williams attacked J. W. Breedlove and criminally assaulted his woman companion on the night of September 13, and that since then W. C. Williams (the Negro) has died." After examining fifty-five white "witnesses" of the lynching, the grand jury reported that it had "obtained insufficient evidence to return any indictments."[4]

The judge, after receiving the reports of the grand jury, thanked the jury for "carrying out the instructions of the court," as follows:

Having completed your labors and made your report, the court wishes to thank you for the splendid and unselfish

---

[3] One may imagine what effect the sight of 1500 white men, questioning their fathers, mothers, and older brothers, had upon the Negro children in this area. The writers have had eyewitness accounts of such "searches"; they take the form of hunting frolics.

[4] *The Times-Picayune* (October 19, 1938), 4.

work you have done during the present two-day special session of the grand jury. The court is aware of the difficulties under which you have labored and believes that you have thoroughly and conscientiously investigated the matters submitted to you by the court for investigation. That means that the court feels that you have fully and honorably discharged your duties under your oaths.[5]

This lynching was considered of so little news value by the white conservative newspaper in New Orleans that it was first reported on the thirteenth page.

Another type of physical punishment used by whites to enforce the subordination of Negroes is starvation. The withdrawing of food or the threat of doing so is a technique used to change human behavior in many societies. It has been used recently with great success in Germany, Czechoslovakia, Spain, and England, as well as in America. When a Hungarian prince, for example, wishes to make his Slovak tenant serfs change their political and national loyalties, he simply refuses them the use of the land.[6] In the same way, a white landlord or employer in the South seldom has to use physical violence to make his Negro employees observe the caste taboos. The threat of legalized force, implicit in his caste position, and his economic power are usually sufficient. Since most Negroes are wage laborers, they depend for food and necessities upon their pay or "advance" from week to week. The white employer can usually enforce any caste demands, therefore, simply by withholding wages or by threatening to discharge the Negro. On the plantation, this compliant behavior is reinforced every week or two when the Negro has

to go to the landlord for credit for food.

Southern color caste must therefore be viewed as a systematic interference in the efforts of a special group of individuals to follow certain biological and social drives. This interference takes the form of a complex of limitations in addition to the accepted controls of our society upon all individuals.

A white or Negro person in the South learns the behavior demanded of him in his caste position chiefly by experiencing (or anticipating) pain or deprivation if he attempts to reach a goal by any other route than that prescribed by the society. To the Negro child, as our cases show, caste presents a group of arbitrary behavioral demands which he is compelled to learn. He is forced into these learning dilemmas both by his parents and by the white children and adults with whom he has contacts. In following the prescribed behavior, he must (1) accept interference with previously established habits, and (2) substitute new forms of response. All learning, after the first learning of infancy, involves the sacrificing by the individual of some of his earlier goal responses. It consequently entails frustration. When the colored child is learning to behave as a lower-caste person, he is finding a method of acting within the frustrating taboos of caste so that he may reach those limited and substitute goals which the society does allow him.

Both the white and the colored child acquire their caste training in two types of relationships: (1) in their family and from nonfamily members of their own caste, and (2) in contacts with members of the other caste. At the age of five or six, the child learns that he must sit only with his fellow caste members on the bus or in the theater, and that he must attend schools which have only children and

5 *Ibid.*
6 Erskine Caldwell and Margaret Bourke-White, *Beyond the Danube* (New York: Viking Press, 1939).

teachers of his own caste. Within his family, he receives instruction in the behavior required toward members of the other caste. As he becomes adolescent, both the definiteness and the parental reinforcements of this instruction increase greatly, for it is then that the occupational and sexual taboos become matters of urgency.

In Negro-white situations, a child learns what behavior is permitted, either (1) when he is allowed to achieve the goal response, or (2) when he experiences punishment in attempting to reach it. In general, the Negro child learns from white people that he cannot be a member of their economic, social, or educational groups. He also learns that he must not be aggressive toward them, but must dramatize his subordinate position by various explicit forms of deference. From his own family, he usually learns that white people are extremely powerful and dangerous and that he must therefore not display aggression toward them. If even the powerful adult cannot resist whites, what can the child hope to gain by attack? He is taught, however, that within the bounds of his caste position he may adopt substitute modes of aggression toward whites. For example, certain well-disguised forms of "getting even," such as sabotage in his work for white people (slowness, lack of punctuality, clumsiness), and the use of flattery, humor, secretiveness, "ignorance," and other behavior for outwitting white people, are learned at an early age. . . . The type of instruction given a Negro child by his parents varies in some degree according to the social class of the parents.

The actual caste behavior of the parents themselves appears to be more important in determining the child's type of accommodation to white people than does verbal instruction on this point. As in other forms of learning by identifying with a person who

has already learned, the child discovers what behavior *will be punished* and what *rewarded* by observing his parents and listening to their accounts of experiences with white people. To be concrete—the child of a Negro domestic servant who hears his mother constantly rehearsing the "injustices" or perhaps the kindness and patronage of her white employer; the boy who hears his father tell angrily of the loss of his job to a white man (and who himself receives less food and heat, and poorer clothes thereafter); the girl whose father is constantly praising his white upper-class patrons and severely criticizing Negroes as a group; and the little boy who hears his mother express anger and humiliation after experiencing some caste punishment in a store or on a bus—these children learn to expect from whites the same punishments or rewards which their parents have received.

The child whose parents are of unlike class origins usually receives one type of caste instruction from his mother and a different type from his father. For example, if the father is of lower-class origin, he will almost certainly tell his son to submit to all white demands unless he is threatened with violence, in which case he should fight. If the mother has been trained in a middle-class family, she will probably teach the son to avoid whites and not to fight them under any circumstances. A child who lives in such a family, or in a family where one parent has been reared in the South and the other in the North, is placed in a continual and almost insoluble dilemma, which may be expected to increase his anxiety and maladaptive tendencies as compared with the child whose parents have the same class and sectional origin.

A second type of conflict in the caste training of the Negro adolescent is especially prevalent in cities. It is the dilemma of the upward mobile child who is beginning to associate with, and to assume the behavior of, a class which is above that of his parents. The first step in such mobility for the mass of *lower-class* colored children in Natchez or New Orleans is to finish a high school course. In this process of educational mobility, the colored adolescent faces a conflict between the caste instruction and example given him by his teachers, who are usually middle-middle class or upper-middle class, and by his parents, who are lower class. Such differences in caste training apply both to etiquette (whether to be deferential to a white person if he seeks to subordinate you, whether to say "Sir" and "Ma'am") and to the choice of an occupation. The middle-class teacher not only gives the colored child instruction in skills associated with the white caste, but he insists upon being called "Mr." or "Miss" by the student. In spite of caste taboos, moreover, he has gained professional status.

In this situation, the Negro child usually identifies with his teachers in caste behavior; that is, he rejects the training and example of his lower-class parents who must be deferential to their white employers and who must accept domestic or manual labor. When he completes high school such a mobile child faces the basic caste restriction against skilled and clerical work for Negroes. In order to achieve middle-class position he must therefore either go on to a higher school and become a teacher or he must obtain a position as a clerk in some Negro business. If he is unsuccessful and has to accept a menial or domestic job under a white supervisor, he experiences a basic frustration upon both caste and class grounds.

By indirection, the caste sanctions also appear within the Negro family and school in the form of distinctions between children upon the basis of their color, hair form, and type of facial contour. It must be remembered that the differentiating marks of the white caste are physical. The Negro *class* sanctions, moreover, are in part organized around differences in color, hair form, and features. It is also true that white people make some distinction in the punishment and patronage of individual Negroes upon the basis of the Negro's approximation to the white physical type. A colored child who is light-skinned with wavy or straight hair therefore has an arbitrary and fortuitous advantage over more Negroid children, both in his own class participation and in his relations with whites.

Colored parents and their children, however, are very reluctant to admit in-family preferences based on color. The lack of evidence from our own informants on this score must be attributed to a general American taboo upon voicing in-family preferences. In America, as is not true in those European societies where the first-born male is given higher privileges than the other offspring, there is a strong social compulsion not to show greater affection for one member of the family than for another. Parents as well as children "cover up" at once when this subject is mentioned, and their subsequent remarks are highly defensive.

In socially withdrawn, light-skinned groups of colored people, such as the colored Creoles in New Orleans and the remnants of the "blue vein" cliques in Old City, however, parents make no effort to conceal their preference for light-skinned children, and their desire to obtain equally light mates for them. Until very recently in Old City, a dark child born to a "blue vein" family was sent away to live with dark relatives in another community. The head of the leading family in this group in 1934 said that only a few years before, "if a child turned out black or dark, it was just too bad for him." His own father had used a shotgun to drive off a brown-skinned suitor of his daughter. Even today in New Orleans, some of the light-skinned Creole families who work as white send any dark baby away to a "dark" branch of the family. The grandparents and parents maintain close surveillance, furthermore, upon the courting of the children to prevent the choice of a dark mate. Since these colored Creoles now attend the same churches, schools, and dances as the rest of the Negroes and increasingly intermarry with them, however, such color distinctions are becoming less rigid.

The importance which color and hair form have for the Negro parent may be most clearly understood from the discussions of colored women or parents concerning a prospective or newborn child. The female interviewers heard several discussions of this kind among upper-class and upper-middle-class Negroes in Old City and in New Orleans. Parents and grandparents were extremely concerned about the color and hair form of the baby, condoling each other if the child was darker or had "worse" hair than had been expected, and felicitating each other if it was lighter or had "better" hair than had been expected. Even before the birth of a child, some upper-class and upper-middle-class parents surveyed in minute detail all the possibilities with regard to the child's color and hair form by recalling these traits in each of their parents and grandparents. It is probably safe to assume that such concern is felt by most upper-class and middle-class Negro parents, even when not verbalized. It is a justifiable point of anxiety, certainly, since it is a vital factor in the child's class and caste opportunities.

The basic value of these physical traits is most clearly and bluntly stated by those lower-class Negro women who are dark-brown or black. One such woman in Old City told her colored employer, "I sho' is sorry I didn' get me uh white man, instid uh gittin' me uh black one, 'n having a whole lot uv black childrun!" The power of light color in aiding the individual to satisfy basic physical and social needs is most clearly seen when the child's father is actually white. Although lower-class colored parents in Old City punish a daughter who has a child by a white man, they nevertheless prefer the child; they prefer it not only for its color but because it attracts vital gifts of money (and therefore of food, shelter, and clothes) from the father. The dark lower-class child in Old City who said mournfully, "Gertrude's father is white, an' she can git ev'ything she wants. Guess I could too, if I had a white daddy!" was expressing the pull of basic biological goals against the weak demands of "respectability."

In New Orleans or Natchez, for a child to come into the world with a dark skin is to have the cards stacked against him from birth. The social and economic world accessible to him is so limited that the chances of his being forced into lower class are about three times as great as those of a white child. It seems clear, furthermore, that the motivation of the Negro child to learn habits of conscientious study, of sexual restraint, of law observance, and of skilled work is necessarily weak, since the upper caste either does not reward his efforts as it does the white child's or it constantly punishes them. We know that effective learning in these fields demands continual impulse control, and that such learning must therefore be reinforced by rewards which are proportionate to the effort and renunciation demanded of the learner. It is the prime function of the caste system to withhold these rewards from Negro children.

the group

fourteen

Although most sociologists accept the *institution* as the basic building block of social structure, there are others who hold that the human group is the more important unit. After World War II there was a vigorous revival of interest in the small group, and systematic investigation was greatly enhanced by the development of laboratory techniques for small-group research. From this work has emerged an image of the group as a microcosm of the larger society, containing most of the important elements of a complete social system. Robert F. Bales was one of the pioneers in elaborating the theory of interaction within groups, and he here presents a succinct summary of several years of research effort. His report also serves as an example of the techniques of laboratory sociology, supplementing the papers on modes of inquiry described in Part Six.

Status, Role, and Interaction

ROBERT F. BALES

During the last ten years, a number of laboratories for the study of social interaction within small groups and organizations have been started in university research centers, hospitals, clinics, and military installations. The studies and experiments I shall describe were conducted in one of these laboratories, which was established in 1947 at Harvard University.

The laboratory consists of a large,

Robert F. Bales, "Task Roles and Social Roles in Problem-Solving Groups," in *Readings in Social Psychology*, 3rd ed., Eleanor E. Maccoby, Theodore M. Newcomb, Eugene L. Hartley, eds. (New York: Holt, Rinehart & Winston, Inc., 1958), pp. 437-447.

well-lighted room for the group under study and an adjoining room for observers who listen and watch from behind windows with one-way vision. The subjects are told at the beginning that the room has been constructed for the special purpose of studying group discussion, that a complete sound recording will be made, and that there are observers behind the one-way mirrors. The purpose of the separation is not to deceive the subjects but to minimize interaction between them and the observing team.

Over a number of years we have evolved a more or less standard type of group and task which has formed the setting for a number of studies. The data I shall report came from several studies, all done under essentially the same conditions, so that a description of the most recent investigation will serve in substance for the others.

Procedures

The sample which provided data for the most recent investigation consisted of thirty five-man experimental groups. Subjects were 150 Harvard freshmen who were recruited by letters sent to a random sample of the entering class which briefly described the experiment as one concerned with group problem solving and decision making. Volunteers were offered a dollar an hour. The groups were randomly composed. Typically the members of a group did not know each other, nor were they introduced to each other. In effect, they were faced with the problem of getting organized as well as with the more obvious problem that was issued to them.

The more obvious problem, which we call the standard task, involved the discussion of a human relations case, a five-page presentation of facts about a problem facing an administrator in his organization. Members were given separate identical copies of the case to read ahead of time and were told that, although each was given accurate information, we intended to leave them uncertain as to whether they each had exactly the same range of facts. The cases were collected after they had been read by the members individually, to prevent direct comparison of typed copies, although members were allowed to take notes. The task defined for each group was to assemble the information, to discuss why the people involved were behaving as they did, and to decide what should be recommended as action for the solution to the problem presented. The groups were asked to time themselves for forty minutes and to dictate the group solution for the sound record in the final one or two minutes of the meeting.

While the group members began to organize themselves and to solve the case problem, the observers got to work in the observation room. They systematically recorded every step of the interaction, including such items as nods and frowns. Each observer had a small machine with a moving paper tape on which he wrote in code a description of every act—an act being

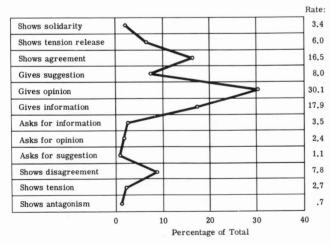

Rate:

		Rate:
Shows solidarity		3.4
Shows tension release		6.0
Shows agreement		16.5
Gives suggestion		8.0
Gives opinion		30.1
Gives information		17.9
Asks for information		3.5
Asks for opinion		2.4
Asks for suggestion		1.1
Shows disagreement		7.8
Shows tension		2.7
Shows antagonism		.7

0   10   20   30   40

Percentage of Total

FIG. 1. Types of interaction and their relative frequencies. This profile of rates is the average obtained on the standard task from twenty-four different groups, four of each size from two to size seven, each group meeting four times, making a total of ninety-six sessions. The raw number of scores is 71,838. [From Robert F. Bales, "How People Interact in Conferences," *Scientific American*, 192 (March, 1955).]

defined essentially as a single statement, question, or gesture. Acts ordinarily occurred at the rate of fifteen to twenty per minute. The recorded information on each act included identification of the person speaking and the person spoken to and classification of the act according to predetermined categories. The categories included attempts to solve either the organizational problems of the group or the task problems by the offering of information, opinions, and suggestions.

Questions and several types of positive and negative reactions completed the set of twelve categories (see Fig. 1). This method is called "interaction-process analysis."[1] The categories are meant to have a general-purpose usefulness for group research and their use is not confined in any way to the laboratory conditions described here, although the best norms exist for the standard task and the group type described here.[2]

As Fig. 1 shows, on the average about half (56 per cent) of the acts during a group session on the standard task fall into the categories of problem-solving attempts; the remaining 44 per cent are distributed among positive reactions, negative reactions, and questions. In other words, the process tends to be two-sided, with the reactions serving as a more or less constant feedback on the acceptability of the problem-solving attempts. The following example will illustrate the pattern of interchange.

Member 1: I wonder if we have the same facts about the problem? [Asks for opinion.] Perhaps we should take some time in the beginning to find out. [Gives suggestion.]
Member 2: Yes. [Agrees.] We may be able to fill in some gaps in our information. [Gives opinion.] Let's go around the table and each tell what the report said in his case. [Gives suggestion.]
Member 3: Oh, let's get going. [Shows antagonism.] We've all got the same facts. [Gives opinion.]
Member 2: (Blushes) [Shows tension.]

A number of interesting generalizations can be made about the way in which rates of activity in the various categories tend to differ according to group size, time periods within a meeting, development of a group over a series of meetings, pre-established status characteristics of members, and the like.[3] The present article, however, will be concerned with a particular set of problems in which the interaction data have played an important part—whether there are tendencies for persons to develop different roles during interaction, even though there are no pre-established status differences, and if so, what kind, and why? There are several plausible views about this set of problems. The following account presents four distinguishable views and shows how research led from one view to another in the course of several studies.

The Hypothesis of a Single-Status Order

Perhaps the most ordinary conception of a group is that it consists of a leader and several followers who fall

[1] Robert F. Bales, *Interaction Process Analysis: A Method for the Study of Small Groups* (Cambridge, Mass.: Addison-Wesley Co., Inc., 1950).
[2] For norms, see Robert F. Bales and Edgar F. Borgatta, "Size of Group as a Factor in the Interaction Profile," in A. Paul Hare, Edgar F. Borgatta, and Robert F. Bales, eds., *Small Groups, Studies in Social Interaction* (New York: Alfred A. Knopf, Inc., 1955), pp. 396-413.

[3] For a short review, see Robert F. Bales "Some Uniformities of Behavior in Small Groups" in Guy E. Swanson, Theodore M. Newcomb, and Eugene L. Hartley eds., *Readings in Social Psychology*, rev. ed. (New York: Holt, Rinehart & Winston, Inc., 1952), pp. 146-159.

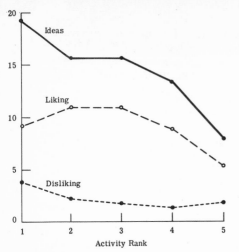

FIG. 2. Average ratings° received on ideas, liking, and disliking by men of each activity rank. [From Robert F. Bales, "The Equilibrium Problem in Small Groups," in Talcott Parsons, Robert F. Bales, and Edward A. Shils, eds., *Working Papers in the Theory of Action* (New York: The Free Press of Glencoe, Inc., 1953), p. 146. Reprinted with permission of The Free Press. Copyright 1953 by The Free Press, a corporation.]

° Each entry at a given activity rank is a mean over twelve sessions for the persons who occupy that rank as of each meeting. (Four separate five-man groups were involved.) The idea index is not actually a rating but an index obtained by adding rankings received (including self-rankings) and subtracting the total from the highest possible, 25. The like and dislike indices are average ratings received, with the highest possible, 28.

into a kind of status order from highest to lowest. The leader is the best-liked member of the group, participates most actively, and is felt to be the best performer of whatever task activities the group undertakes. No matter which of these criteria the researcher takes, he will come out with the same rank order of members. The expectation that most groups are structured like this and that departures from this simple form of organization may be treated as the result of special circumstances may be called the hypothesis of a "single-status order."

This is a plausible hypothesis. It underlies much research on leadership. It is congruent with the ideological position that for good leadership it is very important that a good leader should be an all-around "great man," and it assumes that there are such men, at least relative to the other members in a given group.[4] This hypothesis assumes role differentiation but essentially only along a single quantitative dimension, leadership status.

Early in the research we began to ask group members about their likes and dislikes for each other, their opinions of who had the best ideas and who showed the most leadership, and other similar questions. We wanted to know how these questions related to each other and to our observations of interaction. The question as to whether or not there is role differentiation within a group can be reduced in part to whether group members show some consensus that certain members stand higher than others on a given criterion and whether different criteria give different status orders rather than a single-status order.

When I first began to examine data from our experimental groups, I worked under the assumption that there might be some such thing as a "simply organized group," that is, one in which the rank order of members on activity, task ability, and likeability would coincide, and that these groups would in some sense or other be the most successful or best satisfied.[5]

Figure 2 shows the results which raised a most interesting set of questions. The total interaction initiated by one man in the course of a meeting establishes the basis for ranking him

[4] For some evidence that there are some such men, in relative terms, see Edgar F. Borgatta, Arthur S. Couch, and Robert F. Bales, "Some Findings Relevant to the Great Man Theory of Leadership," *American Sociological Review*, 19 (1954), 755-759.

[5] Robert F. Bales, "The Equilibrium Problem in Small Groups," in Talcott Parsons, Robert F. Bales, and Edward A. Shils, eds., *Working Papers in the Theory of Action* (New York: The Free Press of Glencoe, Inc., 1953).

relative to the others on activity. If there is a strong tendency toward a single-status order, top men on activity should also rank highest in group-member responses to such questions as "who has the best ideas," and should also receive the highest number of "liking" votes and lowest of "disliking."[6] The second man on activity should, on the average, be second highest on the other criteria of excellence, and so on. The rank order on each criterion should be highly correlated to the rank order on the other criteria.

What does Fig. 2 suggest? First, there seems to be a positive correlation between activity rank and idea rank, although the second man seems a little low. But on liking-received rank, there is a marked discrepancy. The top man on activity appears considerably lower than expected on liking received. Both the second and the third men are higher on the average than he. Is the top man doing something to lose likes and provoke dislikes? Here one notes the dislike curve. The differences are small and probably not significant, but they suggest that the top man is possibly the highest on dislikes received. Liking seems to be centering on the second and third man in activity, and they both seem to be lower than expected on idea ranking. Can it be that these men are tending to avoid too heavy an emphasis on the task area for fear of being disliked?

On further investigation of this problem it turned out that something happened in groups over a series of four sessions that was equally thought-provoking. In the first sessions, if a given man held top position on the idea ranking by his fellow members, the probability was about 50-50 that he would *also* hold a top position on

a likeability ranking. But in the second meeting the probability dropped markedly, and by the fourth meeting was only about one in ten. The percentage of cases in which the same man held top position on liking and idea rankings at the same time, divided by session, may be charted as follows:

Sessions

1	2	3	4
56.5	12.0	20.0	8.5

Could it be that there was something about arriving in a top-status position, owing to technical contribution to the task problems of the group, that tended to "lose friends and alienate people"? If so, was another man likely to arise who paid more attention to the social-emotional problems of the group and so tended to collect more liking? The idea that this happens with sufficient frequency that it can be viewed as typical may be called "the hypothesis of two complementary leaders."

The Hypothesis of Two Complementary Leaders

Why, if at all, should groups tend to have two complementary leaders, one a task specialist, the other a social-emotional specialist?[7] Perhaps it would be helpful to look at the interaction of men highest on idea ranking received but not highest on liking received, and vice versa. It may be that men of these two types behave differently, and the differences in behavior may give us some clues as to the reasons for the differences.

Table 1 shows the composite profiles of forty-four matched session

---

[6] The actual questions used are presented in the source indicated in the footnote to Fig. 3. They are omitted [here] for the sake of brevity.

[7] A theory is advanced in Robert F. Bales and Philip E. Slater, "Role Differentiation in Small Decision-Making Groups," in Talcott Parsons, *et al.*, eds., *Family, Socialization, and Interaction Process* (New York: The Free Press of Glencoe, Inc., 1955).

pairs[8] of idea men (who were not best liked in their group) and best-liked men (who were not top in idea ranking). Slater, from whose paper the table is taken, comments: "The most salient general difference in Table 1 is the tendency for the idea man to initiate interaction more heavily in Area B (problem-solving attempts) and the best-liked man in Area A (positive reactions). The idea man also seems to disagree somewhat more, and show a little more antagonism, while the best-liked man asks more questions and shows more tension."[9]

On the receiving end, the situation is largely reversed, with the idea man receiving more agreement, questions, and negative reactions, while the best-liked man receives more problem-solving attempts, and more solidarity and tension release. The general picture is thus one of specialization and complementarity, with the idea man concentrating on the task and playing a more aggressive role, while the best-liked man concentrates more on social-emotional problems, giving rewards and playing a more passive role.

The kind of complementarity that shows in the behavior, then, is a kind that occurs in short interchanges in conversations where a problem-solving attempt by one person is followed by an agreement or disagreement from some other, or where a pleasant remark or a joke by one is followed by a smile or a laugh from the other. Such a division of labor by type of act is very common and easily recognized. There may or may not be a specialization so that one person continues to produce more of one form of behavior than the other.

---

[8] Although the number of *sessions* was forty-four, the number of separate individuals involved was not eighty-eight, since each group ran over four sessions, and some individuals were in the same position more than once.

[9] Philip E. Slater, "Role Differentiation in Small Groups," *American Sociological Review*, **20** (1955), 305. It is not possible to state that all of the detailed differences indicated are significant, because rates in the various categories are interdependent. However, Slater shows that the two types are in general significantly different from each other.

TABLE 1[°] Composite Profiles in Percentages of Forty-four Top Men on Idea Ranking and Forty-four Top Men on Like Ranking for the Same Sessions

	Interaction category	INITIATED		RECEIVED	
		Idea men	Best-liked men	Idea men	Best-liked men
Area A: Positive reactions	Shows solidarity	3.68	4.41	2.57	3.15
	Shows tension release	5.15	6.98	7.95	9.20
	Shows agreement	14.42	16.83	23.29	18.27
Area B: Problem-solving attempts	Gives suggestion	8.97	6.81	7.01	7.22
	Gives opinion	32.74	28.69	25.52	31.09
	Gives orientation	18.54	17.91	14.06	14.54
Area C: Questions	Asks orientation	3.04	3.71	3.62	2.80
	Asks opinion	1.84	2.94	1.94	1.74
	Asks suggestion	.93	1.33	.85	.84
Area D: Negative reactions	Shows disagreement	8.04	7.60	10.65	9.35
	Shows tension increase	1.92	2.16	1.59	1.35
	Shows antagonism	.73	.63	.95	.45

[°] From Philip E. Slater, "Role Differentiation in Small Groups," *American Sociological Review*, 20 (1955), 305.

But now consider an important fact. Almost exactly the same sort of difference in interaction profile tends to be found between high participators and low participators,[10] even if one ignores the idea and like ratings. High participators tend to specialize in problem-solving attempts, low participators tend to specialize in positive or negative reactions or questions. Moreover, the proportion of problem-solving attempts increases when a man is placed with lower participators and decreases when he is working with higher participators. What do these facts suggest?

For one thing, these facts seem to imply that the qualitative differences in the type of act attributed to a given person may be more or less forced by the tendency of others in the group to talk a little or a great deal, thus giving him an opportunity to make the problem-solving attempts or leaving him only in a position to respond to the quicker or more valuable proposals of others.

Insofar as the ratings a man receives are based on the way he behaves, the ratings others give him will surely be dependent on how much he talks. Let us suppose that a man can receive a high rating on ideas only if he makes many problem-solving attempts. He can do this only by talking a good deal. Then, to receive a high rating on ideas he will have to talk a lot. Or, conversely, let us suppose that a man can receive a high rating on liking only if he rewards others by positive reactions. He can do this only if he permits them to make many problem-solving attempts, which in turn requires that he let the other(s) talk a lot. Then, to receive a high rating on liking he will have to talk less.

This line of reasoning seems to fit with the facts so far presented and,

moreover, has a certain plausibility in terms of common organizational arrangements. The husband and wife in many families seem to play complementary roles of the sort described. Many administrators find cases from their experience where organizations in fact have two leaders, one who specializes on the task side, one on the social-emotional side. It is a kind of political maxim that it is almost impossible to elect the person who is technically best suited for an office—he is generally not popular enough. Surely there must be many persons in leadership positions who welcome any theory that explains to them that their lack of popularity is no fault of their own but a result of a specialization that is in the nature of things.

The problem now is that it might be inferred from this ideological version of the theory that there is no essential distinction between sheer activity and ratings received on goodness of ideas and, moreover, that there is a negative correlation between these two and liking received. Is it true that leaders must choose between task effectiveness and popularity?

The Hypothesis of Three Orthogonal Factors

Fortunately, a number of studies in the literature bear on this question, and the results of a number of researchers tend to converge on an answer. When members of small groups are asked to rate and choose each other on a wide variety of descriptive criteria or are assessed by observers, three factors or distinct dimensions generally tend to appear.

Carter[11] indicates the frequency with which these factors are found in reviewing a series of factor analytic

---

[10] See Edgar F. Borgatta and Robert F. Bales, "Interaction of Individuals in Reconstituted Groups," *Sociometry*, **16** (1953), 302-320.

[11] Launor F. Carter, "Recording and Evaluating the Performance of Individuals as Members of Small Groups," *Personnel Psychology*, **7** (1954), 477-484.

studies, such as those of Couch and himself, Sakoda, Wherry, and Clark.[12] A recent study by Wispe[13] may be added to the list.

Carter describes the factors as follows:

Factor I. *Individual prominence and achievement:* behaviors of the individual related to his efforts to stand out from others and individually achieve various personal goals.

Factor II. *Aiding attainment by the group:* behaviors of the individual related to his efforts to assist the group in achieving goals toward which the group is oriented.

Factor III. *Sociability:* behaviors of the individual related to his efforts to establish and maintain cordial and socially satisfying relations with other group members.

These factors seem to represent underlying dimensions in the evaluations persons make of each other, whether as observers or as fellow group members. It may be that the best way of looking at these factors is not as personality traits but as frameworks in which the perceiver responds to personality traits of others.

But the important thing to note is that in these studies the three factors, which I shall call "activity," "task ability," and "likeability," are not, in general, mutually exclusive: a high standing on one does not preclude or interfere with a high standing on the other. Nor are they mutually supportive in general but, rather, they tend to be uncorrelated.

The fact that they are uncorrelated in general does not necessarily mean, of course, that there are no dynamic relationships between the phenomena represented by the factors. It means that there is no simple linear relationship that tends to be found over all populations, so that knowing where a man stands on one does not allow for a prediction of his standing on either or both of the others. If there are dynamic relationships between the factors they must be more complicated, nonlinear, or circumstantial. What suggestions of relationship are there left?

The Hypothesis of Individual Differences in Overtalking

Although it is not true that simply by talking a great deal does one guarantee a high rating on the quality of his ideas, it is still probably true that in groups of the sort we were studying it is very difficult to make a substantial contribution to the task without talking a great deal, especially in the first meeting, and overtalking may be resented by other members as a threat to their own status and a frustration of their own desire to talk. Results of other experimenters provided some findings that are congruent with this line of thought. Let us look for a moment at some of these results.

Leavitt and Mueller[14] explored the effect of one-way communication in a restricted communication situation where the receiver of the information is given no opportunity to "feed back" acknowledgments, questions, or negative reactions to the sender. They find

[12] Arthur S. Couch and Launor F. Carter, "A Factorial Study of the Rated Behavior of Group Members," paper read at Eastern Psychological Association (March, 1952); J. M. Sakoda, "Factor Analysis of O.S.S. Situational Tests," *Journal of Abnormal & Social Psychology*, 47 (1952), 843-852; R. J. Wherry, *Factor Analysis of Officer Qualification Form QCL-2B* (Columbus: Ohio State University Research Foundation, 1950); R. A. Clark, "Analyzing the Group Structure of Combat Rifle Squads," *American Psychologist*, 8 (1953), 333.

[13] Lauren G. Wispe, "A Sociometric Analysis of Conflicting Role-Expectations," *American Journal of Sociology*, 61 (1955), 134-137.

[14] H. J. Leavitt and R. A. H. Mueller, "Some Effects of Feedback on Communication," *Human Relations*, 4 (1951), 401-410.

that an initial reaction of hostility toward the sender tends to appear.

Thibaut and Coules[15] find that receivers who are not permitted to communicate to a person who has sent them an act of hostility show less postexperimental friendliness to the sender than those permitted to reply.

A peripheral position in a restricted network approximates in some ways the position of a receiver with no opportunity for feedback. In an experiment where members were allowed to communicate only in written form through set channels on a task of assembling information, Leavitt[16] finds that members in peripheral positions are less well satisfied with their jobs than those in central positions.

These results suggested to us that the relatively low average of likeability preferences received by top participators might be due to the presence of some men in the total population of top men who overtalk, in the sense that they do not allow an appropriate amount of feedback of objections, qualifications, questions, and countersuggestions to occur. Our method of observation allowed us to examine the amount of interaction a given man received in relation to the amount he initiated. We thus arrived at the hypothesis that the ratio of interaction received to that initiated might help distinguish between those top interactors who were proportionately well liked and those who were not.

In general, as has been indicated, activity, task-ability ratings, and liking ratings appear in many studies as orthogonal factors, uncorrelated with

each other over the total population assessed. It is important to recognize, however, that subparts of a population, or a different population, may show the variables related in a different way. It is the possibility that subparts of our population may show different relationships of these variables that we now explore.

We first make a basic division of the population according to the rank of each person within his own group on the gross amount of participation he initiated and call this his activity. Five ranks are thus recognized, since the groups were five-man groups.

The second division of the population is made within each rank. All the men of each rank are divided into three subpopulations according to their own ratio of amount of participation received from others to the amount of participation they initiate. This ratio is known as the R/I, or the feedback ratio. Within each rank, then, there are three subpopulations of ten men each, low, medium, and high on the feedback ratio.

Figure 3 shows the average values of ratings or ranking received for each of the subpopulations of ten men on liking, disliking, and ideas. The ratings or rankings were given to each man by his four fellow group members and have been converted for plotting in such a way that high numbers mean high average rankings received.

The point of greatest interest is the difference in the relations of liking to activity when the feedback ratio is taken into account. Figure 3 indicates that among the third of the population with a low feedback ratio, the top two men seem definitely lower than would be expected if liking received increased linearly in proportion to activity. The correlation between activity and liking received is near zero.

However, both the medium R/I and the high R/I thirds show a positive

15 J. W. Thibaut and J. Coules, "The Role of Communication in the Reduction of Interpersonal Hostility," *Journal of Abnormal & Social Psychology*, **47** (1952), 770-777.

16 H. J. Leavitt, "Some Effects of Certain Communication Patterns on Group Performance," *Readings in Social Psychology*, 3rd ed., *op. cit.*, Maccoby, *et al.*, eds., pp. 546-563.

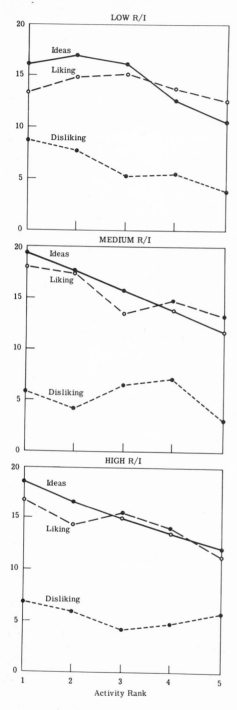

correlation. From these data it is still plausible to suppose that the top man even in the high R/I third shows a little less liking received than one would expect. But the effect is slight.

The data obtained by asking about dislikes present essentially the same picture. The highest participators among the third of the population with the lowest feedback ratio not only are less well liked but are more disliked than their less active colleagues in the same subpopulation. In this third of the population, the more the person talks, the more he is disliked. But in the opposite third of the population, those who have a high feedback ratio, there is no relation between how much a man talks and how much he is disliked.

With regard to idea rankings received, there is a definite indication that the highest participators in the third of the population with the low feedback ratio tend to suffer on idea rankings received, as they do on liking received, although the effect is not so marked. This effect seems to disappear completely in the medium R/I and high R/I groups.

It is plain, however, that there is an appreciable linear correlation between activity and idea rankings received over the total of the three subpopulations. This finding thus differs from other

FIG. 3. Average ratings° received on ideas, liking, and disliking by men of each activity rank, according to their feedback ratio (R/I). [Condensed from Robert F. Bales, "Task Status and Likeability as a Function of Talking and Listening in Decision-Making Groups," in Leonard D. White, ed., *The State of the Social Sciences* (Chicago: The University of Chicago Press, 1956), pp. 148-161.]

° Each entry at a given activity rank is the mean for ten persons. The idea index is not actually a rating, but an index obtained by adding rankings received (including self-rankings) and subtracting the total from the highest possible, 25. The like and dislike indices are average ratings, with the highest possible, 28.

studies which find these two variables to be generally orthogonal. We attribute the correlation in our groups at least partly to the fact that we are dealing in this study with data from first meetings entirely. Data on groups running over four sessions indicate that this correlation tends to fall over time, especially in groups where the initial consensus as to who has the best ideas is low.[17] The correlation between ideas and liking also tends to fall as indicated above in Table 1. In short, the three factors tend to separate out as independent more clearly in later meetings than in the first.

To summarize briefly: In the groups in this total sample there is only a weak correlation between liking received and activity, providing one makes no breakdown into subpopulations. But for about one third of the population there is a positive and linear correlation between how much a man talks and how well he is liked. This is the third who receive more interaction in proportion to the amount they initiate, that is, who have a high feedback ratio. The falling-off of liking received among the individuals who talk the most in total population is attributable especially to the other extreme third of the population, who talk proportionately most above the amount they receive. The same may be said for their rankings.

Conclusion

It appears that activity, task-ability ratings, and likeability ratings should be treated as three distinct factors, since over a large population of members, meetings, and groups they tend to be uncorrelated with each other. If one accepts this assumption, a simple

and very useful classification of role types in small groups suggests itself.

1. A member who is high on all three of the factors corresponds to the traditional conception of the good leader, or the "great man." Such men are found, but, if the factors are uncorrelated, are rare.

2. A member who is high on activity and task-ability ratings but less high on likeability is a familiar type who may be called the "task specialist." This type is not so rare as the first type and may operate effectively in cooperation with the third.

3. A member who is high on likeability but less high on activity and task ability may be called the "social specialist." This type is much less rare than the first type, and groups which operate under the dual leadership of a man of this type and of the second type are common.

4. A member who is high on activity but relatively low on task-ability and likeability ratings may be called an "overactive deviant." This type is not rare. This is the person who, in the leadership literature, is said to show "domination" rather than "leadership."

5. A member who is low on all three may be called an "underactive deviant" and may indeed be a kind of scapegoat. On the assumption that the factors are uncorrelated this type should be as rare as the first type, but since the lack of correlation traces mainly to discrepancies at the upper end of the scales, this type is not actually so rare as the first type and is, in fact, probably very common.

Logically, of course, one can distinguish many additional types. Those mentioned, however, have a certain intuitive distinctness and for present purposes serve to summarize and harmonize the various views on role differentiation that have been examined in this paper.

---

[17] Philip E. Slater, "Role Differentiation in Small Groups," *op. cit.*

the family

fifteen

In American sociology the study of the family has come more and more to focus on interpersonal relations within the family, with special emphasis on the adjustment or "happiness" of the married couple and their children. In the process we have neglected the classic sociological concern with the family as one of the central institutions of society that both reflects and influences the larger social system. In contemporary sociology no one has done more than William J. Goode to redirect our attention to the interaction between family and society. In his contribution to this volume he tests the theory that all societies have a vital interest in fixing responsibility for the child upon some specific individual, and shows how the special social conditions that prevail in the Caribbean have there effectively weakened the application of that principle.

Illegitimacy in the Caribbean

WILLIAM J. GOODE

Over a generation ago Malinowski enunciated a principle which he said amounted to a universal sociological law, that "no child should be brought into the world without a man—and one man at that—assuming the role of sociological father. . . ."[1] This rule is not based on the social disapproval of premarital or extramarital sexual freedom. Malinowski's Trobrianders, for ex-ample, indulged in considerable sex play before marriage, but were shocked at illegitimacy. Rather, the rule expresses the interest of the society in fixing responsibility for the child upon a specific individual. Marriage, therefore, is not primarily the legitimation of sex, but the legitimation of parenthood.[2] Whether Malinowski's principle is indeed a universal sociological law

William J. Goode, "Illegitimacy in the Caribbean Social Structure," *American Sociological Review*, **25** (February, 1960), 21-30.

[1] Bronislaw Malinowski, "Parenthood, the Basis of Social Structure," in V. F. Calverton and Samuel D. Schmalhausen, eds., *The New Generation* (New York: Macaulay Company, 1930), pp. 137-138.

[2] Malinowski was puzzled as to how the Trobrianders could be sexually so free without numerous illegitimates, especially since they denied any connection between sexual intercourse and pregnancy and took no contraceptive precautions. It was not until W. F. Ashley-Montagu's *Coming into Being Among the Australian Aborigines* (London: Routledge & Kegan Paul, Ltd., 1937) that the solution seemed to be clear.

See also M. F. Ashley-Montagu, *The Reproductive Development of the Female* (New York: Julian Press, Inc., 1957).

has not been analyzed, except to the degree that the recurring debate as to whether the "nuclear family" is universal implicitly includes that principle.[3] It seems safe enough to claim at least that all societies have family systems and that possibly a sociological father is required everywhere.[4]

Illegitimacy in the Caribbean

Malinowski's principle is not refuted by data from the United States or western Europe, where illegitimacy rates range from perhaps 4 or 5 per cent to about 11 per cent.[5] However, in the Caribbean area illegitimacy rates are often over 50 per cent, as Table 1 shows.

Under such conditions, doubt may be raised as to whether a "sociological father" exists, and indeed various writers have spoken of a "matri-focal family."[6] Certainly so high a rate of

TABLE 1 Illegitimacy Rates in Selected Caribbean Political Units[*]

Political Unit	Year	Per Cent
British Guiana	1955	35
French Guiana	1956	65
Surinam (excluding Bush Negroes and aborigines)	1953	34
Barbados	1957	70
Bermuda	1957	30
Dominican Republic	1957	61
Guadeloupe	1956	42
Jamaica	1954	72
Antigua	1957	65
Martinique	1956	48
Trinidad and Tobago	1956	47
Grenada	1957	71
Puerto Rico	1955	28
Haiti	—	67-85

[*] All figures except those for Puerto Rico, British Guiana, Surinam, Dominican Republic, Trinidad and Tobago, Grenada, and Haiti were taken from the United Nations Year Book Questionnaire for the years in question. Data were furnished to the U.N. by the statistical offices of the country, and contain all the errors of their own registration procedures. Data for other countries, excluding Haiti and the Dominican Republic, were kindly furnished by the Caribbean Commission. The Dirección General de Estadística of the Dominican Republic graciously sent me the figure for 1957. I have found no recent figure for Cuba; presumably it was 30 per cent in 1939. For Surinam, Rudolf van Lier, Samenleving in ein Gransgebied, 's-Gravenhage: Martinus Nijhoff, 1949, p. 287, gives 70 per cent for 1940. The rate has also dropped in British Guiana from the 41 per cent reported in 1946 in British Guiana Annual Report of the Registrar-General, 1954 (Georgetown, Demerara, British Guiana, 1956, p. 9). I have found no official figure for Haiti, Bastien reports two thirds for Marbial (Remy Bastien, La Familia Rural Haitiana, Mexico: Libra, 1951, p. 85); George E. Simpson reports about 85 per cent for one Haitian area in "Sexual and Family Institutions in Northern Haiti," American Anthropologist, 44 (October-December, 1942), 664.

[3] For a recent discussion of this point, see Melford E. Spiro, "Is the Family Universal?" American Anthropologist, 56 (October, 1954), 839-846.

[4] The most notable case which raises doubts is the Nayar of Malabar Strait. See K. M. Panikkar, "Some Aspects of Nayar Life," Journal of the Royal Anthropological Institute, 48 (July-December, 1918), esp. 260ff; E. Kathleen Gough, "Changing Kinship Usages in the Setting of Political and Economic Change among the Nayar of Malabar," Journal of the Royal Anthropological Institute, 81 (1951), 71-88. Gough's latest report ["The Nayars and the Definition of Marriage," Journal of the Royal Anthropological Institute, 89 (1959), 31] asserts that Nayar marriage does establish paternity legally. Another possible case is the Minang-Kabau; see E. N. Loeb, "Patrilineal and Matrilineal Organization in Sumatra, Part 2," American Anthropologist, 36 (January-March, 1934), 26-56.

[5] In Iceland, illegitimate births constituted 27.9 per cent of live births in 1950, and the rate in Stockholm and a few other areas in Sweden has remained at about 15 per cent in recent years. Cf. Meyer Nimkoff, "Illegitimacy," Encyclopaedia Britannica (1954).

[6] "One of the regularities of social organization, which has appeared in the literature

deviation would suggest that the norm, if it does exist, might have a very dif-

from Herskovits to Henriques, is the concept of the 'matrifocal' family." Vera Rubin, "Cultural Perspectives in Caribbean Research," in Vera Rubin, ed., Caribbean Studies: A Symposium (Jamaica: Institute of Social and Economic Research, 1957), p. 117. Such comments are often applicable as well to one period in the development of the Negro family in this country. Cf. E. Franklin Frazier, The Negro Family in the United States, rev. ed. (New York: Dryden Press, 1948), Part 2, "In the House of the Mother."

ferent meaning than in a society in which the rate is less, say, than 10 per cent. But we must keep in mind that Malinowski was stating a proposition about a *cultural* element: he asserted that the *norm* would always be found, not that the members of the society would obey it under specified conditions.

It is precisely with reference to Malinowski's principle that many students of the Caribbean have taken an opposing position—without developing its implications for family theory. The claim has often been made for various Caribbean lands that when a couple is living together in a consensual union "the family may be said to exist in much the same way as it does in peasant communities throughout the world,"[7] and the child therefore suffers no disadvantage from being illegitimate.[8] Henriques, also writing about Jamaica, comments that there is no moral sanction against "concubinage," by which he means a man and woman keeping house together and raising children, and even claims that respectable black people would rather have their daughter become mistress or concubine to a white or fair colored man than marry a black one.[9] Otherwise put, the consensual union is the marriage form of the lower classes in the Caribbean, and is "sociologically as legitimate" as a legal union. It is, in short, a "cultural alternative," as permissible a way of founding a family as any other.[10] If this interpretation is correct, Malinowski's principle would be erroneous, and one of the apparently major functions of the father would have to be redefined as unessential.

Comments similar to those given above about Jamaica have been made about other Caribbean areas. Herskovits and Herskovits make a similar claim for Trinidad, noting what a "false perspective on the thinking of the people is given by the application of legal terms such as 'legitimate' and 'illegitimate' to the offspring."[11] Similarly, they assert that "there is no social disability imposed by the community because of legitimacy or illegitimacy."[12] The common-law marriage is for many the accepted form.[13]

With respect to Haitian children of a placée union which is legalized, of a legal union, or of a union outside of an existing marriage the claim is made that "none of these classes of children are at any special social disadvantage."[14] With reference to the forms of Haitian unions: "In the main, especially in the countryside, socially sanctioned matings which do not enjoy the approval of the Church endure as long and hold as respected a place in the community. . . ."[15] In a parallel vein, Bastien remarks that when a man has "good intentions" with respect to a girl, but does not have enough money with which to marry, he may "establish himself" with the girl, with marriage as a publicly acknowledged, later

[7] T. S. Simey, *Welfare and Planning in the West Indies* (Oxford: The Clarendon Press, 1956), p. 15.

[8] "The fact of illegitimate birth is one completely taken for granted. An illegitimate child does not consider himself disadvantaged. . . ." *Ibid.*, p. 88.

[9] Fernando Henriques, *Family and Color in Jamaica* (London: Eyre and Spottiswoode, Ltd., 1953), pp. 87, 90.

[10] "Thus, the matrifocal family . . . is a subcultural norm. . . ." John V. Murra,

"Discussion," in *Caribbean Studies, op. cit.,* p. 76.

[11] Melville J. Herskovits and Frances S. Herskovits, *Trinidad Village* (New York: Alfred A. Knopf, Inc., 1947), p. 17.

[12] *Ibid.*, pp. 82-83; see also p. 107.

[13] Lloyd Braithwaite, "Social Stratification in Trinidad," *Social and Economic Studies,* 2 (October, 1953), 125.

[14] Melville J. Herskovits, *Life in a Haitian Valley* (New York: Alfred A. Knopf, Inc., 1937), p. 118.

[15] *Ibid.*, p. 106.

goal, but does not thereby "incur the scorn of the community."[16]

In Martinique, we are told, in place of the rule of legitimacy, which is absent here, other values have emerged such as in-group solidarity, status equality, and conviviality, which express family organization.[17] There is "no unequivocally preferred type of bond between parents."[18] The legitimate and illegitimate share the same status.

Although the illegitimacy rate in Puerto Rico is lower than in the areas noted above, here too the claim has been made that the rule of legitimacy fails. It is said of the consensual union that it is "a cultural alternative," that is, marriage is split into two culturally permissible alternatives.[19] Similarly, ". . . the prevalence of consensual unions ought to be considered in terms of local lower-class conceptions of what is considered 'moral.'" It is not that the lower class prefer illegal behavior, but that consensual unions are not seen as immoral.[20] It is asserted, too, that "the consensual union is considered a binding marriage truly cemented at the birth of the first child."[21]

At first glance, then, Malinowski's rule of legitimacy is refuted. A substantial number of societies in the

West appear not to accept the norm. If this is the case, then several fundamental notions in family theory would have to be discarded.

Yet a closer examination of these and other reports prove conclusively that the norm exists, since in fact marriage is the ideal, and those who violate the rule do suffer penalties. The fact that perhaps a majority of certain of these populations do live in unions outside marriage, at some time in their lives, does not change the normative status of the rule. On the other hand, as we shall later indicate, Malinowski's rule must nevertheless be reformulated.

Let us first look more closely at Jamaica. As against the assertion that illegitimacy is not stigmatized, we note the opposing facts. Both upper- and middle-class opinion is set against "concubinage."[22] The priests may shame the couple about the matter. When a young girl is found to be pregnant, her family is angry.[23] Few men (Rocky Roads) allow their women to bring their illegitimate children into the un-

TABLE 2   British West Indies: Per Cent of Males Ever Married by Age, 1946

Age	Jamaica	Bar-bados	Wind-wards	Lee-wards
20-24	10.1	8.5	4.1	4.0
25-34	21.0	37.6	27.6	27.3
35-44	41.9	61.7	54.9	53.4
45-54	55.0	70.8	68.2	63.7
55-64	66.3	75.2	78.4	75.5
65 and over	74.7	85.2	83.1	78.9

ion, if they do marry.[24] In the same community, illegitimate children are

[16] Bastien, op. cit., pp. 72-73. However, Bastien also presents the prestige rankings of the three forms of matings.

[17] Mariam Kreiselman, The Caribbean Family, A Case Study in Martinique, Columbia University, Ph.D. thesis (1958), pp. 271, 292.

[18] Ibid., p. viii.

[19] J. Mayone Stycos, Family and Fertility in Puerto Rico (New York: Columbia University Press, 1955), p. 110. I assume here the meaning of "culturally equivalent" or "normatively equal."

[20] Sidney W. Mintz, "Cañamelar, The Subculture of a Rural Sugar Plantation Proletariat," in Julian Steward, et al., eds., The People of Puerto Rico (Urbana: University of Illinois Press, 1956), p. 377.

[21] Robert A. Manners, "Tabara: Subcultures of a Tobacco and Mixed Crop Municipality," in ibid., p. 144.

[22] Henriques, op. cit., pp. 87, 164.

[23] Ibid., p. 88. See also Edith Clarke, My Mother Who Fathered Me (London: George Allen & Unwin, Ltd., 1957), p. 99; and Kreiselman, op. cit., p. 189.

[24] Yehudi Cohen, "Structure and Function: Family Organization and Socialization in a Jamaican Community," American Anthropologist, 58 (August, 1956), 669.

illegitimacy in the caribbean   **161**

subjected to more physical rejection and pressures of sibling rivalry.[25] Moreover, as individuals move through the life cycle, an increasing proportion are actually married, a phenomenon which would be inexplicable if the consensual unions were backed by a set of alternative norms. This process is illustrated by the proportions of persons ever married by selected ages in the major areas of the British West Indies, as shown in Table 2.[26] Thus, though the average British West Indian ages at marriage are among the highest in the world (for example, for Jamaica, 34.1 years for males; for Barbados, 31.7; and for Grenada, 33.0[27]), most individuals do marry. In sum, these various mating forms are "not regarded as alternative forms of conjugal associations between which any individual was free to choose."[28]

Similarly, in Trinidad, a couple may finally marry after living together for some time, "for the position it gives the family." Among other things, "marriage is . . . a prestige phenomenon in terms of social or religious values." Though a couple will usually begin life together as "keepers," "such an episode is outside correct procedure." The unmarried keeper woman wears no ring, and only the married woman is called *Madam*.[29] Many people who rise in class find that their new rank is incompatible with the type of union they once entered. Moreover, when working-class women quarrel, one may point out that the other is not properly married.[30]

Although the case of Haiti seems more complex, the same conclusion seems inescapable. The prestige from the legal, Church union is of sufficient significance to "motivate weddings at which the children and even children of the principals act as attendants."[31] The legal union cannot be broken as easily as the plaçage. When the unmarried girl becomes pregnant, she is beaten.[32] The woman in a placée union cannot demand as much from her man, and her children have no right to the name of the father.[33] Most persons would prefer to marry, and this is especially true of women.[34] Contemporary pressures are increasing the proportion who marry, but some gradations of prestige remain.[35] The plaçage is not stable: "perhaps three-fourths of the peasant men, and possibly more, have or have had at one time one or more mates in addition to a legal wife or *femme caille*."[36] "The consciousness

[25] *Ibid.*, 672.

[26] G. W. Roberts, "Some Aspects of Mating and Fertility in the West Indies," *Population Studies*, 8 (March, 1955), 223. The figures for Jamaica in Table 2 presumably refer to 1943.

[27] *Ibid.*, 205. More fundamental data are the actual expressions of norms and ideals, to be found in Judith Blake's *Family Structure: The Social Context of Reproduction*, Columbia University, Ph.D. thesis (1959), a study of the lower-class Jamaican family. It is the first detailed investigation of the mechanisms through which the norms lose much of their coercive power. For a preliminary report from this study, see Blake, "Family Instability and Reproductive Behavior in Jamaica," *Current Research in Human Fertility* (New York: Milbank Fund, 1955), pp. 24-41.

[28] Clarke, *op. cit.*, pp. 77-78. It is significant that Clarke and Blake, who appear to be the only investigators to take seriously the Jamaican's *own* normative statements, assert unequivocally the normative underpinnings of a legal marriage.

[29] Herskovits and Herskovits, *op. cit.*, pp. 82, 84, 87, 93-94.

[30] Lloyd Braithwaite, "Social Stratification in Trinidad," *Social and Economic Studies*, 2 (October, 1953), 125, 126.

[31] Herskovits, *op. cit.*, pp. 106, 107.

[32] *Ibid.*, p. 110; George Eaton Simpson, "Sexual and Familial Institutions in Northern Haiti," *American Anthropologist*, 44 (October-December, 1942), 665.

[33] Herskovits, *op. cit.*, pp. 116, 119.

[34] Simpson, *op. cit.*, 655, 658.

[35] Rhoda Metraux, *Kith and Kin*, Columbia University, Ph.D. thesis (1951), pp. 197, 205-209.

[36] Simpson, *op. cit.*, 656. The *femme caille* shares her consort's house. Bastien, *op. cit.*,

of their social inferiority so troubles . . . [them] . . . that few resist the temptation to explain the cause of their situation. . . ."[37]

In Martinique, too, parents are angry at the pregnancy of the unmarried girl, who may have to leave her home. When talking about the consensual relationships of others, the term "concubine" is used. Many men will promise marriage, but deceive the girl. In a few reported cases of girls having babies, the parents pretended that the children were their own.[38] The consensual union is easily dissolved, and no social obligations are incurred by entering it.[39]

Perhaps more conclusive for Martinique is an important finding, which grew out of an effort to understand the *fête*. In possibly every study of illegitimacy in the Caribbean, people are described as saying—most researchers have accepted this assertion—that they cannot marry because they cannot afford the wedding feast, without which the ceremony is a mockery. The couple will be laughed at later. The "cost of the wedding" is not the church expenses; in every country the Catholic Church (or others, where they are important) has offered nearly free weddings—but with rare acceptance. A few observers have doubted that the expense of the *fête* was the crucial item, even though it is substantial, emphasizing rather that the *fête* is an expression of community solidarity, a *rite de pas-*

sage, and a community validation of the union. Kreiselman is unique among observers in offering and, within limits, testing the hypothesis that most persons who can afford to live *en ménage* can also afford a *fête* and therefore a marriage, but that most who do not marry early or later do not have the same rank.[40]

Whether the rank differences among people of a lower stratum are so crucial, and whether a broad sample of stable consensual unions would show that it is mainly those of equal status who marry, remains to be seen. But if this is the case even in Capesterre (Martinique), the relationship shows that the rule of legitimacy holds there. For the rule has as a major function the prevention of unions between wrong lineages, and in nearly every society the rules of marriage serve to confine legal unions mainly to men and women of equal rank.[41]

In Puerto Rico, there is social disapproval of the consensual union, even though the sanction does not necessarily lead to conformity. Fathers become angry when their daughters elope, and almost everyone pays "lip service" to the superiority of marriage.[42] People may say that they get married in order to baptize the children.[43] Girls

---

p. 73, gives three main categories of unions, in order of social rank: (1) marriage; (2) a union established with the idea of later marriage; and (3) the ordinary plaçage, some forms of which involve several women living apart from one another.

[37] Bastien, *op. cit.*, p. 73.
[38] Kreiselman, *op. cit.*, pp. 188, 189, 199, 201, 223.
[39] *Ibid.*, p. 231. All unions involve social obligations, of course, but the fact that the investigator makes this observation underlines the lack of community support for this type of union.

[40] *Ibid.*, pp. 221-231. After a long consensual union, may marriage occur because the man and woman come to have the same rank?
[41] Perhaps the Natchez were an exception. See Kingsley Davis, "Intermarriage in Caste Societies," *American Anthropologist*, **43** (July-September, 1941), 382ff. Of course, a "free courtship system" achieves the same end; and one may date a person whom one may not marry without censure.
[42] Stycos, *op. cit.*, pp. 108, 110-111.
[43] Eric R. Wolf, "San José: Subcultures of a 'Traditional' Coffee Municipality," in *The People of Puerto Rico*, *op. cit.*, p. 220. In Puerto Rico, the girl is usually a virgin when she enters a consensual union. Bastien makes the same claim for the Marbial area in Haiti, but to my knowledge no observer of other Haitian areas has done so; and Bastien is in-

have "idealized feelings" about marriage ceremonies,[44] and often the girls' parents request or insist upon legal unions.[45]

Two-thirds of both men and women in a national sample of Puerto Rico said that a consensual union is a bad life for a man, and over 80 per cent of the respondents made the same assertion for women.[46] Perhaps a more penetrating test of the normative status of the consensual union may be found in the attitudes expressed about a *daughter* entering a consensual union: only 7.4 per cent of the men and 5.5 per cent of the women admitted that this arrangement would either be "all right" or that "it's up to her; doesn't matter."[47]

We are similarly told that in British Guiana the children born outside wedlock "are not sharply differentiated by any stigma of illegitimacy," while the consensual union is a "socially sanctioned one," and "part of the lower-class tradition."[48] Once again, however, we can note that parents are angry at the daughter and beat her when she becomes pregnant while still in the home. An unmarried mother will usually ask another person to take her illegitimate child to church for baptism.[49] And, although the scholar here quoted agrees with a turn-of-the-century French writer on the Congo who

asserted that among the Bavili "birth sanctifies the child," a man's "outside" children in British Guiana do not rank equally with his legitimate children, and not all of a woman's children remain with her in a new marital union.[50] Moreover, only the married woman is called "Mistress," while her marital rights are clearer and more secure.[51] Marriage confers a different status on the woman. Women wish to marry, and after they have begun to have illegitimate children they understand that they can achieve this status only by gambling that a quasimarital union may develop into a marriage.[52] Finally, most people do marry eventually, and the legal, monogamic union is clearly the ideal.[53]

Differential Intensity of Norm Commitment

Several conclusions and problems emerge from such a confrontation of general assertions with specific observations. In order to proceed to further related propositions, these conclusions may be summarized: (1) Unequivocally, Malinowski's principle of legitimacy holds even for these societies, for which various observers have asserted that it did not hold. Birth out of wedlock is not a "cultural alternative." There is no special approval of the consensual union, no "counter-norm" in favor of such a union. Of course, the parental anger aroused by a clandestine pregnancy will not be repeated when the girl has entered a consensual union. Nevertheless, in none of these societies does the unmarried mother or her

---

consistent. See Bastien, *op. cit.*, pp. 64, 65, 72.

[44] Mintz, *op. cit.*, p. 378.

[45] Elena Padilla Seda, "Nocora: The Subculture of Workers on a Government-Owned Sugar Plantation," in *The People of Puerto Rico, op. cit.*, p. 293.

[46] Paul K. Hatt, *Backgrounds of Human Fertility in Puerto Rico* (Princeton: Princeton University Press, 1952), p. 127.

[47] *Ibid.*, p. 64. I would suppose, however, that the percentage would be much less on the mainland of the United States.

[48] Raymond T. Smith, *The Negro Family in British Guiana* (New York: Grove Press, 1956), pp. 109, 149, 182.

[49] *Ibid.*, pp. 126, 132, 145.

[50] *Ibid.*, pp. 102, 120, 156, 178.

[51] *Ibid.*, pp. 179-180; see also pp. 59, 148-149.

[52] *Ibid.*, p. 138. The highest illegitimacy rate occurs among births to females fifteen to nineteen years of age; British Guiana, *Annual Report . . . , op. cit.*, p. 9.

[53] *Ibid.*, Chap. 5.

child enjoy the same status as the married mother and her legitimate children. A union based on a marriage enjoys more respect than do other types of unions. (2) Equally clear, however, is the corroboration of another principle: that the degree of norm commitment varies from one segment of the population to another. Not only do some individuals reject particular norms, but the members of some strata are less concerned than those of others about given norms.[54] (3) A more specific inference from the latter principle is also corroborated, namely, that the lower social strata are less committed than the middle or upper strata to a variety of family norms, in this instance that of legitimacy,[55] and also obey them less.

More important, however, is a reformulation of Malinowski's principle. As stated, it gives too little emphasis to the real foundation on which it rests, and ignores the differences in norm commitment among different strata, doubtless because neither problem was important in the societies with which Malinowski was concerned. The principle in fact rests primarily upon the function of status placement, not that of locating a father as "protector": the bastard daughter of a count is still illegitimate even if he "protects" her. Violation of the norm creates some status ambiguity with respect to the child, the parents, and the two kin lines. Consequently, (4) commitment to the norm of legitimacy will be greater among the strata or kin lines which enjoy a higher prestige, or in which concern with the kin relation is higher. Although in general this concern is more marked in the upper strata, in every stratum there will be *some* family lines which possess "traditions," pride, a sense of kin identity, and so on. Illegitimacy rates can be expected to be higher among the lower strata in all societies. (5) Correlatively, to the extent that a given society possesses a high proportion of lower strata families who are concerned little or not at all with their lineage, that society will exhibit a higher total rate of illegitimacy than it would have if the proportion were lower.

Given a high rate of illegitimacy, two further inferences may be made. (6) The actual amount of stigma suffered by the average illegitimate child cannot be great, relative to legitimate children in his same stratum and neighborhood. (7) The "matrifocality" of the Caribbean family is merely the result of the mother being left with her children, by either a casual lover, a consensual partner, or husband. The "matriarch" who is in charge has power precisely because no other adult of her generation is there to exercise it. Very likely a different personality configuration as well as a different self-image can and sometimes does develop from this experience.[56] The loyalty of children to the mother is stronger under such a system, since the father is not likely to be around during much

---

[54] Thus, one can find individuals who specifically reject marriage for one reason or another in all these societies. However, the empirical question is: what percentage of the society or stratum? In our society, too, any public opinion poll will locate a few such individuals.

[55] There is substantial literature on this point. See, e.g., William J. Goode, *After Divorce* (New York: The Free Press of Glencoe, Inc., 1956), Chaps. 4-5; Ruth S. Cavan, *The Family* (New York: Thomas Y. Crowell Co., 1953), Chaps. 5-7; and William F. Whyte, "A Slum Sex Code," *American Journal of Sociology*, 49 (July, 1943), 24-31. For other data relevant to the subsequent discussion, see Herbert Hyman, "The Value Systems of Different Classes . . . ," in R. Bendix and S. M. Lipset, eds., *Class, Status, and Power* (New York: The Free Press of Glencoe, Inc., 1953), pp. 426-442.

[56] Nor should the matter of *self-selection* be forgotten. Given the social option, some individuals will find this role more congenial and choose it against other alternatives.

of the infancy and youth of the off-spring.[57]

On the other hand, early in the union, or continuously when the father remains in the union, the male behaves in a fashion which might be called "patriarchal" in the United States. It is possible that some observers have been misled, in their evaluation of the mother's power, by a false image of male behavior in such patriarchal societies as Japan, China, and India, where in fact the older mother is likely to have great authority in the home even when she pays considerable overt deference to the male head of family.

Role Bargaining and Illegitimacy

An "explanation" of these high rates may properly take two directions. One of these would widen our empirical perspective to include other areas of the world, especially the countries south of the Rio Grande where high illegitimacy rates are found, and locate the cultural elements which are common to them. In a related paper, I am making such an analysis, with special reference to the cultural structure of a society and conformity to its norms. This analysis seeks to answer the question: in what types of societies are high rates found?

The second direction is to focus on the more immediate social forces which create a high illegitimacy rate

in the Caribbean. It may be granted that the lower norm commitment in the lower strata of this area would, other things being equal, decrease conformity. Intensity of norm commitment, however, is only one element in the decision to risk pregnancy. The social pattern of primary importance is that the young woman in her courtship behavior must make essentially an *individual role bargain*. This apparent contrast with courtship patterns which produce low illegitimacy rates requires only little attention.

By "making an individual role bargain," I refer to the fact that in any role relationship both ego and alter are restricted in what services they may agree to perform for one another, by the expectations of others and thus by the sanctions which others will apply. For example, father and daughter owe, and feel they owe, certain obligations to one another, and in part these obligations are met because of the rewards and sanctions which either can direct toward the other. However, even if both of them are willing to agree to a different set of obligations—say, those appropriate to lovers—there is a "third layer" of persons who have role relationships with either ego and alter, or both of them, and who will act to force both of them to perform properly. These actions include pressures on ego or alter to punish the other for improper performance.

All courtship systems are market systems, in which role bargains are struck. They differ from one another with respect to the commodities which are more or less valuable on that market (beauty, personality, kinship position, family prestige, wealth) and who has the authority to do the marketing. Modern western societies seem to constitute the only major historical civilization in which youngsters have been given a substantial voice in this bargaining (Imperial Rome might be

---

[57] Although almost every writer points to "some" consensual unions which have "lasted as long as" legal ones, the instability of both types seems indubitable, and consensual unions are less stable; see R. T. Smith, "Family Organization in British Guiana," *Social and Economic Studies*, 1 (1953), 101; Simpson, *op. cit.*, 656; Braithwaite, *op. cit.*, 147; Seda, *op. cit.*, p. 293; Mintz, *op. cit.*, p. 375; Stycos, *op. cit.*, p. 119; Simey, *op. cit.*, p. 16. (Kreiselman, by contrast, asserts stability for both types; *op. cit.*, p. 180). That matrifocality is by default has been noted by others, e.g., Kreiselman, *op. cit.*, p. 282; Simey, *op. cit.*, p. 43; Braithwaite, *op. cit.*, 147.

added by some historians). Even in the United States, however, where this trend is most fully developed, numerous studies have shown that youngsters make their choices within a highly restricted market, with respect to age, race, religion, social class, and so on. Precisely because courtship systems are bargaining systems, apparently hypergamous marriages (the woman marries upward in class) usually are, in most societies, unions in which a high ranking on one or more variables (wealth, beauty) is traded for a high ranking on other variables (power, prestige, race).[58] As a consequence, most marriages occur between individuals of like rank, or at least like bargaining power,[59] whether youngsters or their elders have the greater authority to conduct the bargaining process. When one party has much less bargaining power, he may be unable to pay as much as the other demands, or will have to pay much more than another family with greater bargaining power.

Although these principles hold with respect to both the choice of marital partner and the decision to marry at all, they are upheld, as is any market system, by a set of communitywide or stratumwide set of agreements about *what* is valuable and *how* valuable those characteristics are, and a set of corresponding pressures which prevent the individual from paying too much. In our society, for example, even if a middle-class girl is willing to bear a child outside of marriage, usually her parents will oppose this behavior strongly because she would be giving more than need be under the operating market system.

By contrast, what is striking in the Caribbean community studies are the anonymity and isolation within which the decision is made to enter a union, and the fact that under those social conditions the girl has little chance of being married at all unless she is willing to risk a union outside of marriage. Not only does she become pregnant without her parents' knowing that she is courting, but she is also likely to enter the consensual union without any prior ritual or public announcement.[60]

A synthesis of the factors of importance in the decision to marry or to enter a consensual union can be made from the existing studies (although in many cases needed data are lacking because the appropriate questions were not asked[61]). Especially important are the following five points:

1. The class pattern of marriage has been suggested above. This may be clarified here by noting that not only do middle- and upper-class individuals marry (though of course males from those strata may have mistresses whom they do not marry), but that most members of the lower strata also marry eventually. Some lower-class persons never enter a consensual union, but begin their conjugal career by a wedding. Others begin with a consensual union, but marry sooner or later, usually after the male has somewhat improved his social position. In certain communities which seem to enjoy a higher social standing, a substantial majority of all marital unions are legal.[62]

2. Kreiselman's finding for Martinique concerning marriages between

---

[58] See Davis, op. cit., 386.

[59] Of course, the principle of least interest operates in courtship as in marital conflict; the individual who is more deeply in love has less bargaining power. Willard Waller and Reuben Hill, *The Family: A Dynamic Interpretation* (New York: Dryden Press, 1953), pp. 190-192.

[60] Smith, op. cit., pp. 101, 137.

[61] For Jamaica, as noted in footnote 27, the most complete synthesis has been made by Blake, op. cit.

[62] For example, Orange Grove reported in Clarke, op. cit.; Better Hope reported in Smith, op. cit.; and apparently San José as reported in Wolf, op. cit.

persons of similar rank can be extended to every Caribbean community. Notwithstanding the frequently voiced assumption to the contrary, many fine distinctions of prestige are made within the lower class, in spite of its apparent homogeneity to the (usually white) outside observer.[63] If there were no other index, we could rely on the fact that certain members of the lower class do marry without entering a consensual union.[64] However, other data are also available: for example, the higher ranking of unskilled laborers with *steady* jobs. Granted, these differences are less sharp or refined than the gross differences between upper and lower strata, but within the narrower class horizon of persons in the bottom stratum they may nevertheless loom large. From this fact, we can suppose that when marriage does occur, the man and woman are more likely to be "rank equals," within the more generalized terms proposed above—which include not merely family prestige but also personal qualities such as beauty.[65]

3. Given a system in which consensual unions are common, it follows that the punishments for entering them cannot be severe, and the rewards for marrying cannot be great. (This proposition is an inference from a well-known principle of social control.) Consequently, the girl's parents or relatives (there is no extended kin group which acts as a unit) are punished or rewarded very little if, in turn, they make or fail to make her behavior conform to "ideal" norms.

4. In the Caribbean, there is no "free" adolescent courtship system such as our own, in which an as yet ineligible male is permitted to approach an immature girl, under the protection of her relatives and peer group. Many or most of the men she first meets are ineligible because of the great cost of a wedding. Most of them have not accumulated enough wealth to finance the formal union and to support its subsequent requirement of a higher level of living than a consensual union.[66] Consequently, the girl's first love and sex contacts occur away from home, and without the knowledge of the family. These first contacts take place essentially in social anonymity, so that she must make the best bargain she can, without the family's support.[67] Parental anger, reported in most studies, is at least in part a reaction to the knowledge that the girl has entered the world of adulthood without parental permission and has acted independently while presumably still a child.[68]

5. The Caribbean girl with unusual qualities may be able to demand marriage. However, the average girl has little chance at marriage, early or late, unless she is willing to gamble that a more permanent union will grow from one relationship or another. Without reliable data on the number of unions in the average individual's life, we cannot state what these chances are. Motherhood lowers the girl's value in the market, but if she does not produce a child for the man with whom she is

---

[63] For example, although Smith, *op. cit.*, pp. 218-220 *et passim*, refers to a lack of status differentiation, his detailed descriptions show considerable differentiation.

[64] See, for example, Smith's description (*ibid.*, pp. 169-170) of a formal engagement; Seda's comment that parents may insist on a wedding ceremony (*op. cit.*, p. 293); and Clarke, *op. cit.*, pp. 85-88.

[65] Here the variable of rank is generalized, of course, and Kreiselman's observation (*op. cit.*, p. 278) from Martinique is extrapolated to the rest of the Caribbean.

[66] Cf. Clarke, *op. cit.*, pp. 78, 99; Herskovits and Herskovits, *op. cit.*, p. 84.

[67] Kreiselman, *op. cit.*, p. 99; Herskovits and Herskovits, *op. cit.*, p. 88; Smith, *op. cit.*, pp. 109, 137, 145.

[68] Smith, *op. cit.*, p. 145, makes this point clearly, citing a common statement, "If you want to play a big woman, go find yourself a man."

living, or with whom she has a liaison, her chance of a stable union is low.[69] The decision to marry, within the existing social structure, is his rather than hers, and she gains more from marriage than he does. Consequently, as noted previously, it is the women who press toward marriage, while they must take the only road which can—and, apparently, eventually does—lead to marriage. Meanwhile, however, a woman may have children by several men, and may leave some or all of them with her parents or relatives when entering a new union[70]—a practice often resulting in the "grandmother" family. The widespread adoption pattern in the Caribbean is in part a method of taking care of these children. Ideally, a man wants only his own children in his home, especially if he is marrying.

Summary

Although Malinowski's principle of legitimacy has been called into question by several students of the Caribbean, the detailed descriptions of fam-

[69] At the same time a pregnancy may frighten him away as being too great a burden to assume. Clarke, *op. cit.*, pp. 75, 91, 100-102; Smith, *op. cit.*, p. 138. Blake, *op. cit.*, also reports this fact.

[70] Herskovits and Herskovits, *op. cit.*, pp. 104-105, 131; Clarke, *op. cit.*, p. 91; Smith, *op. cit.*, Chap. 4.

ily and courtship patterns in that area show that it is generally valid. Derived from societies in which conformity to this norm was high, however, the principle requires revision. This should emphasize status placement rather than "paternal protection," and should specify the lower strata as the part of the society in which deviation from the norm is greatest. In addition, revision of the principle should note the weaker norm commitment in these strata, and the resulting lowering of both punishment for deviation and reward for conformity.

The "matrifocal" Caribbean family is a product of an unstable family pattern, in which the mother or grandmother is often in power because no father is there. The courtship pattern is anonymous, so that the young girl must make the best bargain she can, which usually means that she must be willing to risk pregnancy in order to establish a basis for a more stable union. Eventually, most individuals do enter a marriage. The girl is not protected by her relatives or peers in this bargaining. Thus, though the principle of legitimacy is valid, it must be revised. It has also been shown how courtship relations in the Caribbean may lead to a high illegitimacy rate, even when the norm of legitimacy is accepted.

the community

sixteen

Beyond the family and the small group, the most ubiquitous and important social tie is that which links a man to others by virtue of common residence in a "community." When Americans think of relations in their own local community they are most likely to see the problem in terms of "getting on with your neighbors." But our communities are not only collections of friendly neighbors. They are also complex social organizations that control material resources and power, and that often become the focus for intense struggles between factions with competing goals and conflicting objectives. The study of community power structures, and the forces working for stability and change within them, has become one of the most vigorous and exciting areas of sociological work. Peter Rossi here reviews a number of these studies and outlines the main elements we must consider to understand community organization, its stability and change.

Introducing Community Change

PETER H. ROSSI

The title of this paper is in two senses misleading. First, it implies that there is some sort of standard mechanism in all communities which produces the ticking noises we hear when we examine their bodies politic. We are aware of the striking differences among communities; the social forces which they share in common can scarcely be reduced to a machinelike model.

The second sense in which the title

is misleading is its overly ambitious scope. I plan to atone for this deception by discussing some generalizations concerning the forms of decision making in American local communities and indicating what these generalizations imply for techniques of community organization.

These ideas are based on the published literature in this field and data collected by myself and my colleagues in half a dozen studies of communities scattered over the northeastern third of the country.[1] These communities

Peter H. Rossi, "What Makes Communities Tick?" *Public Health Reports*, 77, No. 2 (February, 1962), 117-124.

[1] Peter H. Rossi, "Community Decision Making," *Administrative Scientific Quarterly*, 1 (March, 1957), 415-443; ———, *Industry and Community*, Report No. 64 (Chicago:

vary considerably in size and in economic and social composition, ranging from a neighborhood in Chicago at one extreme to a middle-sized southern Ohio city at the other. They do not constitute any sort of fair sample of United States communities.

Community Social Structure

When compared with the United States community of the nineteenth century, the most striking characteristic of contemporary cities is the relative drop in the importance accorded local government, not only in comparison with state and federal governments, but also in relation to the importance accorded local voluntary associations. To understand what is happening within a contemporary community an investigator cannot confine himself to the official table of organization for municipal government but must also consider a host of voluntary associations which act on behalf of the community and which, with the formal structure of local government, form the basic organizational framework of the local community.

There is no doubt that this is the age of the "community project." Significant community enterprises are often initiated outside the framework of local government, aided and abetted by a proliferation of civic associations and citizen committees.

In many communities the mayor and city council often appear to be dragging their heels while organized prominent citizens exhort the community to push toward progress. The voluntary associations, ranging from the more permanent varieties—the community chest, chambers of commerce, and service clubs—to the *ad hoc* citizens committees, have taken over many of the functions of initiating social change and marshaling community support for such changes that are formally allocated to local government and to political parties. While in many cases these voluntary associations eventually must move local political authorities, the initial spark and much of the task of mobilizing public opinion have been performed in advance by the nonpolitical groups.

My colleague Edward A. Banfield tells me that this is a peculiarly American pattern, not to be encountered in England or in other western nations. In England particularly, local government agencies well staffed with experts are the prime movers of social change in the community.

Another striking characteristic of the American community in comparison with the past is the status gap between the personnel of local government and the local élites of wealth, intellect, and status.[2] The local echelons of the party organizations and the elective offices of municipal, county, and even state governments are manned by persons whose social positions are often several or even many levels below the denizens of the country club, Rotary Club, and the chamber of commerce. The city fathers and the county commissioners are often recruited from among local lawyers of somewhat uncertain income and miscellaneous clientele or from among small proprietors or professional politicians. Money, status, and intellect seem to cluster in one place and po-

National Opinion Research Center, October, 1957), mimeographed; ——— and P. Cutright, "The Impact of Party Organization in an Industrial Setting," in *Community Political Systems*, First International Yearbook in Political Behavior Research, M. Janowitz and H. Eulau, eds. (New York: The Free Press of Glencoe, Inc., 1961), pp. 81-116; ——— and R. Dentler, *The Politics of Urban Renewal: The Chicago Findings* (New York: The Free Press of Glencoe, Inc., 1961).

[2] H. M. Brotz, "Social Stratification and the Political Order," *American Journal of Sociology*, 64 (May, 1959), 571-578.

litical control in another. Such anomalies lead to the hypothesis that things are really not what they seem and that somewhere there are strings by which local government is guided from without.

How things get done has therefore become more and more problematical as the lack of articulation grows between the political élite and the industrial, commercial, and professional élites. It is hard to believe that the corner grocer elected mayor can govern in his own right in a community with branch factories of several national firms, a local élite of some wealth, and several large commercial establishments.

This apparent mushiness to the local community gives rise to problems common to both the community sociologist and the community organizer. It is hard to understand what makes a community tick and it is hard to grasp how to operate the machinery. It is difficult to understand why one community is run with admirable attention to modernization while another, apparently similar, stagnates.

Power Structures

There is a great temptation to resort to the explanation that the ultimate source of innovation and social change in the local community is in either a single individual or in a small group of men. I do not deny that there is evidence that this explanation is warranted in some communities or that some data on all communities tend to support this viewpoint. However, I deny that this is always the case or even that it is the case more often than not.

The existence of power phenomena on the local scene cannot be denied. Citizens are not equally interested and involved in local affairs, and decision makers are not equally sensitive to the opinions of every citizen. It is this inequality of status, wealth, leadership, and involvement which is at the base of community power.

Tied to this inequality are two important issues: first, what accounts for the differentials in effectiveness, and second, over what kinds of decision makers is power particularly effective.

In each of the several communities which we have studied, the wishes and desires of the same types of persons carried particular weight with decision makers. The set of effective power wielders varied somewhat according to the decision maker and the issue. But, in each community it was possible to discern for that particular issue some over-all ranking of effectiveness along which prominent citizens could be ordered unidimensionally.

The way in which the content of an issue determined who would be effective in moving a decision suggests that it would be difficult to define a single over-all pyramidal power structure. Yet, there is an over-all pyramidal structure of power, not of exercised power, but of power potential. In other words, men and social positions could be ranked unidimensionally according to how much weight they could possibly carry, but not according to how much weight they actually throw around. This implies two things: first, the exercise of power is voluntary and some persons of considerable potential elect not to employ it. Second, power rarely is used in all the spheres of community life where it might be employed. In part, this is because partisans seem to specialize in some areas of community life, and in part, some areas of community life are more immune to power.

What are the social positions or the attributes of people who can wield effective influence? Following is a partial catalog of bases of power.

Control over wealth and other resources. This alone is rarely sufficient. Wealth needs to be turned into control over resources or institutions such as banks, land, or mass media that can be used to exercise sanctions or it needs to be accompanied by a tradition of community activity and concern. Thus, in "Bay City," Massachusetts, one wealthy family was powerful because in the past as well as in the present it had contributed heavily to the community by endowing hospitals, playgrounds, and the like, and was recognized as having a claim to be heard. Another family, equally wealthy but without such a history, would have been resented if it had tried to exercise such claims on the community.

Control over mass media. Any newspaper publisher is *ipso facto* powerful whether or not his newspaper wields a great deal of influence with the public. Thus, in a southern Ohio town the newspaper has a poor reputation in the eyes of the public, yet the publisher plays an important role in the community decisions. The controllers of the mass media are in a strategic position because they can either give or withhold attention and approval. These powers are exercised within limits, since a newspaper still must publish some news.

Control over solidary groups. Persons who head cohesive organized groups or who are reputed to have influence over large segments of the public can wield power by threatening to withhold support. Even when support by public opinion is not strictly necessary to the carrying out of a decision-maker role, as in a chamber of commerce campaign to get new industry into town, the threat of withholding public support may be an effective sanction.

Control over values. The social positions of minister, priest, and certain of the professions which are concerned primarily with the interpretation of cultural values wield power by virtue of their right to make value judgments. A minister's moral judgment counts more because this is his specialty.

Control over prestigious interaction. Control over entrée into desirable social circles is an important sanction over the behavior of decision makers. The transformation of a rough-and-tumble labor leader into a tractable and well-behaved member of the community chest board in a large industrial city was accomplished by tempting him into the social circles of high-level management.

In considering this list, it is important to note that it may not be the objective facts which count so much as the reputed facts. For example, the managers of industrial establishments in a southern Ohio city are ranked in power roughly according to the perceived size of each firm. However, size is rarely seen accurately but distorted to fit the rank order of power. Similarly, the Protestant Republican politicians in "Bay City," Massachusetts, saw the Catholic priests as important leaders in the Democratic party who through control over their flocks prevented the politicians' access to the Democratic masses. In fact, a majority of the priests were Republican in their personal political convictions (Bay City Study by J. Leiper Freeman and coworkers, unpublished.)

The manipulation of the appearance of power is, of course, a major technique of the skillful would-be leaders. The source of power which is most easily manipulated in this sense is leadership in organized groups. Few organized groups on the local scene have the power to mobilize public opinion that they are reputed to have.

Who has power over whom? Perhaps the clearest distinction is between the two areas of community life, local government and the voluntary community associations. For local government officials who are ultimately brought to the bar of public opinion on election day, the leaders of solidary groups normally on their side carry the most weight. Insofar as wealth and the mass media are seen as potential influencers of public opinion, they too are powerful. Within the voluntary community associations which depend largely on the bounty of large contributors, wealth and its control play the major role.

Another distinction must be drawn according to types of issues. An issue which divides the community (or which potentially might divide the community, such as integration in public housing or public schools) can be moved to a decision point only by solidary groups. Projects which can be achieved without striking deeply at the gains of one particular group are perhaps best moved by the élite of wealth and status. The best way to get a hospital drive underway is to get together a committee of prominent citizens, but the best way to get a fair employment practices ordinance is to prove that some significant portion of the electorate is for it. This is what is meant by nonpolitical policy issues.

While this diagram of power structures is probably true in a last analysis, ultimate showdown sense, it should not be taken as the norm for day-to-day activities. The potential for power is only intermittently exercised. By and large, a city council goes its own way, the mayor himself makes the major part of his own decisions, the chamber is guided by its full time secretary, and so on. Decisions are made with the potential power structure in mind, but few issues are clear in their implications for the powerful.

A tremendous amount of energy is expended in negotiating consent and support for community projects. The urban renewal of Hyde Park-Kenwood in Chicago, for example, required thousands of hours of negotiation between and among politicians, university officials, community leaders, and downtown businessmen. Much of the negotiation at first glance appeared unnecessary and redundant. The explanation for this activity was the profound uncertainty of the decision makers concerning the ability of individuals and groups to veto the plan. In particular, it was necessary to convince the mayor that no significant group opposed the plan and that positive benefits to the mayor's career could be gained by going along with it. Generally this process consists, in part, of showing that persons in opposition represent only themselves, while the supporters represent widespread consensus among large segments of the population.

The practical significance of this view of community power structure is on a general level. The community organizer bent on getting some change introduced into a community has a wider range of alternative tactics from which to choose than would be possible if a single pyramidal model of community power structure fitted all communities. The community organizer's task is to identify which portions of the potential power structure it is possible to enlist and which would be most effective in moving the community toward a decision.

Two specific tactics are also implied in this model. First, in order to enlist the aid of the voluntary association sector of the local community, it is important to define the issue as noncontroversial and the proposed change as a benefit to all groups or at least a detriment to no groups. Second, it is important to appear to recruit mass support through the aid of reputedly solidary organizations if you want to move local government, and, as a corollary, it is important to move masses of resources if you want to move the voluntary organization sector.

Perhaps the most important task of the community organizer is the negotiation of consent and support from possible sources of opposition. The most successful community organizers whom I have encountered were extraordinarily skilled at this prime task and spent upward of half of their time at it.

Origination of Change

In studying the local community, the topic that engages attention more quickly than any other is how social action, the deliberate changes, comes about.

The first question is where do these changes originate? Typically, there are several sources to be encountered within a community. Individuals in professional occupations centrally concerned with community institutions are a major source of innovations. Part of the responsibility in certain occupations is to constantly propose changes in community institutions. Such professional roles as city managers, school superintendents, public health officers, and the like carry within themselves the notion of constant improvement in services.

For example, the major source of change within school systems stems from the school administrators. School administration as taught within the three graduate schools of education with which I am acquainted is haunted by the dilemma that a superintendent's worth in the profession depends on how many changes he can introduce into his system, but his tenure in the community often depends on completely different criteria. School superintendents and other community professional persons faced with similar dilemmas react to this conflict by an extraordinary mobility rate.

Another point of origin for social action lies in the competition among community leaders. Often enough, local politics appears to be a wild search for issues, with issue after issue being offered up to the public. While few such attempts succeed in capturing public fancy sufficiently to develop into large-scale controversies, this possibility is another specter that haunts every community leader and public official. This anxiety is the ultimate source of the nonpartisan citizens committee and the desire to take politics out of schools, highways, police protection, and the like.

Finally, one must acknowledge the elusive but fairly important role played by general United States value standards. The cult of civic improvement has many devotees in the typical American community. They are found in greatest number within the chamber of commerce and the service clubs. The search for something to do in the way of improvement and amelioration and especially to supply symbols of progress, preferably concrete, provides a constant stream of community projects. Indeed, the demand for community projects is sufficient to support a small industry replete with publications, training sessions, and the like to supply the demand. Certainly the existence of community service organizations like that at Southern Illinois University or at Michigan State University is partially in response to this demand.

Hunter's study of "Regional City,"[3] particularly shows how a group of restless and energetic businessmen spent a significant portion of their time organizing projects to improve their city. In the achievement of an urban renewal project around the University of Chicago, not the least expenditure

[3] F. Hunter, *Community Power Structure* (Chapel Hill: University of North Carolina Press, 1953).

of effort came from the high-level businessmen closely connected with the university.

It is important not to accept a glib but unsophisticated interest explanation for the participation of high-level businessmen in civic activities in the local community. If it is to the interest of business enterprises to expend funds and permit their managers to spend time on community projects, the interest is far from nonspecific to the business enterprise. Furthermore, among those enterprises with fates most closely linked with the local community, the small commercial establishments, civic participation is weakest.

For an explanation of business participation in community projects, it is more useful to look to the social functions of such participation within the business community. Community projects are so much a part of community life, as lived in the middle and upper echelons of the business world, that these projects provide a measure of the prestige positions of firms and business managers on the local scene. Business peers judge the power and prestige of the businessman and his firm in proportion to the importance of their roles in community projects. While the public relations office of the firm may rationalize the expenditure of resources as an investment in community good will, the primary audience in fact turns out to be the rest of the business community; the general public remains virtually unaffected.

In a way, the community chest or the hospital drives are nonwasteful potlatches in which both firms and individuals validate their bids for prestige by the amounts of money they contribute. Conspicuous charity and civic good works in the middle twentieth century have replaced the conspicuous consumption and private piety of the late nineteenth century, aided considerably by the contributions to charity provisions of our income tax laws.

It is characteristic of charities and community projects that those who foot the bill call the tune. These community organizations are not democratic institutions, ultimately responsible to a constituency widely defined. Rather they are ruled by boards and committees who nominate and choose their own successors. Thus a structure of power is more clearly visible in this area of community life than in any other. The boards and committees heavily weighted with large contributors most closely approximate the pyramidal model of a power structure. In this area of community life, wealth and power go hand in hand. Participation in such activities becomes a way of cashing in the resources that one may control, transforming money into prestige. It is this tie-in between prestige and participation in the community affairs which makes it easy to recruit those of high rank in the business and professional worlds to serve on the boards and committees of community organizations.

One latent consequence of this tie-in is that participants in civic activities tend to shy away from the controversial and to stick to things with which no one could possibly disagree. Favorite projects for the chamber of commerce in a southern Ohio community included a clubhouse for youth and rounding up votes for a school bond issue. Nobody in the business community would tackle fair employment laws or even fluoridation for fear that failure of the project would jeopardize the prestige position which participation validates. Similarly, businessmen joined in the fight for urban renewal in Hyde Park-Kenwood only when it was clear that there was no significant opposition to the plan and that the plan would eventually be approved. This pattern is one of the major explanations for the businessman's aversion to politics.

The practical implications of this pattern are considerable. First, it points to a remarkable source of manpower for the citizen committees of community projects. Second, it underscores the necessity for making sure that a project is not going to be controversial if business community support is to be recruited. This gives rise to a new public relations art, that of coopting a sufficient portion of community leadership to take the potential sting out of any proposed community project.

Citizen Participation

Citizen participation is a social invention which is characteristic of United States community life. The idea of ordinary citizens taking part in improving the commonweal is very congenial to our conception of democracy in which superior wisdom is imputed to an enlightened citizenry. According to its proponents, much good is credited to this social invention. A minimum claim is that when the ordinary citizens of a community get together, the final outcome is something that has an easier chance of widespread community acceptance. Some claim that better decisions result. Some extreme proponents have claimed all sorts of miracles; one psychiatrist has claimed that better mental health results in the community when participation really works.

Over the past several years, my coworkers and I have studied the effectiveness of citizen participation in the urban renewal planning of Hyde Park-Kenwood, the neighborhood surrounding the University of Chicago.[4] If ever citizen participation was to achieve its

---

[4] See *The Politics of Urban Renewal, op. cit.*

claimed effects, this was the neighborhood in which success was most likely. The density of liberal, intellectual home owners probably exceeds that of any comparable urban area. In fact, this may be the only urban neighborhood in this country in which intellectuals occupy the highest prestige rank, a phenomenon which results from 85 per cent of the faculty residing within one-half mile of the university.

The area can be characterized as hyperorganized. The local citizens organization, the Hyde Park-Kenwood Community Conference, has 4000 members on its rolls. Block groups affiliated loosely with the conference claim an additional 4000 persons, excluding overlapping membership. Thus approximately 40 per cent of the families in the area are connected organizationally with the conference. Of the nonmembers, "fellow travelers" account for an unknown but undoubtedly large proportion.

The expertise within the membership of the conference is nothing short of fabulous; prominent social scientists, city planners, geographers, real estate moguls, lawyers, all of first rank, are active members and participate vigorously in the conference's many committees. Thousands of man hours and thousands of dollars of foundation funds went into the stimulation and organization of citizen participation in the replanning. Block groups met, considered plans drawn up by professional planners, made recommendations which were carried to the planners, new plans were communicated to the block groups, and so on.

The achievements of the conference must be judged considerable but only in some directions. The plan was changed in numerous minor ways such as which house on a block was to be demolished to provide playground space around a public school. Undoubtedly, the level of anxiety in the neighborhood concerning the meaning of the plan to individual householders was lowered. Intense popular support was mobilized for the final plan. But missing from it were certain points close to the central ideological goals of the conference, such as provisions for middle-income housing and public housing, guarantees surrounding relocations of displaced residents, and the like.

The lesson of Hyde Park-Kenwood for the student of community organization was that citizen participation is a cooptation device which progressively committed the citizens to the plan while their right to dissent was being undercut. This occurred because a large group of citizens, no matter how well trained, working on a part-time basis can only come to a firm consensus on general goals and hence is in an inferior bargaining position vis-à-vis a smaller but full-time group of professionals. (There are, of course, other elements at work in this urban renewal project which complicate the matter and which must be omitted in this short paper.)

The Hyde Park-Kenwood experience raises serious questions in my mind concerning the effectiveness of citizen participation in achieving some of its goals. Grass roots groups like the conference can only react to proposals made by professionals, and, despite the professional competence of members of such an organization, its major function turns out to be that of giving the appearance of consent upward and the appearance of participation downward. While the participation of citizens and their wholehearted involvement made it easier for the plan to be accepted, it can hardly be said to be a plan made by the citizens themselves.

The lesson for the community organizer is plain: the function of citizen participation is to support, not to create. The function of the professional is to create.

Conclusion

In this paper I have tried to draw upon my research experiences to uncover some of the clockwork mechanisms which make some communities tick. There are many brands of clocks in this market, each operating according to somewhat different principles, but just as in the case of time-measuring machines, there are some underlying uniformities.

First, a community is like an iceberg in that the portion which is visible on the surface is only a small part of the total bulk. There is differential influence, power, and authority.

Second, to move the local community toward change from within procedures must be adapted to the various institutions. Politics is the realm of combat and you had better have troops. The community service voluntary areas are the arena of negotiation and some hard cash on your side is handy.

Third, citizen participation is a good way for a professional to operate to get things done, but there is no superior wisdom in the local masses, merely superior strength.

Fourth, the critical role in social change can often be played by the professional who stirs things up, presents, and then organizes mass support.

religion and church

seventeen

Men are oriented not only to other men, but to that which is above and beyond man—to the supernatural. Man's effort to relate himself to the supernatural inevitably involves him in networks of relations with others in more or less formal social arrangements, that is, with *organized* religion. Whereas the psychology of religion has been primarily devoted to understanding its meaning for the individual, sociology has sought to elucidate the significance of religion for the functioning of the social system. The central religious ideas of any group will obviously have an effect on the kind of religious organization they develop. And, as Professor O'Dea makes clear, the social arrangements that characterize any religious community have important implications for the individual's religious experience and for the translation of religious *belief* into religious *action*.

The Social Structure of American Catholicism

THOMAS F. O'DEA

In considering the social structure of American Catholicism it will be necessary to bear two distinctions in mind: the distinction between laity and clergy; and the social distinction between the Catholic community and the rest of the population. First we shall look at the structure of the Church and its lay organizations in this country; second, we shall look at the social stratification of the Catholic population. The second inquiry will concern itself with the distribution of Catholics among the social classes in the country and the social prestige accorded Catholic groups and the various

Thomas F. O'Dea, *American Catholic Dilemma* (New York: Sheed & Ward, Inc., 1958), pp. 109-123.

ethnic groups from which Catholics come.

Within the Church itself there are two definite strata, the clergy and the laity, whose relations to the functioning of the Church—the administration of the sacraments, the liturgy, worship, and the teaching apostolate—are, and have traditionally been, distinct. Rooted in distinctions already to be found in the Gospels, the Acts of the Apostles, and the Epistles of St. Paul, this division into strata had by the second century evolved two recognizable social orders within the Church. Certain specific historical experiences of the Christian body imparted to these concrete social structures a content which tended to increase the difference in function and the social distance between them.

In addition there evolved in time

another stratum within the Church which to some extent cut across the existing strata to create a third grouping. The second and third centuries saw the rise of monasticism. Resisted at first, the monastic order, embodying the counsels of perfection of the New Testament in a life of renunciation of the world, eventually came to be recognized as a way of life superior to that of the world. One result was the tendency for a double pattern of life to be set up, with one, higher, level of spirituality required of [the] religious and another, lower, level required of those "in the world."

One residue of this long historical experience is the attitude which still conceives vocation almost solely in terms of religious or clerical life and leaves the life of the laity in an important sense largely unregulated by the principles which should inform a genuine vocation recognized as such. Another is to be seen in the attitude which would give to the priest or the religious a kind of monopoly of the activities that involve learning and the more serious intellectual and spiritual interests. There is strong evidence to suggest that these two long-term tendencies in Catholic culture continue to prevail in the social structure of the Church. Several years ago a Catholic sociologist made a study whose results showed that Catholics do tend to carry over the paternal relationship of the priest to the layman into spheres where it is inappropriate and may discourage the proper initiative of the layman.[1]

Clergy and Laity in America

The original distinctions, as they assumed institutional form in the second century, tended to make the clergyman the teacher, initiator, and conserver in the intellectual sphere. Monasticism also in time assimilated some share of these functions to itself. In America, where for years the lay Catholic was usually an immigrant, such tendencies could not but gather force. The question therefore arises: to what extent do these distinctions between priest and layman, and the reciprocal expectations derived from them, constitute an element in the problem we are considering?

There is reason to believe that the old expectation that the priest will "know," and that he will take the intellectual initiative when that is necessary, still to a great extent characterizes the relation between priest and laity in the United States. In fact it has been suggested that large numbers of the clergy half-consciously conceive the laity as a kind of spiritual proletariat. They expect little from them in terms of mature Christian knowledge, and in terms of Christian living often not much more than that they will "obey the rules." In some instances which have come to this writer's attention, priests have literally been inhibited from expounding dogma in their sermons by fear of upsetting the faith of the laity. They think it safer that educated Catholics should have only elementary knowledge and immature attitudes in areas where educated Protestants may be well informed—for example, in regard to Biblical criticism. What such priests think the "faith of the laity" *is* in that sense, and what they think it *ought* to be—the real and the latent definitions—would offer an object of sizable dimensions to a research project. Such investigatory efforts will, of course, meet considerable opposition from the kind of priest we have described—from precisely those who need it most. Others whose artificially protected background and excessively formalized training have pre-

[1] John D. Donovan, *The Catholic Priest: A Study in the Sociology of the Professions;* unpublished Ph.D. dissertation, Harvard University, 1951.

vented them from coming to grips with the facts will also resist. Some years ago a study of army attitudes during the Second World War was done by social scientists for the War Department. This investigation was resisted by some army officers on the grounds that "a good officer knows what his men are thinking." This is a typical response from those who feel insecure in any organizational structure. We must expect some analogue of it from certain kinds of clerics. But on the other hand, most will welcome knowledge which will help them and the laity to carry out the Christian tasks that the Church expects of them.

Some years ago a parish priest was shown a copy of one of Father [Joseph Henry] Fichter's studies in parish sociology by one of his assistants who was a student of the subject. Being a gentleman, the pastor merely said, "I hope you do not intend to make that kind of a study here." Yet one might have thought that it is precisely the kind of information a pastor would want to have.

The experience of the Fordham Sociological Laboratory confirms that many pastors have an intelligent attitude toward supporting and making use of such research. But it must unfortunately be admitted that others raise difficulties. Perhaps the favorite approach of this kind is to put forward so-called "theological" arguments. "After all, one cannot study the effects of grace empirically." Such a retort has little bearing on the issue, and one wonders what those priests think has been going on in history, the humanities, and the social sciences for decades. Defensive reactions of this sort tell us much about the latent expectations in some clerical circles; and they also demonstrate how the structure of the clergy, like all occupational and professional structures, can show in places and at times the tendency of the "of-ficeholder" to avoid facing unpleasant facts which may reveal his weakness to himself and his colleagues, even though consideration of them might help him be more efficient in his tasks.

This tendency of many among the clergy to see the laity as needing no advanced religious knowledge—in fact, to feel that it is safer for all concerned if they do not have it—actually does an injustice to the Church. Often the clergyman, busy with his own tasks and conditioned by the selective view of his calling, is slow to see the significance of these issues. I have talked to theologians who, although they thoroughly approve of the new attitudes toward teaching theology to laymen, do not seem at all disturbed that this development should have been so long in coming.

The theological and philosophical preparation of many clergymen has evidently not rendered them aware of what are actually long-term trends in our civilization. Either the fact that it is impossible to produce intelligent Christian laymen without conveying by education an adequate intellectual grasp of Christian thought has never occurred to them, or it has occurred to them but they are opposed to such a course. In most cases the difficulty is the former one, but both offer examples of "clericalism." Clericalism, in this sense, means to be so bound by the status-conditioned view of the office that it becomes impossible to see general problems whole, or with detachment. The result is that the initiative of the Catholic layman may be distrusted by the clergy, while the non-Catholic layman builds a great secular civilization. The problem this presents is serious because it means that members of the clergy so affected have no real grasp of what is going on in the world, no comprehension of what has caused the great setbacks which Christianity has suffered.

Are there perhaps elements in the preparation and formation of the clergy that develop and perpetuate these attitudes? As several observers have already pointed out, the priest is often given a highly formalized education combined with a highly segregated spiritual formation.[2] The consequence may be that little sympathy for the intellectual quest is produced in the student priest, who is thus inadequately prepared to interest himself in and to grasp the problems facing man in the modern world.

. . . The latent level of [the . . . problems which need investigation in connection with Catholic education] will be found to be [most] important, for the attitudes found in the American Catholic milieu generally must to a great extent have their origin in motivations and ideals instilled, sometimes subtly by the very atmosphere, in the elementary school. Is it true that students in the Catholic school tend to feel that because they are taught all or most subjects by a "religious authority" they must accept passively what is given to them? Passive learning, passive acceptance, and memorization appear to play a much larger part than they should in Catholic education in religious matters. Is this carried over into the instruction methods for other subjects? Does our Catholic teaching so combine authoritarianism and the verbal formula as to discourage active inquiry on the part of the student? Is such passivity in religious matters mistaken for faith?—if so, an ironic neo-Lutheranism! Do passivity and the memorization of formulae alienate learning from life for our students?[3]

Does the atmosphere of the school so fill them with oppression that they must seek elsewhere for any of the excitements and pleasures of the mind? Is the Catholic classroom the scene of a joint adventure of teachers and students engaged in confronting God's exciting creation? I am unable to answer these questions, but experience with Catholic faculty members, both clerics and laymen, convinces me that they should be asked and that they deserve investigation. For the Catholic college instructor frequently complains that in all too many cases the attitudes of his students seem to have been conditioned by just such a background as we have proposed for consideration.

A further complication of our problem may be the system of promotions in clerical and religious circles. In every social system we find what sociologists call the institutionalized reward system. There is, moreover, in any institutionalized promotion system, as an unintended concomitant of the very necessary stability that institutionalization provides, a tendency to reward in some form everything that does not threaten the status quo.

A great deal of concrete research in administration has been done by American business organizations precisely on this kind of problem. Certainly the Church will not be any less fearless than such worldly organizations in supporting research to aid its creative self-criticism, as it has already done in the well-known "management audit" of several years ago. Yet too often the very cautious administrative attitudes we wish to study may tend to prevent such study. Some time ago I said to some Catholic sociologists that an important part of any sociological study of institutions was to

---

[2] For a strong statement of this point, the reader might consult the address of Father Gustave Weigel to the Catholic Commission on Intellectual and Cultural Affairs on April 27, 1957. The complete text appears in *Review of Politics* (July, 1957).

[3] For an interesting presentation of this view, the reader is referred to the article on Catholic college education by Daniel and Sydney Callahan in *The Catholic World* (December, 1957).

understand what factors, manifest and latent, affect promotion. When I suggested that this would be a good topic for study in connection with the Church in America, one sociologist who is also a priest agreed but said, "You'll get into trouble if you try to study that." Such attitudes speak volumes if they really are representative of large numbers of administrators.

Related to the problem just discussed is the question of what distortions we have permitted to develop in connection with the conception of Christian obedience. Is it true that in some instances Christian obedience tends to degenerate into the obedience of the military life, or of the unintelligently conducted business firm? I say "unintelligently conducted" because large business shows much more regard for personality factors in the issuing of orders than some of our ecclesiastical bodies seem to do, if some reports are to be believed; and the continuing social science research supported by business in this regard is an important element of the picture. "Seeing Christ in the religious superior" places a tremendous responsibility on the religious superior unless the main purpose of the relationship is purely penitential for the subject. How often in our religious communities are talents in some important field wasted or left undeveloped because the superior must have a teacher of business subjects, to meet a lower-middle class demand, or some minor organization must have an administrator? . . .

One sometimes feels that American Catholicism runs the danger of so overemphasizing the principle of authority as to annihilate the equally vital principle of community which should be its complement. The results of such a deformation can be devastating. Take one example. If a creative theologian should say something that is criticized by authority, this is immediately interpreted by many Catholics—lay and clerical—as meaning that the man, or at least his work, "is condemned." Now since there can be very little creative effort without some error, creativity runs the risk of being "condemned" *per se* in these people's eyes. Thus the equilibrium between Catholic community and authority is destroyed.

When in Catholic society these complementary principles are in balance, the mode of operation is something like this. Between creative thought and authority within the community of the Church there should exist, and essentially does exist, a healthy give and take. Authority is charged chiefly with the conservative function—to preserve that which has been handed down. To creative thought belongs the function of exploring the inexhaustible riches of that deposit and its significance for each succeeding generation. Hence the caution and genuine prudence in the statements of Rome on such problems.

Such a healthy tension between these two principles can become the basis for a creative application of Christianity to every period of history and to every contemporary problem. Yet how is this tension often understood in practice among rank and file in the Church? As a kind of law enforcement —the policeman has apprehended the culprit; the young seminarian has been caught by his superior in an infringement of institutional rules. It is very difficult for even some priests to overcome these immature reactions. The effect is to encourage the doing of nothing, in the creative sense, to make the intellectual quest seem almost sacrilegious. Such attitudes, to the extent that they do in fact exist, will certainly strengthen the tendency to conceive intellectual activity as incompatible with Christianity. They will reward and reinforce inertia. The existence of such patterns is evident, although their full extent can be known only as a result of further empirical studies. . . .

Similar kinds of attitudes are found implicit in the relations between clergy and laity. Father Gustave Weigel has written. "The Americans are also strict believers in the distribution of labor. It seems, in consequence, natural that the priest, one of the people, should lead the religious activities of the people." He points out the way in which American life tends to leave initiative to the expert; how in sports events, the players are instructed in every detail by coaches and are expected to obey these instructions. "Hence, it is not surprising," he continues, "that it works in American Catholicism as well. The modalities of older, European-born pastors who successfully ran their parishes like benevolent despots are no longer popular today and they are a sign of the past. But the modern American pastor does something similar but in a genuinely American fashion. He does not order like a king; he orders like a coach."

Unquestionably such current American tendencies influence parish life, but they build upon the patterns of the past to which Father Weigel alludes. Here we have another example of attitudes from the general American community affecting Catholic predispositions. We saw analogous phenomena in the tendencies toward leveling and the activism which can enter into American Catholic anti-intellectual attitudes.

But it is undeniable that such developments are in marked contrast with other aspects of American life. American soldiers were told over and over again in the Second World War, and there is evidence to support the statement, that the American soldier was capable of initiative and of spontaneously intelligent action when cut off in a small party and isolated from the chain of command. The German and Japanese soldier, according to what we were told, bore a much stronger resemblance to the American parochial situation as Father Weigel describes it than to the American enlisted man and junior officer. He states that "it still remains true that the clergy are all too prone to keep the laity out of tasks of planning, and the laity are only too pliant to accept planning and the competent knowledge for it as the reserve of the priests. There is an energetic passivity in American Catholics, but they are weak in initiative."[4]

American writers and speakers have always attributed the characteristic of initiative to the democratic character of American life and to American free enterprise. Studies in the sociology of business bureaucracy suggest that American businessmen are interested in stimulating initiative and creativity from below and want to understand those elements in organizational structure and bureaucratic attitudes which inhibit it. Catholics can hardly remain indifferent to analogous problems and their solutions.

This lack of initiative which expresses authoritarianism and passivity does not, however, exclude a disregard for genuine authority when it demands initiative and change. "It is noteworthy that up to the present time, the initiative of the Holy See relative to Catholic action and the Apostolate of the Laity has not struck too many sparks on the New England scene," said a recent survey of conditions in that area.[5] "It does seem that Catholics in the Northeast are more reluctant to change established patterns than their

---

[4] Gustave Weigel, S.J., "An Introduction to American Catholicism," in *The Catholic Church, U.S.A.*, Louis J. Putz, C.S.C., ed. (Chicago, Fides Publishers, 1956), pp. 18-19.
[5] Edward G. Murray, S.T.D., "The Catholic Church in New England," in *ibid.*, p. 185.

coreligionists in the Midwest," wrote another observer. "The recent decree of the new Easter liturgy met with slight response in this area, while it was adopted in many dioceses in the West. Generally, the Midwest has taken the lead in the liturgical movement, with Chicago, St. Louis, and St. John, Minnesota, as recognized centers. The same area has been more active in the successful Cana Conferences and Christian Family Movement to promote a spiritual approach to marriage. A recent survey on the teaching of papal social doctrine in Catholic colleges showed that there was a higher proportion of such teaching in the West than in the Northeast. In the whole field of Catholic action, while there would be nuances rather than sharp distinctions, one would discover more conservative tendencies in the East, and greater experimentation in the West."[6] . . .

This area deserves honest investigation and fearless facing of the problems. For some persons, any suggestion of change in this respect arouses the ghost of the old trustee crisis. Yet unless we get more than passivity from the laity, we shall not get spiritual maturity, and without spiritual maturity we shall not produce an intellectual stratum of worth and size.

One recalls the first meeting of President Eisenhower's Cabinet as described in a book published a few years ago. The President, a strong advocate of what he calls the "team," called his Cabinet together to criticize his first inaugural address. When he read it through and was applauded, he responded, "I read it far more for your blue pencils than I did for your applause." He reminded them that "one reason I wanted to read it now is so that you can think it over and be ready to tear it to pieces."[7]

Eisenhower's leadership has been criticized. That of any national leader would be, and in any case not without some justification, for we are all open to criticism. But the President obviously [did] not feel that his constitutional authority [was] endangered by his version of the "team." Perhaps this kind of encouragement of initiative in Catholic circles is even more necessary than in many other groups.

At any rate, the intellectual life is not likely to grow in a situation where community is transformed into bureaucracy and where a clerical monopoly of thinking prevails. Moreover, such clerical monopoly tends to damage the quality of clerical leadership itself. If the laity remain the feet and the clergy the head in terms of constructive thinking, then we shall perpetuate a situation that inhibits the development of intellectual responsibility and creativity on the part of all. Such a condition not only inhibits the development of intellectuals but drives potential intellectuals away from and often into antagonism to the Church.

The Prestige Status of Catholic Groups in the Secular Society

This topic presents another vast research area, and the problems involved will only be sketched here in briefest outline. Professor Kane[8] has shown that American Catholics, despite observable gains, have not shared in the general social mobility to as great a degree as have American non-Catholics. The evidence suggests that Catholics are heavily concentrated in the

---

[6] Joseph N. Moody, "The Catholic Church in the Middle Atlantic Region," in *ibid.*, pp. 192-193.

[7] Robert J. Donovan, *Eisenhower: The Inside Story* (New York: Harper & Row, Publishers, Inc., 1956), p. 2.

[8] John J. Kane, *Catholic-Protestant Conflicts in America* (Chicago: Henry Regnery Co., 1955), pp. 70ff.

lower levels of the social pyramid. This implies that Catholics are not found in large numbers in those social strata whose way of life fosters an interest in intellectual pursuits. For a long period in western civilization, the *rentier* classes have been important in the production of intellectuals. Relatively uninvolved in practical pursuits, with sufficient income and the necessary leisure, and possessing family traditions of culture, such strata offer in many ways the best soil for the growth of intellectually creative individuals.

Although this class is found in greater numbers in Europe than in the United States, it is not unknown in our older metropolitan areas. Catholics are not found in it in any great number, and that is one of the factors inhibiting the development of a Catholic intellectual élite. The upper and upper-middle classes are next in line in the production of intellectually active and creative persons. In these classes also, Catholics are not nearly so numerous as in lower classes.

Upper and upper-middle class families provide about 10 per cent of the children in the United States but send 80 per cent to college. The lower-middle class produces about 30 per cent of American children but sends only 25 per cent of them to college. Classes below this provide 60 per cent of the children but educate only 5 per cent of them in college. Catholics appear to belong mainly to the lower-middle and lower class. This has two meanings: they belong to those classes which produce the largest number of children and which provide them with college education to the least extent.[9]

Thus the position of Catholics in the general American stratification system preserves the picture that we saw earlier in the nineteenth century despite recent social mobility. This fact contributes to the severity of our prob-

[9] *Ibid.*, p. 77.

lem. We must recognize the circular causality involved here. The class milieu has an effect upon the ecclesiastical outlook, as people of lower-middle class origin, clergy and laity, bring the attitudes and latent expectations of their background into the Church and affect Church policies. The resulting policies, by minimizing the importance of the intellectual sphere, inhibit social mobility and tend to keep Catholics in these same classes.

These matters must be given much more attention than they have had among us, and detailed research is of the first importance. Only knowledge and understanding of the concrete situation can enable us to break the vicious circle.

It must be further recognized that in this country Catholics generally descend from ethnic groups whose right to belong has been challenged by nativism in the course of their immigration and assimilation. The resulting lower prestige rating of these groups tends to keep them out of intellectual pursuits which tend to be monopolized by higher-prestige strata. Moreover, their defensiveness can become an obstacle, as we have seen, and their desire to rise quickly can divert them to other ways of life.

One nationality group stands out here as particularly important. The Irish were in many ways the strategic group in relating Catholicism to American life, a fact recorded by all observers of their history in this country. They were the first large group of Catholic immigrants, and in America early arrival has always been of strategic importance. They have produced a disproportionate number of church leaders, priests and prelates. Moreover, their rise to prominence in the Church coincided with a loss in the earlier prestige—tentative though it may have been—that the Church enjoyed in some places in America. It was their immigration in large numbers which fanned the flames of Know-Nothing intolerance. Having come from a background in which Catholicism had been persecuted for centuries and continued to involve legal disabilities, they found themselves here having to defend themselves against native bigotry. Thus the defensive attitude developed in the old country could only be strengthened in the new. The conditions in Ireland had aligned Catholicism in their minds with rising Irish nationalism, despite the fact that the Irish clergy had not always looked favorably upon resistance and reform movements. For the Irishman the sense of Catholicity and of Irishness blended so that his whole conception of his human dignity became involved in his defense of his religion. Perhaps it would not be too strong a statement to suggest that it was his religion that preserved this sense of dignity in the hard years of penal oppression and poverty before his migration and continued to do so in the new conditions across the sea. The Church became for him the institution that enabled him to naturalize himself in this country, and in so doing he naturalized the Church. But he remained partially segregated from important native currents of thought, as we have seen.

The Irish have been the oldest major Catholic group in the United States; they differed from the majority of Catholic immigrants in that they were already English-speaking; they have been dominant in Church leadership; and they have risen in other spheres of life, especially in politics. Yet the Irish have not produced an intellectual group of the proportions which these advantages would have led one to expect. Why is this? Are the Irish authoritarian to the extent of inhibiting inquiry? Are they more dogmatic in nondogmatic areas than others? Has their past of oppression made them more concerned with loyalty than with the content of ideas?

The penal code governing Catholicism in Ireland destroyed for a long time the possibility of lay cultured classes, and to some extent that of a nationally educated clergy. It seems unavoidable that the Irish should have brought attitudes derived from this experience with them to America. To what extent has their experience here modified these attitudes? To what extent is the defensiveness we have been describing attributable to them? And has their dominance in the Church retarded the Church as a whole with respect to the development of a Catholic intellectual life here? Certainly Irish American Catholics (of whom I am one) can openly face these questions, which are being raised by American Catholics who are not of Irish background.

Another important source of difficulties may be found in the background of European priests who came to America in the nineteenth century, especially those who composed the faculties of seminaries. To what extent did these, especially the French, bring to this country attitudes formed in the fierce anticlerical atmosphere of their homeland? Moreover, to what extent did Jansenist tendencies add a disparagement of intellectual activities to the fear of secularism, to make them overdefensive in the attitudes they passed on to their students? The French may in fact have played a double role in this regard, for Irish priests were for generations educated on the Continent, and especially in France. It has been held by a number of students of the period that such priests brought Jansenist inclinations back to Ireland. These questions cannot be further pursued here. Certainly similar questions could be asked of other ethnic groups. Moreover, the peasant background of so many of the immigrants . . . complicates the problems in this area.

From these observations, it is possible to conclude that the status position of American Catholic groups tends to increase the difficulties that we inherit from other aspects of our history. Recent social mobility would suggest that some relief may be granted from that quarter in another generation. But the subject deserves to be carefully studied and research for this purpose to be supported by those genuinely interested in the future prospects of the American Catholic community.

economy

eighteen

Economics is generally defined as the study of the processes whereby goods and services are produced and exchanged. In smaller and simpler societies the economic function is generally less specialized and differentiated from other activities than it is in larger societies. In them it is difficult sharply to distinguish between a man's economic role and his other activities. In the modern world the responsibility for economic affairs has largely shifted into the hands of highly specialized legal persons called "corporations." These have multiplied and grown in size and complexity to a degree wondrous to behold. Ben Seligman presents the major challenges posed for our society by this most remarkable social invention of the modern world. His incisive criticism is in the style of sociological writing that C. W. Mills (Chap. 1) urged as the model for all sociologists.

Who Runs the Giant Corporation?

BEN B. SELIGMAN

In recent years, managerial élites have urgently sought to justify what it is they do. As Wilbert Moore remarked, . . .[1] executives have become worried about the merit of their positions, the salaries they receive but perhaps do not deserve, and the fact that finally they are accountable to no one but themselves. They know that they dispose of vast financial resources and that the economic health of workers, stockholders, and suppliers—as well as entire communities—depends on their decisions. Management, says Moore, is in a "moral crisis."

The older ideology, as reflected in the writings of such economists as

Ben B. Seligman, "The American Corporation: Ideology and Reality," *Dissent,* **11** (Summer, 1964), 316-327.

[1] Wilbert Moore, *Conduct of the Corporation* (New York: Random House, Inc., 1962).

John Bates Clark or Frank H. Knight, now seems inadequate. Clark had announced that by virtue of marginal productivity everyone in society received exactly what he earned, while Knight in his theory converted labor into capital, land into capital, and entrepreneurship into capital, so that in the end capital counted for everything. But all this was too abstruse. The "moral crisis" in the corporation demanded a more supple theory, something not so dense as the Clark-Knight system of apologetics nor quite so rigid as Herbert Spencer's Social Darwinism.

The new outlook started a few years back with books by Adoph Berle, David Lilienthal, and Peter Drucker whose messages were promptly refurbished in *Fortune*. Berle celebrated the soul of the corporation; Lilienthal argued for bigger and better bigness; Drucker turned his lamp on responsibility. And it was amazing how many came away convinced, at least until General Electric, Westinghouse, and few others stubbed their toes over antitrust.

A major theme in this new ideology has been responsibility. The corporation, it was argued, must adapt itself so as to become a domesticated citizen in the contemporary polity. The corporation's very size and its impact on the economy, we were told, willy-nilly enforced proper standards of social conduct. The manager himself, of course, was only a professional, like the nineteenth-century British colonial officer: he possessed certain skills and placed them at the disposal of the ". . . vast clientele he always serves and sometimes leads." He was a highly trained bureaucrat in the best sense, and cheerfully shared the world's burdens.

Frequently, the rhetoric from which these notions were drawn exhibited a defensive and sanctimonious tone. Yet all too often the mood was shattered by such remarks as that of a burgeoning retail magnate who told a reporter some time ago: "We're not going to pay dividends. To hell with the stockholders." Now, this seems to be a truer picture of corporate decision making, for it is self-determined in a manner that locates responsibility in a directorate accountable only to itself. Governance in the corporation, to use Richard Eells' term, is reflexive, that is, it turns inward. The shocked recognition of this seems to have been upsetting to some managerial élites.

How else is one to explain the new corporate literature? Saturated with the message of service, the exploration of "constitutionalism" in the corporation, for example, yet manifests enough buncombe to raise questions of dissimulation. The fact is that those who benefit from corporate affairs are those who shape corporate policy. The literature's purpose is largely to deflect criticism. Here, for example, is Richard Eells, one of the more adroit purveyors of the new corporate ideology: . . .[2]

There is no agreement among corporation theorists as to the definition of terms in the chain of responsibility in corporate governance. *Who* is responsible to *whom* for *what*, and *how* is his responsibility to be enforced? Each of the italicized terms is highly debatable today. As to the first term, the "who" in this formula may refer to board or executive group, or to both. As to the second term, responsibility to "whom" raises arguable issues about the relative positions of various groups of claimants . . . [and] as to the third term . . . one gets answers ranging all the way from . . . maximum profit for stockholders, to the more recent multiple demands of numerous contributor-claimant groups, including the claims of the "general public." As to the fourth term, . . . only the most elementary steps to identify ways and means have yet been taken.

[2] Richard Eells, *The Government of Corporations* (New York: The Free Press of Glencoe, Inc., 1962).

The fundamental issue of control is dissipated in a haze of doubt. Those who bear responsibility for corporate decision making, Eells tells us, cannot be identified. The outcome is to say a corporation does what it does.

Eells, of course, is too astute not to recognize that corporate power must be made to seem legitimate, but his insistence that this requires a "constitution" cannot be validated by parallels with the democratic state, since the corporation hardly can be said to derive its powers from a principle of consent. The fact is that corporate charters are not determined by consensus and in the exercise of authority might does weigh more heavily than right. It is indeed one's location in the corporate hierarchy that determines how power is exercised. To suggest that directors secure their authority from stockholders, or "from society generally," is otiose.

The truth is painfully reached when Eells concedes that corporate decision makers often ". . . create power for the purpose in hand and [then] seek to legitimate the necessary decisions." Yet sheer power has seemed an inadequate base for the illusion of rationality, and so writers on corporations, Eells included, have employed such notions as the principle of balance: the function of the manager, it has been said, is to weigh the contending claims of stockholder, supplier, union, government, and competitor and to parcel out justice to all. But such a version of business democracy sharply clashes with the concession that power is rationalized in *post hoc* fashion. Surely the manner in which the automobile companies all too often have abused their dealers is a better measure of the "balance" managerial élites have had in mind.

A. T. Mason, the noted Princeton law professor, once gave away the whole show, when he said of the welfare state: ". . . [it] must be accomplished under the auspices of competent and efficient business leadership." This seems adequate underpinning for the theme that as long as the corporation is successful, so will the rest of us be. Yet the bitter-end resistance of the big chain stores to the extension of the federal minimum wage law to retail clerks in 1961 suggests how well executives have learned to live with the welfare state.

"Leadership" has become a major preoccupation in the public addresses of such archons of business as Ralph Cordiner, T. V. Houser, and Henry Ford II. (Incidentally, Ford, who has often spoken sternly about corporate men who undermine public confidence, sat stone-faced at a General Electric stockholders' meeting while Cordiner heroically sought to explain away his company's antitrust conviction.) Loren Baritz has demonstrated . . .[3] how much of a fetish "leadership" notions have become among the corporate élite.

But there are still enough executives around who know that the notions of governance, responsibility, and the corporate soul can be overdone. These men, typified by Roger Blough of U.S. Steel, say that the purpose of business is business. They stress the thumbscrew technique in dealing with unions. General Electric, for example, has long practiced through "Boulwareism" a no-nonsense policy that has enabled it to bypass the hundred-odd unions in its plants and virtually dictate bargaining terms. It blends the old paternalism with the new public relations.

Corporate oligarchs have also called into play the behavioral sciences. Personality dynamics, social psychology,

[3] Loren Baritz, *The Servants of Power* (Middletown, Conn.: Wesleyan University Press, 1960).

and cultural patterns have become weapons in extracting more output from workers. The sense of "togetherness" in the plant that the soft sell may create seems to offer just the right mood to frustrate the efforts of the union organizer. Thus, a study of the psychology of rodents can help the manager to manipulate workers to respond properly to appropriate stimuli.

A more elaborate version of this sort of thinking has been developed in recent years by the so-called organization theorists. These writers, e.g., Kenneth Boulding and Herbert A. Simon, insist that their overarching concern is with scientific objectivity, but their ideas can be used effectively to rationalize functioning of the corporation. In organization theory, the corporation is an archetypal structure whose highly integrated and delicately attuned personal relationships demand the elimination of rivalry. Communication is preferred to command. Information must flow through feedbacks to managerial control units. The corporation is seen as a social analogue to the computer. Not only must the productive process be rationalized and centrally directed; the humans themselves must be converted into carefully regulated units of a rigidly defined hierarchy. Since the organization—in this case, the corporation—is a "cooperative system of human activity encompassing psychological, social, biological, and physical relations inherent in cooperative behavior," no deviation from the oligarch's norm should be permitted. The corporate collective now stands as the perfect paradigm for the domicile of an emmet.

The ideological bias involved in these concepts is obscured by an ostensibly neutral or scientific language. The stress placed on manipulative techniques, for example, disguises such issues as the use of hierarchy in sus-taining unequal income distribution. Wages and interest are no longer the outcome of social struggles, as in Ricardo or Marx, but rather "inducements" to complete tasks. Administered prices can be justified by such notable objectives as "desirable levels of internal efficiency." That this constitutes private taxing power, as both David Bazelon and Michael Reagan have demonstrated, is simply ignored. With such formulations, organization theory comes close to apologetics.

Sometimes the whole affair has gone round and round in wondrous circles. Loyalty and teamwork increase satisfaction, which enhances participation, which makes inducements larger, which raises the contribution of work, which reflects an increase in willingness, which leads to an acceptance of corporate goals, which implies loyalty. But, of course, the cost of production could be reduced if satisfaction were available at a low level of inducement: more familiarly, how nice to have lower rates of pay. Obviously, this is an important management goal and if organization theory can show the way, so much the better.

These writings—from the work of Mary Parker Follett and Chester Barnard to James March and Herbert A. Simon—offer the corporate archon a more suitable ideology. By stressing common goals for managers, workers, suppliers, stockholders, consumers—anyone who had anything to do with the corporation—the objectives of the archon become the objectives of all. The problem of power created within the confines of the corporation is dissipated, as it takes its benign and equal place alongside all other groups in society.

Now, it is true that organization theorists are not necessarily liable for the uses to which their scientific ideas are put by corporate ideologues. However, there is not only science but an ethic embedded in organization theory, an ethic that cannot be completely disguised by all the game theoretics and mathematical simulation employed by it. The refined logic has by no means dispelled the aroma of those value judgments that stress harmony and corporate cooperation.

Here then is the new idelogy. But what is the reality of the corporation? Now, there are tens of thousands of these "institutions" inhabiting the economic landscape, as *The Wall Street Journal* never tires of saying, yet only a few seriously affect society and the economy. While only 6 per cent of the corporations reporting to the Internal Revenue Service in 1959 had assets worth over a million dollars, they did account for 70 per cent of corporate receipts. The same few corporations supplied the bulk of the economy's jobs and contributed about 55 per cent of total national income and almost 70 per cent of national income originating in business. All the small corporations and individual proprietorships and partnerships together do not have the impact on our economic and social well-being that a relatively few large corporations have. It is on the latter that the community depends.

Here are some of the giants: General Motors—assets $8.8 billion, sales $12 billion; Standard Oil of New Jersey—assets $10.5 billion, sales $9.3 billion; AT&T—assets $24.6 billion (not counting Western Electric), sales $8.6 billion; Ford—assets $5.1 billion, sales $6.7 billion; Sears, Roebuck—assets $2.5 billion, sales $4.3 billion. All told, there are some fifty names on the billion dollar nonfinancial corporate list for 1961; their sales represent roughly 25 per cent of the gross national product. One might broaden the picture somewhat by taking *Fortune*'s 1962 élite list of 500 leading industrials and the top fifty firms in merchandising, transportation, and utilities. Sales for

this group totalled $337.7 billion or 65 per cent of GNP. (A certain amount of double counting is involved in this arithmetic, but it ought not to reduce the percentage too much. If assets are considered, *Fortune*'s leading corporations, both financial and nonfinancial, may be said to hold perhaps a fourth of the nation's total wealth.)

Such dominant corporations are becoming increasingly important. The elementary fact is that more giants than ever are inhabiting the economic landscape. Fields that were once a haven for small business, such as retailing and service, have been invaded by the giants. In supermarketing, for example, less than 10 per cent of the big chains take in 70 per cent of gross sales. More and more, the small businessman finds it difficult to stay alive: the share of sales made by corporations with assets under $1 million has been declining steadily since the war—from 19 per cent in 1947 to 13 per cent in 1955. It is the huge, sprawling business bureaucracies whose decision makers really move the economy.

How did they get so big? The simplest way would be by an expansion of sales. But this has seldom happened. The most common method for building an industrial empire has been the merger, a device by which business anacondas simply swallow their smaller rivals. Industrial mergers in America came in periodic waves, the first around the turn of the century. Since then, virtually every major enterprise has experienced one or more of these economic fusions. In virtually all instances the motives were purely financial. As one economist put it, ". . . a rising, buoyant securities market made practicable larger and larger units of business enterprise." The archon discovered that really handsome profits might be garnered by selling and buying intangibles, a practice clearly stemming from the changing nature of property itself. And herein lies the reality of the corporation today.

Traditionally, property implied a precise relationship to corporeal objects with an unimpeded right to use, dispose [of], and bequeath real things. As developed by John Locke and in the thinking of the colonists, property meant freedom; it provided a means of earning a living; it meant independence. It gave a man a base from which to speak his piece, a base that was not dominated by either church or state. And it justified Jeffersonian hostility to the corporation, for the latter had been in the main a crown agent and carrier of special privilege. Yet, within three decades of the Constitution's adoption, the corporation had won.

Its legal personality assured by the Fourteenth Amendment and the courts, the corporation lent protective coloration to American industry. Incorporation became an inalienable right, requiring but three names and a modest fee to obtain a charter. Businesses of all kinds and sizes assumed a corporate shape. To be sure, one of the chief attractions was limited liability, restricting the financial responsibility of the "owners" solely to their equity holdings. But the major unintended consequence was to transfer the idea of property from things to pieces of paper. This could be done because in jurisprudence the corporation became a *being*, individual and immortal, and presumably able to manage its affairs as a collective entity and to clothe the spirit of man for all time.

In reality, the stockholders did not own the things that comprised the corporation. A share of stock did not give its holder a right to an aliquot portion of physical assets: it only entitled him to some part of the corporate income, provided the managers were willing to part with it. And if one possessed a share in a holding company, an organization whose assets were merely shares of other corporations, what part of the underlying enterprises did one then own? As the corporation grew and expanded, no one was quite certain who owned what. It was transformed into an institution unto itself, in no way responsible to the shareholder. The latter became less the capitalist and more the speculator whose concern likely was centered on prospective price rises on the stock exchange. The stockholder seldom left a sense of loyalty to the corporation, for he could always sever his connection by simply selling his shares. True, he could vote at the annual meeting, if he got there, but any notion that this would lead to corporate democracy was rather silly, for scattered security holders, whose interest in actual operations was minimal, could exert no influence on internal corporate matters. In fact, most stockholders willingly turned their votes over to incumbent managers through the device of the proxy.

Consequently, there is no need to search for some external principle to justify control, as Eells does in so painful a manner. Boards of directors exercise power because no one else can. As Bertrand Russell once said: "Where no social institution . . . exists to limit the number of men to whom power is possible, those who most desire power are, broadly speaking, those most likely to acquire it." Power in the corporation is now antecedent to profit. Gains are extracted by virtue of strategic control of productive and pecuniary relations; it is no longer a case, as in classical capitalism, of possessing power because a venture is profitable. It is enough to control an enterprise. As a consequence, the nature of the political process in business has been reversed, a turnabout made entirely possible by the corporate proxy! Originally intended as an instrument of convenience for absentee stockholders, the proxy allowed management to perpetuate itself in office.

The new managers also have obliterated the traditional family capitalism of the nineteenth century. Many corporations were once owned by *personal* dynasties: this no longer is the case. The desire to merge and to dominate an industry enforced a turn to the capital markets, resulting for a while in banker-imposed rule. But finance capitalism was surprisingly short-lived, for the new managerial class discovered that with an adequate supply of funds stemming from accumulated profits they could get along quite well without Wall Street tutelage, especially when the corporation itself provided two-thirds of the saving required for investment. (Federal income tax depreciation rules have underpinned a good part of these savings.) Today, it is the paid professional who governs the corporation. In one study of 232 corporate directorates,[4] 58 per cent of board members were classified as executives or former officers while financiers of one sort or another represented but 4.5 per cent and major stockholders less than 20 per cent. It was also evident that the executives had rather small shareholdings in the corporations over which they held sway.

Sometimes a seemingly genuine contest for internal control develops. The solemnity with which these titanic struggles are conducted have all the attributes of a ritualistic dance in which the participants have no freedom to alter preordained motions. The stockholders—allegedly the legal owners—really have little to say about what goes on. The battles for control of the New York Central Railroad, Montgomery Ward, and the Bank of America all looked like political campaigns, with promises of reform, declarations of new deals and new frontiers, and invective against adversaries. Professional proxy gatherers worked like block captains bringing in the vote, while the candidates made grandiloquent speeches.

Power in the corporation, consequently, has little if any relationship to property. Control and expertise are sufficient to legitimate the uses of power. Eells has said quite plainly that knowledge of how a corporation works is a property right which does not demand stock ownership to justify its use. And how right Adolph Berle was when he said that modern capitalism is no longer a system of property relationships, but one rather in which the exercise of power *without* property is the dominant feature. In his words, a relatively small oligarchy of men out of the same milieu, dealing almost always only with each other, and possessing no ownership relation of any sort, represent *the* power center of the corporation. Thus, it is rather a vain hope that the corporation can be "constitutionalized" to make it responsive to the wishes of its "members."

And in fact, it is technically difficult to impose a proper exercise of the corporate franchise. The National City Bank recently listed fifty-six large corporations with more than 50,000 stockholders each, and twenty-seven with over 100,000 stockholders. Democracy in the ordinary meaning of the word, would simply become chaos. The very diffusion of stockholdings makes government in the usual sense impossible. Even the 5 or 6 per cent of stock owners who hold the bulk of outstanding shares are too many to effectively manage a corporation, for they still number over a million persons. Thus, despite some concentration in stock holdings, dispersion is sufficient to create a passive attitude. Further, most stock own-

---

[4] *New University Thought*, 3 (Winter, 1962).

ers are much too concerned with prices on the exchange to be genuinely interested in running a corporation. Besides, such political analogies are false, since shareholders are not the ones governed in a corporation. The governed rather are the direct participants in the economic and industrial activities dominated by the corporation; they are mainly workers and suppliers. It is here that one must begin to talk of democracy in the corporation.

The passive nature of the stockholder, then, allows control to be seized by a managerial corps. Sometimes, more direct devices are employed, as in the case of Sears, Roebuck. In this company, the nation's largest mercantile enterprise, 70 per cent of a $750 million pension fund accumulated since 1916 is invested in Sears' stock, giving the fund more than a fourth of the outstanding shares. This is enough to insure absolute control, particularly when the trustees of the fund are appointed by the Board of Directors of the company itself. It was not until Senator [J. W.] Fulbright questioned this arrangement a few years ago, that employees were allowed to vote for "their" pension trustee. But this in no way has disturbed the self-perpetuating character of the Sears oligarchy. Nor do the voting rights given to future pensioners in similar arrangements in Standard Oil, Union Carbide, or the Celanese Corporation affect the continuing control of managerial insiders, for there would have to be some unity of purpose and some sort of bloc voting for a real change to take place. The likelihood of this ever occurring is dim.

Robert A. Gordon [has] demonstrated . . .[5] that majority ownership was the *least* common mode of control

in the larger nonfinancial enterprises. Minority control was most typical in more than half of the cases studied by Gordon, while stock dispersion was so widespread in another 34 per cent of the cases that management was able to do quite as it pleased.

Might increased common stock purchases by financial intermediaries —banks, insurance companies, investment trusts, mutuals, and pension funds—lead to a new kind of finance capitalism? In fact this is unlikely. True, most of the $30 billion or so of the stockholdings of these institutions are concentrated in a few hundred issues of the "blue chip" variety. But this stems mainly from their search for safety and a good yield. In almost all instances, as Robert Tilove has shown, those who run the "financial intermediaries" usually transmit their proxies to incumbent managements without question. If they dislike what the latter are doing, the stock is simply sold on the exchange. This often does more to rattle a Board of Directors than a threatened proxy fight.[6]

Of course, managers frequently do own stock in their own corporations, yet Gordon's data showed that all the members of his Boards of Directors plus all corporate officers held but about 2 per cent of the voting shares in their firms. In only 20 per cent of the companies studied did management hold more than 10 per cent of voting stock. Mabel Newcomer's *The Big Business Executive*[7] not only verified Gordon's analysis but revealed that

[5] Robert A. Gordon, *Business Leadership in the Large Corporation* (Berkeley: University of California Press, 1961).

[6] *The Wall Street Journal* recently reported several instances in which institutional investors voted against management proposals. This by no means suggests a return to finance capitalism. If the disagreement is sharp, the investor sells the stock anyway. Institutional investors have not yet undertaken proxy contests.

[7] Mabel Newcomer, *The Big Business Executive* (New York: Columbia University Press, 1955).

who runs the giant corporation?   **195**

by 1952, corporate executives owned an even smaller proportion of their company's stock than was the case in the 1930's. This does not mean that officers have no financial stake in their corporations, for 1 per cent of $200 million in outstanding shares is $2 million, and at a 5 per cent yield this brings a neat $100,000 per annum. The executive does indeed have a keen financial interest in his organization, even though he doesn't "own" it. He thus has sufficient reason to welcome the control provided by the modern corporation; when other stockholders try to rebel, he is apt to view their action as a peasants' revolt to be crushed.

This is the reality of the corporation —noncorporeal property, proxies, and the centralization of power. In Michael Reagan's apt phrase, we have now a managed economy in which the central question is: for whom is the managing done? Obviously not for those subject to the archon's power. His rule leads rather to a system of commands and internal sanctions which create a tightly knit operational code. As a result the oligarchs at the top have successfully disenfranchised the mass of stockholders and unless restrained by the countervailing power of a labor union or government agency, are able to injure workers, suppliers, and customers. And contrary to John Kenneth Galbraith's belief, such countervailance is not always forthcoming: as in the case of the electrical conspiracy, "countervailance" often occurs after the damage has been done—if at all.

Joseph Schumpeter, like Galbraith, has argued that bigness in industry has been worthwhile. To Schumpeter, the "creative destruction" practiced by large enterprise acts as a stabilizer for the economy, in that it assures a proper return for a sizable capital outlay. Galbraith has said that only oligopoly—an ugly technical word meaning big business—has been best able to use the unmatched technology with which we have been blessed. Further, corporations are the fount of research and innovation. Yet this seemingly persuasive argument stumbles over the fact that about half the important inventions affecting consumer goods since 1900 have come from the brows of independent researchers working without benefit of a corporate laboratory. Air conditioning, automatic transmissions, cellophane, jet engines, and the quick-freeze were among those that came from old-fashioned inventors or relatively small companies.

To be sure, a fair amount of industrial innovation does today appear as the product of the corporate milieu. But three-fourths of the federal government's enormous outlay for research and development is paid to industry, with much of it directed toward military application. Although the government supplied 56 per cent of research and development monies from 1952 to 1956, 72 per cent of the work was done by private corporations; and if one looks at *applied* research, 75 per cent of the activity is found in the corporation.

But how meaningful is this vast industrial research, amounting to almost $8 billion? Aside from expenditures for defense—perhaps half the research and development outlay by corporations—much of it may be described as glorified waste, the use of scientific techniques for enhancing corporate gain. Much research goes into fancy package design, raising the cost of an item and intended primarily to carve out a little monopoly by making the product unique because it contains some exotic ingredient not found in rival packages. This is then advanced by furious advertising campaigns. Between 1947 and 1957 advertising outlays increased 145 per cent— from $4.2 billion to $10.3 billion, or equal to almost 4 per cent of consumer spending. Moreover, advertising and industrial research often are employed to make a perfectly good product obsolete. This is called "dynamic" obsolescence, and in such industries as appliances and autos it is conceived to be the most noteworthy scientific objective.

It is at this point, in its relationships with the consumer and his family, that the malefic power of the corporation is most clearly exposed. Here countervailing power is utterly absent. Here producer and consumer are revealed as unequal antagonists. One possesses unbounded economic horizons; the other is severely limited in what he can do, dependent on the sale of labor services and subject to ailment and accident. One produces commodities of dubious quality; the other must buy what is available. One is a paragon of efficiency; the other a backward practitioner in the art of spending money. One has vast financial resources at its command; the other, despite the availability of instalment credit, suffers from serious economic disability. One invests in the latest physical equipment; the other frequently is unable to make proper provision for human

capital. One can build new plants in the suburbs; the other must accept such services as the city may offer, and these are usually inadequate. Yet it is the consumer who is supposed to be the beneficiary of what the corporation does. In reality, the consumer has long since lost his sovereignty and his supposed capacity to influence the social and economic order. Estranged from the sphere of production by technology, he has long since forgotten what property means, which itself has been attenuated to the point where it no longer has substance.

Today few persons are able to select alternatives to the estrangement that contemporary economic and political drives impose. Most of them are found in the upper reaches of the corporation; though as propertyless as anyone else, they do possess power and can exercise choice. As C. P. Snow once said in another connection: "One of the most bizarre features of any industrial society in our time is that the cardinal choices [are] made by a handful of men. . . ." And the choice they make frequently signifies disorganization for the great mass of men they seek to control.

the polity

nineteen

The political substructure of society is concerned with the allocation of authority, that is, the legitimate exercise of power. Such authority may be diffused through all levels of society, and is to be found even in the family. Larger and more complex societies, however, develop highly differentiated and specialized organizations which are the main agencies endowed with the right to exercise public power. In democracies the right to such power and its ultimate legitimacy is assumed to rest in the will of the people, and the will of the people is supposed to be expressed through free elections. Understanding the modern polity therefore requires understanding of the forces which govern the outcome of elections. One of the most pervasive determinants of voting behavior is class interest. S. Martin Lipset makes it clear that even in "classless" America, voting is strongly influenced by the socioeconomic status of the voter. The data he presents also serve to give us the main outlines of the system of social *stratification* in American society, relevant to our study of social processes in Part Five.

The Class Basis of Voting in the United States

SEYMOUR MARTIN LIPSET

It often comes as a shock, especially to Europeans, to be reminded that the first political parties in history with "labor" or "workingman" in their names developed in America in the 1820's and 1830's. The emphasis on "classlessness" in American political ideology has led many European and American political commentators to conclude that party divisions in America are less related to class cleavages than they are in other western countries. Polling studies, however, belie this conclusion, showing that in every American election since 1936 (studies of the question were not made before then), the proportion voting Democratic increases sharply as one moves down the occupational or income ladder. In 1948 almost 80 per cent of the workers voted Democratic, a percentage which is higher than has ever been reported for left-wing parties in such countries as Britain, France, Italy, and Germany. Each year the lower paid and less skilled workers are the most Democratic; even in 1952, two thirds of the unskilled workers were for Stevenson, though the proportion of all

Seymour Martin Lipset, *Political Man* (New York: Doubleday & Company, Inc., 1960), pp. 285-294.

manual workers backing the Democrats dropped to 55 per cent in that year—a drop-off which was in large measure a result of Eisenhower's personal, "above the parties" appeal rather than a basic swing away from the Democratic party by the lower strata.[1]

In general, the bulk of the workers, even many who voted for Eisenhower in 1952 and 1956, still regard themselves as Democrats, and the results of the 1954 and 1958 congressional elections show that there has been no shift of the traditional Democratic voting base to the Republicans. Two-thirds of the workers polled by Gallup in 1958 voted for a Democrat for Congress.

The same relationship between class, considered now as a very general differentiating factor, and party support exists within the middle and upper classes. The Democrats have been in a minority among the nonmanual strata, and, except among the intellectual professions, the Democratic proportion of the nonmanually occupied electorate

[1] See Herbert Hyman and Paul B. Sheatsley, "The Political Appeal of President Eisenhower," *Public Opinion Quarterly*, **17** (1953), 443-460. They demonstrate this on the basis of poll results from 1947-48, which already indicated that Eisenhower could win the presidency under the banner of either party.

TABLE 1	Per Cent Republican Voting or Voting Preference Among Occupational Groups and Trade Union Members[*]				
	1940	1948	1952	1954	1956
Business and professional	64	77	64	61	68
White collar workers	52	48	60	52	63
Manual workers (skilled and unskilled)	35	22	45	35	50
Farmers	46	32	67	56	54
Trade union members	28	13	39	27	43

[*] The 1940 figures represent pre-election voting preferences, and are recomputed from Hadley Cantril, *Public Opinion, 1935-1946* (Princeton: Princeton University Press, 1951), p. 602. Since the number of cases is not given in the table, estimates from census data on the relative proportion of persons in a given occupational category were made to facilitate the combination of several of them. The 1948 figures represent the actual voting reported by a national random sample, and are taken from Angus Campbell, Gerald Gurin, and Warren E. Miller, *The Voter Decides* (New York: Harper & Row, Publishers, Inc., 1954) pp. 72-73. The remaining data may be found in an American Institute of Public Opinion news release, October 12, 1958, and also represent actual voting results.

TABLE 2	Relationship Between Size of Firm and Political Party Allegiances of Corporation Executives—1955[*]		
Size of Firm	Repub-lican	Demo-cratic	Inde-pendent
More than 10,000 workers	84%	6%	10%
1000-9999	80	8	12
100-999	69	12	19

[*] Data supplied to author through the courtesy of the Center for International Studies of the Massachusetts Institute of Technology.

declines inexorably with income and occupational status to the point where, according to one study, only 6 per cent of the heads of corporations with more than 10,000 employees are Democrats. Perhaps the best single example of the pervasiveness of status differences as a factor in American politics is the political allegiances of the chief executives of major American corporations. This study, done in 1955 by the Massachusetts Institute of Technology's Center for International Studies, and based on interviews with a systematic sample of 1000 such men, found that even within this upper economic group, the larger the company of which a man was an officer, the greater the likelihood that he was a Republican (see Table 2).

Consistent with these findings are the popular images of typical supporters of each party. The Gallup Poll, shortly before the 1958 congressional elections, asked a nationwide sample what their picture of the typical Democrat was, and received these answers most frequently: "middle class . . . common people . . . a friend . . . an ordinary person . . . works for his wages . . . average person . . . someone who thinks of everybody." The typical Republican, in contrast, is "better class . . . well-to-do . . . big businessman . . . money voter . . . well-off financially . . . wealthy . . . higher class."[2]

All in all, public opinion poll evidence confirms the conclusion reached by the historian Charles Beard in 1917 that "the center of gravity of wealth is on the Republican side while the center of gravity of poverty is on the Democratic side."[3] Beard's conclusions were based on an inspection of the characteristics of various geographical areas, and more recent studies using

[2] American Institute of Public Opinion news release, November 2, 1958. See Angus Campbell, Gerald Gurin, and Warren E. Miller, *The Voter Decides* (New York: Harper & Row, Publishers, Inc., 1954), p. 211, for the 1952 electorate's perception of the support of each party.

[3] Quote is cited by V. O. Key, Jr., in his *Politics, Parties, and Pressure Groups*, 4th ed. (New York: Thomas Y. Crowell Co., 1958), p. 235.

this ecological approach report similar findings. Thus the Harvard political scientist Arthur Holcombe found that among urban congressional districts, "the partisan pattern is the same. The only districts which have been consistently Republican for a considerable period of time are those with the highest rents. . . . The districts which have been most consistently Democratic are those with the lowest rents. . . . The districts with a preponderance of intermediate rents are the districts which have been most doubtful from the viewpoint of the major parties."[4] A detailed survey of party registrations in 1934 in the then strongly Republican Santa Clara County (suburban San Francisco) found a strong correlation between high occupational position and being a registered Republican. About 75 per cent of plant superintendents, bankers, brokers, and managers of business firms identified publicly with the G.O.P., as contrasted with 35 per cent of the cannery and other unskilled workers. Within each broad occupational group, property owners were much more likely to be registered Republicans than those who did not own property.[5]

Although most generalizations about the relationship of American parties to class differences are based on the variations in the backgrounds of their respective electorates, there is some as yet skimpy evidence that the same differences exist on the leadership level,

particularly in the local community. A study of the backgrounds of candidates for nomination for county office in local primaries in three counties in Indiana indicates a close correspondence between the characteristics of leaders and voters. While 76 per cent of those seeking Republican nominations were in professional or business-managerial occupations, 42 per cent of the Democratic aspirants were manual workers (see Table 3). In Milwaukee, Wisconsin, 54 per cent of the officers of the local Democratic party were manual workers or in sales and clerical positions. By contrast these groups represented only 10 per cent among the Republicans, whose leaders were largely professionals or ran business firms.[6]

The relationship of socioeconomic position to political behavior in America as elsewhere is reinforced by religious and ethnic factors. Surveys

TABLE 3   Occupational Backgrounds of Candidates for Nominations for County Office in Three Indiana Counties—1954[*]

OCCUPATION	REPUBLICAN		DEMOCRATIC	
	Number	Per Cent	Number	Per Cent
Professional	23	25.8	17	17.7
Managerial	45	50.6	25	26.0
Clerical-sales	8	9.0	10	10.4
Manual workers	11	12.4	40	41.7
Others	2	2.2	4	4.2
Totals	89	100.0	96	100.0

[*] Frank Munger, Two-Party Politics in the State of Indiana, Harvard University, unpublished M.S. thesis (1955), p. 275; cited in V. O. Key, Jr., op. cit., p. 240.

indicate that, among the Christian denominations, the higher the average income of the membership of a given

[4] Arthur Holcombe, Our More Perfect Union (Cambridge, Mass.: Harvard University Press, 1950), p. 135. See also Samuel Lubell, The Future of American Politics (New York: Doubleday & Co., 1956), pp. 51-55, and Duncan MacRae, Jr., "Occupations and the Congressional Vote, 1940-1950," American Sociological Review, 20 (1955), 332-340.

[5] Dewey Anderson and Percy E. Davidson, Ballots and the Democratic Class Struggle (Stanford: Stanford University Press, 1943), pp. 118-147.

[6] Leon D. Epstein, Politics in Wisconsin (Madison: University of Wisconsin Press, 1938), p. 186.

church group, the more likely its members are to vote Republican. If Christian religious groups in the United States are ranked according to the average socioeconomic status of their membership, they are, reading from high to low, Congregational, Presbyterian, Episcopal, Methodist, Lutheran, Baptist, and Catholic—and this rank order is identical to the one produced when the denominations are ranked by propensity to vote Republican. This suggests that socioeconomic status, rather than religious ideas, is the prime determinant of political values among different denominations. The fact that the Jews, who are one of the wealthiest religious groups in America, are shown by survey data to be most Democratic is probably due . . . to their sensitivity to ethnic discrimination and their lack of effective social intercourse with the upper-status groups in America. But religious beliefs or loyalties, and the political values associated with them, nevertheless seem to have some independent effect on voting behavior. Working-class Protestants belonging to the Congregational or Presbyterian churches are more likely to be Republicans than workers who are Baptist or Catholic. Conversely, wealthy Baptists or Catholics are more apt to be Democrats than equally rich Congregationalists or Episcopalians are.[7]

Roughly speaking, the same differences appear between ethnic groups. Anglo-Saxons are more likely to be Republican than other Americans in the same class position who have a more recent immigrant background. Thus if an individual is middle class, Anglo-Saxon, and Protestant, he is very likely to be a Republican, whereas if he is working class, Catholic, and of recent immigrant stock, he will probably be a Democrat.

Even before the development of the two-party system in its present form, the political issues dividing the society tended to have a class character. Free public schools, for example, did not emerge naturally and logically from the structure and values of American society. Rather, as one historian of American education, Ellwood P. Cubberley, has pointed out: "Excepting for the battle for the abolition of slavery, perhaps no question has ever been before the American people for settlement which caused so much feeling or aroused such bitter antagonism."[8] In large part it was a struggle between liberals and conservatives in the modern sense of the term, although religious issues also played a strong role. "The friends of free schools were at first commonly regarded as fanatics, dangerous to the states, and the op-

[7] For a general study of the politics of the Jews, see Lawrence H. Fuchs, *The Political Behavior of American Jews* (New York: The Free Press of Glencoe, Inc., 1956). See also Werner Cohn, "The Politics of the Jews," in Marshall Sklare, ed., *The Jews: Social Patterns of an American Group* (New York: The Free Press of Glencoe, Inc., 1958), pp. 614-626. See Wesley and Beverly Allinsmith, "Religious Affiliation and Political-Economic Attitudes," *Public Opinion Quarterly*, 12 (1948), 377-389; Paul F. Lazarsfeld, Bernard Berelson, and Hazel Gaudet, *The People's Choice* (New York: Columbia University Press, 1948), p. 22; W. F. Ogburn and N. S. Talbot, "A Measurement of the Factors in the Presidential Election of 1928," *Social Forces*, 8 (1929), 175-183; H. F. Gosnell, *Grass Roots Politics* (Washington: American Council on Public Affairs, 1942), pp. 17, 33-34, 55, 102; S. J. Korchin, *Psychological Factors in the Behavior of Voters*, Harvard University, unpublished Ph.D. thesis (1946), Chap. 5; Louis Harris, *Is There a Republican Majority?* (New York: Harper & Row, Publishers, Inc., 1954), p. 87; A. Campbell, G. Gurin, and W. Miller, *op. cit.*, pp. 71, 79; Bernard Berelson, Paul Lazarsfeld, and William McPhee, *Voting* (Chicago: University of Chicago Press, 1954), pp. 64-71; and Oscar Glantz, "Protestant and Catholic Voting Behavior," *Public Opinion Quarterly*, 23 (1959), 73-82.

[8] Ellwood P. Cubberley, *Public Education in the United States* (Boston: Houghton Mifflin Co., 1954), p. 164.

ponents of free schools were considered by them as old line conservatives or as selfish members of society."[9] Among the arguments presented for free education was that "a common state school, equally open to all, would prevent that class differentiation so dangerous in a republic"; while opponents of such schools argued that they "will make education too common, and will educate people out of their proper station in society . . . [and will] break down long-established and very desirable social barriers."[10] On one side of the issue were the poorer classes; on the other, "the old aristocratic class . . . the conservatives of society . . . taxpayers."[11]

Perhaps no better comment on the meaning of American politics has ever been made than Tocqueville's observation in 1830 about the prominent struggle between aristocracy and democracy:

To a stranger all the domestic controversies of the Americans at first appear to be incomprehensible or puerile, and he is at a loss whether to pity people who take such arrogant trifles in good earnest or to envy that happiness which enables a community to discuss them. But when he comes to study the secret propensities that govern the factions of

America, he easily perceives that the greater part of them are more or less connected with one or the other of those two great divisions which always existed in free communities. *The deeper we penetrate into the inmost thoughts of these parties, the more we perceive that the object of the one is to limit and that of the other to extend the authority of the people.* I do not assert that the ostensible purpose or even that the secret aim of American parties is to promote the rule of aristocracy in the country; but I affirm that aristocratic or democratic passions may be easily detected at the bottom of all parties, and that, although they escape a superficial observation, they are the main points and soul of every faction in the United States.[12]

The relationship between status or class position (as indicated by the three criteria of economic position, religion, and ethnic background) and party loyalty is thus not a new development in American history. Studies of the social bases of the Federalists, America's first conservative party, and the Jeffersonian Democrats in the late eighteenth and early nineteenth centuries indicate that they corresponded closely to the bases of the modern Republicans and Democrats, respectively. The Federalists were backed by the well-to-do farmers, urban merchants, persons of English extraction, and members of such high-status churches as the Congregationalists and the Episcopalians.[13] The Democrats were supported by urban workers, poorer farmers, persons of non-English

[9] *Ibid.*, p. 164.
[10] *Ibid.*, p. 166.
[11] *Ibid.*, pp. 164-165. "The scheme of Universal Equal Education at the expense of the State is virtually 'Agrarianism.' It would be a compulsory application of the means of the richer for the direct use of the poorer classes, and so far an arbitrary division of property among them. . . . Authority—that is, the State—is to force the more eligibly situated citizens to contribute a part of their means for the accommodation of the rest, and this is equivalent to an actual compulsory partition of their substance." Editorial in the *Philadelphia National Gazette* (August 19, 1830), cited in Cubberley, *op. cit.*, p. 182. This indicates that the issue was seen as a left-right one, in the classic economic sense.

[12] Alexis de Tocqueville, *Democracy in America*, Vol. I (New York: Vintage Books, 1955), pp. 185-186 (emphasis added); for similar comments see Harriet Martineau, *Society in America*, Vol. I (London: Saunders and Otley, 1837), pp. 10ff.; and Thomas Hamilton, *Men and Manners in America*, Vol. I (London: T. Cadell, 1833), p. 288.
[13] Manning Dauer, *The Adams Federalists* (Baltimore: The Johns Hopkins University Press, 1953), pp. 24-27, 263.

background such as the Scotch-Irish, and members of the (then) poorer churches like the Presbyterians and the Catholics. The second conservative party, the Whigs, who fought the Democrats from 1836 to 1852, derived their strength from the same group as the Federalists, while the Democrats retained the groups which had backed Jefferson, and added most of the great wave of European immigrants.

Although the Republican party is often thought of as a newly created antislavery party, the research on the pre-Civil War period suggests that it inherited both the support and leadership of the northern Whigs. A detailed study of voting behavior in New York State before the Civil War shows that the Democrats kept their urban lower-class, Catholic, and immigrant support.[14]

The evidence compiled by various social scientists indicates that the men of wealth and economic power in America have *never* given more than minority support to the Democrats. Dixon Ryan Fox, an analyst of New York politics in the first half of the nineteenth century, gathered considerable statistical data which show that the upper-class districts of the various cities of the state voted Federalist and Whig.[15] He quotes a biographer of the wealthy merchants of New York who wrote in the 1860's:

It is a very common fact that for thirty-four years [since the revival of two-party politics in 1828] very few merchants of the first class have been Democrats. The mass of large and little merchants have, like a flock of sheep, gathered either in the Federalist, Whig, Clay, or Republican folds. The Democratic merchants

[14] Research is in process by Lee Benson of the Center for Advanced Study in the Behavioral Sciences.

[15] Dixon Ryan Fox, *The Decline of Aristocracy in the Politics of New York* (New York: Columbia University Press, 1919).

could have easily been stored in a large Eighth Avenue railroad car.[16]

A recent study by Mabel Newcomer of the political views of large business executives in 1900, 1925, and 1950 reports that in all three periods about three quarters of this group were Republicans. Even in 1925, a period not normally considered to be one of political class conflict in America, only 19 per cent of the executives were Democrats. These data certainly underestimate the Republican majority among business executives, since they are based on public party enrollment rather than voting preference and include many registered as southern Democrats who would be Republicans if they were not living in a one-party region.[17]

TABLE 4[°]   Per Cent Democratic Preferences Among St. Paul's School Students

1888	35
1892	37
1900	19
1904	—
1908	17
1912	37
1916	23
1920	13
1924	16
1928	24
1932	18

[°] Recomputed from Arthur S. Pier, *St. Paul's School, 1855-1934* (New York: Charles Scribner's Sons, 1934), p. 181. The original figures are also to be found in E. Digby Baltzell, *Philadelphia Gentlemen* (New York: The Free Press of Glencoe, Inc., 1958), p. 316.

[16] W. Barrett, *Old Merchants of New York*, Vol. I, p. 81, cited in Fox, *op. cit.*, p. 426.

[17] Mabel Newcomer, *The Big Business Executive* (New York: Columbia University Press, 1955), p. 49. In 1928 a survey of those listed in *Who's Who* found that 87 per cent favored Herbert Hoover for President. See Jean-Louis Sevrin, *La Structure interne des partis politiques americains* (Paris: Librairie Armand Colin, 1953), p. 58.

As a final note on the lack of support for the Democrats among the upper class, the straw votes cast for President by the boys attending St. Paul's School, an upper-class private boarding school, are of some interest. From 1888 to 1932 the Republican candidates consistently received the overwhelming majority (see Table 4). Even the conservative Grover Cleveland only secured 35 per cent of the vote of these teen-age scions of the upper class.

Part 5

processes
in
social
systems

One of the persistent dichotomies in sociological thinking is that between the static and dynamic or the structural and the processual. Many a sociologist has gotten himself hopelessly entangled in trying to make clear just what he means by the distinction, yet its perennial character suggests that it springs from something deeply rooted. Whereas structural analysis defines the elements of a social system and the formal relations which bind one status to another, process analysis seeks to describe what actually takes place in the complex web of human interaction. Structures are more or less specific and limited, whereas processes cut across institutions. Certain processes, such as conflict, may be observed in any institution, whereas others, such as diffusion, may be manifested mainly in the relations among a set of institutions.

The classic mode of sociological analysis gave more attention to social processes than to the institutional settings in which they were manifested. Indeed some of the nineteenth-century sociologists argued that it was only in the study of processes, such as cooperation and competition, imitation and diffusion, immigration and assimilation, that sociology could find a subject matter unique to it and not covered by the disciplines concerned with specific institutional realms, such as the economy and the polity. Of the many processes which we might examine, I have chosen in this part to illustrate four which continue to be of major interest in contemporary sociology—conformity, deviance, the related processes of conflict and accommodation, and the ubiquitous theme of social change. But numerous other items in this collection of readings also deal more or less systematically with major social processes. For example, the process of stratification is treated in Lipset's contribution on the class basis of voting in the United States (Chap. 19); conflict is the main concern of L. F. Richardson's piece on the statistics of deadly quarrels (Chap. 26); conformity is the object of study in Asch's research on the effects of group pressure (Chap 20); and socialization is discussed in Aberle and Naegele's study of the middle-class father (Chap. 10).

conformity

twenty

Conformity may well be the most important of all social processes. What gives society structure and provides the indispensable condition of social order is the fact that most individuals conform reasonably well to the expectations laid on them by virtue of the positions they occupy in the social system. Conformity can be won by coercion and the fear of punishment, but no society can rely on this alone unless it is prepared to have every other man a policeman. And then who will police the policemen? Ultimately conformity must rest on a psychosocial condition, the motive, or disposition, to act in accord with the social norms which society seeks to internalize in each of us through the process of socialization. But what then of creative innovation and personal autonomy? David Riesman has made America acutely aware that there is such a thing as a people who conform too well. There are, he argues, many people with a "radar" inside who are mainly tuned into the desires of others. In a now classic experiment, Solomon Asch explores the social conditions under which people can be made to conform so well that they deny the very evidence of their senses. He also calls our attention to the possibility that there is a distinctive conformist personality type.

The Effects of Group Pressure

S. E. ASCH

We shall here describe in summary form the conception and first findings of a program of investigation into the conditions of independence and submission to group pressure.[1]

Our immediate object was to study the social and personal conditions that induce individuals to resist or to yield to group pressures when the latter are perceived to be *contrary to fact*. The issues which this problem raises are of obvious consequence for society; it can be of decisive importance whether or

[1] The earlier experiments out of which the present work developed and the theoretical issues which prompted it are discussed in S. E. Asch, *Social Psychology* (Englewood Cliffs, N.J.: Prentice-Hall, Inc., 1952), Chap. 16. . . .

Based upon data originally reported in S. E. Asch, "Effects of Group Pressure upon the Modification and Distortion of Judgments," in Harold Guetzkow, ed., *Groups, Leadership, and Men* (New York: Russell & Russell, Inc., 1963).

not a group will, under certain conditions, submit to existing pressures. Equally direct are the consequences for individuals and our understanding of them, since it is a decisive fact about a person whether he possesses the freedom to act independently, or whether he characteristically submits to group pressures.

The problem under investigation requires the direct observation of certain basic processes in the interaction between individuals, and between individuals and groups. To clarify these seems necessary if we are to make fundamental advances in the understanding of the formation and reorganization of attitudes, of the functioning of public opinion, and of the operation of propaganda. Today we do not possess an adequate theory of these central psycho-social processes. Empirical investigation has been predominantly controlled by general propositions concerning group influence which have as a rule been assumed but not tested. With few exceptions investigation has relied upon descriptive formulations concerning the operation of suggestion and prestige, the inadequacy of which is becoming increasingly obvious, and upon schematic applications of stimulus-response theory.

Basic to the current approach has been the axiom that group pressures characteristically induce psychological changes *arbitrarily*, in far-reaching disregard of the material properties of the given conditions. This mode of thinking has almost exclusively stressed the slavish submission of individuals to group forces, has neglected to inquire into their possibilities for independence and for productive relations with the human environment, and has virtually denied the capacity of men under certain conditions to rise above group passion and prejudice. It was our aim to contribute to a clarification of these questions, important both for theory and for their human implications, by means of direct observation of the effects of groups upon the decisions and evaluations of individuals.

The Experiment and First Results

To this end we developed an experimental technique which has served as the basis for the present series of studies. We employed the procedure of placing an individual in a relation of radical conflict with all the other members of a group, of measuring its effect upon him in quantitative terms, and of describing its psychological consequences. A group of eight individuals was instructed to judge a series of simple, clearly structured perceptual relations—to match the length of a given line with one of three unequal lines. Each member of the group announced his judgments publicly. In the midst of this monotonous "test" one individual found himself suddenly contradicted by the entire group, and this contradiction was repeated again and again in the course of the experiment. The group in question had, with the exception of one member, previously met with the experimenter and received instructions to respond at certain points with wrong—and unanimous—judgments. The errors of the majority were large (ranging between one-half and one and three-quarters inch) and of an order not encountered under control conditions. The outstanding person—the critical subject—whom we had placed in the position of a *minority of one* in the midst of a *unanimous majority*—was the object of investigation. He faced, possibly for the first time in his life, a situation in which a group unanimously contradicted the evidence of his senses.

This procedure was the starting point of the investigation and the point of departure for the study of further problems. Its main features were the following: (1) The critical subject was submitted to two contradictory and irreconcilable forces—the evidence of his own experience of a clearly perceived relation, and the unanimous evidence of a group of equals. (2) Both forces were part of the immediate situation; the majority was concretely present, surrounding the subject physically. (3) The critical subject, who was requested together with all others to state his judgments publicly, was obliged to declare himself and to take a definite stand vis-à-vis the group. (4) The situation possessed a self-contained character. The critical subject could not avoid or evade the dilemma by reference to conditions external to the experimental situation. (It may be mentioned at this point that the forces generated by the given conditions acted so quickly upon the critical subjects that instances of suspicion were infrequent.)

The technique employed permitted a simple quantitative measure of the "majority effect" in terms of the frequency of errors in the direction of the distorted estimates of the majority. At the same time we were concerned to obtain evidence of the ways in which the subjects perceived the group, to establish whether they became doubtful, whether they were tempted to join the majority. Most important, it was our object to establish the grounds of the subject's independence or yielding —whether, for example, the yielding subject was aware of the effect of the majority upon him, whether he abandoned his judgment deliberately or compulsively. To this end we constructed a comprehensive set of questions which served as the basis of an individual interview immediately following the experimental period. Toward the conclusion of the interview each subject was informed fully of the purpose of the experiment, of his role and of that of the majority. The reactions to the disclosure of the purpose

TABLE 1   Lengths of Standard and Comparison Lines

Trial	Length of Standard Line (in Inches)	Comparison Lines (in Inches)			Correct Response	Group Response	Majority Error (in Inches)
		1	2	3			
1	10	8¾	10	8	2	2	—
2	2	2	1	1½	1	1	—
3	3	3¾	4¼	3	3	1*	+¾
4	5	5	4	6½	1	2*	−1.0
5	4	3	5	4	3	3	—
6	3	3¾	4¼	3	3	2*	+1¼
7	8	6¼	8	6¾	2	3*	−1¼
8	5	5	4	6½	1	3*	+1½
9	8	6¼	8	6¾	2	1*	−1¾
10	10	8¾	10	8	2	2	—
11	2	2	1	1½	1	1	—
12	3	3¾	4¼	3	3	1*	+¾
13	5	5	4	6½	1	2*	−1.0
14	4	3	5	4	3	3	—
15	3	3¾	4¼	3	3	2*	+1¼
16	8	6¼	8	6¾	2	3*	−1¼
17	5	5	4	6½	1	3*	+1½
18	8	6¼	8	6¾	2	1*	−1¾

° Starred figures designate the erroneous estimates by the majority.

of the experiment became in fact an integral part of the procedure. The information derived from the interview became an indispensable source of evidence and insight into the psychological structure of the experimental situation, and in particular, of the nature of the individual differences. It should be added that it is not justified or advisable to allow the subject to leave without giving him a full explanation of the experimental conditions. The experimenter has a responsibility to the subject to clarify his doubts and to state the reasons for placing him in the experimental situation. When this is done most subjects react with interest, and some express gratification at having lived through a striking situation which has some bearing on them personally and on wider human issues.

Both the members of the majority and the critical subjects were male college students. We shall report the results for a total of fifty critical subjects in this experiment. In Table 1 we summarize the successive comparison trials and the majority estimates. The reader will note that on certain trials the majority responded correctly; these were the "neutral" trials. There were twelve critical trials on which the responses of the majority responded incorrectly.

The quantitative results are clear and unambiguous.

1. There was a marked movement toward the majority. One third of all the estimates in the critical group were errors identical with or in the direction of the distorted estimates of the majority. The significance of this finding becomes clear in the light of the virtual absence of errors in the control group, the members of which recorded their estimates in writing. The relevant data of the critical and control groups are summarized in Table 2.

2. At the same time the effect of the majority was far from complete.

TABLE 2   Distribution of Errors in Experimental and Control Groups

Number of Critical Errors	Critical Group* (N = 50) F	Control Group (N = 37) F
0	13	35
1	4	1
2	5	1
3	6	
4	3	
5	4	
6	1	
7	2	
8	5	
9	3	
10	3	
11	1	
12	0	
Total	50	37
Mean	3.84	0.08

* All errors in the critical group were in the direction of the majority estimates.

The preponderance of estimates in the critical group (68 per cent) was correct despite the pressure of the majority.

3. We found evidence of extreme individual differences. There were in the critical group subjects who remained independent without exception, and there were those who went nearly all the time with the majority. (The maximum possible number of errors was 12, while the actual range of errors was 0–11.) One fourth of the critical subjects was completely independent; at the other extreme, one third of the group displaced the estimates toward the majority in one half or more of the trials.

The differences between the critical subjects in their reactions to the given conditions were equally striking. There were subjects who remained completely confident throughout. At the other extreme were those who became disoriented, doubt-ridden, and experienced a powerful impulse not to appear different from the majority.

For purposes of illustration we include a brief description of one independent and one yielding subject.

Independent

After a few trials he appeared puzzled, hesitant. He announced all disagreeing answers in the form of "Three, sir; two, sir"; not so with the unanimous answers on the neutral trials. At Trial 4 he answered immediately after the first member of the group, shook his head, blinked, and whispered to his neighbor: "Can't help it, that's one." His later answers came in a whispered voice, accompanied by a deprecating smile. At one point he grinned embarrassedly, and whispered explosively to his neighbor: "I always disagree—darn it!" During the questioning, this subject's constant refrain was: "I called them as I saw them, sir." He insisted that his estimates were right without, however, committing himself as to whether the others were wrong, remarking that "that's the way I see them and that's the way they see them." If he had to make a practical decision under similar circumstances, he declared, "I would follow my own view, though part of my reason would tell me that I might be wrong." Immediately following the experiment the majority engaged this subject in a brief discussion. When they pressed him to say whether the entire group was wrong and he alone right, he turned upon them defiantly, exclaiming: "You're *probably* right, but you *may* be wrong!" To the disclosure of the experiment this subject reacted with the statement that he felt "exultant and relieved," adding, "I do not deny that at times I had the feeling: 'to heck with it, I'll go along with the rest.'"

Yielding

This subject went with the majority in eleven out of twelve trials. He appeared nervous and somewhat confused, but he did not attempt to evade discussion; on the contrary, he was helpful and tried to answer to the best of his ability. He opened the discussion with the statement: "If I'd been first I probably would have responded differently"; this was his way of stating that he had adopted the majority estimates. The primary factor in his case was loss of confidence. He perceived the majority as a decided group, acting without hesitation: "If they had been doubtful I probably would have changed, but they answered with such confidence." Certain of his errors, he explained, were due to the doubtful nature of the comparisons; in such instances he went with the majority. When the object of the experiment was explained, the subject volunteered: "I suspected about the middle—but tried to push it out of my mind." It is of interest that his suspicion did not restore his confidence or diminish the power of the majority. Equally striking is his report that he assumed the experiment to involve an "illusion" to which the others, but not he, were subject. This assumption too did not help to free him; on the contrary, he acted as if his divergence from the majority was a sign of defect. The principal impression this subject produced was of one so caught up by immediate difficulties that he lost clear reasons for his actions, and could make no reasonable decisions.

A First Analysis of Individual Differences

On the basis of the interview data described earlier, we undertook to differentiate and describe the major forms of reaction to the experimental situation, which we shall now briefly summarize.

Among the *independent* subjects we

distinguished the following main categories:

(1) Independence based on *confidence* in one's perception and experience. The most striking characteristic of these subjects is the vigor with which they withstand the group opposition. Though they are sensitive to the group, and experience the conflict, they show a resilience in coping with it, which is expressed in their continuing reliance on their perception and the effectiveness with which they shake off the oppressive group opposition.

(2) Quite different are those subjects who are independent and *withdrawn*. These do not react in a spontaneously emotional way, but rather on the basis of explicit principles concerning the necessity of being an individual.

(3) A third group of independent subjects manifests considerable tension and doubt, but adhere to their judgment on the basis of a felt necessity to deal adequately with the task.

The following were the main categories of reaction among the *yielding* subjects, or those who went with the majority during one half or more of the trials.

(1) *Distortion of perception* under the stress of group pressure. In this category belong a very few subjects who yield completely, but are not aware that their estimates have been displaced or distorted by the majority. These subjects report that they came to perceive the majority estimates as correct.

(2) *Distortion of judgment*. Most submitting subjects belong to this category. The factor of greatest importance in this group is a decision the subjects reach that their perceptions are inaccurate, and that those of the majority are correct. These subjects suffer from primary doubt and lack of confidence; on this basis they feel a strong tendency to join the majority.

(3) *Distortion of action*. The subjects in this group do not suffer a modification of perception, nor do they conclude that they are wrong. They yield because of an overmastering need not to appear different from or inferior to others, because of an inability to tolerate the appearance of defectiveness in the eyes of the group. These subjects suppress their observations and voice the majority position with awareness of what they are doing.

The results are sufficient to establish that independence and yielding are not psychologically homogeneous, that submission to group pressure and freedom from pressure can be the result of different psychological conditions. It should also be noted that the categories described above, being based exclusively on the subjects' reactions to the experimental conditions, are descriptive, not presuming to explain why a given individual responded in one way rather than another. The further exploration of the basis for the individual differences is a separate task.

Experimental Variations

The results described are clearly a joint function of two broadly different sets of conditions. They are determined first by the specific external conditions, by the particular character of the relation between social evidence and one's own experience. Second, the presence of pronounced individual differences points to the important role of personal factors, or factors connected with the individual's character structure. We reasoned that there are group conditions which would produce independence in all subjects, and that there probably are group conditions which would induce intensified yielding in many, though not in all. Secondly, we deemed it reasonable to assume that behavior under the experimental social pressure is significantly related to certain characteristics of the individual. The present account will be limited to the effect of the surrounding conditions upon independence and submission. To this end we followed the procedure of experimental variation, systematically altering the quality of social evidence by means of systematic variation of the group conditions and of the task.

The Effect of Nonunanimous Majorities

Evidence obtained from the basic experiment suggested that the condition of being exposed *alone* to the opposition of a "compact majority" may have played a decisive role in determining the course and strength of the effects observed. Accordingly we undertook to investigate in a series of successive variations the effects of *nonunanimous* majorities. The technical problem of altering the uniformity of a majority is, in terms of our procedure, relatively simple. In most instances we merely directed one or more members of the instructed group to deviate from the majority in prescribed ways. It is obvious that we cannot hope to compare the performance of the same individual in two situations on the assumption that they remain independent of one another; at best we can investigate the effect of an earlier upon a later experimental condition. The comparison of different experimental situations therefore requires the use of different but comparable groups of critical subjects. This is the procedure we have followed. In the variations to be described we have maintained the conditions of the basic experiment (e.g., the sex of the subjects, the size of the majority, the content of the task, and so on) save for the specific factor that was varied. The following were some of the variations studied:

1. *The presence of a "true partner."* (a) In the midst of the majority were *two* naïve, critical subjects. The subjects were separated spatially, being seated in the fourth and eighth positions, respectively. Each therefore heard his judgments confirmed by one other person (provided the other person remained independent), one prior to, the other after announcing his own judgment. In addition, each experienced a break in the unanimity of the majority. There were six pairs of critical subjects. (b) In a further variation the "partner" to the critical subject was a member of the group who had been instructed to respond correctly throughout. This procedure permits the exact control of the partner's responses. The partner was always seated in the fourth position; he therefore announced his estimates in each case before the critical subject.

The results clearly demonstrate that a disturbance of the unanimity of the majority markedly increased the independence of the critical subjects. The frequency of promajority errors dropped to 10.4 per cent of the total number of estimates in variation (a), and to 5.5 per cent in variation (b). These results are to be compared with the frequency of yielding to the unanimous majorities in the basic experiment, which was 32 per cent of the total number of estimates. It is clear that the presence in the field of *one other* individual who responded correctly was sufficient to deplete the power of the majority, and in some cases to destroy it. This finding is all the more striking in the light of other variations which demonstrate the effect of even small minorities provided they are unanimous. Indeed, we have been able to show that a unanimous majority of three is, under the given conditions, far more effective than a majority of eight containing one dissenter. That critical subjects will under these conditions free themselves of a majority of seven and join forces with one other person in the minority is, we believe, a result significant for theory. It points to a fundamental psychological difference between the condition of being alone and having a minimum of human support. It further demonstrates that the effects obtained are not the result of a summation of influences proceeding from each member of the group; it is necessary to conceive the results as being relationally determined.

2. *Withdrawal of a "true partner."* What will be the effect of providing the critical subject with a partner who responds correctly and then withdrawing him? The critical subject started with a partner who responded correctly. The partner was a member of the majority who had been instructed to respond correctly and to "desert" to the majority in the middle of the experiment. This procedure permits the observation of the same subject in the course of the transition from one condition to another. The withdrawal of the partner produced a powerful and unexpected result. We had assumed that the critical subject, having gone through the experience of opposing the majority with a minimum of support, would maintain his independence when alone. Contrary to this expectation, we found that the experience of having had and then lost a partner restored the majority effect to its full force, the proportion of errors rising to 28.5 per cent of all judgments, in contrast to the preceding level of 5.5

per cent. Further experimentation is needed to establish whether the critical subjects were responding to the sheer fact of being alone, or to the fact that the partner abandoned them.

3. *Late arrival of a "true partner."* The critical subject started as a minority of one in the midst of a unanimous majority. Toward the conclusion of the experiment one member of the majority "broke" away and began announcing correct estimates. This procedure, which reverses the order of conditions of the preceding experiment, permits the observation of the transition from being alone to being a member of a pair against a majority. It is obvious that those critical subjects who were independent when alone would continue to be so when joined by a partner. The variation is therefore of significance primarily for those subjects who yielded during the first phase of the experiment. The appearance of the late partner exerts a freeing effect, reducing the level of yielding to 8.7 per cent. Those who had previously yielded also became markedly more independent, but not completely so, continuing to yield more than previously independent subjects. The reports of the subjects do not cast much light on the factors responsible for the result. It is our impression that some subjects, having once committed themselves to yielding, find it difficult to change their direction completely. To do so is tantamount to a public admission that they had not acted rightly. They therefore follow to an extent the precarious course they had chosen in

TABLE 3   Errors of Critical Subjects with Unanimous Majorities of Different Size

Size of Majority	Control	1	2	3	4	8	10-15
N	37	10	15	10	10	50	12
Mean number of errors	0.08	0.33	1.53	4.0	4.20	3.84	3.75
Range of errors	0-2	0-1	0-5	1-12	0-11	0-11	0-10

order to maintain an outward semblance of consistency and conviction.

4. *The presence of a "compromise partner."* The majority was consistently extremist, always matching the standard with the most unequal line. One instructed subject (who, as in the other variations, preceded the critical subject) also responded incorrectly, but his estimates were always intermediate between the truth and the majority position. The critical subject therefore faced an extremist majority whose unanimity was broken by one more moderately erring person. Under these conditions the frequency of errors was reduced but not significantly. However, the lack of unanimity determined in a strikingly consistent way the *direction* of the errors. The preponderance of the errors, 75.7 per cent of the total, was moderate, whereas in a parallel experiment in which the majority was unanimously extremist (i.e., with the "compromise" partner excluded), the incidence of moderate errors was 42 per cent of the total. As might be expected, in a unanimously moderate majority, the errors of the critical subjects were without exception moderate.

The Role of Majority Size

To gain further understanding of the majority effect, we varied the size of the majority in several different variations. The majorities, which were in each case unanimous, consisted of two, three, four, eight, and ten to fifteen persons, respectively. In addition, we studied the limiting case in which the critical subject was opposed by one instructed subject. Table 3 contains the mean and the range of errors under each condition.

With the opposition reduced to one, the majority effect all but disappeared. When the opposition proceeded from a group of two, it produced a measurable though small distortion, the errors

being 12.8 per cent of the total number of estimates. The effect appeared in full force with a majority of three. Larger majorities did not produce effects greater than a majority of three.

The effect of a majority is often silent, revealing little of its operation to the subject, and often hiding it from the experimenter. To examine the range of effects it is capable of inducing, decisive variations of conditions are necessary. An indication of one effect is furnished by the following variation in which the conditions of the basic experiment were simply reversed. Here the majority, consisting of a group of sixteen, was naïve; in the midst of it we placed a single individual who responded wrongly according to instructions. Under these conditions the members of the naïve majority reacted to the lone dissenter with amusement. Contagious laughter spread through the group at the droll minority of one. Of significance is the fact that the members lacked awareness that they drew their strength from the majority, and that their reactions would change radically if they faced the dissenter individually. These observations demonstrate the role of social support as a source of power and stability, in contrast to the preceding investigations, which stressed the effects of social opposition. Both aspects must be explicitly considered in a unified formulation of the effects of group conditions on the formation and change of judgments.

The Role of the Stimulus Situation

It is obviously not possible to divorce the quality and course of the group forces which act upon the individual from the specific stimulus conditions. Of necessity the structure of the situation molds the group forces and determines their direction as well as their strength. Indeed, this was the reason that we took pains in the investigations described above to center the issue between the individual and the group around an elementary matter of fact. And there can be no doubt that the resulting reactions were directly a function of the contradiction between the observed relations and the majority position. These general considerations are sufficient to establish the need to vary the stimulus conditions and to observe their effect on the resulting group forces.

Accordingly we have studied the effect of increasing and decreasing the discrepancy between the correct relation and the position of the majority, going beyond the basic experiment which contained discrepancies of a relatively moderate order. Our technique permits the easy variation of this factor, since we can vary at will the deviation of the majority from the correct relation. At this point we can only summarize the trend of the results, which is entirely clear. The degree of independence increases with the distance of the majority from correctness. However, even glaring discrepancies (of the order of three to six inches) did not produce independence in all. While independence increases with the magnitude of contradiction, a certain proportion of individuals continues to yield under extreme conditions.

We have also varied systematically the structural clarity of the task, employing judgments based on mental standards. In agreement with other investigators, we find that the majority effect grows stronger as the situation diminishes in clarity. Concurrently, however, the disturbance of the subjects and the conflict quality of the situation decrease markedly. We consider it of significance that the majority achieves its most pronounced effect when it acts most painlessly.

Summary

We have investigated the effects upon individuals of majority opinions when the latter were seen to be in a direction contrary to fact. By means of a simple technique we produced a radical divergence between a majority and a minority, and observed the ways in which individuals coped with the resulting difficulty. Despite the stress of the given conditions, a substantial proportion of individuals retained their independence throughout. At the same time a substantial minority yielded, modifying their judgments in accordance with the majority. Independence and yielding are a joint function of the following major factors: (1) *The character of the stimulus situation.* Variations in structural clarity have a decisive effect: with diminishing clarity of the stimulus conditions the majority effect increases. (2) *The character of the group forces.* Individuals are highly sensitive to the structural qualities of group opposition. In particular, we demonstrated the great importance of the factor of unanimity. Also, the majority effect is a function of the size of group opposition. (3) *The character of the individual.* There were wide and, indeed, striking differences among individuals within the same experimental situation.

deviance

twenty-one

No set of social norms, not even that most widely held and deeply honored, is ever adhered to in all times and places by all those under its command. When society's standards are violated we speak of "social deviance," although the term is generally reserved for those violations which a given society takes quite seriously. Crime and delinquency, homicide and suicide are easily recognized by everyone as deviant. Homosexuality and drug addiction earn the same classification in the judgment of most ordinary citizens, and in the United States—though not in England—the law follows public opinion in this matter. By expanding the list we can comfortably convince ourselves that deviance is something manifested mainly by "sick" or "queer" people on the fringes of society. But Edwin Sutherland forces us to deal with deviance on the part of our most respected citizens at the very core of the social establishment.

White Collar Crime

EDWIN H. SUTHERLAND

This paper is concerned with crime in relation to business. The economists are well acquainted with business methods but not accustomed to consider them from the point of view of crime; many sociologists are well acquainted with crime but not accustomed to consider it as expressed in business. This paper is an attempt to integrate these two bodies of knowledge. More accurately stated, it is a comparison of crime in the upper or white collar class, composed of re-

Edwin H. Sutherland, "White Collar Criminality," *American Sociological Review*, 5 (February, 1940), 1-12.

spectable or at least respected business and professional men, and crime in the lower class, composed of persons of low socioeconomic status. This comparison is made for the purpose of developing the theories of criminal behavior, not for the purpose of muckraking or of reforming anything except criminology.

The criminal statistics show unequivocally that crime, *as popularly conceived and officially measured*, has a high incidence in the lower class and a low incidence in the upper class; less than 2 per cent of the persons committed to prisons in a year belong to the upper class. These statistics refer to criminals handled by the police, the criminal and juvenile courts, and the prisons, and to such crimes as murder, assault, burglary, robbery, larceny, sex offenses, and drunkenness, but exclude traffic violations.

The criminologists have used the case histories and criminal statistics derived from these agencies of criminal justice as their principal data. From them they have derived general theories of criminal behavior. These theories are that, since crime is concentrated in the lower class, it is caused by poverty or by personal and social characteristics believed to be associated statistically with poverty, including feeblemindedness, psychopathic deviations, slum neighborhoods, and "deteriorated" families. This statement, of course, does not do justice to the qualifications and variations in the conventional theories of criminal behavior, but it presents correctly their central tendency.

The thesis of this paper is that the conception and explanations of crime which have just been described are misleading and incorrect, that crime is in fact not closely correlated with poverty or with the psychopathic and sociopathic conditions associated with poverty, and that an adequate explanation of criminal behavior must proceed along quite different lines. The conventional explanations are invalid principally because they are derived from biased samples. The samples are biased in that they have not included vast areas of criminal behavior of persons not in the lower class. One of these neglected areas is the criminal behavior of business and professional men, which will be analyzed in this paper.

The "robber barons" of the last half of the nineteenth century were white collar criminals, as practically everyone now agrees. Their attitudes are illustrated by these statements: Colonel Vanderbilt asked, "You don't suppose you can run a railroad in accordance with the statutes, do you?" A. B. Stick-

ney, a railroad president, said to sixteen other railroad presidents in the home of J. P. Morgan in 1890, "I have the utmost respect for you gentlemen, individually, but as railroad presidents I wouldn't trust you with my watch out of my sight." Charles Francis Adams said, "The difficulty in railroad management . . . lies in the covetousness, want of good faith, and low moral tone of railway managers, in the complete absence of any high standard of commercial honesty."

The present-day white collar criminals, who are more suave and deceptive than the "robber barons," are represented by Krueger, Stavisky, Whitney, Mitchell, Foshay, Insull, the Van Sweringens, Musica-Coster, Fall, Sinclair, and many other merchant princes and captains of finance and industry, and by a host of lesser followers. Their criminality has been demonstrated again and again in the investigations of land offices, railways, insurance, munitions, banking, public utilities, stock exchanges, the oil industry, real estate, reorganization committees, receiverships, bankruptcies, and politics. Individual cases of such criminality are reported frequently, and in many periods more important crime news may be found on the financial pages of newspapers than on the front pages. White collar criminality is found in every occupation, as can be discovered readily in casual conversation with a representative of an occupation by asking him, "What crooked practices are found in your occupation?"

White collar criminality in business is expressed most frequently in the form of misrepresentation in financial statements of corporations, manipulation in the stock exchange, commercial bribery, bribery of public officials directly or indirectly in order to secure favorable contracts and legislation, misrepresentation in advertising and salesmanship, embezzlement and misapplication of funds, short weights and measures and misgrading of commodities, tax frauds, misapplication of funds in receiverships and bankruptcies. These are what Al Capone called "the legitimate rackets." These and many others are found in abundance in the business world.

In the medical profession, which is here used as an example because it is probably less criminalistic than some other professions, are found illegal sale of alcohol and narcotics, abortion, illegal services to underworld criminals, fraudulent reports and testimony in accident cases, extreme cases of unnecessary treatment, fake specialists, restriction of competition, and fee-splitting. Fee-splitting is a violation of a specific law in many states and a violation of the conditions of admission to the practice of medicine in all. The physician who participates in fee-splitting tends to send his patients to the surgeon who will give him the largest fee rather than to the surgeon who will do the best work. It has been reported that two thirds of the surgeons in New York City split fees, and that more than one half of the physicians in a central western city who answered a questionnaire on this point favored fee-splitting.

These varied types of white collar crimes in business and the professions consist principally of violation of delegated or implied trust, and many of them can be reduced to two categories: misrepresentation of asset values and duplicity in the manipulation of power. The first is approximately the same as fraud or swindling; the second is similar to the double cross. The latter is illustrated by the corporation director who, acting on inside information, purchases land which the corporation will need and sells it at a fantastic profit to his corporation. The principle of this duplicity is that the offender holds two antagonistic positions, one of which is

a position of trust, which is violated, generally by misapplication of funds, in the interest of the other position. A football coach, permitted to referee a game in which his own team was playing, would illustrate this antagonism of positions. Such situations cannot be completely avoided in a complicated business structure, but many concerns make a practice of assuming such antagonistic functions and regularly violating the trust thus delegated to them. When compelled by law to make a separation of their functions, they make a nominal separation and continue by subterfuge to maintain the two positions.

An accurate statistical comparison of the crimes of the two classes is not available. The most extensive evidence regarding the nature and prevalence of white collar criminality is found in the reports of the larger investigations to which reference was made. Because of its scattered character, that evidence is assumed rather than summarized here. A few statements will be presented, as illustrations rather than as proof of the prevalence of this criminality.

The Federal Trade Commission in 1920 reported that commercial bribery was a prevalent and common practice in many industries. In certain chain stores, the net shortage in weights was sufficient to pay 3.4 per cent on the investment in those commodities. Of the cans of ether sold to the army in 1923-25, 70 per cent were rejected because of impurities. In Indiana, during the summer of 1934, 40 per cent of the ice cream samples tested in a routine manner by the Division of Public Health were in violation of law. The Comptroller of the Currency in 1908 reported that violations of law were found in 75 per cent of the banks examined in a three-month period. Lie detector tests of all employees in several Chicago banks, supported in almost all cases by confessions, showed that 20 per cent of them had stolen bank property. A public accountant estimated, in the period prior to the Securities and Exchange Commission, that 80 per cent of the financial statements of corporations were misleading. James M. Beck said, "Diogenes would have been hard put to it to find an honest man in the Wall Street which I knew as a corporation lawyer" (in 1916).

White collar criminality in politics, which is generally recognized as fairly prevalent, has been used by some as a rough gauge by which to measure white collar criminality in business. James A. Farley said, "The standards of conduct are as high among office-holders and politicians as they are in commercial life," and Cermak, while mayor of Chicago, said, "There is less graft in politics than in business." John Flynn wrote, "The average politician is the merest amateur in the gentle art of graft, compared with his brother in the field of business." And Walter Lippmann wrote, "Poor as they are, the standards of public life are so much more social than those of business that financiers who enter politics regard themselves as philanthropists."

These statements obviously do not give a precise measurement of the relative criminality of the white collar class, but they are adequate evidence that crime is not so highly concentrated in the lower class as the usual statistics indicate. Also, these statements obviously do not mean that every business and professional man is a criminal, just as the usual theories do not mean that every man in the lower class is a criminal. On the other hand, the preceding statements refer in many cases to the leading corporations in America and are not restricted to the disreputable business and professional men who are called quacks,

ambulance chasers, bucket-shop operators, dead-beats, and fly-by-night swindlers.[1]

The financial cost of white collar crime is probably several times as great as the financial cost of all the crimes which are customarily regarded as the "crime problem." An officer of a chain grocery store in one year embezzled $600,000, which was six times as much as the annual losses from 500 burglaries and robberies of the stores in that chain. Public enemies numbered one to six secured $130,000 by burglary and robbery in 1938, while the sum stolen by Krueger is estimated at $250,-000,000, or nearly 2000 times as much. *The New York Times* in 1931 reported four cases of embezzlement in the United States with a loss of more than a million dollars each and a combined loss of $9 million. Although a million-dollar burglar or robber is practically unheard of, these million-dollar embezzlers are small fry among white collar criminals. The estimated loss to investors in one investment trust from 1929 to 1935 was $580,000,000, due primarily to the fact that 75 per cent of the values in the portfolio were in securities of affiliated companies, although it advertised the importance of diversification in investments and its expert services in selecting safe securities. In Chicago, the claim was made six years ago that householders had

---

[1] Perhaps it should be repeated that "white collar" (upper) and "lower" classes merely designate persons of high and low socioeconomic status. Income and amount of money involved in the crime are not the sole criteria. Many persons of "low" socioeconomic status are "white collar" criminals in the sense that they are well dressed, well educated, and have high incomes, but "white collar" as used in this paper means "respected," "socially accepted and approved," "looked up to." Some people in this class may not be well dressed or well educated, nor have high incomes, although the "upper" usually exceed the "lower" classes in these respects as well as in social status.

lost $54,000,000 in two years during the administration of a city sealer who granted immunity from inspection to stores which provided Christmas baskets for his constituents.

The financial loss from white collar crime, great as it is, is less important than the damage to social relations. White collar crimes violate trust and therefore create distrust, which lowers social morale and produces social disorganization on a large scale. Other crimes produce relatively little effect on social institutions or social organization.

White collar crime is real crime. It is not ordinarily called crime, and calling it by this name does not make it worse, just as refraining from calling it crime does not make it better than it otherwise would be. It is called crime here in order to bring it within the scope of criminology, which is justified because it is in violation of the criminal law. The crucial question in this analysis is the criterion of violation of the criminal law. Conviction in the criminal court, which is sometimes suggested as the criterion, is not adequate because a large proportion of those who commit crimes are not convicted in criminal courts. This criterion, therefore, needs to be supplemented. When it is supplemented, the criterion of the crimes of one class must be kept consistent in general terms with the criterion of the crimes of the other class. The definition should not be the spirit of the law for white collar crimes and the letter of the law for other crimes, or in other respects be more liberal for one class than for the other. Since this discussion is concerned with the conventional theories of the criminologists, the criterion of white collar crime must be justified in terms of the procedures of those criminologists in dealing with other crimes. The criterion of white collar crimes, as here proposed, supplements convictions in the criminal courts in four respects, in each of which the extension is justified because the criminologists who present the conventional theories of criminal behavior make the same extension in principle.

First, other agencies than the criminal court must be included, for the criminal court is not the only agency which makes official decisions regarding violations of the criminal law. The juvenile court, dealing largely with offenses of the children of the poor, in many states is not under the criminal jurisdiction. The criminologists have made much use of case histories and statistics of juvenile delinquents in constructing their theories of criminal behavior. This justifies the inclusion of agencies other than the criminal court which deal with white collar offenses. The most important of these agencies are the administrative boards, bureaus, or commissions, and much of their work, although certainly not all, consists of cases which are in violation of the criminal law. The Federal Trade Commission recently ordered several automobile compaines to stop advertising their interest rate on instalment purchases as 6 per cent, since it was actually 11.5 per cent. Also it filed complaint against *Good Housekeeping,* one of the Hearst publications, charging that its seals led the public to believe that all products bearing those seals had been tested in their laboratories, which was contrary to fact. Each of these involves a charge of dishonesty, which might have been tried in a criminal court as fraud. A large proportion of the cases before these boards should be included in the data of the criminologists. Failure to do so is a principal reason for the bias in their samples and the errors in their generalizations.

Second, for both classes, behavior which would have a reasonable expectancy of conviction if tried in a criminal court or substitute agency should be defined as criminal. In this respect, convictability rather than actual conviction should be the criterion of criminality. The criminologists would not hesitate to accept as data a verified case history of a person who was a criminal but had never been convicted. Similarly, it is justifiable to include white collar criminals who have not been convicted, provided reliable evidence is available. Evidence regarding such cases appears in many civil suits, such as stockholders' suits and patent infringement suits. These cases might have been referred to the criminal court but they were referred to the civil court because the injured party was more interested in securing damages than in seeing punishment inflicted. This also happens in embezzlement cases, regarding which surety companies have much evidence. In a short consecutive series of embezzlements known to a surety company, 90 per cent were not prosecuted because prosecution would interfere with restitution or salvage. The evidence in cases of embezzlement is generally conclusive, and would probably have been sufficient to justify conviction in all of the cases in this series.

Third, behavior should be defined as criminal if conviction is avoided merely because of pressure which is brought to bear on the court or substitute agency. Gangsters and racketeers have been relatively immune in many cities because of their pressure on prospective witnesses and public officials, and professional thieves, such as pickpockets and confidence men who do not use strong-arm methods, are even more frequently immune. The conventional criminologists do not hesitate to include the life histories of such criminals as data, because they understand the generic relation of the pressures to the failure to convict. Similarly, white collar criminals are relatively immune because of the class bias of the courts and the power of their class to influence the implementation and administration of the law. This class bias affects not merely present-day courts but to a much greater degree affected the earlier courts which established the precedents and rules of procedure of the present-day courts. Consequently, it is justifiable to interpret the actual or potential failures of conviction in the light of known facts regarding the pressures brought to bear on the agencies which deal with offenders.

Fourth, persons who are accessory to a crime should be included among white collar criminals as they are among other criminals. When the Federal Bureau of Investigation deals with a case of kidnaping, it is not content with catching the offenders who carried away the victim; they may catch and the court may convict twenty-five other persons who assisted by secreting the victim, negotiating the ransom, or putting the ransom money into circulation. On the other hand, the prosecution of white collar criminals frequently stops with one offender. Political graft almost always involves collusion between politicians and business men, but prosecutions are generally limited to the politicians. Judge Manton was found guilty of accepting $664,000 in bribes, but the six or eight important commercial concerns that paid the bribes have not been prosecuted. Pendergast, the late boss of Kansas City, was convicted for failure to report as a part of his income $315,000 received in bribes from insurance companies, but the insurance companies which paid the bribes have not been prosecuted. In an investigation of an embezzlement by the president of a bank, at least a dozen other violations of law which were related to this embezzlement and involved most of the other officers of the bank and the officers of the clearing house, were discovered, but none of the others was prosecuted.

This analysis of the criterion of white collar criminality results in the conclusion that a description of white collar criminality in general terms will be also a description of the criminality of the lower class. The respects in which the crimes of the two classes differ are the incidentals rather than the essentials of criminality. They differ principally in the implementation of the criminal laws which apply to them. The crimes of the lower class are handled by policemen, prosecutors, and judges, with penal sanctions in the form of fines, imprisonment, and death. The crimes of the upper class either result in no official action at all, or result in suits for damages in civil courts, or are handled by inspectors and by administrative boards or commissions, with penal sanctions in the form of warnings, orders to cease and desist, occasionally the loss of a license, and only in extreme cases by fines or prison sentences. Thus, the white collar criminals are segregated administratively from other criminals, and largely as a consequence of this are not regarded as real criminals by themselves, the general public, or the criminologists.

This difference in the implementation of the criminal law is due principally to the difference in the social position of the two types of offenders. Judge Woodward, when imposing sentence upon the officials of H. O. Stone and Company, bankrupt real estate firm in Chicago, who had been convicted in 1933 of the use of the mails to defraud, said to them, "You are men of affairs, of experience, of refinement and culture, of excellent reputation and standing in the business and social world." That statement might be used as a general characterization of white collar criminals for they are oriented basically to legitimate and respectable careers. Because of their social status they have a loud voice in determining what goes into the statutes and how the criminal law as it affects themselves is implemented and administered. This may be illustrated from the Pure Food and Drug Law. Between 1879 and 1906, 140 pure food and drug bills were presented in Congress and all failed because of the importance of the persons who would be affected. It took a highly dramatic performance by Dr. Wiley in 1906 to induce Congress to enact the law. That law, however, did not create a new crime, just as the federal Lindbergh kidnaping law did not create a new crime; it merely provided a more efficient implementation of a principle which had been formulated previously in state laws. When an amendment to this law, which would bring within the scope of its agents fraudulent statements made over the radio or in the press, was presented to Congress, the publishers and advertisers organized support and sent a lobby to Washington which successfully fought the amendment, principally under the slogans of "freedom of the press" and "dangers of bureaucracy." This proposed amendment, also, would not have created a new crime, for the state laws already prohibited fraudulent statements over the radio or in the press; it would have implemented the law so it could have been enforced. Finally, the Administration has not been able to enforce the law as it has desired because of the pressures by the offenders against the law, sometimes brought to bear through the head of the Department of Agriculture, sometimes through congressmen who threaten cuts in the appropriation, and sometimes by others. The statement of Daniel Drew, a pious old fraud, describes the criminal law with some accuracy, "Law is like a cobweb; it's made for flies and the smaller kinds of insects, so to speak, but lets the big bumblebees break through. When technicalities of the law stood in my way, I have always been able to brush them aside easy as anything."

The preceding analysis should be regarded neither as an assertion that all efforts to influence legislation and its administration are reprehensible nor as a particularistic interpretation of the criminal law. It means only that the upper class has greater influence in molding the criminal law and its administration to its own interests than does the lower class. The privileged position of white collar criminals before the law results to a slight extent from bribery and political pressures, principally from the respect in which they are held and without special effort on their part. The most powerful group in medieval society secured relative immunity by "benefit of clergy," and now our most powerful groups secure relative immunity by "benefit of business or profession."

In contrast with the power of the white collar criminals is the weakness of their victims. Consumers, investors, and stockholders are unorganized, lack technical knowledge, and cannot protect themselves. Daniel Drew, after taking a large sum of money by sharp practice from Vanderbilt in the Erie deal, concluded that it was a mistake to take money from a powerful man on the same level as himself and declared that in the future he would confine his efforts to outsiders, scattered all over the country, who wouldn't be able to organize and fight back. White collar criminality flourishes at points where powerful business and professional men come in contact with persons who are weak. In this respect, it is similar to stealing candy from a baby. Many of the crimes of the lower class, on the other hand, are committed against persons of wealth and power in the form of burglary and robbery.

Because of this difference in the comparative power of the victims, the white collar criminals enjoy relative immunity.

Embezzlement is an interesting exception to white collar criminality in this respect. Embezzlement is usually theft from an employer by an employee, and the employee is less capable of manipulating social and legal forces in his own interest than is the employer. As might have been expected, the laws regarding embezzlement were formulated long before laws for the protection of investors and consumers.

The theory that criminal behavior in general is due either to poverty or to the psychopathic and sociopathic conditions associated with poverty can now be shown to be invalid for three reasons. First, the generalization is based on a biased sample which omits almost entirely the behavior of white collar criminals. The criminologists have restricted their data, for reasons of convenience and ignorance rather than of principle, largely to cases dealt with in criminal courts and juvenile courts, and these agencies are used principally for criminals from the lower economic strata. Consequently, their data are grossly biased from the point of view of the economic status of criminals, and their generalization that criminality is closely associated with poverty is not justified.

Second, the generalization that criminality is closely associated with poverty obviously does not apply to white collar criminals. With a small number of exceptions, they are not in poverty, were not reared in slums or badly deteriorated families, and are not feeble-minded or psychopathic. They were seldom problem children in their earlier years and did not appear in juvenile courts or child guidance clinics. The proposition, derived from the data used by the conventional criminologists, that "the criminal of today was the problem child of yesterday" is seldom true of white collar criminals. The idea that the causes of criminality are to be found almost exclusively in childhood similarly is fallacious. Even if poverty is extended to include the economic stresses which afflict business in a period of depression, it is not closely correlated with white collar criminality. Probably at no time within fifty years have white collar crimes in the field of investments and of corporate management been so extensive as during the boom period of the 'twenties.

Third, the conventional theories do not even explain lower-class criminality. The sociopathic and psychopathic factors which have been emphasized doubtless have something to do with crime causation, but these factors have not been related to a general process which is found both in white collar criminality and lower-class criminality and therefore they do not explain the criminality of either class. They may explain the manner or method of crime —why lower-class criminals commit burglary or robbery rather than false pretenses.

In view of these defects in the conventional theories, an hypothesis that will explain both white collar criminality and lower-class criminality is needed. For reasons of economy, simplicity, and logic, the hypothesis should apply to both classes, for this will make possible the analysis of causal factors freed from the encumbrances of the administrative devices which have led criminologists astray. [Clifford R.] Shaw and [Henry D.] McKay and others, working exclusively in the field of lower-class crime, have found the conventional theories inadequate to account for variations within the data of lower-class crime and from that point of view have been working toward an explanation of crime in terms of a more general social process. Such efforts will be greatly aided by the procedure which has been described.

The hypothesis which is here suggested as a substitute for the conventional theories is that white collar criminality, just as other systematic criminality, is learned; that it is learned in direct or indirect association with those who already practice the behavior; and that those who learn this criminal behavior are segregated from frequent and intimate contacts with law-abiding behavior. Whether a person becomes a criminal or not is determined largely by the comparative frequency and intimacy of his contacts with the two types of behavior. This may be called the process of differential association. It is a genetic explanation both of white collar criminality and lower-class criminality. Those who become white collar criminals generally start their careers in good neighborhoods and good homes, graduate from colleges with some idealism, and with little selection on their part get into particular business situations in which criminality is practically a folkway and are inducted into that system of behavior just as into any other folkway. The lower-class criminals generally start their careers in deteriorated neighborhoods and families, find delinquents at hand from whom they acquire the attitudes toward, and techniques of, crime through association with delinquents and in partial segregation from law-abiding people. The essentials of the process are the same for the two classes of criminals. This is not entirely a process of assimilation, for inventions are frequently made, perhaps more frequently in white collar crime than in lower-class crime. The inventive geniuses for the lower-class criminals are generally professional criminals, while the inventive geniuses for many kinds of white collar crime are generally lawyers.

A second general process is social disorganization in the community. Differential association culminates in crime because the community is not organized solidly against that behavior. The law is pressing in one direction, and other forces are pressing in the opposite direction. In business, the "rules of the game" conflict with the legal rules. A businessman who wants to obey the law is driven by his competitors to adopt their methods. This is well illustrated by the persistence of commercial bribery in spite of the strenuous efforts of business organizations to eliminate it. Groups and individuals are individuated; they are more concerned with their specialized group or individual interests than with the larger welfare. Consequently, it is not possible for the community to present a solid front in opposition to crime. The Better Business Bureaus and Crime Commissions, composed of business and professional men, attack burglary, robbery, and cheap swindles, but overlook the crimes of their own members. The forces which impinge on the lower class are similarly in conflict. Social disorganization affects the two classes in similar ways.

I have presented a brief and general description of white collar criminality on a framework of argument regarding theories of criminal behavior. That argument, stripped of the description, may be stated in the following propositions:

1. White collar criminality is real criminality, being in all cases in violation of the criminal law.

2. White collar criminality differs from lower-class criminality principally in an implementation of the criminal law which segregates white collar criminals administratively from other criminals.

3. The theories of the criminologists that crime is due to poverty or to psychopathic and sociopathic conditions statistically associated with poverty are invalid because, first, they are derived from samples which are grossly biased with respect to socioeconomic status; second, they do not apply to the white collar criminals; and third, they do not even explain the criminality of the lower class, since the factors are not related to a general process characteristic of all criminality.

4. A theory of criminal behavior which will explain both white collar criminality and lower-class criminality is needed.

5. An hypothesis of this nature is suggested in terms of differential association and social disorganization.

conflict and accommodation

twenty-two

One of the most frequent and telling criticisms directed against the contemporaneously dominant functionalist school of sociology is that it neglects the role of conflict in society. Those who emphasize that conflict is a ubiquitous feature of human existence and of social life are hardly lacking in evidence for their point of view. History and contemporary life provide no end of examples, and elsewhere in this volume (Chap. 26) we are treated to ample documentation in the paper by L. F. Richardson on "The Statistics of Deadly Quarrels." Yet for the conflict school of sociology to win its share of sociological attention, it must go beyond pointing to the fact of conflict and offer theories and data bearing on its origins and causes and the forms of its social expression. Lewis Coser makes a substantial contribution through his explication of the conditions under which conflict may be terminated. We thus come to understand better not only social conflict, but its resolution through the process of *accommodation*.

On Terminating Conflict

LEWIS A. COSER

Certain social processes are finite, i.e., they are defined by their transitory character and the manner of their termination is institutionally prescribed. Courtship ends when union with the beloved has been attained in marriage; formal education ends when the educational goal has been reached and examinations or commencement exercises mark completion of the process. Other social processes, however, such as friendship or love, have no precise termination point. They follow a law of social inertia insofar as they continue to operate if no explicit provision for stopping their course is made by the participants. Social conflict is such a process. While in a game, for example, the rules for the process include rules for its ending, in social conflict explicit provisions for its termination must be made by the contenders. If no mutual agreements are made at some time during the struggle, it "ceaseth only in death" or in total destruction of at least one of the antagonists. The termination of conflict hence presents problems that do not arise in finite processes.

Lewis A. Coser, "The Termination of Conflict," *Journal of Conflict Resolution*, 5 (December, 1961), 347-353.

Various types of conflicts can be classified according to the degree of their normative regulation. Fully institutionalized conflicts, such as duels, may be said to constitute one extreme of a continuum while absolute conflicts, in which the goal is the total destruction of the enemy rather than a mutually agreed-upon settlement, fall at the other extreme. In the second type, agreement is reduced to a minimum; the struggle ceases only upon the extermination of one or both of the contenders. As Hans Speier has said, "peace terminating an absolute war is established *without* the enemy."[1]

It stands to reason that conflicts of this kind—at least between contenders with a rough equality of strength—are exceedingly costly and exhausting. If the contenders wish to prevent their struggle from becoming a zero sum game in which the outcome can only be total defeat or total victory, they have a common interest in establishing mechanisms which can lead to an agreed-upon termination of the struggle. The fact is that most conflicts do indeed end long before the defeated has been totally crushed. "Resistance to the last man" is almost always a

[1] Hans Speier, *Social Order and the Risks of War* (Norwalk, Conn.: George W. Stewart, Publisher, Inc., 1952), p. 223.

phrase. As long as one belligerent survives in one's camp further resistance is always possible; yet combat usually ceases long before this point is reached. This is so because both parties agree upon norms for the termination of the conflict.

While absolute conflicts allow practically no agreements as to their termination, certain types of highly institutionalized conflicts have built-in termination points. Trials by ordeal, duels, and other agonistic struggles are centered upon symbolic endings which give the gamelike features and determine the outcome automatically. A score is kept, a goal line established, maximum injury is conventionally fixed. When the score adds up to a certain number, when a certain type of injury has been established, or the goal line has been crossed, the conflict is over and the loser as well as the winner can easily perceive the outcome of the contention.

In conflicts not fully institutionalized, assessment of relative strength is not an easy matter so that the loser may not in fact concede that he has lost, nor may he even be aware of it. Therefore, it is to the interest of both contenders that the point at which victory is attained or the point beyond which no more gains can be anticipated be marked as clearly as possible so as to avoid unnecessary exertions on both sides. Termination of conflict becomes a problem to be solved by both parties.

The termination of conflict is a social process dependent upon, but not directly deducible from its pursuits. It is, as Georg Simmel has noted, "a specific enterprise. It belongs neither to war nor to peace, just as a bridge is different from either bank it connects."[2]

To be sure, the outcome of a conflict is related to the goals of the antagonists and to the means by which it is fought; its duration and intensity will depend on objectives and available resources plus the time and effort required to achieve a decision. But the termination of the conflict, that is agreement as to what constitutes a true decision, highlights some factors which are not deducible from its pursuit and must hence be studied separately.

For all except absolute conflict, termination involves a reciprocal activity and cannot be understood simply as a unilateral imposition of the will of the stronger on the weaker. Therefore, contrary to what common sense might suggest, not only the potential victor but also the potential vanquished makes crucial contributions to the termination. As a military commentator has pointed out, "war is pressed by the victor, but peace is made by the vanquished. Therefore, to determine the causes of peace, it is always necessary to take the vanquished's point of view. Until the vanquished quits, the war goes on."[3] Victory, in other words, involves the yielding of the vanquished. By the very act of declaring himself beaten, he achieves a last assertion of power. With this act, as Georg Simmel has said, "he actually makes a gift to the victor."[4] The capacity of making gifts is a measure of autonomy.

If both victor and vanquished are to make a contribution to the termination of their conflict they must arrive at some agreement. Thomas Schelling has recently argued persuasively that "limited war requires limits . . . but limits require agreement or at least some kind of mutual recognition and

[2] Georg Simmel, *Conflict*, Kurt H. Wolff, trans. (New York: The Free Press of Glencoe, Inc., 1955), p. 110.

[3] H. A. Calahan, *What Makes a War End* (New York: Vanguard Press, 1944), p. 18.
[4] Simmel, *op. cit.*, p. 114.

acquiescence."[5] This applies not only to the conduct but also to the termination of conflicts. In order to end a conflict the parties must agree upon rules and norms allowing them to assess their respective power position in the struggle. Their common interest leads them to accept rules which enhance their mutual dependence in the very pursuit of their antagonistic goals. Such agreements make their conflict, so to speak, self-liquidating. To the degree that such rules are provided, the conflict is partly institutionalized and acquires some of the features of the agonistic struggle alluded to earlier.

Agreements as to goals and determination of outcome shorten the conflict. Once a goal has been reached by one of the parties and this accepted as a clue to the acceptance of defeat by the other, the conflict is ended. The more restricted the object of contention and the more visible for both parties the clues to victory, the higher the chances that the conflict [will] be limited in time and extension. Emile Durkheim's dictum concerning human needs, "The more one has, the more one wants, since satisfaction received only stimulates instead of filling needs" is applicable in this connection. Agreed-upon limits upon the "appetites" of the contenders place normative restrictions upon a process which does not inherently contain self-limiting properties. The history of trade unionism provides interesting examples.

Struggles engaged in by business unionism, given its limited goals, provide for the contending parties an opportunity for settlement and furnishes them at the same time with recognizable signals as to the opportune moment for ending a conflict. Revolutionary syndicalism, on the other hand, has always been plagued by the problem of ending strike action. Since its goal is the overthrow of the capitalist order rather than improvements within it, it cannot accept as the end of the conflict outcomes which would constitute victories from the point of view of business unionism. Revolutionary syndicalism is faced with the dilemma that no outcome of a strike, short of the overthrow of capitalism, can be considered an acceptable form of conflict resolution so that its strategy is foredoomed to failure. Not sensitized to clues which would allow them to conclude that a victory has been reached, unable to recognize peace overtures or concessions from the adversary, revolutionary syndicalists are not in a position to take advantage of partial gains. Paradoxically, in this case, those who are under ordinary conditions the *weaker* party demand "unconditional surrender" of the stronger so that they make it inevitable that the struggle can cease only upon total exhaustion.

The above examples illustrate how closely specific outcomes are related to the aims of the contenders. The smaller the sacrifice a party demands from the opponent, the more limited the aims, the higher the chances that the potential loser will be ready to give up battle. The loser must be led to decide that peace is more attractive than the continuation of the conflict; such a decision will be powerfully enhanced if the demands made upon him are not exorbitant.[6] When the war aims of the winning side are limited as, say, in the Spanish-American War or the Russo-Japanese conflict of 1905, the making of peace is relatively easy. Once the Japanese war aims—the stopping of Russian penetration into the Far East—had been reached, Japan could afford to make the first move for peace by appealing to Theodore

[5] Thomas Schelling, *The Strategy of Conflict* (Cambridge, Mass.: Harvard University Press, 1960), p. 53.

[6] Calahan, *op. cit.*, p. 253, *et passim*.

Roosevelt to act as a mediator. Once Cuba was liberated and the Spanish fleet defeated, American war aims were attained and the United States had no interest in continuing the war through an attack upon the Spanish mainland.

It remains, however, that no matter how the activities of the potential winner have facilitated an early termination of the conflict, the final decision to end the war remains with the potential loser. How, then, is the loser moved to decide that he has, in fact, lost? Not only the objective situation but the perception of the situation is crucially important since only the latter will bring forth the requisite admission of defeat. "If an opponent," writes Clausewitz, "is to be made to comply with our will, we must place him in a situation which is more oppressive to him than the sacrifice we demand."[7] This elegantly phrased dictum is, however, meaningless unless the criteria be specified that determine how the antagonist will in fact assess the situation. Different contenders might arrive at variant estimates as to the degree of oppressiveness of a situation and of the value of the sacrifice demanded. Since such assessments are difficult to make and do not depend on rational calculations alone, they are greatly facilitated by the availability of symbolic signposts.

Whenever wars have been strictly limited, as in eighteenth-century warfare, some visible event, such as the taking of a particular fortress, the reaching of some natural barrier, and the like, symbolized to both parties that the desired objective has been reached by one of them and that the conflict could now be considered solved through the subsequent acquiescence of the loser. When such mutually acceptable symbolic clues are not avail-

able, the resolution of the conflict will be more difficult.

The nature of such symbolic clues may vary considerably[8] and it is hence important that the potential winner ascertain which clues will be accepted by the potential loser as symbols of defeat. If in the common consciousness of the citizens, the capital symbolizes the very existence of the nation, then its fall will be perceived as defeat and will lead to the acceptance of the terms of the victor. The fall of Paris in 1871 and 1940 symbolized to the bulk of Frenchmen the end of the war despite the fact that Gambetta had rallied significant numbers of undefeated troops in the provinces, and that de Gaulle appealed for the continuation of the war from London. Only a relatively small number of Frenchmen refused to accept the fall of Paris as a symbol of defeat. In less centralized nations, however, where the capital has no such symbolic significance, its fall is not perceived as a decisive event. Pretoria and Bloemfontein fell to the British in 1900, yet Boer resistance, rather to the surprise of the British, continued for two more years. The British failed to understand that, to the rural Boers, the vast countryside rather than the cities symbolized the nation; to them the war ended only when want of forage, capture, and overwork decimated the Boer horses. In a country in which men were bred in the saddle, the decimation of horses symbolized defeat.[9] Similarly, the sacking of Washington in 1812 did not signal defeat to Americans, for whom the open spaces of the country rather than the federal capital symbolized national independence. In other situa-

[7] Karl von Clausewitz, *On War*, Vol. I (London: Routledge & Kegan Paul, Ltd., 1956), p. 5.

[8] One must further distinguish between purely symbolic events, such as the capture of a flag, and events which, as in the examples that follow, have realistic as well as symbolic significance.

[9] Calahan, *op. cit.*, p. 114.

tions the capture of charismatic war lords rather than any taking of a locality will symbolize defeat.

The structure of the opposing camp furnishes clues as to meaningful symbols of defeat and victory. It is hence of the utmost importance for both sides to have as much knowledge as possible about the characteristic features of their respective structure and symbols. When ignorant armies clash [by] night, their pluralistic ignorance militates against their ability to come to terms short of mutual exhaustion.

The contenders' ability to make use of one another's symbols of defeat and victory does not only depend on their awareness of the structure of the opposing camp, but also on the dynamics within each camp. Internal struggles may be waged over what set of events may be considered a decisive symbol of defeat. A minority may consider that resistance can be continued even though the majority has accepted defeat. Subgroups may consider that the decision makers have betrayed the cause by agreeing to end the conflict. Peace terms provide ample material for internal conflict within each of the contending camps. These terms are, moreover, likely to be defined and redefined in the course of the conflict in tune with the fortunes of battle. Different parties may disagree violently on whether a given event is to be considered decisive or of only incidental significance. Such contentions are likely to be the more deep-going the less integrated the social structure. In integrated structures internal contentions may vitalize and strengthen the groups' energies, but if divergencies as to appropriate action affect the basic layers of common belief, symbolizations of victory and defeat are also likely to be basically divergent.[10] In

highly polarized social systems where a number of internal conflicts of different sorts are superimposed upon one another, there exists hardly any common definition of the situation binding all members of the society to commonly held perceptions.[11] To the extent that a society or group is rent into rival camps so that there is no community of ends between the parties, if one party is not willing to accept the definition of the situation which the other propounds, the making of peace becomes an almost impossible enterprise. In such situations a prior settlement of scores within, an unambiguous definition or redefinition of the balance of power between contending groups, may be the precondition for concluding peace without. The Russian provisional government after the March, 1917, revolution being continuously goaded and challenged by the growing Bolshevik party, was unable either to wage war effectively or to conclude peace; once the Bolsheviks had seized power their definition of the situation prevailed and peace could be concluded at Brest Litovsk.

Even when such deep-going fissures are not present in a social structure, the ever-present divergencies between the perspectives of the leaders and the led, between those in authority and those submitted to it,[12] require considerable effort on the part of the leaders to make the led accept their definition of the situation. Just as at the beginning of the struggle the leaders must convince the led that the sacrifice demanded of them will redound to their benefit and that the conflict concerns [the] wide interests of all rather than the narrow interests of the top stratum, so the leaders must also

---

[10] Lewis A. Coser, *The Functions of Social Conflict* (New York: The Free Press of Glencoe, Inc., 1956), pp. 72-80.

[11] *Ibid.*, pp. 76ff.; and Ralf Dahrendorf, *Class and Class Conflict in Industrial Society* (Stanford: Stanford University Press, 1959), pp. 213ff.

[12] Dahrendorf, *op. cit.*, Chap. 5.

be able to convince the led that the acceptance of defeat is warranted and even desirable from the point of view of the total system rather than in terms of special leadership interests. To make defeat palatable may require as much effort as to make war desirable.

Leaders will typically differ from the led not only in terms of social perspectives but also in regard to their cognitive horizon so that leaders may be able to assess consequences and relative advantages more rationally than the led. A leader foreseeing a defeat which is not as yet visible to his followers must adjust his strategy to the need of convincing the followers. In such an effort it might be advantageous to him to construe partial defeat in such a way as to make it appear as at least a partial victory. Often the led, like the mark in a con game, might have to be cooled out by being told that what they experience as a loss is "really" a partial victory.[13]

Contentions within enemy camps as to the proper definition of the situation once again highlight the importance of symbolizations. The leader will have to rely on his ability to manipulate the symbolic system by which the led define the situations if he is to soften the blow that defeat implies. In labor-management conflicts, for example, events which may appear to an outsider as having only peripheral importance may in fact have highly charged emotional significance to the participants. The return to work of a few strikers or, alternatively, the success of a demonstration or the support of public officials or the reactions of an organ of public opinion, may be invested by the rank and file with high symbolic significance and trigger off a return to work or a revival of the will

to victory. This is why it is important for the leaders to manage the symbols that structure the perception of the led. The strike leader must know how to end a strike at the opportune moment, but his knowledge would serve him but little if he did not also have the ability to communicate his knowledge to the led. This may often involve the highlighting for the rank and file of a partially attained victory in order to divert attention from a partially suffered defeat.

This is the stuff of which compromises are made. Often seen by the rank and file as a "betrayal" by the leaders, they actually derive from the structural circumstance that the leaders' position allows them a view of the total situation which is denied to the led. Moreover, leadership roles require to so manage intragroup tensions as to keep the group united in adversity even though this might entail certain sacrifices insofar as the attainment of the group's goals are concerned. "System maintenance," to use [Talcott] Parsons' terminology, may sometimes require lowered task performance.

Indeed, most conflicts end in compromises in which it is often quite hard to specify which side has gained relative advantage. Hence, one must distinguish between the will to make peace and the will to accept defeat. Quite often the former may be present although the latter is not. The parties to the conflict may be willing to cease the battle when they recognize that their aims cannot be attained or that they can be attained only at a price which they are not willing to pay, or, more generally, when they conclude that continuation of the conflict is less attractive than the making of peace. In neither of these cases would they be willing to accept defeat although they are willing to stop short of victory. In such situations they may be impelled to explore the chances for

[13] Erving Goffmen, "On Cooling the Mark Out," *Psychiatry*, **15** (November, 1952), 451-463.

a compromise. The willingness to negotiate a compromise, that is to stop chasing the mirage of victory, will, of course, depend on correct assessment of the situation, and such assessment, just as in the cases discussed earlier, will be facilitated by the availability of indices of relative standing in the battle. It is one of the key functions of the mediator to make such indices readily available to both parties. To the extent that the contenders share a common system of symbols allowing them to arrive at a common assessment, to that extent they will be able to negotiate. Symbols of defeat and victory thus turn out to be of relevance in order to stop short of either.

Relative appraisal of power is difficult before the contenders have measured their respective strength in conflict. But accommodation may be reached once such an assessment has been achieved. Such redefinitions in the course of a struggle often bring to the fore elements which remained hidden during its onset. Accommodation is facilitated if criteria are available which allow the contenders to gauge the situation. The chance of attaining peace without victory depends on the possibility of achieving consensus as to relative strength and on the ability to make this new definition "stick" within each camp. When the United States chose the neck of Korea as their symbolic standing place in the Korean War, they succeeded in conveying to the other side as well as to the American people their determination to hold it. When enough blood had been let and it became clear to both sides that the other could be beaten only at a cost that neither was willing to incur, negotiations got down to a compromise that took into account the real balance of political and military power and proved acceptable at home. "Peace through stalemate," writes B. H. Liddell-Hart, "based on a coincident recognition by each side of the opponent's strength, is at least preferable to peace through common exhaustion."[14]

Although it is true that in many cases an assessment of the relative strength of the opponents is possible only in conflict, it is also true that their travail may be shortened if clear symbolizations of outcome and relative strength are readily available. When recourse to such measures of success or failure has been highly institutionalized, the duration of the conflict can be shortened and its intensity limited. In this sense, research directed toward an understanding of those symbols which move men to accept compromise or even defeat might be as valuable as research to uncover symbols which incite to war.

[14] B. H. Liddell-Hart, *Strategy: The Indirect Approach* (London: Faber and Faber, Ltd., 1955), p. 370.

social change

twenty-three

Robert MacIver has said that discovering the "principles of change" is potentially the most illuminating task of the social scientist, and yet the most elusive. Many a young sociological knight, who has proudly ridden out proclaiming his intention at last to capture and tame this dragon, later crawled back with his lance broken, his armor badly dented, and the dragon still breathing fire in freedom. A *general* theory of change may be so elusive as to escape us forever, but sociologists have made substantial progress in developing more limited models of change which seem to apply quite well to selected events in a narrow range of time. In this chapter such a model is developed and tested against the facts of social change in Soviet Russia from 1890 to 1950.

Social Change in Soviet Russia

ALEX INKELES

Even in the case of so imposing, rapid, and extensive a social revolution as that experienced in the Soviet Union, one discerns a host of changes which can be equated with the broader sweep of social change that affected western society in the last century. In the realm of authority, for example, there has been a shift from traditionally legitimated authority to a system of formal rational-legal authority although with a large admixture of charismatic legitimation. In the economic sphere the transition has been from

Alex Inkeles, "Social Change in Soviet Russia," *Freedom and Control in Modern Society*, Morroe Berger, Theodore Abel, and Charles H. Page, eds. (Princeton: D. Van Nostrand Co., Inc., 1954), pp. 243-264.

the predominantly agricultural to the heavily industrialized, with a concomitant change in agriculture from small-scale units and a limited if not primitive technology to large-scale units worked primarily by machine. Accompanying these alterations in the economic structure there has been a characteristic trend in the direction of urbanism, with the development of large-scale urban aggregates. The extended family has been largely broken up, to be replaced by more or less isolated conjugal family units, and women in enormous numbers have been drawn into the occupational system. In interpersonal relations the "familistic," or what Talcott Parsons calls the particularistic, patterns of an earlier era have been ever pushed into the background to be replaced increasingly by formal, impersonal, or "universalistic" relationship patterns under the impact of increasing role specialization and spreading bureaucratization and technicization. A relatively stable system of social stratification, based largely on role ascription and traditional criteria for the assignment of prestige, has been replaced by extensive social mobility with status largely assigned on the basis of achievement in turn intimately linked with the attainment of education and technical skill.

In the realm of values and fundamental "life ways," religion has lost ground to the progressive secularization of values; and distinctive national folk cultures, with their infusion of religious prescription, have in significant degree given way to a more or less uniform national culture with the predominance of rational legal norms for regulating individual behavior. The relaxed, nonstriving, undisciplined personality type which was modal, if not actually favored, has fallen into official disfavor relative to the model of the disciplined, goal-oriented, striving, energetic, optimistic "new Soviet man." Even that respect in which social change in the Soviet Union is frequently taken to be most distinctive—namely, the presence of a conscious and centrally determined plan for change—can be said to have its historical parallels, to which Kroeber calls attention, in Russia in the person of Peter, elsewhere in the Meiji modernization of Japan, and more recently in the wholesale social change in Turkey effected by Kemal Ataturk.

Although it may be comforting to be able thus to reduce the discrete aspects of changes in Soviet society to relatively standard descriptive categories, our understanding of the total phenomenon of social change in the Soviet Union is thereby only slightly enhanced. For such an approach fails adequately to deal with the unique *combination* of those elements which the Soviet revolution represents. No less than inventions in material culture, the social invention of the revolutionary process takes its character from the unique combination of elements already at hand rather than from the generation of entirely new patterns of social relations.

In the Soviet case we have the distinctive combination of planned social change instituted from above, centrally directed and executed by a body whose occupational role is that of effecting change, backed by the power and all the economic and political force which a totalitarian regime can muster, guided by a central theory or ideology, carried out at a relatively unprecedented rate, and extending into every dimension of social life. Even leaving aside the distinctive element of the Marxist orientation of the Soviet revolution, it is most doubtful that any program of this type on such a scale and of such intensity can be found in recorded history. Yet this is not to be taken as an event never reasonably expected to recur. Indeed, its significance comes largely from the fact that its leaders see it as a model for programs of social change in time to encompass the major part, if not all, of the world's peoples and societies. Furthermore, in many areas of the world it is apparently perceived as a model by revolutionaries who are already in power or who are making a significant bid to gather power into their hands. Consequently, although unique for its early season, the Soviet revolution may become a widespread standard for social change in the next half century. Thus, added to its intrinsic interest as a social phenomenon is its continuing political significance. We are under double incentive, therefore, to seek in the Soviet revolution the reflection of those "principles of change" which

Robert MacIver set as the hardest yet potentially the most illuminating task of the social scientist.

The Russian revolution cannot properly be conceived of as merely an event of precisely limited duration in the same sense as the American revolution. It is rather a process of substantial duration, and one which affected all the major institutional components of the society in which it occurred. Indeed, it is not one process, but a complex of processes operating at different levels and rates. For example, political authority has never really in any fundamental sense undergone a transformation in Soviet society. From the earliest days control has been exercised by a small group of tightly organized, highly conscious and purposeful ideologists with a marked drive for political power. Such change as did occur was in the direction of making explicit and concrete the basic implications and propensities of the Leninist position which Stalin carried to its logical conclusion.

In contrast, Soviet policy in regard to the family has undergone profound change during the course of the revolution. Stimulated by Engels' hostility to the "bourgeois" monogamous family and his prediction that many of its functions would wither away to be replaced by state care and raising of children, and spurred on by Lenin's assertion that to be a socialist one must believe in complete freedom of divorce, the Soviet regime initially subjected the family to a frontal attack including divorce by post card, and legal and free abortion. But today not only is abortion no longer free, it is a serious offense except under certain extreme circumstances, and divorce is at least as difficult and expensive to obtain as in the great majority of states in the United States. The family as an institution is reconstituted in the eyes of the regime, defined as a pillar on which the society rests. Parents are hailed as the partners of the state in the bringing up of healthy, patriotic, obedient citizens devoted to work.

In the rural areas of the Soviet Union we are treated to still another level and rate of change. For here is a vast and complex form of social organization for agricultural production built at untold cost by a process of forced change on an enormous scale, followed by years of experimentation and adjustment, and by the regime's testimony proved in the test of war as successful in meeting its social functions. Nevertheless, it is inherently unstable, is clearly viewed by the leadership as transitory, and is marked for further radical transformation.

To understand this complex, to discover the essential pattern, we must discern the elements which have entered into the process of social change in Soviet society. Three main elements may be analytically distinguished, which have been in interaction with varying degrees of intensity throughout the history of Soviet social development. The first of these we term Bolshevik ideology, the conceptual apparatus, the aspirations and objectives of the power élite. The second we may designate as the social structure which the new authority inherited, in a sense, when it seized power in revolutionary Russia. The third is constituted by the new institutional forms and social forces set in motion by the revolutionary upheaval itself, and particularly by the early efforts of the Bolshevik leadership to place its program in operation. From the interaction of these elements, from the changes wrought in and on each, has emerged the structure of Soviet society as we know it today.

Can we discern in the interaction of the elements we have distinguished any pattern that would have more general application to revolutionary programs committed to the radical transformation of society? Viewed in the perspective of more than thirty years of development, the Soviet revolution suggests the existence of a patterned sequence of revolutionary social transformation which may have general relevance. The major determinant of that sequence appears to be the differential adaptability of social organization to consciously directed social change. In a sense the problem is one of delineating the timetable of social revolution and the limits on its effect and extent. Essentially, we seek an answer to the question: What in the old social structure can the revolution sweep away almost at once, what basic social changes can it effect in a relatively short course of time, and what institutional forms and behavioral patterns are most persistent and may be changed by the revolutionary process only in the very long run, if at all?

The different levels of change are, of course, not restricted to completely discrete time periods, but rather overlap substantially. Nevertheless, some rough congruence can be established between the major processes of revolutionary development and certain broad time periods. In a double sense, therefore, we may speak of the revolutionary timetable, from which we can read both the place of departure and the destination (or direction) of change, and the approximate time of initiation and termination of the various processes of change. The following exploration of the levels of social change in Soviet society will, therefore, distinguish three major time periods of revolutionary development in the Soviet Union: an initial period, termed the period of the seizure of power, lasting until roughly 1924; an intermediate period, termed the period of the consolidation of power, running until 1936; and a third, or current period, called the period of the stabilization

of social relations. Such a division of Soviet development into stages and time periods, however, must be clearly recognized as a construct we impose on the data. Least of all should it be taken as a "timetable" in the sense that it provided an advance schedule for the Communist party. On the contrary, the stages of Soviet development were almost certainly not foreseen by the men who came to power in October, 1917. Indeed, it may be said that it is precisely the fact of their inability accurately to anticipate the long-range development of Soviet society that makes more comprehensible many acts of the Bolshevik leadership which subsequently required radical alteration and adjustment.

The initial period of revolutionary development, the period of the seizure of power, begins before the revolution with the emergence of the revolutionary party, and witnesses the formulation and elaboration of its ideology and program of action, with successive adjustments in both political organization and ideology to meet the exigencies of the local situation and to incorporate the lessons of experience. The period includes, of course, the actual revolutionary seizure of power, and continues until the formally proclaimed seizure of power is rendered truly factual by the destruction, or at least the neutralization, of effective organized opposition. In the Soviet case this period may be dated as beginning roughly in 1898 with the formation of the Russian Social Democratic party, certainly no later than 1902-03 when the Bolshevik faction, under Lenin's leadership, split with the Menshevik group; and it extends through the October, 1917, revolution and the subsequent period of Civil War and foreign intervention. In its last phases this period saw the calculated and ruthless overthrow and supplanting of the independent emergent political entities on the periphery of the former Tsarist empire, climaxed by the bloody and arbitrary destruction of the Menshevik social-democratic government of Georgia. The end of the period may be symbolized by the adoption of the Constitution of the Union in 1924, which established the unquestioned hegemony of the central power in the federated structure of Soviet Russia.

In the broad social and economic realm this period is characterized by the destruction or radical transformation of many of the gross institutional features of the old social order, and the primarily proclamatory initiation of the revolutionary features of the new social order. Perhaps the most important, certainly the first, major change involved the structure of power relationships through the transfer of political authority from the provisional government to the workers' and peasants' government of Russia, meaning, in effect, the Communist party. Following closely on the transfer of formal governmental authority, and intimately associated with it, came the basic shift in the structure of property relationships, beginning with the nationalization of all land and its expropriation without compensation and the abolition in perpetuity of the right of private property. The establishment of workers' control over industry and related establishments was in turn followed by confiscation and nationalization of most industry. Nationalization of the banks, the effective confiscation of important holdings of individuals therein, the elimination of the rights of inheritance, and the proscription on hiring the labor of others completed the radical transformation of property relationships. Similar structural changes were effected in the nation's legal system, with the outright abolition of "all existing general legal institutions," the repudiation of the existing legal codes, and their replacement with a new system of people's courts and the rule of "revolutionary legal consciousness."

The changes in the locus of authority, the transfer of property, the dissolution of the old legal system, in effect meant the destruction of the old formal class system. But this was further advanced by a decree abolishing all classes, divisions, ranks, and distinctions save that of "citizen of the Russian republic," extending to the abolition of even military ranks and titles. Finally these transformations reached to the realm of thought, belief, and interpersonal relations with the separation of church and state and at least the formal declaration of freedom of conscience, the institution of civil marriage, virtually complete freedom of divorce, the legalization of abortion, and the declaration of absolute equality for women in all legal, political, and economic relations.

The second major period of revolutionary development, the period of the consolidation of power, beginning in 1924, extends through the latter part of the new economic policy and the massive programs of industrialization and forced collectivization, down to the formal declaration of the establishment of socialism embodied in the so-called Stalin Constitution of 1936. The revolution had been fought to a successful issue. The old society was a bombed-out shell, with only here and there a torn wall still standing, although a certain subterranean structure or foundation stood relatively undamaged and firm, and represented a phenomenon yet to be dealt with by the regime.

The task of revolution shifted to that of building the new society on the ruins of the old. Lenin was not unaware that the revolution was only a surface phenomenon so long as it was restricted to the formal destruction of the old social order. Many a revolution before had seen the rapid restoration of the old order despite the most sweeping formal legal changes. Indeed, Lenin was wont to speak of what he termed a peculiar "Bolshevik conceit" implicit in the assumption that revolution could be effected by decree rather than by the systematic construction of new institutional forms and patterns of social organization and human relationship. It is in this period, therefore, that we find the extensive social experimentation and innovation which produced the main institutional forms that we recognize today as the characteristic features of Soviet society. Indeed this period may be regarded as the second Soviet revolution (the first having been the revolution in the structure of formal power and authority): the social revolution, the revolution in the forms and patterns of social and economic organization.

By the late 1920's, in the agricultural realm, for example, the land was nationalized and the land owner gone from the countryside. But in most essential respects the forms of rural social and economic organization remained much as they had been before the revolution. The old patterns of social differentiation were still much in evidence. In 1927, 8 per cent of the peasants were still landless, 20 per cent were classified as semiproletarians, and over a third of the households were still obliged to hire their animal power and farm implements from the rich peasant or "kulak." Only about 3 per cent of the peasant households were joined in state or cooperative farms. As Sir John Maynard has phrased it, ten years after the revolution "the countryside was back in prewar days, minus the landlord."

It was into this situation that the regime moved with its astounding program of forced collectivization on a scale unprecedented in history and with a ferocity and intensity such that even Stalin had to draw back, call a temporary halt, and cry "dizzy with success." Some 25,000,000 farm families, constituting more than 100,000,-000 souls, were forced in the span of a few short years radically to change the whole pattern of their lives. Five million of these people, those in the families designated as "kulak," were dispossessed outright of their land and property, and a large proportion forcibly transplanted to other parts of the country. The Russian countryside glowed red—the sky with flames of burning peasant huts and government buildings, the ground with the blood of cattle slaughtered by the peasants and peasants slaughtered by the militia and the flying squads of Communist workers and the agitated peasant "Committees of the Poor." Between 1928 and 1933 the cattle population fell from 70 to 38,000,000, sheep and goats from 147 to 50,000,000, and pigs from 26 to 12,000,000. Losses of this magnitude for a predominantly agricultural country are so staggering as to be very nearly beyond comprehension. They meant for the country at large a drastic and violent decline in the supply of animal food and industrial raw materials, and for the villages in addition a colossal loss of draught power and animal fertilizer. Once again famine stalked the land.

Yet out of this chaos and destruction there emerged a new form of social organization which constitutes one of the major institutional complexes of Soviet society, incorporating well over half the population. The *kolkhoz* or collective farm system is a distinctive form of social organization, with its *kolkhoz* chairman, general meeting, advisory council, and other administrative forms; its brigades and links for the organization of the work group; its labor day, piece rate, and bonus system of remuneration; its social insurance funds, communal buildings, peasant reading huts, radio loudspeaker nets, and other instrumentalities for the provision of social services and facilitation of communication by the regime; its complicated contracts with the machine tractor stations and state breeding farms, and with government agencies which control production and regulate delivery to the state of assigned quotas of produce; its *usadba* or private garden plot, and other forms for relating the private economy of the peasant to the collectivized, state-oriented segment of the agricultural economy. All these are examples of the diverse institutional arrangements which had to be devised to convert the idea of collective farming into an adequate form of social organization capable of effecting agricultural production in accord with the interests of the regime, which would yet have an essential minimum of congruence with the needs and expectations of the peasants. Thus we see in the agricultural realm the characteristic pattern of the second phase of revolutionary development—to meet newly created or perceived needs, new forms of social organization are devised, tested, reformed and reshaped, and finally woven into some viable system of social institutions for relating men to men, to the machinery of production, and to the larger society.

Certainly less violent, but perhaps no less spectacular, was the industrial transformation of Soviet society effected by the five-year plans. In the course of the first five-year plan more than 20,000,000,000 rubles were invested in industrialization, above 80 per cent of that sum going to heavy industry alone. The gross product of large-scale industry as evaluated in fixed prices was by Soviet report more than doubled, and although there is much doubt as to the accuracy of the figure it does reflect the magnitude of

development, which is also apparent in the fact that the industrial labor force doubled in size from 11 to 22,000,000 workers and employees.

In contrast to the situation in agricultural production, the regime was faced with much less of a task of creating institutional forms *de novo*, for there was at hand both the model of industrial organization in prerevolutionary Russia and throughout the western world as well as Soviet experience gained in the years of state industrial administration since 1917. At the same time, the leaders' experience was largely limited to restoring to its former level an already established industrial structure, whereas they were now faced with the rather different task of building a new industrial system. The problem was intensified not only by the greater magnitude and complexity of the new industrial order, but also by the fact that many of the industries now introduced were new to the Russian scene. Consequently, in this area as well there arose imposing problems of evolving new forms of social organization, and of integrating the new molecular institutions with the molar social system.

The result was a vast amount of experimentation, invention, revision, and readjustment in the social and organizational forms which constituted the structure of Soviet industry. For example, to find the most efficient formula for relating the discrete industrial enterprises to each other the regime abolished the chief administrations or *glavks* and replaced them with combines in May, 1929, only to abolish the combines in turn and replace them in 1934 with the previously abolished chief administrations now reconstituted in revised form. As might be expected, the greatest uncertainty centered on problems of managerial responsibility, with a constant strain manifested between the demands of efficient, authoritative management on the one hand, and on the other the requirement for central control by higher economic organs and for supervision and political surveillance by the local party and trade union organizations. There was, consequently, a long history of experimentation and halting development before there emerged the current Soviet variant on the common pattern of responsible plant management, which they termed *edinonachalie*, or one-man management.

A comparable range of problems was met in the effort to establish measuring instruments and standards for evaluating progress and making investment decisions. In time the regime was forced to adopt elaborate indices of qualitative and quantitative production, to set and manipulate prices, and to evolve a system of cost accounting, although many of the devices adopted had been assumed by Marxian economics to be unnecessary in a socialist economy. Comparable experimentation occurred in the effort to integrate the worker into the requirements of the evolving system of factory production. This produced in time the elaboration of work norms and quotas, the extensive piece rate system, the bonuses, socialist competition, the labor book, and other characteristic features of labor organization in the Soviet factory. The trade unions did not escape the process of adaptation, and were forcibly reoriented from concentration on protecting the rights of workers and collective wage bargaining to emphasis on maximizing production, inculcating labor discipline, etc.

By the mid-1930's the process of tearing down the old social structure was complete in virtually all its phases, and the main foundations of the new social order laid down. The factories were built, and the peasants organized in collective farms under firm state control. The first process, that of tearing down the old social structure, was particularly facilitated by the release of revolutionary energies and by the natural destructive forces set in motion with the loosening of social bonds characterizing revolutionary periods. The second process, that of laying the foundations for the new social order, was greatly facilitated by the devotion and extra human effort of a small minority—even though a minority of several millions—pushing on the rest of the population by example, persuasion, and where necessary by force. This was the "heroic" phase of the revolutionary process.

But neither revolutionary fervor nor extra human effort constitute[s] a firm basis for the persistent, day-to-day operation of a large-scale social system. The political and economic development of the revolution had now run far ahead of the more narrowly "social." In the haste of revolutionary experiment, no systematic attention had been given to the congruence of the newly established institutional forms with the motivational systems, the patterns of expectation and habitual behavior, of the population. Furthermore, as the new institutions began to function they produced social consequences neither planned nor anticipated by the regime. The leaders found themselves somehow compelled to bring these elements into line. For they found that it was one thing to build large factories and form collective farms, but quite another matter to get those institutions to function persistently at reasonable levels of efficiency. They came slowly to realize that it was one matter to enroll the peasants in collectives and to mobilize million of workers in industry, but yet another matter to induce them to labor discipline and high productivity. This realization was symbolized in Stalin's declaration in 1935 that, whereas in the first years of the plan it was technique that was decisive, in the new period "cadres [personnel] decide everything."

We enter therefore the current, but what is also in a sense the last, phase of revolutionary development in the Soviet Union, the period of the stabilization of social relationships. It is this period that answers in large part the question: What elements in the old social order tend to persist despite the revolution, and are changed, if at all, only in the long run? It appears that despite the massive destruction of the main formal elements of the old social structure and the extensive elaboration of new social forms, a large number of basic attitudes, values, and sentiments, and of traditional modes of orientation, expression, and reaction tend to be markedly persistent. Although the revolution effected a radical shift in the locus of power, the traditional attitudes of the population to authority and authority figures cannot be assumed to have undergone a comparable transformation. The change in the formal pattern of property relationships was equally fundamental, yet there is little evidence that the common man's "sense" of property, his attitude toward its accumulation, possession, and disposition, was altered in significant degree. In brief, we come in contact here with national character or better the modal personality patterns of the population, which show a marked propensity to be relatively enduring despite sweeping changes in the formal structure of society. Certain core or primary institutional forms, notably the kinship structure and the pattern of interpersonal relations within the family, show a comparable resistance and delayed reaction to change despite the revolutionary process.

Such persistent elements in the social system have a major impact on the revolutionary ideology and the new institutional patterns created under its imperative in the earlier phases of the revolution. The interaction of these forces of course changes both elements, but if we are to judge by Soviet experience the accommodations and adjustments come sooner and are more extensive in the new institutional forms than in the traditional primary institutions and their associated behavioral patterns. The really massive attack on the problem, the large-scale conscious adjustments to meet this situation, appear to be delayed until the later stages of revolutionary development. This delay occurs in part because realization of the need for such adjustments comes but slowly to practical men in the habit of effecting social change by decree, and in part because the initial focus is so heavily on the destruction of the old society and the institution of the major formal structure of the new social order. In the case of a Marxist-oriented revolution, furthermore, there is the added influence of an ideology which predisposes the leaders to assume that fundamental changes in the patterns of human relations, seen by them as part of the dependent "superstructure" of society, must follow naturally and inevitably from changes in the formal political and economic system.

In any event, from the early 1930's there began, in regard to a large number of Soviet institutions, a series of fundamental policy changes which many saw as the restitution of the old social order, others as the betrayal of the revolution. The "great retreat," as [Nicholas S.] Timasheff has labeled it, represented the regime's effort to place social relations on a stable basis adequate to the demands of a large-scale industrialized, hierarchic, authoritarian society. In the last analysis it was designed to produce disciplined, compliant, obedient individuals with respect for authority, who yet had a strong sense of individual responsibility and were active, goal-oriented, optimistic, stable.

Appropriately, basic changes came earliest in the realm of education, which witnessed rapid abandonment of progressive education and its replacement by traditional subjects organized in standard curricula, a formal system of examinations and grades, and perhaps most important, the restoration of the authority of the teacher. History was rewritten to reconstitute the role of the individual as an historical force, the great national leaders of the past were restored and now glorified, and the inculcation of patriotism became a prime responsibility of the school. The family, as already indicated, was restored to grace and defined as a pillar of the state, the authority of parents emphasized and their role defined as partner of the state in the upbringing of disciplined, loyal, patriotic citizens devoted to hard work and exemplary social behavior. The law was fetched out of the discard heap of the revolution and given an honored place as an essential ingredient of the new social order. Social stratification emerged in an elaborate and refined system of gradation of income and status which gave rise to a full-blown system of social stratification on the classic model of western industrial society. Accompanying these changes, and in a sense symbolizing the whole range of development, was the profound reorientation of Soviet psychology. The old determinist attitude toward human behavior was condemned and replaced wholesale by a psychology which emphasized individual responsibility and the ability of man to shape his own personality and behavior by the action of his will. The whole trend was perhaps climaxed by the startling accommodation with the Church which the regime made during the later years of World War II and in the postwar years.

Thus virtually all the novel and radical orientations of the regime to interpersonal relations and primary social groupings, which for many people were the distinguishing characteristics of the revolution, were replaced by traditional orientations of a distinctive conservative cast. There emerged by the time of World War II a definite and relatively stable social structure which was a distinctive mixture of the old social order and of the new institutional elements which had emerged out of the commitments of the revolutionary ideology. Both elements were, however, greatly transformed, adapted to the inherent demands of large-scale organization and the traditional motivational and behavioral patterns of the population. In significant degree the revolutionary process inside Russia had come to an end.

Although the pressure on the Soviet leaders to adapt the patterns of social relations better to suit them to the demands of the new industrial order is clearly evident, it is by no means equally clear why the course of action adopted involved so marked a restoration of previously scorned patterns of social organization. Their availability may perhaps be attributed to the inherent resistance of primary relationship patterns to social change. Since the regime shifted its policies after little more than two decades of rule, during part of which time its preoccupation with merely staying in power drew off much of its energy, it is hardly to be expected that radical transformations in popular values and attitudes should have occurred in anything but a small segment of the population. Furthermore, the widespread absence of enthusiasm, indeed the active hostility, of large segments of the population to the Bolsheviks and their program, undoubtedly acted to heighten allegiance to old values and ways of life as a kind of stubborn, mute resistance to the regime which could be expressed more or less safely because it was so covert. Finally, one should not neglect the fact that in times of rapid change and general social disorganization there is a widespread tendency to find a modicum of security in ritualistic adherence to familiar values and patterns of life.

The resistance offered, and consequent strain posed, by these persistent orientations undoubtedly forced some direct compromises on the regime. The granting to the collective farm peasant of the right to a private plot, and later the right to sell his surplus more or less freely in the peasant market, can both at least in large measure be explained as such forced compromises. But the changes in policy toward the family, the restoration of law, the reorientation of the school system, the reintroduction of ranks and distinctive uniforms in the military services can hardly be fully explained as the product of any inescapable compromise on the regime's part with the demands of the populace. The stimulus for most of the changes came directly from the central authorities; they were another manifestation of what Stalin has called "revolution from above." Indeed, in the case of the law making abortion illegal, the measure was forced through despite obvious widespread resistance on the part of major segments of at least the urban women.

The explanation of such changes must, therefore, be sought primarily in changed orientations of the Bolshevik leadership, changes in their conception of the nature of Soviet society and their role in it. Although Lenin was an exceedingly hard and ruthless politician, there were elements of radical "libertarian," indeed utopian, thought in his conception of the new society under socialism. These "libertarian" sentiments were given full expression by Lenin only during the brief period immediately preceding and following the revolution, particularly in his *The State and Revolution*. Yet we cannot dismiss them entirely. Although those thoughts represented a definitely minor mode in the total pattern of Lenin's thinking, they did constitute one facet of his intellectual makeup. Thus, alongside of Lenin's view of the mass man as inert, lacking in consciousness, and requiring stimulation and direction from without, another element of Lenin's view of human nature treated man as essentially spontaneously "good," and capable of tremendous works of creative social living once freed from the constraints, pressures, and distorting influences of capitalist society. He envisioned a relatively "free" society, in which the oppression of the state would be directed primarily against the former possessing classes, whereas the proletarian masses would enjoy a new birth of freedom. Lenin therefore assumed a high degree of direct mass participation in the processes of industry and government, epitomized in his statement that every toiler and cook could help run the government. He assumed that personal motivation would also undergo a transformation, and that men would work harder and better than ever before, because now they would be working "for themselves." Finally, the general problem of social control would diminish in importance, partly because of the new motivations of man under conditions of freedom, and partly because the community of men would take it directly into its own hands to deal with those who violated social norms.

The realities of maintaining power and governing the former Russian Empire under the conditions of civil war and general social disorganization assured that whatever the real weight of the views Lenin expressed in 1917, little was done to implement them on any significant scale. Nevertheless, Lenin apparently was clearly still motivated by some of this earlier thinking, as evidenced by his continued emphasis on mass participation, although in definitely more circumscribed and limited form than he had earlier envisioned. There is some evidence for believing, furthermore, that the apparent disillusion, the sense of doubt and perhaps defeat, which he experienced before his death in 1924, was related to his feeling that so far as the encouragement of man's free development was concerned, Soviet society was not going in the direction he had hoped.

Lenin's successors, Stalin and his coterie, at no time revealed a philosophic orientation to the problems of man's role in society which was at all comparable to that revealed, however briefly, by Lenin in 1917. They were hardly social radicals in the sense that Lenin was. They came to power by means of their talent for controlling and manipulating the party apparatus, wielding traditional instruments of power. They effected their program by force, and came through further experience to rely on the efficacy of organization and discipline, and to respect rules, order, training, and duty. Their approach to institutional forms was exceedingly pragmatic, their faith being largely in institutions that "worked"—that is, accomplished the functions assigned them in the social realm—so long as those institutions were consonant with the general goal of maintaining the Communist party in power, and facilitating the transformation of Soviet society into a large-scale industrial power, state-socialist in form.

This new leadership was faced, in the late 1920's and early 1930's, with a distinctive problem in Soviet development which heightened the probability that its basic propensities in the treatment of people would be maximally expressed. The rate of industrial expansion in the initial plan period was much more intense than had been earlier expected or, indeed, planned. This rate of development, imposed as it was on a system already operating with a most meager margin of popular consumption, created enormous, seemingly insatiable and self-perpetuating demands for the sacrifice of individual comfort and freedom of choice. Unless the pace of industrialization [was] to be significantly relaxed, a possibility the Stalin leadership apparently rejected outright, continued functioning of the system required absolute control of every resource including in the first instance human resources. The problem of social control became central to the Stalin group, and the answer it posed to the problem was consistent with the patterns it had manifested in its own ascent to power within the Communist party. Thus, however limited their chances for survival even under continued Leninist rule, the radical libertarian aspects of the earlier stages of the revolution fell a certain victim to the combination of circumstances represented by the propensities of the Stalinist group and the demands of the forced pace of industrialization which that group set.

The type of authority which the Stalinist leadership represented, and the pattern of institutional relations it had forged in Soviet society, required obedience, loyalty, reliability, unquestioning fulfillment of orders, adherence to norms and rules, willingness to subordinate oneself to higher authority, and other personal qualities suitable to an authoritarian system. In fact, however, the supply of such people was exceedingly limited.

The Stalinist faction was obliged, rather, to deal with two main types. First, more limited in number but widely present in positions of responsibility and trust within the élite, were the goal-oriented idealists, who found it difficult to compromise principle and to accept the apparent sacrifice of basic revolutionary goals for short-run intermediate objectives. Although these people were most prominent among the older generation of Bolsheviks, the Soviet school and the Young Communist League continued to attract and develop such individuals in substantial numbers. Second, the great mass of the rank and file of the population posed a related but different problem. Here, the widespread traditional Russian characteristics of evasion and suspicion of authority, avoidance of responsibility, lack of discipline and striving, were not being systematically countered by Soviet education, nor discouraged by Soviet law and custom through rigorous sanctions. Indeed, the system of progressive education probably seemed to the Stalin leadership to reinforce many of these basic orientations, and the beleaguered family was hardly a model of "proper" authority relations.

The problem posed by the core of goal-oriented idealists was of course summarily resolved by the ruthless method of the great purge in the mid 1930's, and by the reorientation of party and Komsomol selection and training. The problem posed by the rank and file of the population, and particularly by the growing generation of young people, many of whom were expected to enter the Soviet élite, was not resolvable by such simple means. The Stalinist leaders recognized that marked changes would be required in both the initial training of young people and in the environment in which those individuals would live as adults. The restoration of law, the reintroduction of ideas of guilt and personal responsibility, the intensification of sanctions, the imposition of firmer discipline, were therefore largely rational selections of means for the given end.

The restitution of the family and the changes in educational policy may be understood in much the same way. The leadership was concerned with developing disciplined, orderly, hardworking, responsible individuals who respected and feared authority. The restoration of the teacher's authority along with the reintroduction of regular curricula, examinations, school uniforms, student "passports," and the rest was apparently a product of careful calculation relative to the attainment of the goals indicated.

In seeking to achieve those goals it is not surprising that Soviet leaders should have looked to the past for models which had proved that they could "work" and which might be expected to take more "naturally" with the people. It is not at all necessary to assume, as some have, that this tendency arose because the Bolshevik leaders had "mellowed" as their stay in power extended itself, and that they consequently came to value traditional Russian forms as ends in themselves. Indeed, it is perfectly clear from the marked selectivity in the choice of elements from the past to be reconstituted, that only those were chosen which could serve the current objectives of the regime. The Bolsheviks restored many old forms, but they were not restorationists. Although the forms utilized were conservative they were adopted to serve the radical end of remaking Soviet man in a new mold of subservience, and although tradition was emphasized the Soviet leaders sought to manipulate it and not to follow it.

There were, of course, other alternatives open. Particularly in the case of the family, the regime could conceivably have attempted to bring up all children in state institutions in an effort to develop precisely the type of human material it desired. Indeed, the development of such institutions on a limited scale in the postwar period, in the form of the Suvorov and Nakhimov military schools, reveals the probable attraction of this solution for the present Soviet leaders. But the cost and burden for the state would have been enormous, the alienation of the population extreme, and the effect on the birth rate severe. Since the family could therefore not easily be replaced, the leaders acted instead to convert it to their purpose of raising a work-loving, loyal, disciplined, authority-fearing generation. Again, although the solution adopted may have been conservative, it hardly derived from any desire to return to the old way of life. Rather, it was an adaptation to the purposes of the regime of established and tested institutional forms. Indeed, it may be said that a characteristic of the last fifteen years of Soviet rule has been the increasing precision with which the leadership has come to manipulate institutions and juggle situations in order to harness private motivation for the purposes of the regime.

Marx was much more concerned with elaborating the developmental "laws" of capitalism than he was [with] outlining the institutional structure of socialist society. Indeed he tended to regard such efforts in a class with utopianism. Lenin, in his turn, was much more concerned with developing a model of the revolutionary political party, and with the strategy and tactics for the revolutionary seizure of power, than with detailing the pattern of social relations that should exist in the new society. Yet they left a sufficiently large number of explicit prescriptions and prognostications about the institutional forms of socialist society to permit a meaningful comparison between their expectations and the reality of Soviet social organization. Barrington Moore, attempting such an assessment in his *Soviet Politics,* has concluded that of all the aspects of Bolshevik doctrine the transfer of the means of production to the community as a whole represents the main instance of close congruence between prerevolutionary anticipations and postrevolutionary facts. Although many might produce a more extended list, there certainly is no doubt that the expectations concerning the school, the family, the organization of industry, mass political participation, social equality, and even religion, are hardly met by contemporary social reality in the Soviet Union.

In the light of this fact, what remains of the characterization of Soviet society as the product of planned social change? Certainly little, if anything, if our measure be the congruence between the current social structure of the U.S.S.R. and the specific institutional patterns called for in the social blueprint of Marxist-Leninist doctrine to which Soviet leaders ostensibly adhered. Long-range planning in this sense in the Soviet Union has been largely limited to the pursuit of very general goals, which were themselves frequently subject to change. It is perhaps more appropriate, therefore, to describe the pattern of social change in the Soviet Union as one in which the forces which produced change were centrally planned, or better set in motion, rather than to speak of the precise resultant institutional patterns themselves as having been planned. Thus, Stalin decreed the forced collectivization, and in some degree he planned and controlled the stages of its execution. But apparently no one in the Soviet regime had a plan for the detailed, or even for the broad, structure of human relations within the collective farm. The collective farm system as the complex of social organization which we know today was planned by no one. It grew out of a continuous process of accommodation and adjustment between the regime's interest in production and its control, the requirements of efficient organization within the structure of large-scale farm units, and the persistent desires, needs, interests, and expectations of the people who worked the farms.

The relatively unplanned development of the internal organization of the collective farm, however, represents only one aspect of advance social planning in the U.S.S.R. In particular, this type of development was most characteristic of the middle period of Soviet history, which we have termed the period of the consolidation of power. In the more recent period, as the preceding discussion of the changes in family, education, law, etc., sought to emphasize, there has been a marked tendency for the "revolution from above" to become ever more precise in effecting change rationally designed to achieve specific social ends. Furthermore, evidence from both published Soviet sources and interviews with former Soviet citizens strongly supports the premise that the regime has been surprisingly successful in its attempt to build "stability" in social relations.

There remains, nevertheless, the striking basic change in policy concerning the role of certain institutional complexes in the larger society, such as the family, education, and the law, about which Marxist-Leninist doctrine had been relatively specific. The importance, for understanding this development, of the change in the composition and life situation of the Bolshevik leadership has already been indicated. That change in leadership is a necessary but not a sufficient explanation of the "great retreat" of the 1930's. One must in addition give proper weight to the distinctive historical phenomenon with which Soviet development confronts us.

It is possible to discuss here only two of the crucial historical factors. In the first place, we must recognize the exceedingly limited experience of the Bolshevik leaders in the administration of a large-scale government apparatus imposed on a highly heterogeneous society. The Communist party was a training ground only for the revolutionary seizure of power and for the explosive destruction of the old social order, and its personnel was both attracted to and selected by it on those grounds rather than on grounds of actual experience in or potentialities for administration and social construction. In the second place, it must be recognized that in the eyes of most Marxists, indeed to some extent in the eyes of the Bolshevik leaders themselves, the Russian revolution was an accident if not a mistake. Initially the Soviet leaders firmly believed that they could not stay in power and could hardly proceed to build socialism, unless revolution soon came to the advanced countries of western Europe which would aid and support the Soviet regime. Even the limited guidance Marxist doctrine offered as to the program to be applied after the proletariat came into power was intended for and assumed to be applicable only in an "advanced" capitalist country with widely developed industry, a well-trained and disciplined working class, an efficient and functioning administrative apparatus. None of these requisites was available to be taken over by the Communist "vanguard of the proletariat" in Russia, and indeed what did exist was in a state of deterioration and disorganization at the time the Bolsheviks seized power.

The Bolshevik leaders, however, were perhaps understandably not prepared to relinquish power even though their own theory defined their position as an historical anomaly. Indeed, after an initial period of about six months of relatively cautious activity, they launched that overzealous and rigid implementation of the main features of the Marxist revolutionary program of social change which characterized the years of "war Communism." The personal qualities of the Bolshevik leaders and their experience in seeking to seize power had led them to raise to the level of principle the ideas of not compromising and of pushing ahead at all costs. Further the early radical policy was in part a response to the pressures created by the Civil War and the foreign intervention, which required absolute state controls. It was also in part a response to the apparent wave of revolutionary sentiment in the mass of the population, which the Bolshevik leaders sensed and by which they were somewhat carried away. In addition, however, one detects in the absolute quality of the policies of the war Communism period a desperate effort on the part of the Soviet leaders to prove both to themselves and to "history" the legitimacy of their revolution through great works of social transformation in the direction indicated by Marx.

In any event, whatever the potentialities of a Marxist program of revolutionary social change, it was certainly inappropriate to the conditions which existed in Russia in 1917. This incongruity was magnified by the explosive and wholesale character of the Bolshevik destruction of the old social order, and by the intensity of the pace with which the program was put into effect. It was perhaps inevitable, therefore, that social disorganization and a host of crises should have assailed the regime. And when the unworkability under Soviet conditions of the initial program of social radicalism became unmistakable, the reaction against it and its wholesale replacement with new action programs displayed that same sweeping, explosive nature which characterized the action patterns of a leadership trained predominantly in the absolute use of force.

Yet beyond the specific historical circumstances which attended the Russian revolution and the distinctive features of the Bolshevik leadership, one may discern the effects of a crucial lack of sensitivity and awareness of the salient characteristics of social organization which one need not expect to be limited to Communist social engineering. The Soviet leaders failed, for example, to give adequate consideration to the interrelatedness of the elements of the social system; that is, they failed to recognize the extent to which it was indeed a *system* such that basic changes in any major institution would have important implications for the functioning of other institutions and hence for the structure as a whole. Thus, they initially showed no real awareness of the implications of their family and educational policy for the rest of the system—in particular, the impact it would have on the fundamental attitudes toward authority which would be inculcated in youths raised in an atmosphere of distrust and suspicion of the earliest authority models, the parent and teacher. They neglected to weigh the influence of inherited motivational systems, and the culturally determined behavior patterns and expectations of the population. Thus, in their policy in regard to the remuneration of labor both in industry and agriculture they were faced with a prolonged struggle with apathy, lack of incentive, and consequent low productivity and high mobility of labor, which in significant measure resulted from the absence of any correspondence between the system of rewards which they had devised and the expectations of the population. They overestimated the ability of formal verbal pressures, of propaganda, significantly to affect behavior in the absence of legal sanctions and social norms, even when the behavior required ran counter to the existing personal motivation of individuals, and particularly when that motivation was lent support by pressures generated in the life situation of individuals. Hence, the failure of their propaganda efforts against abortion when it was legal and free, and when the individuals concerned had strong desires to avoid having children in the face of the pressures of inadequate income, housing, and other requirements of stable family life.

Perhaps least of all were they prepared to anticipate the possible diverse social consequences of any specific social action, or to recognize the imperatives which inhered in certain forms of social organization once they were instituted. Thus, they did not anticipate, and had no advance program to meet, the implications of the commitment to develop large-scale industry, with its inherent demands for hierarchical authority, technical competence, labor discipline, and the integration of complex tasks, and which therefore required the training of new personnel, inculcation of new habits of work, development of chains of command and channels of communication, of systems for allocating rewards, and other adjustments. From these commitments were to rise consequences, such as the rapid social stratification of the population, having far-reaching implications both for the revolutionary ideology and for the structure of the old social system on which it was imposed.

These are but a few examples of what might be termed the "lessons" of centralized social planning as they emerge from Soviet experience. . . . They are stated here in relatively value-neutral terms and, therefore, do not express the political reality of Soviet society with its monopoly of power, its secret police and forced labor, its censorship and absence of personal liberty and freedom, and its sacrifice of human comfort and dignity to the demands of a totalitarian power group. Crucial as they may be, such features of Soviet totalitarianism do not exhaust the significance of Soviet society and its changes. Efforts at large-scale social planning will undoubtedly be made in different political and cultural environments. And those efforts will also be obliged to deal with the realities of social organization, of culture, and of human psychology. It is a political decision whether or not such programs are undertaken, but once they are, an understanding of the dynamics of social systems can contribute to minimizing the resultant social disorganization and the consequent human travail. Certainly further study of Soviet efforts at planned social change can be expected to contribute to our understanding of the dynamics of social systems and the forces which must be reckoned with by those who seek consciously to change and direct such systems.

Part 6

modes
of
inquiry
in
sociology

It has been argued that the theoretical disagreements which seem so deeply to divide social scientists are in fact quite unimportant in comparison with differences in the mode of inquiry they adopt. Without forcing ourselves to decide the relative importance of these two aspects of sociological work, we can nonetheless acknowledge that the methods a sociologist mainly relies on certainly influence his choice of subject and the whole style of his sociological analysis. There is a definite tendency for the men who investigate certain problems to prefer certain techniques of investigation and vice versa. This has led to something of a stereotyped conception of "hard" and "soft" sociology, the former including, especially, research on small groups, public opinion studies, and studies of social stratification, and the latter including studies of organizations, the local community, the family, and the national society. Even if this division were an accurate reflection of reality, and that is itself doubtful, there is no reason why the differentiation need exist. The interaction of small groups can be and has been studied by laboratory experiment, by participant observation in street corner gangs, and through the analysis of the record of historically important conferences. Public opinion can be and is studied not only through public opinion polls, but also through participation in communities, talks with élites, and the analysis of official and public media of communication.

The distinction between hard and soft fields, and hard and soft methods, is mischievous and misleading. I have chosen the particular examples of important methods of social research appearing in this and other parts of this book in order to make clear the wide range of methods which may be used in any sociological investigation on whatever subject. While using the public opinion survey, Paul Lazarsfeld is concerned with subtle themes, such as "political apprehensiveness" and "political permissiveness." Charles Tilly, dealing with an historical question, uses census data, economic reports, information on the class background of legislators, and indices of the integration of city and countryside. L. F. Richardson works with mathematical models, but they here help explain the causes of wars. Elsewhere in our reader Oscar Lewis (Chap. 6), studying a small community in Mexico, uses police records, economic marketing data, and some of the sampling methods of public opinion polls. Robert Bales (Chap. 14) and Solomon Asch (Chap. 20) examine ideas as soft as the "great man theory of leadership" and the concept of "conformity," but each approaches his problem through use of the most rigorous techniques of laboratory investigation.

modern empiricism

twenty-four

There are many persistent misconceptions which the uninitiated entertain about modern methods of research in sociology. One impression is that of a rather crude instrument incapable of dealing with subtle qualities of social life or with important public issues. Others rather emphasize the esoteric, almost occult, nature of statistical analysis which seems to them to get further and further from simple exposition and clear meaning. No doubt there are those who abuse the questionnaire and misuse statistics, just as there are essayists who produce impenetrable prose and poets who write miserable verse. But it is a serious mistake to assume that these qualities are inherent in modern empirical methods. To make the point I have chosen a selection by Paul F. Lazarsfeld, who is not only one of the most vigorous and inventive contributors to modern empirical methodology, but also an eminent sociologist in the pure sense.

Exploring the Academic Mind

PAUL F. LAZARSFELD

WAGNER THIELENS, JR.

. . . An index of apprehension [has been] developed, permitting the characterization of each social science teacher in our sample according to the level of apprehension he felt at the time of the study. The items in the index were originally chosen, on common sense grounds, as typical expres-

Paul F. Lazarsfeld and Wagner Thielens, Jr., *The Academic Mind* (New York: Free Press of Glencoe, Inc., 1958). Copyright © 1958 by The Free Press, a corporation. Reprinted by permission.

sions among teachers of what might ordinarily be meant by this term. Then, to determine more precisely the meaning of the classification, . . . we cross-tabulated the apprehension index against other characteristics of our respondents, including their interest in matters of civil liberties and their experiences in the realm of academic freedom. *We concluded that the apprehension we measured was a combination of fear for one's own professional security and an objective con-*

cern with the state of academic freedom in general. For most professors it was not a paralyzing apprehension, since it left room for a considerable readiness to defend their rights and to express their own opinions, especially in the confines of the campus. . . .

Keeping still to the over-all statistical picture, the causes of teachers' apprehension were then considered. To organize our material we followed the well-established idea that all human experiences are determined by two broad groups of elements: the characteristics of the people themselves and those of the environment in which they live and work. . . . The pivotal attribute of the social science teacher turned out to be his permissiveness. . . .

[The rating of the social science professors as to their "permissiveness" was based on their answers to a set of questions concerning politics, controversy, and nonconformity on the campus. One question dealt with whether students should be allowed to form a Young Communist League, a second asked whether a professor should be fired if he admitted being a Communist. Another set inquired about allowing Owen Lattimore to speak on campus, permitting the Young Socialist League on campus, firing a store clerk who admitted being a Communist, and the relative advantages of having radical and nonconformist teachers among social scientists. Those who answered all five questions in the liberal direction (22 per cent) were classified as "highly permissive," and so on down to the group who answered all five questions in the opposite way (14 per cent) and were therefore classified as "clearly conservative." It was later observed that the more permissive professors more often voted Democratic, more often approved discussion of controversial matters in the classroom,

and more often felt it to be the teacher's responsibility to prepare students to participate in future social improvements.—A.I., Ed.]

. . . We would like to examine more fully some of the determinants and consequences of apprehension. The full complexity of the situation we set out to study is still bound to elude us in one single inquiry. And yet, we can indicate some lines for future work by discussing two sets of data in more detail.

To begin with, there is a marked difference in apprehension between younger and older teachers. This finding, if not a particularly surprising one, nevertheless turns out not to be simply explained. Quite an array of data will be introduced in order to interpret it. Our conclusion from this discussion will be [an] emphasis on . . . the mutual support which creates a common climate of opinion and morale among social scientists. This emphasis will be further justified by [a discussion of] age differences . . . in terms of permissiveness.

Next, we shall use an important illustration to elaborate on the . . . pressures on teachers. . . . This will provide a background for some data on the interplay between the incidents occurring on a campus, the extent to which they are perceived by various kinds of teachers, and their resultant bearing on the spread of apprehension.

In short, [we will] direct special attention to the social context of apprehension.

Age and Apprehension

. . . Younger teachers are likely to be more permissive than older ones. We would expect, because of this, that they are also more apprehensive. This is indeed the case: 53 per cent of the teachers aged forty or younger are apprehensive, compared to 46 per cent

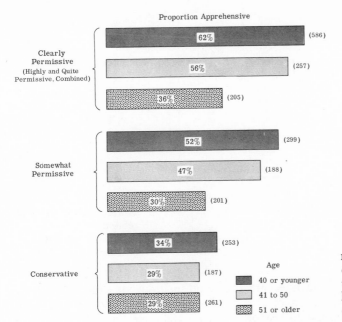

Proportion Apprehensive

Clearly Permissive
(Highly and Quite Permissive, Combined)

62% (586)
56% (257)
36% (205)

Somewhat Permissive

52% (299)
47% (188)
30% (201)

Conservative

34% (253)
29% (187)
29% (261)

Age
■ 40 or younger
□ 41 to 50
▨ 51 or older

FIG. 1. On each level of permissiveness, older teachers are less apprehensive than younger ones.

of those between forty-one and fifty, and 31 per cent of those over fifty. However, even when the factor of permissiveness is eliminated, age continues to play a role. The three parts of Fig. 1 show this, for they reveal that among the professors on each level of permissiveness, the younger respondents are more often apprehensive.

Why do younger teachers show more apprehension? Because they lack the security of tenure will be the first answer which comes to mind. But surprisingly enough, this is not the correct explanation. When the proportions of apprehensive respondents for those who have and who do not have tenure are compared, within each age group the differences are small and inconsistent. Among both those with and without tenure, however, the younger teachers remain more apprehensive than the older ones.

Thus the role of tenure should not be overrated. It is true that ousting a

teacher is legally more difficult for a school if he has tenure. But on the one hand, life can be made unpleasant for a professor even though he does not lose his job; on the other [hand], flagrant discrimination, if brought to light, is not easily defended even when directed against a person without tenure.

Another possibility deserves exploration. As a professor grows older he is likely to have published more, he becomes better known, and so might feel more secure because he can count on the support of his academic public. Also, his publications sometimes provide him with independent income, and thus perhaps with a cushion against temporary unemployment.

Our productivity index suitably represents a professor's publications. The questionnaire also asks: "Do you have any outside sources of income besides your salary?" Since outside income can, of course, come from other sources,

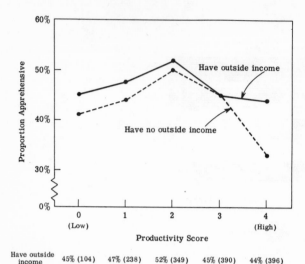

Have outside income	45% (104)	47% (238)	52% (349)	45% (390)	44% (396)
No outside income	41% (116)	44% (221)	50% (255)	45% (190)	35% (126)

FIG. 2. Apprehension as related to productivity and the availability of outside income.

such as consultations or investments, this more general formulation of the question permits an additional test of whether economic security affected professorial apprehension during the difficult years. The results of Fig. 2 are quite surprising in one respect.

Looking first along the two lines, in each case the most apprehension is found among the professors of medium productivity. This makes intuitive sense: quite likely these individuals have expressed themselves enough in public to become controversial, but have not acquired enough status to take attacks with relative equanimity.[1] The surprise comes when, on each productivity level, it develops that respondents with outside income in no way show a lower frequency of apprehension, but in most cases a slightly higher one. Outside income is often derived from consultations. We have noticed before that men and women

who do such outside work are likely to be more permissive. We took this as a sign of their greater sensitivity to a diversity of demands; it would also make them more alert to civil liberties problems, overbalancing whatever security they might derive from their additional income. In their net effect, then, none of the elements of objective security—tenure, professional status, outside income—which come with higher age are noticeably related to apprehension.[2] These factors, therefore, cannot explain why it declines so markedly with age.

The Role of Integration

Rather, we submit, it is a special kind of psychological security that

---

[1] Since productivity is of course cumulative with age, Fig. 2 had to be set up separately for the different age groups. Since the pattern remains the same, the figures need not be shown here.

[2] One other indicator of objective security was investigated. Because an unmarried teacher has fewer responsibilities than his married colleagues, we thought that he might be less apprehensive. Not to confuse the problem, the analysis was restricted to men and excluded teachers at Catholic schools, who often were priests. When the factor of age is kept constant, there is only a 3 per cent average difference in the apprehension of married and unmarried men.

plays a role here. Sociologists might call it a sense of social integration. The newcomer at a school, unacquainted with the traditions of his profession or of his college, feels insecure. He doesn't quite know what is expected of him, and even if he is told, can't judge what latitude he has for individual variations. The older a man gets and the longer he has taught at the same place, the more at home he is likely to feel. It is the difference between the well-known apprehension of the first-time weekend guest and the experienced visitor who, as the saying goes, "knows the ropes."

While tightly knit proof of this idea is not possible with the data on hand, two questionnaire items are suggestive indicators of this integration: the number of years a respondent has taught at his present college, and the way he feels about the relations among faculty members. We can use them to make several points. First, let us notice that the longer a professor teaches at a col-

lege, the more satisfied he is with the social climate in the faculty. Among those on a campus for five years or less, 20 per cent considered faculty relations fair at best; this proportion diminishes to 10 per cent among teachers with more than ten years' residence. Doubtless this is partly a question of self-selection; teachers who feel especially uneasy are likely to leave or to be forced out by conflict. And for those who remain on the campus, it is probably also a matter of personal adjustment.

In any case, apprehension is related to both of these integration factors. Fig. 3 classifies all respondents by their length of residence at the present college and their judgment of faculty relationships, and reports the proportion of apprehensive teachers for the nine resulting combinations.

The separation of the three lines shows that apprehension is more frequent among respondents who consider relations among faculty members less

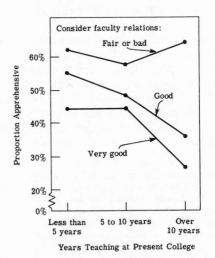

FIG. 3. The longer social scientists have taught at a college, and the better they feel about faculty relations, the less apprehension they experience.

Consider faculty relations—	Less than 5 years	5 to 10 years	Over 10 years
fair or bad	61% (159)	58% (137)	62% (73)
good	55% (349)	49% (409)	36% (326)
very good	44% (281)	44% (322)	26% (347)

satisfactory.[3] Undoubtedly, this works both ways: A satisfying personal environment puts a man more at ease; this enables him to look at other people with more trust and he thus encourages their good will. And inversely, apprehension and interpersonal difficulties can reinforce each other.

Reading along the two lower lines of Fig. 3, we find that the longer teachers have taught at a school, the less apprehensive they are. The top line is interesting: for the minority of 369 respondents in whose judgment faculty relations are not good at all, apprehension is about equally high, regardless of the length of time they have taught at their colleges.

This is, then, how we think the more widespread apprehension of younger teachers can be explained. They were newcomers at their schools, inexperienced in the rules of the game, and uncertain about the support they could count on, and so the events of the difficult years were bound to appear more threatening to them than to their older colleagues.

Since the uncertainties of a beginning career are in themselves something of a trial for young teachers, it can only be regrettable if these teachers are put under additional stress by outside forces. Under such circumstances it would seem important that the American Association of University Professors, as the major professional organization of college teachers, pay special attention to the newcomers.

We [have] found . . . that permissive social scientists are more likely to belong to the A.A.U.P.; because younger teachers are more permissive, one might expect that they are, therefore, more often A.A.U.P. members, and that this would help alleviate their apprehension. Actually, the opposite is true. Membership is more frequent among older teachers; and it is especially rare exactly among the younger people who have not yet been able to achieve attention through professional activities. The question arises whether the A.A.U.P. has not missed out in attracting the very social scientists who need help most.

The importance to teachers of a sense of social belonging is reinforced by one more finding. We [have found] that our social scientists have what we call a feeling of occupational inferiority: they think that community leaders, especially businessmen and politicians, attribute little prestige to the professor when he is put beside three comparable occupations.[4] Apprehension is the greater, the more pronounced this feeling of low standing. Figure 4 selects as an example the image professors have of how businessmen judge them. The respondents are divided according to the prestige they attribute to themselves: they may expect high esteem (first or second rank) or low (third or fourth).

We know that the more permissive professors are more pessimistic about their prestige; now Fig. 4 shows that on each level of permissiveness apprehension is more frequent among teachers for whom this occupational inferiority feeling is pronounced. Additional tables . . . show that the image

[3] Turning to our seventy-seven largest samples, we can classify the colleges according to the proportion of social scientists who think that faculty relations are fair at best; formation of these rates helps to eliminate the biases of individuals and so to describe the actual state of affairs. In the most satisfied schools (rate below 10 per cent), 45 per cent of the respondents are apprehensive, while in the most dissatisfied ones (rate above 30 per cent), the proportion of apprehensives is 52 per cent; the increase in the intermediate groups is proportional.

[4] The prestige attribution . . . was obtained in the following way: The imaginary judges were to rank the college professor as compared to a lawyer, a manager of a branch bank, and an account executive in an advertising agency.

of the Congressman's judgment, as we might expect in the difficult years, is more salient: the average difference in apprehension is 11 per cent, twice as large as that found for the businessman at the bottom of Fig. 4. For the trustees, the figure is also 11 per cent. It is because of the current special importance of Congressmen, and the perennial significance of the trustee, that we choose the less obviously meaningful figure of the businessman to mirror the professor's sense of community integration.[5]

---

[5] Several hundred respondents said they didn't know how outsiders would rank their profession. Invariably, these teachers were less apprehensive than those who expressed an opinion, even an optimistic one. They might be persons who "just don't give a damn" what other people think about them, and, being less concerned about the opinion of others,

The meaning of integration, it is true, has now changed. . . . Earlier, we talked about respondents' integration among their peers. Now we talk about the way they feel their profession is integrated in the larger community. Still, in this more general way, Fig. 4 shows again the sociopsychological determination of apprehension. Mutual support within the college makes for less apprehension, just as lack of support by the larger community (or teachers' doubts to this effect) makes for more.

Age and Permissiveness

The importance of one's social environment can be shown in still an-

---

are less apprehensive in terms of our index. Whatever the interpretation, the data are consistent.

Proportion Apprehensive

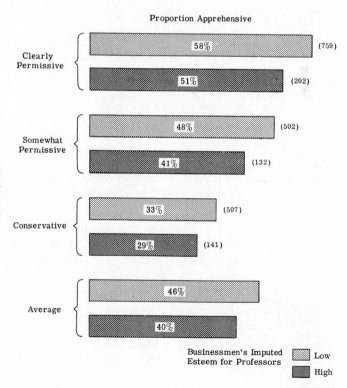

FIG. 4. Social scientists who have a greater occupational inferiority feeling are more frequently apprehensive.

other way. We have so far treated as "obvious" our finding that permissiveness decreases with age. But is it? Actually, two competing explanations come to mind. Perhaps as we grow older our individual enthusiasm for and belief in innovation declines just like other elements of our vitality. Or it may be that growing up in a basically conservative society explains this trend; would a country where something like a permanent revolution prevailed not show a very different "effect" of aging?[6]

A cross-sectional survey does not permit a definitive answer, but we have some evidence that the environment in which a man lives does, indeed, affect the role of age. While our respondents are all part of the same essentially conservative society, they work in colleges with quite different climates of opinion. We turn again to our seventy-seven schools with thirteen

---

[6] We are reminded here of the study by Theodore Newcomb, *Personality and Social Change*. He showed that in Bennington College, where the prevailing environment established by the faculty was nonconservative, the students became *less* conservative from year to year. For a summary, see *Readings in Social Psychology*, Guy Swanson *et al.*, eds. (New York: Holt, Rinehart & Winston, Inc., 1952). Where Newcomb followed the same students over a period of four years, we compare social scientists of different ages today. It could be that thirty years ago colleges were more likely to favor the appointment of conservatives. However, a detailed analysis of our age figures shows a steady decline of permissiveness with age, and this makes it more probable that the age results in Fig. 1 reflect a true biographical trend. This conclusion is also in harmony with what is known about the effect of age on the population at large. So we shall accept our data as evidence that the average novice starts out with a high degree of permissiveness and is likely to be more conservative toward the end of his career. We don't need to worry about another historical factor, the often-discussed role of the depression generation. They now would be in the age group 40-to-50, but we find the highest proportion of permissives in the youngest age group, who were adolescents just before the Second World War.

or more interviews, permitting us to develop characterizing rates. We can distinguish permissive colleges, where 60 per cent or more of the social scientists are clearly permissive; conservative schools where this rate is 39 per cent or less; and a middle group, where the permissive sector is from 40 to 59 per cent. Figure 5 reports the relation between age and permissiveness in these three groups of institutions.

In order to summarize the information in a compact way, the figure presents, for each type of school, the average permissiveness score for each age level. . . . These averages may provide a more sensitive measure of differences than percentages.[7]

Let us begin by comparing the first two age groups. Between the youngest and the middle age categories we find the following decline of average individual permissiveness: fifteen points (3.13 minus 2.98) in highly permissive colleges, thirty-two points in the medium school group, and thirty-six points in the most conservative schools. Thus the trend toward conservatism among older teachers is markedly smallest in the permissive colleges and highest in the conservative schools. Comparing next the middle and oldest age categories, we still find that the professors in the most permissive institutions show only a decline of twelve points after the age of fifty, while in the medium college group the decline is thirty-six points. The only place where the figures seem to run against the general trend is with the oldest teachers in the conservative schools, whose permissiveness score does not again drop sharply. Special tabulations suggest that this may be due to the fact that we do not have a larger number of "restrictive" items in our index.

---

[7] . . . Highly permissive respondents were given a score of four, and the clearly conservative one of zero.

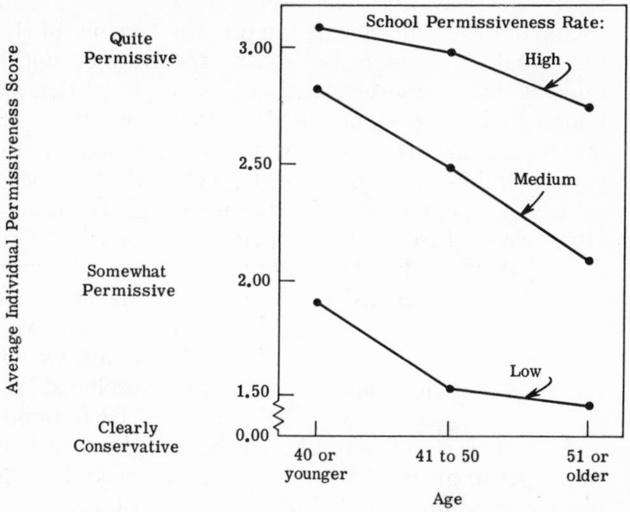

FIG. 5. The average level of permissiveness according to age, in three groups of colleges.

School Permissiveness Rate:	Average Individual Permissiveness		
High (60% or more clearly permissive)	3.13 (347)	2.98 (146)	2.76 (136)
Medium	2.81 (290)	2.49 (177)	2.13 (194)
Low (up to 39%)	1.90 (245)	1.54 (151)	1.46 (159)

On two of these items (disapproval of a guest speech and of the formation of a Socialist League), the oldest professors in the conservative schools are not more prohibitive than the age group between forty and fifty. Probably a greater variety of such items would be needed to bring out an extremely low level of permissiveness. On the other hand, it is of course possible that there is a limit below which the conservative attitude of a social scientist cannot go in the contemporary American scene. In this case, the bottom right percentage of Fig. 5 might not be a statistical artifact, but the measure of a cultural ceiling which limits the degree to which age and social environment may induce a conservative position. Only future studies can clarify this point. However, apart from this one exception, Fig. 5 shows again that the social context in which these social scientists work has a pronounced influence on their attitudes. The proverbial conservative trend of age is much smaller in a highly permissive environment.

The relatively small conservative age shift in the most permissive and, as we know, most prominent colleges has a considerable bearing on [the fact that] the more prominent social scientists are likely to be highly permissive. From this we deduce that for many of the less committed teachers, permissiveness is often tied up with the image of professional success. This might seem to be contradicted by the fact that on the whole the older and presumably more powerful members of the profession are more conservative. . . . This tendency is weakest in the leading colleges, which are surely the most visible to those younger teachers oriented toward the profession at large.

So far the notion of social context has meant relationships with other people: how long one has worked with them, the way one gets along with them, and the influence of the prevailing climate of opinion. But during the difficult years another element was bound to be important and therefore deserves special attention: the series of attacks and accusations against teachers which beset a number of campuses. How were these episodes perceived and what effect did they have on our respondents' apprehension?

The Impact of Incidents

A teacher who ha[s] himself been the target of an incident [is] especially likely to be apprehensive. But how [do] his colleagues react to the episode? [Do] they know of it at all? And if so, [do] they too become more apprehensive?

. . . Some teachers . . . report many of these episodes; others . . . notice nothing. It is not surprising to learn that a respondent's general ideology affect[s] his perception of the local situation: the more permissive respondents notice more incidents.

To bring this selective perception clearly to the fore, Fig. 6 introduces two precautions. Only those incidents are considered which are reported by at least two people—corroborated incidents, we will call them for short. And excluded as interested parties are the 269 respondents who were themselves the target of any kind of personal attack. By keeping the objective situation constant, each part of Fig. 6 shows that permissive teachers noticed more incidents than conservative respondents. For instance, at all schools where there were from one to three corrobo-

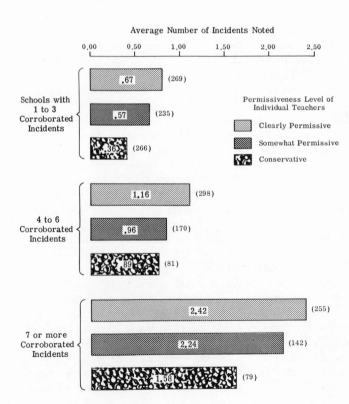

Average Number of Incidents Noted

Schools with 1 to 3 Corroborated Incidents

.67 (269)
.57 (235)
.36 (266)

Permissiveness Level of Individual Teachers

Clearly Permissive
Somewhat Permissive
Conservative

4 to 6 Corroborated Incidents

1.16 (298)
.96 (170)
.89 (81)

7 or more Corroborated Incidents

2.42 (255)
2.24 (142)
1.58 (79)

FIG. 6. Within the same objective situation, permissive teachers noticed more incidents.

rated incidents,[8] an average of .67 incidents was reported by clearly permissive respondents (two reports for every three teachers), compared to an average of .36 for conservative professors (about one for every three).

Does the number of incidents which come to a professor's attention increase his apprehension even if he is not himself involved? The matter is not easy to resolve. Even if apprehension and the number of perceived incidents turn out to be correlated, we cannot be sure how this connection comes about; the apprehensive teacher is their selective perception. If, then, the number of incidents is still related to increased apprehension, we can well argue that a threat to colleagues spreads apprehension among all social scientists. The facts are summarized in Fig. 7, which is again restricted to corroborated incidents and excludes all respondents who were accused or attacked themselves.

Looking at the separation between the three lines, we see again our familiar finding that permissiveness is strongly associated with apprehension. The new information is to be found

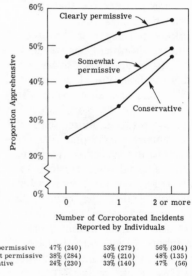

FIG. 7. The more incidents professors learn about, the more apprehensive they are.

	0	1	2 or more
Clearly permissive	47% (240)	53% (279)	56% (304)
Somewhat permissive	38% (284)	40% (210)	48% (135)
Conservative	24% (230)	33% (140)	47% (56)

Number of Corroborated Incidents
Reported by Individuals

more sensitive to academic freedom problems and therefore undoubtedly is quicker to notice if a colleague encounters difficulties. But we can take account of this, at least to a considerable degree, by a separate study of professors on different levels of permissiveness. This should help to discount

[8] A detailed tabulation of colleges for each exact total number of corroborated incidents leaves the pattern of Fig. 6 unchanged.

reading across each line. Regardless of teachers' own ideological position, and despite the fact that none of the individuals considered here has personally experienced difficulties, the more that incidents involving colleagues occur around them, the more apprehensive they are.

But Fig. 7 also tells an unexpected story. The effect of campus events is greatest, not upon the more permissive, but upon the more conservative professors. In the top line the figures increase by 9 per cent, in the bottom one by 23 per cent. The most probable explanation is as follows: A highly permissive teacher is concerned with civil liberties in general; he pays attention to events in other colleges and to discussion on the national level. His apprehension is considerable even if nothing especially dramatic happens on his own campus; local events increase his apprehension only slightly. But a conservative professor is less alert to civil liberties issues. If his own college is quiet, then his apprehension is low. Only if casualties occur nearby does he begin to worry, and then his attitude comes to resemble that of his highly permissive colleagues.

This differential effect of the objective campus environment has considerable implications, and needs to be documented as well as our data permit. We shall, therefore, show that the administration's performance also affects the conservative more than it does the permissive professors.

For each of the seventy-seven schools in which we conducted thirteen or more interviews, we can report what we previously called the protection rate: the proportion of respondents who feel that their administration would support them wholeheartedly in the event they were accused of being leftists. Thus these colleges can be classified into four groups, ranging from poorly protected to highly protected schools.

One would expect that the more protected a faculty, the lower the apprehension felt by its members. And in general this is indeed the case. But it is not true for our two most permissive categories of teachers (who together make up what we have called "clearly permissive" teachers). Their apprehension is practically unaffected by the protectiveness of the administration; but among the remainder the proportion of apprehensive professors decreases markedly.

In general, then, apprehension increases with the number of incidents on the campus and is relieved by an administration's protective performance. . . . The relatively similar amounts of apprehension on all levels of college quality [can be] explained as the result of a balance between attack and defense. The . . . important aspect of Fig. 7 is the differential reactions of professors with varying degrees of permissiveness. Conservative teachers are quite strongly affected by local events. Permissive social scientists, on the other hand, show a high apprehension which is little influenced by events on their own campuses. Several previous findings make highly plausible our surmise that the reaction of these men and women is more affected by what happens in their profession at large. Permissive social scientists are more interested in following civil liberties news; they put much more emphasis on general professional privileges than on the public relations problems of their own college[s]; their publication record shows that they are more oriented toward a nationwide audience. All this fits in with a way of looking at the world which has been given considerable attention by social analysts.

historical research

twenty-five

There are two main problems in historical research: first, to establish the facts of historical sequence, that is, to demonstrate what really happened and when; and second, to explain why things happened as they did. It has long been assumed that neither sociologists, nor indeed other social scientists, such as economists, had much to do with either problem. Establishing the facts was largely a matter of digging in government archives, and explanations were largely a matter of finding heroes and villains, uncovering the unique or accidental, or pointing to the self-evident facts. Now a new history is coming to the fore in which these conceptions are being profoundly changed. Charles Tilly's study of the rebellion against the French revolution points to the importance for historical scholarship of a different order of fact—such as the social class composition of the population, the economic relations between city and countryside, and the shifting pattern of control over public office—which sociologists are especially well qualified to collect. And the way of explaining the facts shifts from the personal and the accidental, from themes such as "traditionalism" in religion or "royalism" in politics to differences in social organization in different parts of the country. As Dr. Tilly says: "The strategic questions to ask and answer are, in fact, not doctrinal. They are basically sociological."

Counterrevolution in France

CHARLES TILLY

Through a species of dialectic, counterrevolutions often reveal the character of the revolutions against which they are directed. Resistance to a revolution may show, more clearly than its apparently unanimous acceptance, which elements of the population are the revolution's propelling force. For this reason, the Vendée, the massive revolt which broke out in the west of France in 1793, is of particular interest to those who wish to understand the French revolution. Albert Mathiez himself said that the counterrevolution had "the gravest consequences for the further development of the revolution."[1]

Charles Tilly, "Some Problems in the History of the Vendée," *American Historical Review*, **67** (October, 1961), 19-33.

[1] Albert Mathiez, *La Révolution française* (Paris, 1954), Vol. II, p. 201.

Yet much of the traditional history of the Vendée is of little help in understanding the revolution. Let us leave aside the dramatic military history of the counterrevolution, over which there is not much dispute, and the questions of hagiography, which so easily trip up the wanderer among so many heroes and exploits. These matters, although they probably fill nine-tenths of the mountain of books written on the Vendée, are not very important for the general history of the revolution. That leaves the perplexing problem of the origins and development of the counterrevolution. Those historians who have faced this problem seriously are a mere handful in the throng who have written accounts of the Vendée, but even they have not found a satisfying solution.[2]

It is not simply a question of finding a new interpretation of old facts. Much of the essential information is still embedded in the documents of the departmental archives of the West, in a form that only long and tedious research can release. But a recent revival of work on the old regime and the revolution in the West makes it seem feasible and desirable now to restate the essential questions and to indicate the direction a reinterpretation of the Vendée should take.[3] That is the purpose of this paper.

There are three problems that ought to attract our attention: the distinguishing characteristics of those sections of the West in which the counterrevolution flourished; the formation and composition of the two competing parties, revolutionary and counterrevolutionary; the relationship between developments before 1793 and the outbreak of the rebellion. It may be wise to begin by explaining why these problems are important, and why they are difficult.

Why did the counterrevolution occur where it did? The importance of this question seems self-evident. It implies, first, that a sound explanation of the Vendée must also account for the existence of militantly republican areas (such as the Loire Valley, the Poitevin Plain, and the coastal marshes) in the heart of the West and, second, that any successful study of the problem must be a comparative one. Yet despite the obvious character of these remarks, the historians of the Vendée have generally neglected the comparative problem, or given it only languid obeisance in their introductory remarks.[4] Furthermore, past neglect of the value of precise and detailed comparison has left us with nothing but general impressions, no more reliable for their frequent repetition, on such

---

[2] The most solid accounts are all over thirty years old: Léon Dubreuil, *Histoire des insurrections de l'Ouest* (Paris, 1929); Émile Gabory, *La Révolution et la Vendée* (Paris, 1925); Pierre de la Gorce, *Histoire religieuse de la Révolution française* (Paris, 1911-1923), Vol. III; Célestin Port, *La Vendée angevine* (Paris, 1888).

[3] Among the recent relevant studies are: Paul Bois, *Paysans de l'Ouest* (Le Mans, 1960); Joseph Denecheau, "La vente des biens nationaux dans le district de Vihiers," Mémoire pour le Diplôme d'Études Supérieures d'Histoire, Université de Poitiers, 1955; Marcel Faucheux, *Un ancien droit ecclésiastique perçu en Bas-Poitou: Le boisselage* (La Roche-sur-Yon, 1953); Louis Merle, *La mé-*

tairie et l'évolution agraire de la Gâtine poitevine de la fin du moyen âge à la Révolution (Paris, 1958); Charles Tilly, "The Social Background of the Rebellion of 1793 in Southern Anjou," Ph.D. thesis (1958), Harvard University.

[4] It was only by this sort of negligence that Dubreuil could attribute a crucial role in the fomentation of the counterrevolution to the influence of the bishops of the West over the lower clergy, and via the lower clergy over the general population, when the populations and the priests of each of the dioceses most directly involved—those of Angers, Luçon, Nantes, and La Rochelle—were sharply divided into revolutionary and counterrevolutionary territories. Dubreuil, *op. cit.*, esp. Vol. I, pp. 39-45.

fundamental questions as the ownership of the land, the material condition of the peasantry, and the sale of Church properties during the early revolution.

The first element conspicuously absent from the traditional analyses of the Vendée is therefore a detailed and systematic comparison of social organization in the revolutionary and counterrevolutionary sections of the West.

The illusion of unanimity in the counterrevolution has drawn the attention of historians away from the composition and formation of the revolutionary and counterrevolutionary parties within the territory of the rebellion. To be sure, all recent writers have recognized that even in the midst of the Vendée, a number of cities were "patriot" (that is, revolutionary) outposts; they have also noted that the "patriots" were recruited particularly among the bourgeoisie. But we need to know more than that: first of all, about the party divisions outside the cities, for the vision of a countryside uniformly opposed to the revolution is just as much a mirage as the vision of a Vendée without patriot cities. Then, it is clearly necessary to specify who were the activists on both sides, to deal separately with the positions of peasants, artisans, various types of bourgeois. Finally, we need to know how and when the parties formed. The answers to these essential questions lie in the forbidding, but finally rewarding, analysis of innumerable, apparently petty events of the years before 1793.

A satisfactory solution to these first two sets of problems would leave still pending the analysis of the events that led directly to the outbreak of the counterrevolution. Historians of the Vendée have generally assigned each of the major groups—for example, clergy, bourgeois, and peasants—a unitary attitude. They have then pictured "outside" events such as the sale of Church properties or the death of the king as revealing, activating, or at times modifying the expression of these unitary attitudes. To some extent this form of simplification is necessary both as a dramatic device and as an economical summary of the facts. But in using this too convenient form of analysis, Émile Gabory, Pierre de la Gorce, Léon Dubreuil, and the other writers on the Vendée have identified their social categories too carelessly (confusing, for example, peasants and artisans), assigned them positions and motives with insufficient evidence, and said very little about the relations among the members of the various categories in the years before the counterrevolution. As a result, the available accounts do not show how the fundamental events of the revolution affected their solidarity or hostility in the country communes that eventually revolted.

We may conclude that solving the puzzle of the Vendée is more complicated than a simple choice between the formulae now available: the far-flung noble plot, the agitation of the clergy, the "royalism" of the region, the defense of the clergy by the common people, the distaste of peasants for military service.

In fact, the bankruptcy of these "solutions" should be a sufficient warning against investing all in any sonorous slogan. In commenting on each of the three major problems already outlined, I shall suggest some less engaging, more ponderous, perhaps more honest, ways of dealing with them. The themes of the commentary will be: that there was a basic difference in social organization between the revolutionary and counterrevolutionary areas; that within the territory of the counterrevolution, party divisions followed identifiable lines of class and locality; that the revolt of 1793 was the culmination of a long and bitter series of combats between a small revolutionary party, essentially drawn from the mercantile bourgeoisie, which had assumed control of the political apparatus, and a larger, more disparate, counterrevolutionary party. In presenting these themes, I shall draw particularly on developments in Anjou, south of the Loire, the heartland of the insurrection.[5]

The counterrevolution was a creature of the *bocage*, the granite-based mass of land south of the Loire, which is settled in relatively dispersed hamlets and isolated farms and is covered with small fields surrounded by high hedgerows. The revolution was generally successful in the areas of river valley and plain, with their concentrated settlements and open fields. This observation in itself is commonplace. What is important is that the differences in habitat were accompanied by differences in the positions of the major social classes.

The *bocage* enclosed a considerable number of nobles, frequently resident, who owned most of the land exploited by the peasants, while in valley and plain the nobles were much more frequently weak and absent.[6] The

peasants of the *bocage* were mainly subsistence farmers, living on medium-sized rented or sharecropped family farms, selling enough cattle to cover rents, taxes, and little more. The principal intermediary between peasant community and outside world was the curé.

Valley and plain included large ecclesiastical properties as well as considerable bourgeois and peasant holdings, often extremely fractionated. Along the Loire the rich lands of such abbeys as Fontevrault and St. Florent often adjoined the plots of *bécheurs* and *laboureurs à bras*—peasants with holdings small and fruitful enough to be worked profitably by a man with a spade and his own two arms, instead of by a great team of six, eight, or even ten oxen, as in the *bocage*. The crops of these areas were often specialized and destined for urban markets: wine, wheat, flax, hemp. Their producers included a much larger proportion of day laborers and of owners of small pieces of land than in the *bocage*. This summarizes the agricultural complex.

There was also an industrial complex, and the surprising fact is that industry was more developed in the *bocage*, at least in those sections that

---

[5] The following conclusions are based mainly on the documents of the departmental archives of Maine-et-Loire, but also on those of other departmental archives of western France and of the Archives Nationales. The generalizations of this paper are meant for the section south of the Loire that joined the great rebellion of March, 1793, and not necessarily for the areas of *Chouannerie*—persistent harassment of the patriots by small bands of raiders, without open and general warfare—north of the Loire. *Chouannerie* raises a whole new set of problems, to the solution of which the recent thesis of Bois (*op. cit.*) has made a significant contribution.

[6] R. H. Andrews, *Les paysans des Mauges au* XVIIIe *siècle* (Tours, 1935); Marcel Garaud, "Le régime agraire et les paysans de Gâtine au* XVIIe *siècle," *Bulletin de la Société des Antiquaires de l'Ouest*, **2** (1954),

643-682; J. Levainville, "Les Mauge: Notes de géographie humaine," *Annales de géographie*, **14** (1905), 310-317; Merle, *Métairie et l'évolution*; Louis Poirier, "Bocage et Plaine dans le Sud de l'Anjou," *Annales de géographie*, **43** (1934), 22-31; Henri Sée, "L'économie rurale de l'Anjou dans la première moitié du XIXe siècle," *Revue d'histoire économique et sociale*, **15** (1927), 104-22; André Siegfried, "Le régime et la division de la propriété dans le Maine et l'Anjou," *Annales du musée social* (1911), 195-215. Bois's solid and devastating re-examination of Siegfried's conclusions concerning the Sarthe (*Paysans de l'Ouest*, esp. pp. 61-98) is an eloquent warning that Siegfried's observations of the areas south of the Loire need verification and that nothing could be more welcome than a careful and comprehensive study of property ownership and control in the whole region.

joined most actively in the counter-revolution. By far the most important was the textile industry, called the manufacture of Cholet, but actually scattered among more than 10,000 looms in a wide territory around that city. In the perspective of France as a whole, or even of the West, the manufacture of Cholet was of secondary importance. In the area of the rebellion there was, nevertheless, a growing class of merchants and clothiers, and in a great many communes weavers comprised 20 per cent of the working population. The features of this domestic production of kerchiefs and colored cloth that make it interesting for the present discussion are that it drew much of its raw material from outside the *bocage*, particularly from the Loire Valley, and that it placed its finished products on a national and world market, particularly via the port of Nantes. This means that in the *bocage* there was a small but prospering group of merchants who had relatively little to do with the local peasants, but much to do with both the local weavers and their colleagues outside the *bocage*. It also means that the cities, small as they were, were devoted to a commerce that drew their interests far outside the region.

This rapid summary indicates the essentials of the contrast: the plain and valley, combining peasant proprietors and day laborers who produced for outside markets, a relatively strong bourgeoisie, and extensive ecclesiastical properties; the *bocage*, populated with subsistence farmers dependent on noble landlords, a parish clergy with a strong hand in local affairs, a growing semirural proletariat attached to the textile industry, and a small but rising mercantile bourgeoisie. These facts alone would probably permit us to predict that the bourgeois would have an easier time developing a following and

encouraging support for the revolution in the first set of areas, and would meet greater resistance from nobles and clergy and receive less support from the rest of the population in the *bocage*.

It is essential to notice that the contrast between the two sections of the West, "blue" and "white," revolutionary and counterrevolutionary, existed long before the revolution and persisted long after it. Religious practice and political preference have followed the same frontiers well into the twentieth century.[7] An adequate analysis of the counterrevolution must therefore provide an understanding both of the temporary circumstances that agitated the West in 1793 and of the enduring characteristics of those sections that joined the rebellion.

The parties of *patriotes* and *aristocrates* formed early in the revolution, although it is not yet clear how widespread identification with one or the other was before the first applications of the Civil Constitution of the Clergy and the first sales of Church property, both early in 1791. These constituted the first deep thrusts of the revolution into the heart of the countryside and were, therefore, the first occasions on which many countrymen had to declare their positions publicly. From that time on, what there was of a third party was inexorably ground to dust

[7] See Joseph Denecheau, "Les élections de 1869 dans le département de Maine-et-Loire," unpublished Mémoire complémentaire, Université de Poitiers, 1958; Marcel Faucheux, "Les élections de 1869 en Vendée," *Bibliothèque de la Révolution de 1848*, **21** (1959), 127-162; Gabriel Le Bras, *Études de sociologie religieuse* (Paris, 1955-1956), Vol. I, esp. p. 306; Abel Châtelain, "Évolution des densités de population en Anjou (1806-1936)," *Revue de géographie de Lyon*, **31** (1956), 43-60; André Siegfried, *Tableau politique de la France de l'Ouest sous la Troisième République* (Paris, 1913).

between the turning stones of revolution and counterrevolution.[8]

The great majority of the clergy, particularly the secular clergy, belonged to the counterrevolutionary party. This may seem quite normal, until we recognize that it set off the *bocage* distinctly from the surrounding area. The most convenient indication is the oath aligning the clergy with the Civil Constitution, generally administered at the beginning of 1791. In the districts where the rebellion arose, the proportion of the clergy taking the oath was under 15 per cent, while in the surrounding "patriot" districts, it was generally well over 50 per cent.[9] In fact, the constitutional clergy who were brought in to replace those who had refused the oath were commonly curates and monks from the districts outside the *bocage*.

Nobles of the region were even more uniformly opposed to the revolution. Despite the common supposition that the nobles agitated and even organized the rebellion, however, they were very little in evidence in the party conflicts of 1791 and 1792. A number of the great nobles who were to be counterrevolutionary chiefs, such as Henri de la Rochejaquelein and Artus de Bonchamp, were with the king until late in 1792, many more nobles had emigrated long before the counterrevolution, and the rest had retired to their chateaux without meddling much in local affairs.

According to the paradoxical terminology of the time, the bulk of the peasants of the *bocage* were "aristocrats," opponents of the revolution. Here again is a remarkable contrast with the surrounding territories, where the peasants formed revolutionary clubs, bought Church properties, and gave all the other usual signs of support for the revolution.

The bourgeois, particularly merchants, clothiers, and others involved in commerce and industry, were the heart of the patriots. In southern Anjou, we find *négociants* and *marchands* everywhere in the lists of local officeholders and of purchasers of Church properties on the counterrevolutionary side of the line, while in the patriot country near Saumur, we find rather more lawyers, administrators, and substantial farmers. In many parts of the *bocage* the few bourgeois were the only adherents of the revolution.

Artisans are at once the most troublesome and the most interesting category. The auxiliary artisans (those who rendered services to the agricultural population, as did shoemakers, smiths, masons, or potters) resembled the peasants in political behavior. But the industrial artisans (weavers, spinners, and dyers) are another problem. Part of the problem is a simple matter of identification, since the most prosperous master weavers are practically

---

[8] The available evidence on party alignments is varied: a considerable number of reports on local affairs by communal and district officials, commonly submitted after some dispute over the application of revolutionary changes in the commune, and particularly dealing with the two groups of priests, those who had accepted the Civil Constitution and those who had not, the Constitutionals and the Refractories; the records of communal, cantonal, and district elections from 1789 to 1793, including the lists of officeholders and protestations concerning the manner in which they were elected; the records of the organization and recruitment of the National Guard and of the departmental battalions of volunteers; reports on counterrevolutionary manifestations and attacks on patriots before 1793. From the period of the counterrevolution itself, we have: a number of local and regional compilations of the names of participants in the rebellion, drawn particularly from the interrogations of refugees and prisoners; registers of refugees from the rebellion, such as a "liste des bons patriotes de St. Macaire" prepared to facilitate the return of the Republic to a commune near Cholet at the end of the great war of 1793. A(rchives) D(épartementales de) Maine-et-Loire, I L 1159.

[9] Charles Tilly, "Civil Constitution and Counter-Revolution in Southern Anjou," *French Historical Studies*, 1 (1959), 172-199.

indistinguishable from the poorer merchants, while the poorest rarely appear in the available documents. The more serious complication is that weavers and their confreres appeared on both sides of the party line between 1789 and 1793. On the one hand, it is evident that where there were many artisans, there were patriot strongholds. Cholet, Chemillé, Mortagne, and Bressuire are cases in point. Furthermore, a large proportion of the local National Guard companies and of the volunteers from the *bocage* were artisans.[10] This much is evidence of alignment with the patriots. On the other hand, a very large share of the leaders of demonstrations against the patriots in 1791 and 1792, and an exceptional number of local chiefs of the insurrection itself in 1793, were also artisans, for reasons which are now examined.

It is important to note that the textile industry of the *bocage*, after decades of energetic growth, began to falter just about the beginning of the revolution. No one has paid much attention to this local crisis (while the pains that the textile industry of France as a whole was suffering in the same period are well known). Therefore no one has traced its probable connection with the origins of the counterrevolution. The first signs appear in local reports for 1788; at the end of that year the merchants complained that business was falling off.[11] According to the accounts of the most important government bureau, at Cholet, production was down 25 per cent in 1789. By 1790 a report from Vihiers left no doubt of the gravity of the situation:

One can see from this account of the present state of the manufacturing and commerce of Vihiers how much they have fallen and continue to decline. This failure strikes the poorest class of people, the workers of the countryside, who are out of work and lack the resources to live and support their families.[12]

In the responses of the communes of Anjou to the 1790 questionnaire of the *Comité de Mendicité* of the *Constituante*, it was precisely those communes and cantons where weaving had flourished that reported the highest proportions of individuals needing assistance. These localities unanimously blamed the recent debacle of cloth and kerchief manufacturing in terms like those of the report from the commune of Andrezé:

We should observe that Cholet's commerce has fallen off entirely, so far as cloths and kerchiefs, which supported all the people of our *bourgs*, are concerned; the greater number have been out of work for two years, and reduced to begging, this causes many revolts over the movement of grains [out of the territory].[13]

Artisan discontent with this situation broke out in demonstrations against the bourgeois of Chemillé, Trémentines, and other textile centers. In fact, in the district of Cholet—the cradle alike of the textile industry, of resistance to the revolution before 1793, and of the counterrevolution itself— every locality that reported more than a quarter of its population needing assistance in 1790 was the scene of at least one "insurrection," and a center of exceptional agitation, between then and the counterrevolution.[14] It is therefore not entirely unreasonable to entertain the hypothesis that the industrial artisans were the most discontented class of the *bocage* during the early revolution, that they expressed their discontent in exceptional political ac-

10 AD Maine-et-Loire I L 566[16]ff.
11 AD Indre-et-Loire C 135.
12 AD Maine-et-Loire I L 546.
13 *Ibid.*, I L 402.
14 That is, the communes of Chemillé, St. Pierre de Chemillé, Vezins, Mazières, Maulèvrier, and St. Macaire.

tivity, that although at the beginning many of them cast their lot with the revolution, the fact that the revolution did much for the merchants and very little for them eventually encouraged a sizable number of them to turn bitterly to the opposition. The virtual absence of industrial artisans in the valley and plain meant that this type of unemployment could not have the same divisive effects in the revolutionary sections of the West as in the counterrevolutionary country of the *bocage*.

This description of party divisions in the *bocage* has one implication that has remained unrecognized too long: the division between *patriote* and *aristocrate* reached into the interior of every locality of the area that joined the counterrevolution. The revolution made itself felt through the presence of small patriot cities and of a nucleus of patriots in almost every parish of the *bocage*.

As one might expect, it was particularly the cities, centers of trade and industry (such as Montaigu and Cholet), rather than strongholds of the nobility (such as Beaupréau and Châtillon), that breathed patriotic fire. It was the bourgeois of Cholet who were able to report in 1790 that "public spirit [that is, support of the revolution] has undeniably made more progress here than in any of the surrounding parishes and cities."[15] For this, they themselves doubtless deserved most of the credit.

But it was not just a matter of the scattering of cities, with their spirited patriots and National Guards, through the *bocage*. To understand the ecology of counterrevolution in the Vendean countryside, one must avoid the image of concentrated peasant villages surrounded by fields and substitute for it a picture of a rural community composed of a central settlement, the

bourg, usually containing less than half the population, with the rest of the population distributed through tiny villages, hamlets of two or three dwellings, and isolated farms. The bourg's size and importance varied with the amount of commercial and manufacturing activity in the commune, but in every commune the homes and activities of the bourgeois and the artisans were concentrated there. The bourg was the last outpost of the revolution.

The effect of this arrangement was to divide almost every commune of the *bocage* socially and physically, to make the confrontation and conflict of the two parties an everyday matter, and to heighten the sense of encirclement and desperation of the country patriots. For they, in contrast with their urban comrades, were in direct, constant contact with their political enemies and were frequently the weaker party. The bourgeois of the small cities and bourgs, surrounded by inimical countrymen, beat the patriotic drums all the more loudly, to keep their enemy at a distance and, perhaps, to fortify their own sense of purpose and solidarity. As a result, much of the local history of the early revolution in the *bocage* is of the clash between country and city and between bourg and hinterland, of the attempt of a small, weak, yet articulate and officially dominant group of urban bourgeois to bring the great changes of 1789 and 1790 to a recalcitrant countryside. Far from being the unanimous voice of an undivided region against an external enemy, the counterrevolution was a cry of vengeance against the enemy within.

Two general observations clarify the tumultuous history of the early revolution in the *bocage*: the bourgeoisie acquired political power, to the virtual exclusion of all other classes; the dominant fact of the period was a series of conflicts between parties already fairly well defined by early in 1791, a series

---

15 Archives Nationales D^{IV} ^{bis} 67.

of which the counterrevolution was the most vicious episode.

The vocabulary of class conflict should not obscure the fact that the immediate issue was rather more political than economic. The rising bourgeois of the *bocage* found themselves in a country where they had little influence over the peasantry, intensely religious, dominated by its curés, where it was usual to say that the priest "governed" his parish. In fact, an extraordinary number of curés of the *bocage* became mayors of their communes at the first elections, in 1790.[16] The bourgeois sought to displace the parish priest of the *bocage* from the political position he had already lost peaceably and imperceptibly, over a long period of time, in the other sections of the West.

The bourgeois won a temporary victory. The Civil Constitution of the Clergy, enacted by the *Constituante* during 1790 and put into motion in the West early in 1791, essentially transformed the parish priest into a civil servant, into an employee of the local political authorities. Indeed, the fact that they had much more to lose, and could count more surely on the support of their parishioners, largely accounts for the greater rate of rejection of the Civil Constitution by the priests of the *bocage* than by those of valley and plain. For the curés of the *bocage*, the oath solicited in January, 1791, was not only a question of conscience, but also a question of capitulation to the local bourgeoisie. But the

bourgeoisie, backed by the armed force of the nation, succeeded in forcing many of the curés into hiding and the rest into exile and in substituting for them more cooperative priests from elsewhere who had taken the oath.

At the same time, the bourgeois were taking over the political offices offered by the revolution. It is no news that the clergy were out of office after 1790, since rejection of the oath automatically disqualified the priests. The remarkable feature of the political changes between 1789 and 1792 is the displacement of the peasants by the bourgeoisie. If we compare the deputies to the provincial assemblies for the Estates General of 1789 with the cantonal electors of 1790-1792 in two districts of Anjou, the one (Cholet) the very center of the counterrevolution and the other (Saumur) a solidly revolutionary territory, we find the following situation:[17]

---

[16] See the reports in *ibid.*, D^IV2.

[17] Compiled mainly from election minutes, AD Maine-et-Loire II B 1320-21, I L 321-24; F. Uzureau, "Les élections du Tiers-État et la Sénéchaussée d'Angers (1789)," *Anjou historique, 3* (1903), 134-158; F. Uzureau, "Les élections des administrateurs du district de Saumur (1790)," *ibid., 15* (1915), 470-484; F. Uzureau, "Les élections des administrateurs du district de Cholet (1790)," *ibid., 30* (1930), 87-90. The occupational information in the election records is fragmentary, and even after extensive searching in other documents for information on the individuals named, I have had to exclude from these calculations 155 of 412 officeholders in the district of Saumur, and sixty-five of 299 in the district of Cholet, who remain unidentified by occupation or class. It would be quite possible and quite rewarding, although depressingly time-consuming, to prepare the same kinds of statistics for communal offices.

	Cholet				Saumur		
Year	Bourgeois	Peasant	Other	Year	Bourgeois	Peasant	Other
1789	57%	38%	5%	1789	62%	28%	10%
1790	64%	22%	14%	1790	88%	9%	3%
1791	80%	4%	16%	1791	89%	—	11%
1792	77%	14%	9%	1792	82%	4%	14%

It would be impetuous to generalize from this one comparison, but it will serve to suggest that the revolution brought the bourgeois the political positions they desired, and it did so more rapidly in the revolutionary areas than in the counterrevolutionary ones.

Paul Bois, in noticing the decline of the rural electorate, has interpreted these changes as a sign of peasant apathy.[18] The election records, however, indicate that at first the two parties struggled for control of the political machinery and that the later withdrawal of the peasants was more in protest than in disinterest. Two features of the law favored the departure of all *aristocrates* from all electoral assemblies after 1790: the necessity of being signed up for the National Guard and the requirement of a civic oath. The first was believed to align the citizen with the agents of the revolution, and the second to signify public acceptance of the Civil Constitution of the Clergy. The year 1791, however, witnessed both the organization of "counterrevolutionary" National Guard companies, who dispensed with the civic oath, as at St. Pierre-de-Chemillé, and electoral assemblies at which the oath was unceremoniously omitted, as at Jallais.[19] In the latter case, some of the citizens later complained that "at the time of the primary assembly, insidious maneuvers convinced them by taking the oath required before the naming of electors, they would be renouncing their religion [and] the greater number, misled, refused it. . . ."[20] Most of them apparently remained "misled," since of the twenty-seven who ventured out to the cantonal elections of 1792 (as opposed to over one hundred at the 1791 assembly), ten withdrew when the chairman de-

manded the individual rendering of the oath. By that time, in Jallais as in most other places in the *bocage*, only the patriots were left.

The cantonal elections have received considerable attention because they involved enough people to make some summary statistics feasible and because they named the men who would in turn elect the district and department officials. At the level of district and department, and to a lesser extent at the level of the individual commune, the same eventual dominance by bourgeois patriots took place. The disappearance of the rest of the population from these offices was encouraged by simple unwillingness to do the work of the revolution, as testifies the frequency with which municipal officers resigned when they were called on to install the constitutional curé.[21]

There is one crucial element to add to this description: the loss of effective control of the population. As the patriots assumed control of local offices, they discovered they did not have the means to do the work of the revolution. They met passive resistance everywhere, were unable to collect taxes, quell disturbances, protect the constitutional curés. The use of their most powerful weapon, the calling in of the National Guard of one of the region's cities, served in the long run to estrange them further from the populations they were supposed to govern. In this context one can appreciate the plaint of the four patriot municipal officers of St. Lambert-du-Lattay in July, 1791. After the "aristocratic" faction had withdrawn its participation in communal affairs:

No matter what comes up, only the four writers are there to handle the parish business. Just imagine how much fear or

---

18 Bois, *op. cit.*, pp. 261-291.
19 AD Maine-et-Loire I L 568, I L 323, I L 324.
20 *Ibid.*, I L 323.

21 See the November, 1791, report of the *directoire* of Vendée in Charles-Louis Chassin, *La préparation de la guerre de Vendée* (Paris, 1892), Vol. II, p. 120.

respect is given them. People never stop insulting our curé. We would like to put him under the protection of the law but we cannot. We ask you, gentlemen, can twelve patriots stand up to 800 aristocrats?[22]

Small wonder, then, that the patriots of the little bourgs of the Vendée, with a growing sense of isolation and despair, turned to their urban allies for aid, and by doing so widened the chasm between the parties. They hated and feared each other as only feuding neighbors can.

The account I have given should make clear that the party conflict that eventuated in the struggle of 1793 began long before that "spontaneous" revolt, that it was the irritating presence of the enemy in almost every bourg that gave the conflict much of its bitterness, and that the most important public issue separating the parties was —as it was for a century after the revolution—the relationship of Church and state. It was at the nearly simultaneous application of the Civil Constitution of the Clergy and sale of Church properties that neutrality became impossible. There is no real distinction between the categories of patriots, supporters of the constitutional clergy, and purchasers of Church properties. In the *bocage* they were the same group, their core the merchants of the cities and largest bourgs. Outside the *bocage* few citizens were forced to make a politically significant choice between the old clergy and the new, and a wide range of the population, including peasants, bought Church properties.

It is true that the usual paltry properties of the *bocage* curé were less tempting than the extensive lands of the religious establishments in the surrounding plains and valleys. Possibly the sentiment of many peasants toward

the purchasers was less moral indignation than envy and disappointment, for some peasants did buy during the first few weeks of the sales. In the area that later joined the counterrevolution, nevertheless, the purchase of Church properties was an almost certain sign of alignment with the patriot party.

From that point on, the threat of counterrevolution grew. Most of the conflicts between *patriotes* and *aristocrates* before 1793 were limited in scope and consequences, but there were enough of them, and a sufficient number involving violence or threats of violence to indicate that the matter was serious. In the coastal Vendée alone, for example, in the short period from mid-April to mid-May, 1791, there were armed demonstrations against the patriots at Challans, St. Gilles, Palluau, Apremont, St. Jean-des-Monts, Machecoul, and St. Christophe-du-Ligneron.[23] Toward the end of the same year the great processions and pilgrimages that had started as fairly peaceful affirmations of attachment to the old religious order grew much more warlike, becoming occasions for threats and imprecations against the local patriots, and for the display of crude but ominous weapons. The most serious example of the violent encounters between patriots and their enemies that anticipated the counterrevolution was the attack on Châtillon and Bressuire in August, 1792, which may have involved as many as 6000 rebels, and left several hundred dead.

In this setting, the violent resistance of the Vendée to conscription in March, 1793, is not too difficult to understand. No doubt the boys of the *bocage* did not like the idea of military service, but that fact hardly distinguished them from the youth of the surrounding regions, where the draft proceeded peace-

---

[22] AD Maine-et-Loire I L 349.

[23] Archives Nationales D^XXIX 15; Chassin, *Préparation de la guerre*, I, 245ff.

fully. It was the first time that the patriots had tried to impose a drastic and unpopular measure on the whole countryside simultaneously; even the deportation of the clergy had been partial, had operated in irregular stages, and had depended on the cooperation of the priests themselves. This time the fragments of the counterrevolutionary party were able to coalesce.

Furthermore, the law essentially exempted the patriots by excusing public officials and mobilizing the National Guard "in place." In the *bocage* this meant that only the *aristocrates* were eligible. Nothing could have more effectively brought into the open the cleavage between the parties. The people called for the buyers of Church properties and the chiefs of the National Guard to go first; near Tigny a gang of young men "went to Coquin's inn to drink, and the idea there was that if they let recruitment go on the patriots would have the upper hand and the aristocrats would be *foutu*, and if they took thirty-five today they would take as many more a month from now. . . ."[24] In short, this was the latest and gravest of the series of conflicts between the patriots and aristocrats of the Vendée.

One last observation reinforces the impression of continuity between the party battles of 1791-1792 and the outbreak of the counterrevolution. The first violent events of the counterrevolution were demonstrated by countrymen who disarmed the patriots of their bourgs and then proceeded to do the same to the patriots of the nearest city; events at Cholet, Machecoul, Montaigu, and St. Florent fit this pattern. The first "battles" of the counterrevolution were actually massive but haphazard forays by country people into the patriot bourgs and cities of the Vendée, their prime targets the homes and headquarters of the bourgeois.

---

[24] AD Maine-et-Loire I L 1018.

Nowhere in this essay will the reader find the old theme of royalism as a "motive" for the Vendée; nor will he find religion in the abstract. This is not to say that the peasants and artisans who rose in March, 1793, were indifferent to questions of politics and religion. On the contrary, they cursed the republicans and hailed the *bons prêtres* with ferocious energy. But the unity of the counterrevolutionaries at the beginning of their adventure was rather in opposition to the regional and local patriot minority than in either a common ideology or a theoretical opposition to the revolution in general. The ideology of the "Catholic and Royal Army" emerged from the stress of battle and from the need of the combatants to explain to themselves and to others what they were doing. It is therefore risky to take the rebels' own later pronouncements for explanations of the counterrevolution.

The strategic questions to ask and answer are not, in fact, doctrinal. They are basically sociological: the special features of the counterrevolutionary areas, the composition of the parties, the conditions that permitted violent opposition to the patriots to develop. Firm answers to questions of this nature require the long, tedious, systematic, even statistical, analysis of masses of documents. But we may anticipate the conclusions of that essential research in at least these respects: the enduring difference in social organization between the revolutionary and counterrevolutionary areas of the West, the revolution succeeding only where commercial and urban influence, and therefore bourgeois power, had advanced as it had elsewhere in France; the existence of a large number of small, irritating, local patriot parties, limited primarily to the mercantile bourgeoisie; the progressive embitterment of relations between the two contending parties, to the point of violent counterrevolution in 1793.

mathematical models

twenty-six

The development of mathematical models as a mode of inquiry in the social sciences is now very fashionable. Followers of this tendency rather scorn any analysis not presented in terms of such models as old fashioned, imprecise, and lacking both rigor and elegance. They hold out the promise of an unusually productive new era for social science. Critics of the model builders point out that data which can be translated into the terms of the mathematical models are not available and may be intrinsically unobtainable, so that model building becomes a perhaps harmless but also useless and empty game. In the hands of a clever man with respect for the facts and with access to data in usable form, however, mathematical analysis has demonstrated its power to test popular assumptions and give new insights. L. F. Richardson uses as a model the Poisson distribution and a variation on Bernoulli's approach to the binomial distribution of probability to test some popular ideas about the duration and frequency of wars, and comes up with some startling and sobering conclusions.

The Statistics of Deadly Quarrels

L. F. RICHARDSON

Introduction

There are many books by military historians dealing in one way or another with the general theme "wars, and how to win them." [Our] theme . . . is different, namely, "wars, and how to take away the occasions for them," as far as this can be done by inquiring into general causes. But is there any scope for such an inquiry? Can there be any general causes that

L. F. Richardson, "Statistics of Deadly Quarrels," *Psychological Factors of Peace and War*, T. H. Pear, ed. (New York: Philosophical Library, Inc., 1950), pp. 239-245, 248-255.

are not well known, and yet of any importance? Almost every individual in a belligerent nation explains the current war quite simply by giving particulars of the abominable wickedness of his enemies. Any further inquiry into general causes appears to a belligerent to be futile, comic, or disloyal. Of course an utterly contradictory explanation is accepted as obviously true by the people on the other side of the war; while the neutrals may express chilly cynicism. This contradiction and variety of explanation does provide a *prima facie* case for further investigation. Any such inquiry should be so conducted as to afford a hope that critical individuals belonging to all nations will ultimately come to approve of it. National alliances and enmities vary from generation to generation. One obvious method of beginning a search for general causes is therefore to collect the facts from the whole world over a century or more. Thereby national prejudices are partly eliminated.

Collections of Facts from the Whole World

Professor Quincy Wright[1] has published a collection of *Wars of Modern Civilization*, extending from 1482 to 1940, and including 278 wars, together with their dates of beginning and ending, the name of any treaty of peace, the names of the participating states, the number of battles, and a classification into four types of war. This extensive summary of fact is very valuable, for it provides a corrective to those frequent arguments which are based on the few wars which the debater happens to remember, or which happen to support his theory. Wright explains his selection by the statement that his list:

"is intended to include all hostilities involving members of the family of nations, whether international, civil, colonial, or imperial, which were recognized as states of war in the legal sense or which involved over 50,000 troops. Some other incidents are included in which hostilities of considerable but lesser magnitude, not recognized at the time as legal states of war, led to important legal results such as the creation or extinction of states, territorial transfers, or changes of government."

Another worldwide collection has been made by L. F. Richardson for a shorter time interval, only 1820 onward, but differently selected and classified. No attention was paid to legality or to important legal results, such concepts being regarded as varying too much with opinion. Instead attention was directed to deaths caused by quarrelling, with the idea that these are more objective than the rights and wrongs of the quarrel. The wide class of "deadly quarrels" includes any quarrel that caused death to humans. This class was subdivided according to the number of deaths. For simplicity the deaths on the opposing sides were added together. The size of the subdivisions had to be suited to the uncertainty of the data. The casualties in some fightings are uncertain by a factor of three. It was found in practice that a scale which proceeded by factors of ten was suitable, in the sense that it was like a sieve which retained the reliable part of the data, but let the uncertainties pass through and away. Accordingly the first notion was to divide deadly quarrels into those which caused about 10,000,000 or 1,000,000 or 100,000 or 10,000 or 1000 or 100 or 10 or 1 deaths. These numbers are more neatly written respectively as 10^7, 10^6, 10^5, 10^4, 10^3, 10^2, 10^1, 10^0 in which the index is the logarithm of the number of deaths. The subsequent discussion is abbreviated by the introduction of a technical term. *Let the "magnitude" of any deadly quarrel be defined to be the logarithm, to the base ten, of the number of persons who died because of that quarrel.* The middles of the successive classes are then at magnitudes 7, 6, 5, 4, 3, 2, 1, 0. To make a clean cut between adjacent classes it is necessary to specify not the middles of the classes, but their edges. Let these edges be at 7·5, 6·5, 5·5, 4·5, 3·5, 2·5 . . . on the scale of magnitude. For example, magnitude 3·5 lies between 3162 and 3163 deaths, magnitude 4·5 lies between 31,622 and 31,623 deaths, magnitude 5·5 lies between 316,227 and 316,228 deaths, and so on. Rich-

[1] Quincy Wright, A *Study of War* (Chicago: Chicago University Press, 1942).

ardson's collection has not yet been published *in extenso*, but various extracts from it have appeared in print, and it will be available in microfilm. . . .

These two worldwide collections provide the raw material for many investigations. Three, which have already been published by learned societies, are summarized below. Others relating to language, religion, and common government will be offered in microfilm.

The Distribution of Wars in Time

This aspect of the collections is taken first, not because it is of the most immediate political interest, but almost for the opposite reason, namely, that it is restfully detached from current controversies.

Before beginning to build, I wish to clear three sorts of rubbish away from the site.

1. There is a saying that "if you take the date of the end of the Boer War and add to it the sum of the digits in the date, you obtain the date of the beginning of the next war, thus $1902 + 1 + 9 + 0 + 2 = 1914$." Also $1919 + 1 + 9 + 1 + 9 = 1939$. These are merely accidental coincidences. If the Christian calendar were reckoned from the birth of Christ in 4 B.C., then the first sum would be $1906 + 1 + 9 + 0 + 6 = 1922$, not $1914 + 4$.

2. There is a saying that "every generation must have its war." This is an expression of a belief, perhaps well founded, in latent pugnacity. As a statistical idea, however, the duration of a generation is too vague to be serviceable.

3. There is an assertion of a fifty-year period in wars which is attributed by Wright[2] to Mewes in 1896. Wright mentions an explanation by Spengler of this supposed period, thus: "The warrior does not wish to fight again himself and prejudices his son against war, but the grandsons are taught to think of war as romantic." This is certainly an interesting suggestion, but it contradicts the other suggestion that "every generation must have its war." Moreover, the genuineness of the fifty-year period is challenged. Since 1896, when Mewes published, the statisticians have developed strict tests for periodicity.[3] These tests have discredited various periods that were formerly believed. In particular the alleged fifty-year period in wars is mentioned by Kendall[4] as an example of a lack of caution.

Having thus cleared the site, let us return to Wright's collection as to a quarry of building material.

The Distribution of Years in Their Relation to War and Peace

A list was made of the calendar years. Against each year was set a mark for every war that began in that year. Thus any year was characterized by the number, x, of wars that began in it. The number, y, of years having the character x was then counted. The results were as follows.[5]

---
[2] *Ibid.*, p. 230.

[3] See, for example, M. G. Kendall, *Advanced Theory of Statistics*, Part II (London: Charles Griffin & Co., Ltd., 1946).

[4] M. G. Kendall, *Journal of the Royal Statistical Society*, **108** (1945), 122.

[5] L. F. Richardson, *Journal of the Royal Statistical Society*, **107** (1945), 242.

Years from 1500 to 1931 Inclusive (Wright's Collection)

Number, x, of outbreaks in a year	0	1	2	3	4	>4	Totals
Number, y, of such years	223	142	48	15	4	0	432
Y, as defined below	216·2	149·7	51·8	12·0	2·1	0·3	432·1

It is seen that there is some regularity about the progression of the numbers y. Moreover, they agree roughly with the numbers Y. These are of interest because they are calculated from a well-known formula, called by the name of its discoverer the "Poisson distribution" and specified thus

$$Y = \frac{N\lambda^x}{(2 \cdot 7183)^\lambda \, x!}$$

in which N is the whole number of years, λ is the mean number of outbreaks per year, and x! is called "factorial x" and is equal, respectively, to 1, 1, 2, 6, 24, when x equals 0, 1, 2, 3, 4. Similar results were obtained from Richardson's collection both for the beginnings and for the ends of fatal quarrels in the range of magnitude extending from 3·5 to 4·5, thus:

perfectly with the formulae that are accepted as representing them. In the paper cited,[6] the disagreement with Wright's collection is examined by the χ^2 test and is shown to be unimportant. It should be noted, however, that the application of this standard χ^2 test involves the tacit assumption that there is such a thing as chance in history.

There is much available information about the Poisson distribution; about the theories from which it can be derived; and about the phenomena which are approximately described by it.[7] The latter include the distribution of equal time intervals classified according to the number of alpha particles emitted during each by a film of radioactive substance.

In order to bring the idea home, an experiment in cookery may be sug-

Years 1820 to 1929 Inclusive							
x outbreaks in a year	0	1	2	3	4	>4	Total
y for war	65	35	6	4	0	0	110
Poisson	64·3	34·5	9·3	1·7	0·2	0·0	110·0
y for peace	63	35	11	1	0	0	110
Poisson	63·8	34·8	9·5	1·7	0·2	0·0	110·0

The numbers in the rows beginning with the word "Poisson" were calculated from the formula already given, in which N and λ have the same *verbal* definitions as before, and therefore have appropriately altered *numerical* values. Such adjustable constants are called parameters.

If every fatal quarrel had the same duration, then the Poisson distribution for their beginnings would entail a Poisson distribution for their ends; but in fact there is no such rigid connection. The durations are scattered: Spanish America took fourteen years to break free from Spain, but the siege of Bharatpur was over in two months. Therefore the Poisson distributions for war and for peace may reasonably be regarded as separate facts.

Observed numbers hardly ever agree

gested. Take enough flour to make N buns. Add λN currants, where λ is a small number such as 3. Add also the other usual ingredients, and mix all thoroughly. Divide the mass into N equal portions, and bake them. When each bun is eaten, count carefully and record the number of currants which it contains. When the record is complete, count the number y of buns, each of which contains exactly x currants. Theory would suggest that y will

[6] *Ibid.*

[7] H. Jeffreys, *Theory of Probability* (Oxford: Oxford University Press, 1939); M. G. Kendall, *The Advanced Theory of Statistics* (London: Charles Griffin & Co., Ltd., 1943); W. Shilling, *Journal of the American Statistical Association*, **42** (1947), 407-424; H. Cramér, *Mathematical Methods of Statistics* (Princeton: Princeton University Press, 1946).

be found to be nearly equal to Y, as given by the Poisson formula. I do not know whether the experiment has been tried.

A more abstract, but much more useful, summary of the relations, is to say that the Poisson distribution of years follows logically from the hypothesis that there is the same very small probability of an outbreak of war, or of peace, somewhere on the globe on every day. In fact there is a seasonal variation, outbreaks of war having been commoner in summer than in winter, as Q. Wright shows. But when years are counted as wholes, this seasonal effect is averaged out; and then λ is such that the probability of a war beginning, or ending, during any short time dt years is $λdt$.

This explanation of the occurrence of wars is certainly far removed from such explanations as ordinarily appear in newspapers, including the protracted and critical negotiations, the inordinate ambition and the hideous perfidy of the opposing statesmen, and the suspect movements of their armed personnel. The two types of explanation are, however, not necessarily contradictory; they can be reconciled by saying that each can separately be true as far as it goes, but cannot be the whole truth. A similar diversity of explanation occurs in regard to marriage: on the one hand we have the impersonal and moderately constant marriage rate; on the other hand we have the intense and fluctuating personal emotions of a love story; yet both types of description can be true.

Those who wish to abolish war need not be discouraged by the persistent recurrence which is described by the Poisson formula. The regularities observed in social phenomena are seldom like the unalterable laws of physical science. The statistics, if we had them, of the sale of snuff or of slaves, would presumably show a persistence during the eighteenth century; yet both habits have now ceased. The existence of a descriptive formula does not necessarily indicate an absence of human control, especially not when the agreement between formula and fact is imperfect. Nevertheless, the Poisson distribution does suggest that the abolition of war is not likely to be easy, and that the League of Nations and its successor the United Nations have taken on a difficult task. In some other fields of human endeavor there have been long lags between aspiration and achievement. For example, Leonardo da Vinci drew in detail a flying machine of graceful appearance. But four centuries of mechanical research intervened before flight was achieved. Much of the research that afterward was applied to airplanes was not at first made specifically for that object. So it may be with social science and the abolition of war.

The Poisson distribution is not predictive; it does not answer such questions as "when will the present war end?" or "when will the next war begin?" On the contrary, the Poisson distribution draws attention to a persistent probability of change from peace to war, or from war to peace. Discontent with present weather has been cynically exaggerated in a comic rhyme:

As a rule a man's a fool:
When it's hot he wants it cool,
When it's cool he wants it hot,
Always wanting what is not.

A suggestion made by the Poisson law is that discontent with present circumstances underlies even the high purposes of peace and war. There is plenty of psychological evidence in support. This is not the place to attempt a general review of it; but two illustrations may serve as pointers. In 1877 Britain had not been engaged in any considerable war since the end of the conflict with China in 1860. During the weeks of national excitement in 1877 preluding the dispatch of the British Mediterranean squadron to Gallipoli, in order to frustrate Russian designs on Constantinople, a bellicose music hall song with the refrain:

We don't want to fight, but, by Jingo, if we do:
We've got the men, we've got the ships, we've got the money too.

was produced in London and instantly became very popular.[8]

Contrast this with the behavior of the governments of Britain, China, [the] U.S.A., and [the] U.S.S.R. in 1944, after years of severe war, but with victory in sight, who then at Dumbarton Oaks officially described themselves as "peace-loving."[9]

Chance in history. The existence of a more or less constant λ, a probability per time of change, plainly directs our attention to chance in history. Thus the question which statisticians are accustomed to ask about any sample of people or things, namely "whether the sample is large enough to justify the conclusions which have been drawn from it" must also be asked about any set of wars.

Have wars become more frequent? In particular the discussion of any alleged trend toward more or fewer wars is a problem in sampling. No definite conclusion about trend can be drawn from the occurrence of two world wars in the present century, because the sample is too small. When, however, the sample was enlarged by the inclusion of all the wars in Wright's collection, and the time was divided into two equal intervals, the following result was obtained.

The increase from 143 to 156 can be explained away as a chance effect.

This was not so for all subdivisions of the time. When the interval from 1500 to 1931 was divided into eight consecutive parts of fifty-four years each, it was found that the fluctuation, from part to part, of the number of outbreaks in Wright's collection was too large to be explained away as chance. The extremes were fifty-four outbreaks from 1824 to 1877, and sixteen outbreaks from 1716 to 1769. Other irregular fluctuations of λ were found, although less definitely, for parts of twenty-seven and nine years.[10] All these results may, of course, depend on Wright's selection rules. The problem has been further studied by Moyal.[11] . . .

* * * * *

Which Nations Were Most Involved?

This section resembles quinine: it has a bitter taste, but medicinal virtues. The participation of some well-known states in the 278 "wars of modern civilization" as listed by Wright is summarized and discussed by him.[12]

Over the whole time interval from 1480 to 1941 the numbers of wars in which the several nations participated were as follows: England (Great Britain) 78, France 71, Spain 64, Russia (U.S.S.R.) 61, Empire (Austria) 52, Turkey 43, Poland 30, Sweden 26, Savoy (Italy) 25, Prussia (Germany) 23, Netherlands 23, Denmark 20, United States 13, China 11, Japan 9.

It may be felt that the year 1480 has not much relevance to present-day affairs. So here are the corresponding

Dates of beginning	1500 to 1715	1716 to 1931
Numbers of wars	143	156

---

[8] *Encyclopedia Britannica*, 13th ed., Vol. XIV, p. 69.

[9] H.M. Stationery Office, London, Cmd. 6666.

[10] *Journal of the Royal Statistical Society*, **107**, 246-247.

[11] J. E. Moyal, *ibid.*, **112** (1950), 446-449.

[12] *A Study of War, op. cit.*, pp. 220-223, 650.

numbers for the interval 1850 to 1941, almost within living memory: Great Britain 20, France 18, Savoy (Italy) 12, Russia (U.S.S.R.) 11, China 10, Spain 10, Turkey 10, Japan 9, Prussia (Germany) 8, USA 7, Austria 6, Poland 5, Netherlands 2, Denmark 2, Sweden 0.

It would be difficult to reconcile these numbers of wars in which the various nations have participated with the claim made in 1945 by the Charter of the United Nations[13] to the effect that Britain, France, Russia, China, Turkey, and [the] U.S.A., were "peace-loving" in contrast with Italy, Japan, and Germany. Some special interpretation of peace-lovingness would be necessary: such as either "peace-lovingness" at a particular date; or else that "peace-loving" states participated in many wars in order to preserve world peace.

It would be yet more difficult to reconcile the participations found by Wright with the concentration of Lord Vansittart's invective against Germans, as though he thought that Germans were the chief, and the most persistent, cause of war.[14]

In fact no one nation participated in a majority of the wars in Wright's list. For the greatest participation was that of England (Great Britain), namely in seventy-eight wars; leaving 200 wars in which England did not participate. The distinction between aggression and defense is usually controversial. Nevertheless, it is plain that a nation cannot have been an aggressor in a war in which it did not participate. The conclusion is, therefore, that no one nation was the aggressor in more than 28 per cent of the wars in Wright's list.

Aggression was widespread. This result for wars both civil and external agrees broadly with Sorokin's findings after his wide investigation of internal disturbance. He attended to Ancient Greece, Ancient Rome, and to the long interval 525 to 1925 in Europe. Having compared different nations in regard to internal violence, Sorokin concluded that "these results are enough to dissipate the legend of 'orderly' and 'disorderly' peoples. . . . All nations are orderly and disorderly according to the times."[15] . . .

There does not appear to be much hope of forming a group of permanently peace-loving nations to keep the permanently aggressive nations in subjection; for the reason that peace-lovingness and aggressiveness are not permanent qualities of nations. Instead the facts support Ranyard West's[16] conception of an international order in which a majority of momentarily peace-loving nations, changing kaleidoscopically in its membership, may hope to restrain a changing minority of momentarily aggressive nations.

The Number of Groups on Each Side of a War[17]

Wars can be classified according to the number of organized groups of people on the two sides: for example, one government vs. one set of insurgents, or two states vs. one state, or five nations vs. three nations, or in general r belligerent groups vs. s belligerent groups. Then the number of wars of the type "r vs. s" can be counted, for each r and s, and the results can be

---

[13] H.M. Stationery Office, London, Cmd. 6666, Articles 3 and 4 together with the list of states represented at the San Francisco Conference.

[14] Sir Robert (now Lord) Vansittart, *Black Record* (London: Hamish Hamilton, Ltd., 1941).

[15] Pitirim A. Sorokin, *Social and Cultural Dynamics* (New York: American Book Co., 1937).

[16] R. West, *Conscience and Society* (London: Methuen & Co., Ltd., 1942).

[17] Being an abstract of L. F. Richardson's paper in the *Journal of the Royal Statistical Society*, **109**, 130-156.

written in a table of rows and columns. As there was no good reason for distinguishing 2 *vs.* 1 from 1 *vs.* 2 the observed number of wars of this type was bisected, and half of it was written in each of the two possible places; and so in general whenever *r* was not equal to *s*. This analysis was applied to both Wright's and Richardson's collections with the following results.

Quarrels of Magnitudes Greater than 3·5 which Ended from 1820 to 1939 Inclusive (Richardson's Collection)

	1	2	3	4	5	6
6	0·5	0	0	0	0	0
5	1	0·5	0	0	0	0
4	2·5	0·5	0·5	0	0	0
s3	2·5	1	0	0·5	0	0
2	12	3	1	0·5	0·5	0
1	42	12	2·5	2·5	1	0·5

r

There were also beyond the bounds of the above table: 2 wars of 7 *vs.* 1; 1 war of 9 *vs.* 1; 1 war of 15 *vs.* 5; thus making a total of ninety-one wars.

Wars Not Marked Civil in Wright's List from 1480 to 1941 Inclusive

	1	2	3	4	5	6
6	1	0·5	0	0	0	0
5	1·5	0·5	0·5	0	0	0
4	6	0	0·5	0	0	0
s3	6	3	1	0·5	0·5	0
2	14	4	3	0	0·5	0·5
1	117	14	6	6	1·5	1

r

There were also in Wright's list beyond the bounds of the above table one war of each of the following types: 7 *vs.* 1, 8 *vs.* 1, 11 *vs.* 1, 16 *vs.* 1, 20 *vs.* 1, 7 *vs.* 3, 8 *vs.* 5, 20 *vs.* 5, 33 *vs.* 5, 35 *vs.* 7, 9 *vs.* 8, thus making a total of 200 wars.

The above two tables, though based on different definitions of war, have a strong resemblance. In both the com-

monest type is 1 *vs.* 1, and the next commonest 2 *vs.* 1. Both distributions are tolerably well fitted by the formula

$$(\text{number of wars of type } r \text{ vs. } s) = \frac{5}{9} \frac{(\text{whole number of wars})}{(rs)^{2.5}}$$

Professor M. S. Bartlett has pointed out to me that, according to this law, any cell frequency is equal to the product of the marginal totals for its row and its column, divided by the total for the whole table; so that the variable *r* would be said to be "statistically independent" of the variable *s*. Apart from this bit of insight, the formula is empirical: it describes the facts, but does not explain them. Although tables in rows and columns, including especially correlation tables, are a common feature of works on statistics, yet a frequency distribution of this particular shape was certainly not well known. No readymade theory, which might have illuminated the causes of wars, was available. So rival theories were made on purpose, under the guidance of the following leading ideas:

1. International relations have not been so deterministic as to justify any theory which would offer to predict exactly what must happen at any date.

2. A theory, however, should indicate what probably would happen. It ought to agree with the historical facts collected from any sufficiently long interval, say, from one hundred years or more.

3. That because a nation cannot be at war all by itself, therefore the probabilities of war must be attached to pairs of nations, and not to nations singly.

4. In the course of a century the same nation may have been peace-loving on several occasions, and aggressive on several others. These characteristics are not sufficiently permanent to form the basis of a long-term theory.

Klingberg[18] has published a summary of the opinions of 220 outstanding students of international affairs about the chance of war between pairs of states. Considerable fluctuations of opinion occurred in a few years. It would be an instructive adventure to begin at the opposite extreme by first regarding all nations as of similar pugnacity, and later introducing only such discriminations between nations as are called for by the statistics of r vs. s.

5. That any type of war, such, for example, as 2 vs. 1, comprises many mutually exclusive varieties of conceivable war, which could be specified by naming the two belligerents and the one. The number of such mutually exclusive varieties can be formulated; and so in general for r vs. s.

6. A remarkable feature is that 1 vs. 1 has been much the commonest type; and that in general the more complicated types have been rarer than the simpler types. This is a characteristic of lack of organization, of chaos. In the molecular chaos of a gas, collisions of molecules two in a bunch are much more frequent than collisions three in a bunch. Mathematically the characteristic of chaos is that the probability of a complicated event contains among its factors the probabilities of simpler events.

7. These ideas combine to give an expression of the following form for the probability of a war of the type r vs. s

$$(\text{number of mutually exclusive varieties}) \times p^x \times (1 - p)^y$$

where p is the probability of war between any pair of nations, x is the number of pairs that are in the war, and $(1 - p)^y$ is the probability that the neutrals would keep out. Any such theory may be called, in musical terminology, a variation on the theme by Bernoulli concerning the binomial distribution of probability.

These general ideas were developed in connection with successive special hypotheses until a combination was found which agreed with the facts. For some theories the appropriate facts were numbers of wars, for others durations of wars. It was quite interesting to notice the manner in which some hypotheses failed. The details can be seen in the original paper, to which the numerals refer. In one theory (8), which is called "a simple chaos between sixty nations" it is supposed for simplicity that p, the probability of war inside a pair of nations, is the same for all pairs and at all times. But it was impossible to find any number p that would agree with all parts of the distribution of durations of wars classified as r vs. s. Most of the misfits could have been avoided if the number of nations in the world had been about six or ten instead of about sixty. The next three theories (9, 10, 11) are devices for reducing the number of nations in effective contact with one another. Thus in theory 9 an approximate agreement would be achieved if there were in the world only about ten bellicose nations, all the others being permanently nonbelligerent. It is, however, impossible to sort the nations into these two supposed categories; for the total number of names of belligerents, including names of insurgents, but not counting any name twice, was found to be, not ten, but 108, for the ninety-one wars that ended from 1820 to 1939 according to Richardson's list.

To circumvent this obstacle a different device (10) was next considered for reducing the effective number of belligerents. It was supposed that disputes had occurred in localities scattered at random over the globe so that altogether they concerned numerous possible belligerents; but that each dis-

18 F. L. Klingberg, *Psychometrika*, 6 (1941), 335-352.

pute was localized so that it concerned only eight nations or other possible belligerent groups; and that the probability of war about that dispute was 0·35 for every pair that could be formed from the eight groups. These remarkably simple hypotheses led to a good agreement with the facts in Richardson's collection, provided $r + s \leqq 8$. But the theory denied the possibility of any war involving more than eight belligerents, and so in particular that of the First World War.

The failure of these three theories (8, 9, 10) showed the need for a more inclusive hypothesis designed to explain both the localization of most wars and the occasional occurrence of long-range or world wars, in the era before aviation became dominant. Accordingly, in theory 11 the world was supposed for simplicity to consist of only three sorts of nations, namely eleven landlocked, forty-four local-coastal, and five powers capable of reaching any coast by sea. This hypothesis greatly complicated the mathematics; for different sorts of pairs of nations were contemplated, each with its appropriate, but at first unknown, probability of war. The probability of any event is here defined to be the fraction of time during which the event occurred in the course of any very long historical interval. For comparison, the historical data in Richardson's collection had to be rearranged as durations of wars. Moreover, the former type 1 vs. 1 had now to be divided into three subtypes, namely:

A long-range power vs. a long-range power;

A long-range power vs. a short-range power;

A short-range power vs. a short-range power;

and so on for the more complicated types. The classification became four-dimensional; the type r vs. s being

analyzed into subtypes such as r_1 and r_2 vs. s_1 and s_2.

The probabilities were deduced from the historical data. For type 1 vs. 1 the deduction was definite and unique. For type 2 vs. 1 the deduction was a compromise fitted to redundant data. For type 3 vs. 1 various difficulties increased. The comparison of theory with fact was carried as far as type 2 vs. 2. Beyond that the historical facts would be described statistically as "outliers" in the sense that the classification of them contained many empty compartments with rare observations irregularly dispersed. Similar ragged appearances are usually to be seen in the outer regions of any diagram of observed frequencies. In particular the First World War, which was regarded as 15 vs. 5, was isolated in the four-dimensional classification, being surrounded on all sides by many empty cells; one cannot easily say how many. A comparison of theory 11 with the fact of the First World War would involve a difficult summation of probabilities over the outer regions of the classification, both empty and occupied. Theory 11 certainly admits the possibility of such a war; but a quantitative study of outliers was not attempted.

The probability, x, of war between two long-range powers was found to be only of the order of 0·001. The probability, y, of war between a long- and a short-range power was found rather discordantly to be 0·002 or 0·015 or 0·009; on the average one may say that y was of the order 0·01, about ten times as great as x. The probability, z, of war between neighboring powers was found to vary conspicuously with circumstances, thus:

Number, rs, of pairs of opposed belligerents	1	2	3	4
z	0·008	0·020	0·046	0·119?

On the average z was decidedly greater than y, and all the more so than x. That is to say *propinquity tended to war*.

Theory 12 was an amendment to theory 11 such that the variation of z with rs was simply accepted and explained as due to the infectiousness of fighting.

Theory 13 was called "a uniform chaos modified only by infectiousness"; that is to say geographical barriers were ignored, and every nation was supposed (as also in theory 8) to be in contact with every other nation. Aviation may make it so in future; but for the years before 1929 theory 13 definitely misfits the history. So one should return to theory 12 which is called *"chaos restricted by geography and modified by infectiousness"*; for of all these theories it is the only one which has survived the test of quantitative comparison with historical fact. The possibility remains that someone may invent a different theory which may fit the facts as well or better.

Historians will doubtless be keenly aware of many relevant considerations which have been ignored in the foregoing batch of theories. But a theory is not necessarily to be despised for what it leaves out. This may be gathered from the history of the explanation of the moon's motion.[19] Sir Isaac Newton began the explanation by considering an idealized moon moving uniformly in a circle about the earth as center. As a description that was crude, for Hipparchus in the second century B.C. had known better. Yet Newton's first simple explanation is so interesting that it is still regularly taught to physics students. It has also been fertile. In 1913 Bohr used it, along with brilliantly novel ideas, to explain the motion of an electron around the nucleus of an atom. Meanwhile a succession of astronomers have labored to improve lunar theory. In the present century E. W. Brown put in all the relevant considerations. Brown's theory is so accurate that it is used in the computation of the *Nautical Almanac*. But, as Brown's theory involves 1500 terms, it is not teachable to scientists in general.

------

[19] John Jackson in *Encyclopaedia Britannica*, 15th ed., Vol. XIV, pp. 780-781.